Crossroads of Knowledge in Early Modern Literature

Volume 4

This series rewrites the story of early modern epistemology by examining the intervention of the 'literary' in a wider conversation about the process, ethics and psychology of knowing, more obviously ongoing across Theology, Natural Philosophy, Economics and Law. Each volume focuses on a particular interdisciplinary threshold, with literature as a running thread, reading these cognate fields as coeval but distinct, and charting certain elusive and ordinarily unassimilable aspects of the experience and texture of knowing by using a unique interdisciplinary route.

Subha Mukherji · Dunstan Roberts
Editors

Literature and the Legal Imaginary

Knowing Justice

palgrave
macmillan

Editors
Subha Mukherji
Fitzwilliam College
University of Cambridge
Cambridge, UK

Dunstan Roberts
University of Cambridge
Cambridge, UK

ISSN 2946-4455 ISSN 2946-4463 (electronic)
Crossroads of Knowledge in Early Modern Literature
ISBN 978-3-031-74095-4 ISBN 978-3-031-74093-0 (eBook)
https://doi.org/10.1007/978-3-031-74093-0

This Palgrave Macmillan imprint is published by the registered company Springer Nature Switzerland AG
The registered company address is: Gewerbestrasse 11, 6330 Cham, Switzerland

Acknowledgements

The editors would like to thank the contributors for their good humour and their commitment to this project on its journey to completion.

All images are either in the public domain or obtained with the permission of the relevant copyright holders, as indicated in the relevant chapters.

The research for the series, and for this volume, has received funding from the European Research Council under the European Union's Seventh Framework Programme (FP7/2007-2013)/ERC grant agreement no. 617849.

Contents

Part I Introduction

1 **Knowing Justice: Literature and the Legal Imaginary** 3
Subha Mukherji

Part II Legal Imaginaries

2 **Solomon, Trajan, and the Figure of Justice: Narrative Backgrounds to an Early Modern Allegory** 27
Julie Stone Peters

3 **Law of Nature in Inns of Court Drama** 55
Doyeeta Majumder

4 **Escalus' Dream: Re-imagining Shakespeare's States** 79
Richard K. Sherwin

Part III Text, Knowledge, Hermeneutics

5 **The Letter and the Spirit: Portia's Case** 109
Regina Schwartz

6 **Configuring God as Law: Richard Hooker's Poetics of Law** 127
Torrance Kirby

7 **The Common Consent of Words: An Aristotelian Element of Hobbesian Legal Rhetoric** 143
Charles McNamara

Part IV Play and Pleasure

8 **Doublings: Comedy, Office, Law** 165
Peter Goodrich

9 **Ludic Legal Pedagogy: Mooting in Early Modern England** 197
Maksymilian Del Mar

10 **"A Delightful Measure": Imagining Barfield's Poetic Jurisdiction** 217
Gary Watt

Part V Law and Poetics

11 **Gottfried von Strassburg's *Tristan* and the Allegory of Law** 241
Conrad van Dijk

12 **The Versification of Legal Codes** 263
Valérie Hayaert

13 **Towards a Poetics of Equality in Nineteenth-Century English Literature** 283
Jan-Melissa Schramm

14 **The Beatitude of the Berrigans: Jurisprudential Drama and the Poetics of Martyrdom** 305
Alex Feldman

Part VI Afterword

15 **Afterword** 333
Kathy Eden

Index 337

Editors and Contributors

About the Editors

Subha Mukherji is Professor of Early Modern Literature and Culture at the University of Cambridge. She has researched and published on various aspects of Renaissance English literature, including law and theatre, Shakespeare, early modern genres, and literary epistemologies. She has also published on migration and art forms, the poetics of space across cultures, and contemporary Indian art. She is writing a book entitled *Knowing Encounters: Questioning Knowledge in Early Modern Literature*, and editing Shakespeare and Fletcher's *Henry VIII*. She was Principal Investigator of the ERC-funded project, *Crossroads of Knowledge in Early Modern England*; this book completes a mini-series emerging from that project: 'Crossroads of Knowledge in Early Modern Literature' (Springer/Palgrave).

Dunstan Roberts has published widely on the history of books, libraries, and reading in the early modern period. He is currently cataloguing the early modern manuscripts at Queens' College, Cambridge, and is in the process of completing a book-length study of the library of Edward, 1st Lord Herbert of Cherbury (1582–1648).

Contributors

Maksymilian Del Mar is Professor of Legal Theory and Legal Humanities at Queen Mary University of London. He works on the theory and history of imagination, knowledge, emotion, rhetoric, law, embodiment, pedagogy, and sociality.

Conrad van Dijk is the author of *John Gower and the Limits of the Law* and the online writing guide *The Nature of Writing*. His research covers topics as diverse as literature and law, twentieth-century Christian fiction (primarily G. K. Chesterton and C.S. Lewis), and children's literature.

Kathy Eden is Chavkin Family Professor of English and Professor of Classics at Columbia University. Her fields of study include Renaissance humanism, the history of rhetoric, and the classical tradition.

Alex Feldman is Senior Lecturer (Assoc. Prof.) in English Literature at the University of Haifa. His research, published in *Law & Literature*, *Law, Culture and the Humanities*, *Modern Drama*, *Comparative Drama Modernism/modernity,* and elsewhere, focuses upon representations of law and justice in theatre. His first book was entitled *Dramas of the Past on the Twentieth-Century Stage: In History's Wings* (Routledge, 2012), and he is currently working on two projects: *Terence Rattigan: New Critical Perspectives*, co-edited with Dan Rebellato, under contract with Cambridge University Press, and a monograph entitled *The Rigging of the Law*, tracing jurisprudential drama's development on the modern and contemporary stage.

Peter Goodrich is Professor of Law and Director of the Program in Law and Humanities at Cardozo School of Law, New York and Visiting Professor in the School of Social Science, NYU Abu Dhabi. He is an ardent advocate of argute alliterations and of the silent p, as in raspberry, psittacist, Ptolemy, and rhubarb. Chef, film-maker, and essayist, his most recent book, *Vision in Decision: On the Judicial Use of Images* was published by Oxford University Press in 2023.

Valérie Hayaert is a classicist, historian, and humanist researcher of the early modern European tradition, whose research interests lie at the intersection between Art and Law. Her first book, *Mens emblematica* (2008), examined the playful yet serious pictorial tradition surrounding humanist lawyers, and her latest book, *Lady Justice: An Anatomy of Allegory* (2023), takes a uniquely interdisciplinary view of the figure of justice in the fifteenth and sixteenth centuries. Her current research looks at justice on the stage. She teaches Law at the University of Warwick.

Torrance Kirby is Professor of Ecclesiastical History and sometime Director of the Centre for Research on Religion at McGill University, Montreal. DPhil in Modern History, Oxford University (1988). Fellow of the Royal Historical Society, life member of Corpus Christi College, Cambridge, and McCord Fellow of the Princeton Centre of Theological Inquiry. Recent books include *Persuasion and Conversion: Religion, Politics and the Public Sphere in Early Modern England* (2013), *The Zurich Connection and Tudor Political Theology* (2007), and *Richard Hooker, Reformer and Platonist* (2005). His most recent book is an edition of selected *Sermons at Paul's Cross, 1521-1642* (OUP, 2017).

Doyeeta Majumder completed her first two degrees from Jadavpur University and her Ph.D. from the University of St Andrews. Having taught at the University of Edinburgh, and then at Shiv Nadar University, Delhi, she is now Assistant Professor of English Literature at her alma mater—Jadavpur University. Her research interests include early modern law and literature, political and juridical theory, intellectual history, and translation studies. Her monograph, entitled *Tyranny and Usurpation: The New Prince and Lawmaking Violence in Early Modern Drama*, was published by Liverpool University Press in 2019.

Charles McNamara is Director of Greek and Latin and Lecturer in the Department of Classical and Near Eastern Religions and Cultures at the University of Minnesota. Previously he was Robert Belknap Core Faculty Fellow at Columbia University and Postdoctoral Research Fellow for the *Thesaurus Linguae Latinae* at the Bayerische Akademie der Wissenschaften.

Julie Stone Peters is H. Gordon Garbedian Professor of English and Comparative Literature at Columbia University, Affiliated Faculty member at Columbia Law School, and Global Professorial Fellow at Queen Mary University School of Law. She is the author, most recently, of *Law as Performance: Theatricality, Spectatorship, and the Making of Law in Ancient, Medieval, and Early Modern Europe* (Oxford UP, 2022) and *Staging Witchcraft Before the Law: Skepticism, Performance as Proof, and*

Law as Magic in Early Modern Witch Trials (Cambridge UP [Elements], 2024).

Jan-Melissa Schramm is Professor of Literature and Law at the University of Cambridge. She specialises in the history of the English novel and the wider cultural relations of law and the humanities, mostly within the eighteenth and nineteenth centuries. Her research has addressed a wide range of themes and topics within this broader field, including sacrifice, mercy, forgiveness, censorship, internationalism, and institutional reform.

Richard K. Sherwin is Wallace Stevens Professor of Law Emeritus at New York Law School. His scholarly writings explore the rich and varied relationship between law and culture, focusing in particular on legal narrative, visual communication, the legitimation process, and the genealogy of law's sovereignty. Recent books include *A Cultural History of Law in the Modern Age* (Bloomsbury 2019/2023), *Visualizing Law in the Age of the Digital Baroque* (Routledge 2011), and *When Law Goes Pop* (Chicago 2000).

Gary Watt is Professor in the School of Law at the University of Warwick. He was the co-founding editor of the journal *Law and Humanities* and General Editor of Bloomsbury's *A Cultural History of Law.* As a National Teaching Fellow and national 'Law Teacher of the Year' (2009), he for many years delivered rhetoric workshops for the Royal Shakespeare Company. He has a monograph on Shakespeare and the law with Bloomsbury Arden Shakespeare and another forthcoming with Oxford Shakespeare Topics. His most recent book, *The Making Sense of Politics, Media, and Law* (Cambridge, 2023), arose from a Leverhulme Major Research Fellowship.

Regina Schwartz is Professor of Literature, Religion and Law at Northwestern University. Her research, publications and teaching span Literature and Ethics, Early Modern Literature, Law and Literature, Critical Theory, Classical and Biblical Literature, and Poetry and Poetics. Her publications include *Sacramental Poetics at the Dawn of Secularism: When God Left the World (Stanford University Press, 2008), Loving Justice, Living Shakespeare* (Oxford University Press, 2017), and (co-ed. with Patrick McGrath) *Toward a Sacramental Poetics* (Notre Dame Press, 2021).

List of Figures

Fig. 1.1	Philip Galle after Pieter Bruegel the Elder, Justice from The Seven Virtues (c. 1559) (Public Domain image courtesy of the National Gallery of Art, Washington, DC)	2
Fig. 2.1	"Justitia" with scenes from the Judgment of Solomon and Justice of Trajan. Gregor Reisch, *Margarita philosophica* (1505) (Courtesy of Ghent University Library, MS BHSL.HS.0007, verso of unnumbered leaf between fol. 312 and fol. 313)	29
Fig. 2.2	*Bible moralisée* (thirteenth century). Vienna Österreichische Nationalbibliothek, Cod. 2554, fol. 50r (details). Left: Solomon hands the living child to the true mother, while the false mother protests. Right: Jesus hands the living child to Ecclesia while Synagoga mourns (Courtesy of the Vienna Österreichische Nationalbibliothek)	36
Fig. 2.3	Prayer book cover showing Henry VIII as Solomon in the Judgment of Solomon (c.1540). British Museum, 1894,0729.1 (© The Trustees of the British Museum)	42
Fig. 2.4	The Judgment of Solomon as a fairy tale pastoral in the advertisement for Elizabeth I's Great Lottery (1567). *A Very Rich Lotterie Generall* (London: Henrie Bynneman, 1567) (Detail from extra sheet following Folger Shakespeare Library, STC 8000 Bd. in STC 7758.3 Vol. 1 [flat]. Image number 43893)	43

Fig. 2.5 Coin issued for the coronation of thirteen-month-old King James VI of Scotland in 1567, with a hand pointing toward the naked sword piercing the crown and Trajan's motto: "*Pro me si mereor in me*"; use this sword for me, but against me if I deserve it. British Museum, SSB,27.9 (© The Trustees of the British Museum) 48
Fig. 8.1 *In vitam humanam*, from Andrea Alciato, *Livret des emblemes* (1536) (With permission of the University of Glasgow Archives and Special Collections) 168
Fig. 8.2 *In vitam humanam*, from Andrea Alciato, *Emblemata* (1584) (With permission of the University of Glasgow Archives and Special Collections) 170
Fig. 8.3 *Democritus et Heracletus*, from Johann Theodor de Bry, *Proscenium vitæ humanæ* (1627) (Courtesy of Herzog August Bibliothek) 172
Fig. 8.4 *Consuetudo est altera natura*, from Jacobus Bornitius, *Emblemata ethico-politica* (1664) (Hathi Trust, public domain) 174
Fig. 8.5 Title page, from Johann Flitner, *Nebulo nebulonum* (1620) (Hathi Trust, public domain) 177
Fig. 8.6 *Inverte, et avertes*, from Jacob Cats, *Silenus Alcibiadis* (1620) (Hathi Trust, public domain) 180
Fig. 8.7 *Hic de cæruleis prædicat anatibus*, from Johann Flitner, *Nebulo nebulonum* (1664) (Hathi Trust, public domain) 182
Fig. 8.8 *Hic garriendo literas perforat,* from Johann Flitner, *Nebulo nebulonum* (1634) (Courtesy of Herzog August Bibliothek) 183
Fig. 8.9 *Hic garriendo literas perforat,* from Johann Flitner, *Nebulo nebulonum* (1664) (Hathi Trust, public domain) 186
Fig. 8.10 *Allegory of Fortuna and Justitia*, Anonymous (1534) (Courtesy of the Metropolitan Museum of Art, public domain) 187
Fig. 8.11 *Iustitiæ languor*, from Johann Theodor de Bry, *Proscenium vitæ humanæ* (1627) (Hathi Trust, public domain) 188
Fig. 8.12 *Iustitia et Prudentia*, Hendrick Goltzius (Courtesy of the Rijksmuseum, Amsterdam) 189
Fig. 8.13 *Justitia*, Maratti, Royal Collection (Courtesy of the Royal Collection Trust. © His Majesty King Charles III 2024) 191
Fig. 8.14 Anonymous drawing attributed to Lambert Lombard (© The Trustees of the British Museum) 192

Fig. 8.15 *Democritus, Time and Fortune*, Guillaume Perrière, *Morosophie* (1553) (With permission of the University of Glasgow Archives and Special Collections) 194
Fig. 12.1 Paul Baudry, *La glorification de la Loi* (1881) (Copyright Paris, Cour de cassation) 278

PART I

Introduction

Fig. 1.1 Philip Galle after Pieter Bruegel the Elder, *Justice* from *The Seven Virtues* (c. 1559)
(Public Domain image courtesy of the National Gallery of Art, Washington, DC)

CHAPTER 1

Knowing Justice: Literature and the Legal Imaginary

Subha Mukherji

This engraving, based on a sketch by Pieter Bruegel the Elder and part of a series on 'The Seven Virtues' (1559–1560), is an allegory of justice as well as a scene of judgement. It is a crowded spectacle. The foreground is filled with judges and legal officials on the right. On the left, scenes of torture and punishment dominate: a man is being racked while fluid is forced down his throat and what looks like molten wax is dripped onto his thighs. Another man is being flogged on a stage surrounded by gaping spectators in the middle ground. Curiously, the bustle and the physicality of these judicial events are interspersed with depictions of the textual activities of law. On the far left, a man with a quill enters details into a large, limply bound volume, documenting either penal procedures or information extracted from the torture victim. In the foreground to the right, a figure holding an unbound document appears to be dictating to a scribe seated at the adjacent table, and—just behind them—two men

S. Mukherji (✉)
Faculty of English, University of Cambridge, Cambridge, UK
e-mail: sm10014@cam.ac.uk

S. Mukherji and D. Roberts (eds.), *Literature and the Legal Imaginary*, Crossroads of Knowledge in Early Modern Literature 4,
https://doi.org/10.1007/978-3-031-74093-0_1

sit at a writing desk within a flimsy wooden lean-to, while two others stand over them, one of them holding up a parchment sheet with seals hanging from it. Formally dressed and often armed officers of the state appear throughout. But in the middle of this legal field full of folk—almost hidden—we see Justitia (or 'Justicia'), blindfolded, with a sword in one hand and scales in the other, standing front and centre. The scene is ostensibly a representation of justice, being dispensed impartially and authoritatively. But if so, then it surely evokes criminal justice in its institutionalised form, rather than as a personification of justice as a virtue. The Latin inscription at the bottom suggests that this spectacle of exemplary social justice, grim as it is, is necessary: 'The aim of law is either to correct him who is punished, or to improve others by his punishment; or, following the removal of the culprit, so that the remaining people can live more securely'.[1] But what is overwhelming about this penal landscape is its severity and the sense of justice as a bureaucratic machine. The vivid social space in which the allegorical figure of justice is placed allows realistic evocations of visceral brutality to play against the positive symbolic meanings of sword and blindfold. The shadow of punishment all but overwhelms the symbolism of justice, as we see the letter of the law swamping the spirit of equity. An empty set of shackles lies close to where Justicia stands, and the finely balanced scales which she holds in her right hand hang perilously close to the head of the man who turns the wheel of the rack. Even the pedestal on which she stands has a ring set in it—presumably so that it could be used to restrain a prisoner. Is Justice purely an admonitory figure, or is she herself on trial, with the cross on the hill in the upper left corner of the image evoking the execution of an innocent man who stood for the forgiveness of all mankind's sins? The image teeters between an exemplary depiction and a critique of a criminal justice system that was Judaeo-Roman in origin and at odds with Christian notions of mercy and grace. Like the photographic 'scenes' that pricked Roland Barthes through 'the co-presence of two discontinuous elements', this tense heterogeneity is the site of the adventure of this painting, and its hermeneutic invitation.[2]

[1] The Latin inscription reads: 'Scopvs legis est, avt vt evm qvem pvnit emendet, avt poena / eivs caeteros meliores reddet avt svblatis malis caeteri secvriores vivant'.

[2] Roland Barthes, *Camera Lucida: Reflections on Photography* (London: Vintage Books), 23.

It is interspaces such as these, which elude the formal discourses of law or legal history, that are brought into view at the boundaries between judicial procedure, legal thinking, and imaginative practice. The knowledges generated here are located between ideology and the real processes of law. *Knowing Justice* seeks to understand and inhabit this threshold, and to tune into the collective understanding of law as social action. But the law, in early modern England—the focus of this book though not its horizon—was also an imaginative resource and a repository of structures of feeling. These are functions that can only be grasped from a variety of sources examined together, and often best through literary mediation because literature shares the representational modes and structures of law but not its methods or ends. Our use of 'legal imaginary' gathers up the meanings of the phrase which have accumulated since Cornelius Castoriadis's formulation of it in 1975—variations on the idea that we make the world we live in by collectively imagining it as well as acting in it.[3] The conditions of such a construction are conceptualised according to the point of view and discursive position: Jacques Lacan's psychoanalytical approach employs the imaginary (interlinked in a triad with the symbolic and the real) in the construction of the psyche and the self in the world, and Julia Kristeva relates it to semiotics on the one hand and transference on the other.[4] For Jean-Paul Sartre, the imaginary lies

[3] The genealogy of the term 'imaginary' goes back to '*imaginaire*', as used by Cornelius Castoriadis in *L'Institution imaginaire de la société (1975)*, translated into English by Kathleen Blamey as *The Imaginary Institution of Society* (Cambridge, MA: MIT Press, 1987). For a recent formulation of the relation between social representation theory and social imaginaries, see Angela Arruda, 'Image, social imaginary and social representations', in Gordon Sammut, Eleni Andriouli, George Gaskell, and Jaan Valsiner, eds., *The Cambridge Handbook of Social Representations* (Cambridge: Cambridge University Press, 2016), Chap. 9 (128–42). For a helpful overview of the meanings and evolution of the social imaginary, see Paul James, 'The Social Imaginary in Theory and Practice', in Chris Hudson and Erin K. Wilson, eds., *Revisiting the Global Imaginary: Theories, Ideologies, Subjectivities (Essays in Honour of Manfred Steger)* (Basingstoke: Palgrave Macmillan, 2019). On the contiguous discourse of social construction theory, see Peter L. Berger and Thomas Luckmann, *The Social Construction of Reality: A Treatise in the Sociology of Knowledge* (New York: Doubleday & Company, 1966).

[4] Jacques Lacan, *Écrits* (Paris: Editions du Seuil, 1966) and *The Language of the Self, The Function of Language in Psychoanalysis*, trans. Anthony Wilden (Baltimore and London: The Johns Hopkins University Press, 1968); see also Fredric Jameson, 'Imaginary and Symbolic in Lacan', in *The Ideology essay of Theory, Essays 1971–1986, Volume I:*

at the heart of a theory of total perception.[5] While there are overlaps across these and other variations, it is the sociological sense of 'imaginary'—perhaps most notably explored in modern times by Charles Taylor and Manfred Steger—that is most relevant to this book: the layers of social meaning that can only be understood through a convergence, even collation, of epistemological methods.[6] We veer away from flat description to layered analysis, cognisant of the plurality of concept, practice, and representation. In using a literary lens, we treat apparent binaries or distinct registers as interlinked constituents of an ecology forming the shared and composite understanding of the law: letter and spirit, text and performance, norms and deviations, agreement and exception, custom and nature, earthly and divine, levity and gravity, comedy and tragedy, doctrine and aesthetics, concept and form, images and stories, protests and prophecies, polity and play, regulation and rights. In tune with the complex saturation of this legal imaginary—based on the operation of law but exceeding it in its imaginative remit—this volume navigates the gap between the idealised neutrality of law and its messy, embodied realities, between abstract jurisprudence and the affective, composite, social event of justice or judgement. Its understanding of 'literature', likewise, is capacious: including imaginative writing and practice, literary strategies used by law and its cognate disciplines, and hermeneutic and critical methods that are traditionally regarded as literary. Its notion of epistemology, meanwhile, encompasses not simply the condition of judicial knowledge but also its process, psychology, and ethics; it attempts to know justice at the same time as it attends to what justice knows, fails to know, or resists knowing.

The essays in this collection are bound by a shared preoccupation with the knowledge, judgement, and poetics that the intersection of legal and literary discourses and practices brings under a spotlight. Together, these

Situations of Theory (Minneapolis: University of Minnesota Press, 1988), 85; For Kristeva's imaginary, see Julia Kristeva, 'Psychoanalysis and the Imaginary', in George Levine, *Constructions of the Self* (New Brunswick, NJ: Rutgers University Press, 1992), 285–98.

[5] Jean-Paul Sartre, *The Imaginary: A Phenomenological Psychology of the Imagination* (New York: Routledge, 2010).

[6] Charles Taylor, *Modern Social Imaginaries* (Durham: Duke University Press, 2004); Manfred B. Steger, *The Rise of the Global Imaginary: Political Ideologies from the French Revolution to the Global War on Terror* (Oxford: Oxford University Press, 2008).

dimensions reveal vital facts about what law and literature have historically done for each other, and what they can do for each other in our critical appreciation of cultural dynamics—two levels of interdisciplinary operation that we consistently keep in view. Recalibrating the fundamental assumptions in law and literature studies in relation to the current state of the field, this book charts a way forward from debates about whether the two disciplines are bound by similarities or contrasts, and whether the field is based on fantasising relationality (as judge Richard Posner would have it) or asserting difference (as in Julie Stone Peters's identification of 'shared longing' rather than 'shared content'), to address both complicity and critique.[7] Though literature and law both speak, as the jurists would put it, from the space of truth and are both potentially active and decisive, there are significant distinctions between formal and judicial resolution. While some of us have pointed towards this in our individual research, it is vital now to thematise it and to interpret cultural texts and practices in light of the paradoxical combination of proximity and rivalry in this interrelation which can be traced all the way back to its classical origins.[8] It is against this basic methodological framework that we re-examine our close readings and place them in a wider context of the kind which Franco Moretti called 'distant reading'.[9] It provides an architecture within which we might encounter and extract knowledges that have been obscure or unavailable—perhaps even repressed.

Related to this is the relative claims of the two disciplines to a representation of the 'real'. Peters's provocatively diagnostic article cited above—'Law, literature and the Vanishing Real: On the future of an Interdisciplinary Illusion'—is a brilliant but bleak survey from 2005 which argued that each discipline was drawn to the other because it yearned for a supplement. In the case of law, it proposed, literature seemed able to reconnect codified legal thinking and practice to an affective and ethical reality; for literary critics, law offered the promise of grounding the aesthetic in the active, of mooring the imaginative in the 'real world

[7] Richard Posner, *Law and Literature: A Misunderstood Relation* (Cambridge, MA: Harvard University Pres, 1988); Julie Stone Peters, 'Law, Literature and the Vanishing Real: On the Future of an Interdisciplinary Illusion', *PMLA*, 120:2 (March 2005), 442–53 (448–49).

[8] See Peter Goodrich's foundational article: 'Law', in Thomas O. Sloane, ed., *Encyclopedia of Rhetoric* (Oxford: Oxford University Press, 2001).

[9] Franco Moretti, *Distant Reading* (London: Verso, 2013).

of law and politics', and of bolstering the general with the technical.[10] Peters was pointing up the irony of a project setting out to traverse disciplinary borders ending up exaggerating those very boundaries through an imaginary projection of disciplinary antithesis, and thus undoing its own premises. There is much here that still merits reflection even as the dialogue continues to evolve, and which has already fed into some of the most provocative and polemical work in the field. Indeed, some of the implications of Peters's observation are especially suggestive in thinking about the early modern period. The challenge is to take what this approach offers and to understand what it is reacting to, while steering clear of self-defeating projection. The line that critics such as Peter Goodrich have taken in the past, positing an antinomy between empiricist epistemology and exemplary indetermination, can indeed risk a sentimental aggrandisement of the non-veridical nature of the domain of fiction, if essentialised as a feature of the relation between law and literature.[11] It can, by the same token, amount to a liberal humanist demonisation of the law. Much of the recent scholarship has been anxious to avoid such mystification, and has either emphasised the analogy that Richard Weisberg saw in his suggestively named rebuttal of Posner, *Poethics*, or restated it in terms of an implication in a shared process.[12] Witness Bradin Cormack's presentation of his thesis in his *A Power to do Justice* (2007): '[...] the literary engagement with early modern jurisdiction becomes exemplary, not (according to a familiar historicist model) because literature supports or resists particular developments in Tudor or Stuart laws and governance, but because it is implicated in the same process of shaping unruly practice for which jurisdiction itself stands'.[13] Luke Wilson's earlier, influential book, *Theaters of Intention* (2000), acknowledges the relatively hermetic nature of common law discourse and

10 Peters, 'Law, Literature and the Vanishing Real', 446.

11 Peter Goodrich, *Legal Discourse: Studies in Linguistics, Rhetoric and Legal Analysis* (Basingstoke: Macmillan, 1987); Peter Goodrich, *Oedipus Lex: Psychoanalysis, History, Law* (Berkeley: California University Press, 1995); Peter Goodrich, 'Gay Science and Law', in Victoria Kahn and Lorna Hutson, eds., *Rhetoric and Law in Early Modern Europe* (New Haven/London: Yale University Press, 2001), 95–124.

12 Richard Weisberg, *Poethics and Other Strategies of Law and Literature* (New York: Columbia University Press, 1992).

13 Bradin Cormack, *A Power to do Justice: Jurisdiction, English Literature, and the Rise of the Common Law, 1509–1625* (Chicago: Chicago University Press, 2007), 3–4.

qualifies the glib reciprocal argument of the eighties about the comparable influence of each discipline upon the other, but nonetheless 'insists on understanding early modern English theatre and law as institutions which, despite deep and abiding dissimilarities, show a common preoccupation with representations of human action, ... shaped by evolving articulations of intention' (3).[14]

The findings of our book are suggestive in this regard. For instance, it acknowledges the play at the heart of what we might think of as a regulatory discipline—both performance and pleasure—that the interface of legal and imaginative practice generates, and understand its formal and ethical yield. As several of the essays here indicate, the *tone* of the engagement with play and purpose has shifted on both sides of the interdiscipline: it is no longer about the anxiety that Peters wrote about two decades ago, the perceived lack within their own discursive field which led lawyers to look to literature for a humane enhancement, and literary critics to look to law for praxis. What we hear from our authors' engagements is, rather, a more relaxed and inquisitive awareness of both affinities and differences, and a positive, proactive, and dialogic crossing of the threshold, freed from the constriction of a troubled binary that was of its time. It is not just the lawyers (such as Peter Goodrich, Maksymilian del Mar, and Gary Watt) who—true to Peters's model—emphasise play, nor only literary scholars (such as Doyeeta Majumder) who like to show how apparently frivolous entertainments within legal institutions are engaged in serious legal and political thought. Richard Sherwin, a former legal practitioner, chooses imaginative constructs—'dream' and 'character'—as interrogative devices for the most serious questions of life and death, governance, and ethics. Play is not conceptualised by this volume, across 'legal' and 'literary' contributions, as a function outside of the law, to which the law must turn to fill an affective-ethical hole in its own centre. It is, rather, an aspect of law that scholars are in a position to address with the benefit of historical understanding, in the expanding *inter*space between the disciplines, and liberated from the constraints of *intra*-disciplinary investments. These essays are an invitation for us to fine-tune our paradigm of pleasure and play vis-à-vis solemnity and the reality factor in our mapping of legal-literary conversations—then and now.

[14] Luke Wilson, *Theaters of Intention: Drama and the Law in Early Modern England* (Stanford: Stanford University Press, 2000), 3.

In Renaissance England, the interrelation between law and imaginative practice was inflected by the specific imperatives of legal, theatrical, and fictional practice: the flourishing of drama allowed literature to be mimetic of courtroom practice in novel and vivid ways—a kinship strengthened by the overlap in the cultural geographies of law and drama; the return to classical authorities generated new kinds of fiction and friction between common and Roman law and a newly sharpened awareness of the complex intimacy between forensic and theatrical practice; and the Reformation provoked reconfigurations of legal hermeneutics and the relation between the spirit and the letter of the law. Despite a freshly felt sympathy, a crucial distinction remained between a discipline that seeks actively to arrive at a verdict and one that seeks to complicate it. This combination provoked the complexity of literary engagements with law's methods of knowing, primarily in the theatre but spreading across literary genres. Not only did literature provide law with a humanistic space for exploring empathy, as Martha Nussbaum has argued in a twentieth-century context in *Poetic Justice;*[15] the law provided structures of cognition and feeling to literary practice too. This book tunes into the full range of affects and exchanges that this dynamic entailed, and how they were represented and in turn conditioned representation itself. It aims, ultimately, at a nuanced understanding of the granular constitution of the legal imaginary of a culture.

While our nucleus lies in the early modern period (with eight of our essays taking it as their primary focus), we look before and after, and our contributors bring an awareness of their place in a long tradition of thought, as well as an alertness to the diachronic nature of the interdiscursive entanglement that they address, whether through a focus on its historical specificities or on its *longue-durée* evolution.

Structure and Content

The volume is divided into six Parts, with four sections of thematically grouped essays forming the core, framed by this introductory chapter and the Afterword (Parts I and VI). Part II—the first section of essays—offers us ways of understanding the 'legal imaginary': a collective picture of the values, practices, structures of thought, and modes of representation

[15] Martha Nussbaum, *Poetic Justice: The Literary Imagination and Public Life* (Boston: Penguin Random House, 1995).

through which law is understood by a culture; a view that includes but is not limited to institutions and procedure, and accommodates an osmotic sense of law as both lived experience and symbolic form, official as well alternative jurisdictions. In her essay, 'Solomon, Trajan, and the Figure of Justice', Julie Stone Peters puts pressure on the familiar ideological alignment of judgement and knowledge by crossing them with uncontainable emotion, dramatic action, and spectacular violence. Examining a pictorial representation of iconic legal stories, she opens up its relationship with other *forms* through which the law was imagined: theatrical renderings such as royal entertainments, a scene in Spenser's *Faerie Queene*, a sermon, and a travel guide. These apparently disparate yet legally engaged texts raise questions about what counts as historical evidence, about the functions of the affective and the sensory in the scene of law, and about the opposition between doctrinal and aesthetic knowledge and judgement. Majumder's essay examines the tragedies produced by the law students at the Inns of Court to unearth competing hermeneutic claims around the law of nature, revealing the imaginative space opened up by natural law within the positivist common law of early modern England. Sherwin's 'Escalus' Dream' offers a revisionary reading of Shakespeare's *Measure for Measure* to demonstrate the mutual constitution of states of mind and states of polity and the competing imaginaries of law. Together, these essays are suggestive of a new archive of materials that we might want to institutionalise to understand the law in this larger, more humane, and representationally attuned way.

The essays in Part III—'Text, Knowledge, Hermeneutics'—reflect on the epistemological implications of the law, the stakes of text and interpretation, and the individual and communal elements of legal knowledge. Ranging from Biblical to secular and civil applications of legal hermeneutics and ways of communicating jurisprudence, they offer provocative counterpoints to one another as well as referring out to other overlapping disciplinary thresholds. Regina Schwartz probes the relation between religion and law, taking the Pauline phrase 'letter and spirit' as her punctum and using Shakespeare's *The Merchant of Venice* as her test case for exploring its translation from scripture to equity. Torrance Kirby also dwells on the interface of law and theology, interrogating the tension between Richard Hooker's legal ontology and his reformed doctrine of salvation. But he teases out the 'poetics of law' emerging internally from the dynamic between a proto-scholastic conception of ineffable juridical wisdom, and the visible, audible, order of law. This is shown to have implications not only for legal epistemology but also for the modes of representation—literal or figurative—that enact and express the process of knowing. Charles McNamara expands our interdisciplinary remit by showing how Hobbes's civil science relies crucially on the Aristotelian forensic-rhetorical concept of *homologoumena* or agreement in making 'common opinion' the key tool for communicating—and indeed, proving—law's truths. Explaining the apparently inexplicable centrality of Aristotle in Hobbes's scientific phase, when he translated *Rhetoric* into *A Briefe of the Art of Rhetorique*, McNamara challenges and complicates the temptingly tidy narrative of a Hobbesian turn from civil law to science.

Part IV—'Play and Pleasure'—also revises a historiographical orthodoxy: this time about the register of law itself. The essays here offer an alternative perspective to the received narrative of the solemn business of the law, though their routes into the dynamic between gravity and levity are distinct. Peter Goodrich focuses on humorous doubling in the discourse of law to explore the early modern legal profession's expansion and recasting of a comedic dimension that went back to the classical tradition of *res levem*, emerging out of Roman games and the *officium ludicrae*. Through an exploration of English lawyers' practice of mock trials, revels, saturnalia, and jocastic customs, Goodrich reveals the ways in which the ludic provided a supplement as well as a challenge. Leavening the monumental in law with the momentuous, forms of play are shown to have served as a revisionary, processive, and revitalising force that helped the classically melancholic science of law renew itself by stepping outside of the literally legal and tuning into the enigma, ambiguity, and uncertainty that bind law and life. Del Mar, in a similar key, shows how the mooting exercises at the Inns of Court modelled knowledge as play, and how intrinsic play was to the making of lawyers and legal practice. The argument, illustrated by a close reading of a fourteenth-century moot, brings alive the affective, sensory, and communal dimensions of pleading, and the need for legal pedagogy to accommodate, indeed embrace, the inventive, embodied, and interactive. Gary Watt, on the other hand, close-reads the 'poetic jurisdiction' of the Oxford 'Inkling', Owen Barfield, to reformulate an essential difference between law and poesy—with law seeking to close down ambiguity and poetry forever opening it up. But it is this very antinomy, he argues, that generates pleasure and performance through freeing frisson and, paradoxically, has the potential to unlock what Watt calls the 'first voice' of law, which is a poetic and participatory voice.

Part V, 'Law and Poetics', follows naturally from the previous one: the four essays here all examine the role of poetics in the learning and reception of the law, as well as in imagining, reimagining, supplementing, or challenging it, exploring nothing short of an alternative jurisdiction to positive law. Conrad van Dijk uncovers medieval engagements with the 'state of exception' that Giorgio Agamben designates as a modern phenomenon. Through Gottfried von Strassburg's *Tristan*, van Dijk shows how dire legal need can translate into the metaphor of courtly love, thereby intimating an unsuspected formal affinity between law and love. Valérie Hayaert, like van Dijk, ranges from the thirteenth to the nineteenth centuries to examine the durability of a tradition largely overlooked: the versification of legal codes, whether to aid memory or pedagogy. Jan-Melissa Schramm spots a gap in the historiography of human rights and plugs it by unearthing the abiding but 'forgotten' engagement with universal rights in the literary and theological thought of nineteenth-century England and its incipient internationalism. Alex Feldman unpacks the centrality of the Christian story—in particular, of Christ's trial and martyrdom—to the legal theatre of modernity and the hagiographic drama that forms its source. Like Watt, he focuses on a singular figure: Daniel Berrigan, poet, Jesuit priest, and peace activist, and his documentary verse-drama, *The Trial of the Catonsville Nine* (1970) which was inspired by a landmark law case about the Catonsville protest against the Vietnam War. Feldman shows how the play in turn forged an aesthetically hybrid medium to offer a tool of knowing injustice: a powerful, prophetic interrogation of the American government's exploitation of the earth and its resources. The essays in this section stretch our temporal span from the medieval period to the twentieth century, often looking before and after and intimating previously unsuspected trajectories.

The volume is rounded off by Kathy Eden's Afterword which draws together the interests of the collection as a whole by reflecting on the deep homologies between literature and the law. Going back to Plato, Aristotle, Quintilian, and Philip Sidney, it reflects on the shared status of the two disciplines and practices as human constructs—'*made things*'—and on their common interest in dialogic form. Ultimately, it suggests the necessity of employing intrinsically poetic methods in mediating between the generalities of law and the particularity of human action. It is *poeisis* which is seen to give the law its powers of imagination, and the essays are read as a collective exploration of the variable but essential entanglement of legal and literary imagination.

Interconnections

The section divisions are one way of grouping our essays, but not the only one. They have proved to be thresholds to be crossed and spoken across. The more we have pondered the resonance of the individual arguments, the more we have been struck by the way they forge parallel connections, and come together to form an ecology of ideas about how the regulatory instinct at the heart of law interacts with the poetic, how the veridical and judicial impulses of literary genres complicate any straight-forward polarity between the disciplines, and how the differences between the legal and the poetic can themselves be generative of imaginative affordance and ethical lucidity. Collectively, they invite and initiate a refinement of our understanding of the structure of this interdiscipline, and of the reconceptualisation of knowledge and knowability at the interface between the two cultural practices and intellectual disciplines.

Feldman's essay, for instance, demonstrates how the lyric potency and liturgical affect of legal performance in *The Trial of the Catonsville Nine* forges an alternative episteme to the epistemology of the positive law through a chiasmus between semiotic power and political vulnerability. This is aligned with the divine mandate which drives the defendants, thus intimating a gap between secular procedure and an inwardly apprehended judicial order through an act that carries a performative knowledge that is at once an evocation and a fantasy. While it is palpably affined to essays such as Schramm's which are engaged with juridical poetics, it also speaks to Majumder's exposition of how the drama of the Inns created an 'exceptional' space for natural law within an institution structured by positive law. Her essay, in turn, is in implicit dialogue with van Dijk's exploration of the literary negotiation of exception as a site which reveals a fundamental dimension of the relation between law and literature: allegory. But to him, allegory is both a structure of relation that forms a bridge between two domains, and a reading practice that is at once demanded and generated by this interdiscipline. Thus, it is also in dialogue with the essays that address hermeneutics more explicitly across legal discourse and humanistic works.

On another axis, Feldman's interest in the paradoxical relation between liberal traditions and Christian impulses in twentieth-century jurisprudential drama cuts across to Kirby's exploration of the creative tension in Hooker between the hidden law of nature and the revealed law of scripture. In effect, this is a tension between knowability and mystery that entwines early modern law and religious imagination. Thus, it belongs in some senses, with Peters's essay too, which implicitly taps into the shared discursive interests between law and natural philosophy, focusing as it does on a telling juxtaposition of text and image about legal knowledge and judgement in a scientific textbook. But, in another direction, it links up with Schwartz's and Majumder's discussions, as all three engage with the theological origin that gives rise to the notion of the mystical foundations of law—akin, in our times, to Jacques Derrida's *force de loi*.[16] Schwartz addresses a paradigm and a distinction that reverberates through centuries of Biblical hermeneutics and legal debate.

But interconnections also take the form of provocation. Does Goodrich's argument, for instance, pose a challenge to law's spiritual origins in the way it gets at the doubleness inherent in legal performances? Along with del Mar's essay, it opens up the seriousness of judicial play and the performative pleasure through which the business of judgement finds its voice and its way in the world. In a similar vein, Valérie Hayaert focuses on the value of versification in the transmission of legal codes, raising suggestive questions about the impulses underlying such a sustained symbiosis between law and poetics: is it a want in law that is really a lack, or is it in fact a desire to tap into a mutually enriching affinity? Gary Watt's essay enters into a playful but provocative conversation with all three of these by positing the very polarity between legal and poetic investments in the process of truth-finding to be a source of imaginative energy. While Watt focuses on a twentieth-century literary poet and solicitor as his point of entry, his thesis goes back to an ancient complexity and paradox of interrelation, but shines the spotlight not on the *agon* but the *jouissance* of the interspace between regulation and play.

[16] Jacques Derrida, *Force de loi: Le "Fondement mystique de l'autorité"* (Paris: Galilée, 2005; first pub. 1995). For an English translation, see Derrida, 'Force of Law: "The Mystical Foundation of Authority"', in Drucilla Cornell, Michael Rosenfeld, and David Gray Carlson, eds., *Deconstrauction and the Possibility of Justice* (London: Routledge, 1992), 3–67.

Cross-temporal tracking of the interrelation between law and poetics is a feature of our volume. Van Dijk, like Watt, traces the prehistory of a contemporary concept back to medieval maxims and romance and considers the long-running, cross-historical notion of necessity creating legal exception. Del Mar not only illuminates an epistemic structure familiar to Renaissance legal training but also places it in an extended history, tracing its beginnings back to the twelfth century, before honing in on a fourteenth-century moot for illustration. Hayaert commands a similar span with regard to versification, tracing the entanglement between poetry and jurisprudence across six centuries of cognate practice. Meanwhile, McNamara's revisionist essay traces the genealogy of Hobbesian civil science, revealing diachronic evolutions of legal knowledge as well as demonstrating, somewhat surprisingly, that, even in the age of Enlightenment, the common opinions of the masses constituted an important evidential standard to be met in legal proceedings.

Peters's essay demonstrates vividly how visual representation, alongside a range of literary genres, enables an attunement into the texture of the early modern legal imaginary, and the dynamic—often unstable—relation between forms of knowledge and acts of judgement. While obviously in dialogue with the work of the visual culture and iconography of law, most notably that of our own Valérie Hayaert,[17] in its intuition of the tension between the poetics and praxis of law, this reading also brushes against Watt's discussion of the sweet enmity between poetic and legal jurisdictions.

Schramm, in identifying specific poetic and fictional forms as the repositories of the forgotten rhetoric of rights in post-Revolutionary England, partakes of an inquiry into legal poetics shared by essays which focus on imaginative forms in other periods, such as varieties of dramatic genres, travel manuals, romance, epic, and didactic literature. Richard Sherwin, who is not only a legal academic but, like Schramm, a barrister-turned-scholar, finds that it is drama, and intrinsic dramatic devices such as character, language, and action, that allow him to interrogate most effectively the performative self-constitutions of law and political legitimacy. It is the relatively neglected character of Escalus in *Measure for Measure* that he foregrounds as the agent of reimagining political power and the counterpoint to the Duke's enactment and manipulation of law's knowledge.

[17] See Valérie Hayaert, *Lady Justice: An Anatomy of Allegory* (Edinburgh: Edinburgh University Press, 2023).

Schwartz also finds in Shakespeare's play the most suggestive gloss on the relation between the letter and the spirit of law.

And finally, the essays by McNamara, Sherwin, and Schramm come together in a different orbit to promise an assurance of law's common and communal elements that recalls Hannah Arendt's legal communitarianism—a commitment, throughout her corpus, to the role of law and judgement in human togetherness; this shared hope is also, and more directly, informed by Martha Nussbaum's belief in the imbrication of justice with social good.[18]

While our groupings set up a dialectical framework against which the essays take their place, our readers can choose their own path through the collection, or, 'With windlasses and with assays of bias, | By indirections find directions out'.[19]

Our Book in the Field

The interdiscipline of law and literature has come of age. Since the vexations of the early 1990s, when Posner declared it a 'misunderstood relation', it has evolved into a thriving field across periods, with the English Renaissance proving to be one of the most fecund areas of enquiry.[20] With this progress and the authority and intellectual security it has given us, however, come new responsibilities as well as new freedoms. What can we now see about this interdiscipline—both in primary practice and in academic response—that we could not have had clarity about at the movement's inception? What are the disciplinary anxieties that we should now shake off? Have new ones emerged which we need to examine and seek to understand? What urgencies demand address now? And what does work on interactions between the legal and literary imagination in other

[18] See especially, Hannah Arendt, *Responsibility and Judgment*, ed. Jerome Kohn (New York: Shocken Books, 2003); Hannah Arendt, 'The Nation' [Book Review], *Review of Politics*, 8:1 (January 1946), 138–41; *The Origins of Totalitarianism* (New York: Meridian Books, 1978); Martha Nussbaum, *Poetic Justice*, and *Political Emotions: Why Love Matters for Justice* (Cambridge, MA: Harvard University Press, 2013); and Martha Nussbaum, *Anger and Forgiveness: Resentment, Generosity, Justice* (Oxford: Oxford University Press, 2016).

[19] William Shakespeare, *The Riverside Shakespeare: Second Edition*, ed. G. Blakemore Evans, et al. (Boston, MS: Houghton Mifflin, 1997), 1200 (*Hamlet*, II.i.62–63).

[20] Posner, *Law and Literature: A Misunderstood Relation*.

periods or cultures put in perspective for anglophone early modernists? This book enters the field with these questions in its frame.

The larger terrain to which this book belongs—law and the humanities—has also received recent boosts, thanks to the rethinking and re-energising impact of collections such as the compendial *Oxford Handbook of Law and Humanities*, edited by Simon Stern, Maksymilian del Mar, and Bernadette Meyler (2020).[21] Our volume introduces certain distinctive foci to this subject: it explores the epistemic dimensions of this cross-disciplinary meeting point; commits itself to understanding and capturing the *imaginaire* that legal practices can make available, and which literary and artistic constructions of intention, affective subjecthood, proof, and justice seize on; and attempts to understand this interrelation in its full, multidirectional dynamics, as a two-way process that is determined by disciplinary investments and facilities, encompasses analogy and difference, and eschews both a rationalist resistance to humanistic input and a sentimental aggrandisement of the ethical and epistemic superiority of literature over law. Our point of entry is provided by the specific questions of what literature (including theatrical production) does to—and with—positivist or indeed probabilistic assumptions, and how legal practice understood in its widest sense engages the literary imagination to temper, texture, or complicate its own approaches towards knowing and the knowable. Thus, our intervention reframes the field and re-examines some of the fundamental components of the dialogue between the two discourses and cultural practices in a historical context.

Issues of knowledge are of course implicit in Lorna Hutson's pioneering work, *The Invention of Suspicion* (2007) and in her more recent volume, the rich and dense *Circumstantial Shakespeare* (2015), as well as in Subha Mukherji's *Law and Representation in Early Modern Drama* (2006).[22] But *Knowing Judgements* tries to extract the implications of this conjunction for the larger interdiscipline. It is also unusual in its attention to genealogies. *The Oxford Handbook of Law and Humanities*, for instance, locates the historicisation of the humanities in the

[21] Simon Stern, Maksymilian del Mar, and Bernadette Meyler, eds., *The Oxford Handbook of Law and Humanities* (Oxford: Oxford University Press, 2019).

[22] Lorna Hutson, *The Invention of Suspicion: Law and Mimesis in Shakespeare and Renaissance Drama* (Oxford: Oxford University Press, 2007); Lorna Hutson, *Circumstantial Shakespeare* (Oxford: Oxford University Press, 2015); Subha Mukherji, *Law and Representation in Early Modern Drama* (Cambridge: Cambridge University Press, 2006).

twenty-first century, with Rens Bod's *New History of the Humanities* (2013) and the journal *The History of the Humanities* (launched in 2016) laying the foundation stones for the field.[23] Our volume focuses, instead, on the legal humanities as a practice that brings into view a much older historiography, one that includes and narrativises formative shifts and evolutions of an interdisciplinary relation over time. It also takes a small step towards a wider interdisciplinarity, if only on an indicative scale: given the more comprehensive interdisciplinary project on *Crossroads of Knowledge in Early Modern England* out of which this volume—and the series it completes—emerges, we intimate the interfaces of the specific dialogue between law and literature with other disciplines of knowing—most notably, science and theology.

Particular highlights in the field of law and literature in recent years have included Jessica Winston's *Lawyers at Play* (2016), Bernadette Meyler's *Theaters of Pardoning* (2019), Penelope Geng's *Communal Justice in Shakespeare's England* (2021), and Julie Stone Peters's *Law as Performance* (2022).[24] We have been beneficiaries of each one of these books, in ways big and small. But our scope is more inclusive and, as a collection, we are taking a wider perspective to understand law as an imagined social whole.

Majumder and del Mar both extend the existent research on the dramatic culture of the Inns of Courts and are, thus, in dialogue with, as well as in debt to, Winston's foundational work. But their foci are specific, and their temporal spans are different, with del Mar taking the discussion of moots back to the fourteenth century. And while Winston's book brings alive the vitality of the literary culture of the Inns, and excavates its role in the formulation of political debate in sixteenth-century England, del Mar is interested in the element of play at the heart of legal learning, and Majumder's focus on the performance of tragic plays by law students raises previously unaddressed questions not only about the

[23] Rens Bod, *A New History of the Humanities: The Search for Principles and Patterns from Antiquity to the Present* (Oxford: Oxford University Press, 2013).

[24] Jessica Winston, *Lawyers at Play: Literature, Law, and Politics at the Early Modern Inns of Court, 1558–1581* (Oxford: Oxford University Press, 2016); Bernadette Meyler, *Theaters of Pardoning* (New York: Cornell University Press, 2019); Penelope Geng, *Communal Justice in Shakespeare's England: Drama, Law, Emotion* (Toronto: Toronto University Press, 2021); and Julie Stone Peters, *Law as Performance: Theatricality, Spectatorship, and the Making of Law in Ancient, Medieval, and Early Modern Europe* (Oxford: Oxford University Press, 2022).

kernel of literary genres *in* law, but also about the generic place of the idealised law of nature in the real world of legal training and practice.

Meyler presents a focused study of acts of clemency on the early modern stage and in the no less theatrical domain of contemporary politics. Her work focuses on a number of plays to argue that the early–mid-seventeenth century exhibits a movement from pardons being bestowed on individual malefactors to pardons being granted to larger groups of people, often with an emphasis on the good done to the commonwealth as a whole, rather than on the divine mercy exemplified by the sovereign—a trend which, she argues, both reflected and influenced the status of the pardon in the increasing fractious world of contemporary politics. This central narrative is situated against an impressive literary and intellectual historical background. Her delineation of the intellectual trajectory of the theatre of pardon and her thematisation of a possible genre are compelling and generative. But it is precisely such full-length studies, examining a single idea, that we hope our curated but eclectic gathering of individual chapters will help to generate in the work of our readers.

Geng focuses specifically and persuasively on the attenuation of communal justice in the course of the Elizabethan and Jacobean periods, and the drama's registration of this. In its intuition of the theatre's interrogation of the increasing specialism of legal expertise, her book comes close to our methodological concerns about the transactions at the interface of law and literature. Indeed, Schramm, McNamara and Sherwin's essays are all implicitly in dialogue with her preoccupation with communal justice. But our compilation is engaged in a more collaborative and syncretic act of recovery, though necessarily less sustained and more in the nature of provocative case studies.

Meanwhile, Peters's book is a brilliant unpacking of the very theatricality of law itself, its mise-en-scène, illuminating the aesthetic power of legal performance, the unruly autonomy and surplus of performance that tell us things about the law that doctrine cannot, and the often troubled self-reflexivity that law's performances entail. While her own essay in our volume emerges from these interests, it extends them by considering a range of literary genres and the unresolved but fertile tensions in imaginative depictions of the scene of judgement. Both the courtroom and its aesthetic representation become sites of what Èdouard Glissant might call a 'poetics of relation' as well as an epistemological event.[25] Thus, our volume at once looks forward, suggesting future directions of research, and looks backward in a sense, to reflect on, complicate, and draw out the implicit intimations of recent and ongoing work. It harnesses the energies of the current field and runs with them.

A longer view back across the last fifteen to twenty years of major interventions and directions in the field may be helpful for readers unfamiliar with the interdiscipline. Lorna Hutson's *The Oxford Handbook of English Law and Literature, 1500–1700* (2017) was a major and significant contribution to the field, not least for its evident scope and breadth. Our volume, arriving a few years down the line, builds on the findings of this collection, and fine-tunes its perspectives in light of what happens to the field in the intervening years. It is also thematically more tightly focused and complements the *Handbook* and looks back at it in dialogic mode. Christopher Warren's *Literature and the Law of Nations, 1580–1700* (2015) is another book of interest and relevance. It shares our literary focus but places literary culture in relation to global legalities, and specifically to the emergence of international law. Thus, it gives us methodological grist and provides an intertext for Schramm's essay in our volume, though it remains overall a different enterprise. On another axis, Hayaert's work on legal emblems in Renaissance Europe represents an invaluable perspective on the visual structures of early modern English law, revisited in our volume by Peters and Hayaert herself, and the way in which that links up inalienably with the humanistic imagination. Hayaert and Goodrich's co-edited volume, *Genealogies of Legal Vision* (2014) and Hayaert's recent *Lady Justice* (2023) also provide us with a capacious context.

Derek Dunne's *Shakespeare, Revenge Tragedy and Early Modern Law* (2016) engages with legal culture in challenging the critical orthodoxy of the participatory nature of revenge.[26] While we welcome its revisionist claim about popular participation, it confirms our feeling that much of the work on the early modern part of this turf is focused on drama, and most often on Shakespeare: we open these discussions out to a cross-generic consideration and break newer grounds. Lorna Hutson's *Circumstantial*

[25] Édouard Glissant, *Poetics of Relation* (Ann Arbor: University of Michigan Press, 1990).

[26] Derek Dunne, *Shakespeare, Revenge Tragedy and Early Modern Law: Vindictive Justice* (Basingstoke: Palgrave Macmillan, 2016).

Shakespeare is a seminal contribution to both Shakespeare studies and aspects of law and literature, in showing how the forensic idea of 'circumstances' was deployed to create dramatic character by conjuring a vivid hinterland of motive and intention. In its interest in the classical rhetorical tradition, it complements Quentin Skinner's *Forensic Shakespeare* (2014).[27] We share both volumes' belief in the relevance of the tradition of judicial rhetoric to the English theatrical culture of the Renaissance. But our collective volume, by its very nature, has a wider remit, in terms of both literary genres and legal topics. We are also in a position to draw out, from collaborative close readings, the implications of the paradoxical relation between law and the performative. Knowability is central to this enterprise, as it is tied up with the notion of accessing other people's emotions, and the slippery relations between reading, representation, and reception. The readership is now ready for this enquiry to be taken further and in specific directions. Bringing together legal academics, literary critics, theologians, and former legal professionals, our book should appeal to lawyers, literary scholars, and historians, as well as to scholars of law and literature; indeed the hope is that it forges a wider community around this still-intriguing interface.

It is significant that the field has become self-reflexive in recent years, and several notable books, articles, and journals, as well as conferences and research centres, are geared towards examining the state of the field and its possibilities. This is symptomatic of a discipline that has firmly established itself, but finds itself at a juncture where it needs to interrogate, revise, and readjust its basic premises, and adapt to cultural change. The turf wars of the late 80s and 90s saw excellent critical thinking on what was at stake for the interdisciplinary subject and its two constituents; in Weisberg's *Poethics*, for instance, and Goodrich's polemical, provocative, and controversial books, *Legal Discourse* and *Oedipus Lex*, in the first wave of explorations of the premises of the field. The retrospective *re*-assessments were most clearly initiated, perhaps, with Peters's 'Law, Literature and the Vanishing Real' (2005), discussed early in this chapter. Since then we have had several reflective surveys and re-evaluations: from Subha Mukherji's 'Understood Relations' (2009) to Greta Olson's

[27] Quentin Skinner, *Forensic Shakespeare* (Oxford: Oxford University Press, 2014).

'Futures of Law and Literature' (2015).[28] Much of this self-reflection has taken place in the wider fields of law and cultural studies, and law and the humanities: journals such as *Law and Humanities* edited by Paul Raffield and Gary Watt, *Law, Culture and the Humanities*, edited by Austin Sarat, and the *Yale Journal of Law & the Humanities* have carried a significant volume of the discussions, the majority of which address the modern world. Edited collections such as Austin Sarat's *Law and the Humanities: An Introduction* (2014) have begun to appear in the conversation.[29] Goodrich's Berkeley-based journal, *Law and Literature* (1989–), was a pioneering forerunner to many of these. *Knowing Justice* seeks to situate early modern studies firmly on this wider, cross-temporal map. While it is not exhaustive in its comparatism, it gestures before and after in an indicative spirit, joining up pre-modern narratives and techniques of law and literature to modern, post-modern, and contemporary ones, through precise and often passionate case studies. Our examination of the symbiosis between the compelling narratives and mental images of law and literature probes continuities and changes through to our own times. It opens up the complex sensory prehistory of the affects of the courtroom explored in the contemporary context by legal scholarship such as Richard Sherwin's *Visual Persuasion* project or his *Visualising the Law in the Age of the Digital Baroque* (2011).[30] Relatedly, we pitch into the emerging interest in law and emotion, signalled, for example, by the History of Law and Emotions Research Cluster at The Centre for Medieval and Early Modern Law and Literature at the University of St Andrews, with input from the University of Sydney node of The Australian Research Council's Centre for the History of Emotions. The new focus on affective influences on legal knowledge as well as the affective matter at the heart of the law is attested also by articles such as Susan Bandes and Jeremy Blumenthal's 'Emotion and the Law' (2012),

[28] Subha Mukherji, '"Understood Relations": Law and Literature in Early Modern Studies', *Literature Compass*, 6 (2009), 706–25; Greta Olson, 'Futures of Law and Literature: A Preliminary Overview from a Culturalist Perspective', in Christian Hiebaum, Susanne Knaller, and Doris Pichler, eds., *Recht und Literatur im Zwischenraum: Aktuelle inter- und transdisziplinäre Zugänge = Law and Literature In-Between: Contemporary Inter- and Transdisciplinary Approaches* (Bielefeld: Transcript, 2015), 37–69.

[29] Austin Sarat, ed., *Law and the Humanities: An Introduction* (Cambridge: Cambridge University Press, 2014).

[30] Richard Sherwin, *Visualising the Law in the Age of the Digital Baroque* (New York: Routledge, 2011).

Eric Posner's 'Law and the Emotions' (2000), Terry Maroney's 'Law and Emotion' (2006), Richard Sherwin's 'Law in the Flesh' (2014), and Rachel Holmes and Toria Johnson's *In Pursuit of Truth* (2018).[31] Our book responds to the invitation of this sub-field for early-period literary and legal scholars, to step infill the gaps and join later-period specialists, as suggested by Renata Grossi in her 'Understanding Law and Emotion'.[32] Peters's essay in our book, and in less obvious ways those of Goodrich, Feldman, and van Dijk's, are wholly in tune with this movement but offer new provocations.

The present volume is thus a response to the challenges and stimuli which have arisen in the field during the last few decades. It delves into origins, points towards possibilities, explores performance, and probes form—forms of, and in, law, as well as literary forms. And all the while, it reflects on the evolving, outmoded, and possible methods of interdisciplinarity itself.

[31] Susan A. Bandes and Jeremy A. Blumenthal, 'Emotion and the Law', *Annual Review of Law and Social Science*, 8 (2012), 161–81; Eric A. Posner, 'Law and the Emotions' (University of Chicago, John M. Olin Law & Economics Working Paper no. 103 (2000)); Terry A. Maroney, 'Law and Emotion: A Proposed Taxonomy of an Emerging Field', *Law and Human Behaviour*, 30 (2006), 119–42; Richard Sherwin, 'Law in the Flesh: Tracing Legitimation's Origin to "The Act of Killing"', *No Foundations: An Interdisciplinary Journal of Law and Justice*, 11 (June 2014), 38–60; Rachel Holmes and Toria Johnson, 'In Pursuit of Truth', *Forum for Modern Language Studies*, 54:1 (January 2018), 1–16 (editors' introduction to special issue: *In Pursuit of Truth: Law and Emotion in Early Modern Europe*).

[32] Renata Grossi, 'Understanding Law and Emotion', *Emotion Review*, 7:1 (2015), 55–60.

PART II

Legal Imaginaries

CHAPTER 2

Solomon, Trajan, and the Figure of Justice: Narrative Backgrounds to an Early Modern Allegory

Julie Stone Peters

Figure 2.1 represents "Justitia" (Justice) with scenes from two stories—the Judgment of Solomon and the Justice of Trajan—which it places in the background to illustrate the meaning of the allegorical figure. Appearing on the cover of my recent book, it represents one of the book's central contentions: that behind the concept of law as sober and dispassionate justice lie the messy and contentious realities of law-in-action, a domain of dramatic expression and sensory, affective, embodied experience.[1] The image, however, invites consideration of a number of other issues that I do not address in the book but that lie at the heart

[1] Julie Stone Peters, *Law as Performance: Theatricality, Spectatorship, and the Making of Law in Ancient, Medieval, and Early Modern Europe* (Oxford: Oxford University Press, 2022).

J. S. Peters (✉)
Columbia University, New York, NY, USA
e-mail: peters@columbia.edu

S. Mukherji and D. Roberts (eds.), *Literature and the Legal Imaginary*, Crossroads of Knowledge in Early Modern Literature 4,
https://doi.org/10.1007/978-3-031-74093-0_2

of this collection: the connections between knowledge and judgment, imagination and jurisprudence, literature and law.

Scholars of the early modern period have noted the importance of Solomon as a model for the English monarchy, but have paid little attention to the equally important figure of Trajan, who often appeared side-by-side with Solomon in texts and images. In the Justitia image, the two stories at once illustrate the allegorical figure of Justitia and articulate the relationship between two different meanings of the word "judgment" for law: judgment-as-knowledge (arrival at the verdict) and judgment-as-execution (enactment of the sentence). I argue, among other things, that the difference between these two legal conceptions of judgment—surprisingly unremarked by legal historians and theorists—offers a key to understanding the relationship between law's epistemological and penal functions, and that a number of key ethical and political concepts hinge on this difference as well. My essay uses the Justitia image as a starting place for exploring the relationship between these two forms of judgment as they appear in these two stories and in the broader early modern legal imaginary. It then turns to consider the particular significance of these stories for the Tudor-Stuart monarchy, where they offer two very different visions of justice and of the relationship between sovereign prerogative and the law: visions that are in fact antithetical and that continue to appear in our own battles over authority, right, and justice.

Scenes of Justice: Two Stories Confront an Allegory

"Justitia" and the Ideology of Justice in the Margarita Philosophica *(1505)*

The Justitia illustration appears in a 1505 manuscript of Gregor Reisch's *Margarita philosophica* (*Philosophical Pearl*), a popular introduction to the liberal arts first published in 1503.[2] It illustrates Reisch's heavily

[2] Gregor Reisch, *Margarita philosophica* (1505), Ghent University Library, MS BHSL.HS.0007, verso of unnumbered leaf between fol. 312 and fol. 313. Available online: https://lib.ugent.be/viewer/archive.ugent.be%3A403E45D4-8200-11E3-9D7A-455ED43445F2#?c=&m=&s=&cv=318&xywh=-144%2C0%2C8002%2C4869, accessed 30 August 2023. Unlike the other illustrations, which replicate the composition of the woodcuts in the original 1503 edition, the image of Justitia is original to the manuscript. On the *Margarita philosophica* generally, see Andrew Cunningham and

Fig. 2.1 "Justitia" with scenes from the Judgment of Solomon and Justice of Trajan. Gregor Reisch, *Margarita philosophica* (1505) (Courtesy of Ghent University Library, MS BHSL.HS.0007, verso of unnumbered leaf between fol. 312 and fol. 313)

ideological discussion of "Justice" (*Iusticia*). There, justice appears not as an abstract virtue but as the concrete product of juridical institutions, consisting (for Reisch) of justice of two kinds: "legal justice," which punishes "an impious act of whatever kind against the law" and "pure justice," which, through law, "gives a stable ... order to things that are not [naturally] ordered." The allegorical figure of Justice represents this union of law and justice: "Justice ... assigns to everyone what they deserve and does not claim anything to herself," writes Reisch (paraphrasing Aristotle). She "has no malice" and is "oblivious to her own good," dedicated only to "fairness," along with all the other virtues: "religion, devotion, observance, obedience, protection, penitence, gratitude, truth, ... generosity, friendship, reliability, equity and all the others." In her perfect virtue, she belongs to the sphere "of the holy."[3]

The illustrator clearly read Reisch's text carefully before designing the Justitia image, which translates Reisch's orthodox allegory into visual form. Serenely regal in her crown and ermine-trimmed robe, Justitia sits on her throne-like tribunal, whose acorns symbolize the "penitence" she demands of those who offend "religion, devotion, observance, obedience." On the one hand she holds a book of law, representing knowledge and the rules that produce "stable ... order." On the other, she holds a holy sword representing judgment: her power to punish "impious act[s]." Dispassionate, upright, motionless, "steady and perpetual," Justitia is here (as Aulus Gellius described her) "dignified, holy, austere ... lofty, and powerful," full of "force and majesty": "an awe-inspiring virgin with penetrating eyes."[4]

But what exactly are her eyes penetrating? An attentive observer might notice that all of the other allegorical figures in the 1505 manuscript are busily engaged in their respective activities: Music directs the musicians; Geometry shows her students how to draw with a compass; Astronomy

Sachiko Kusukawa's introduction to Gregor Reisch, *Natural Philosophy Epitomised: A Translation of Books 8–11 of Gregor Reisch's Philosophical Pearl (1503)*, trans. and ed. Cunningham and Kusukawa (Abingdon, Oxon: Routledge, 2016), ix–lxvi.

[3] Reisch, *Margarita philosophica* (Freiburg: Johannes Schott, 1503), sig. bbiiv–r (translations mine).

[4] Valérie Hayaert, *Lady Justice: An Anatomy of Allegory* (Edinburgh: University of Edinburgh Press, 2023), 81 (quoting Gellius's *Attic Nights* 14.4). Hayaert notes that this passage was regularly quoted by humanist lawyers and orators.

points her astrolabe at the stars.[5] Justitia alone sits aloof on her throne, looking away through half-hooded eyes. Gazing toward the infinite, she seems to illustrate Reisch's pious, anti-ocular precept: "wisdom can never be seen with the eyes of the body," only "by the intellect ... inspired without mediation by the 'Father of lights.'"[6] But meanwhile, two highly interesting scenes are unfolding behind her: full of seething emotion, dramatic action, and spectacular violence. The image seems to draw our eyes past the static figure on the throne, urging us to use "the eyes of the body" to look at the scenes in the background and learn how the law really works. Justitia, of course, does not see these scenes, which take place quite literally behind her back. Is it possible that, for all her regal dignity, she is no different from the famous figure of "Justice blindfolded by the Fool" in Sebastian Brant's *Ship of Fools*?[7] What might she see if she would only turn around and look?

What she would see are scenes from two stories familiar to most early modern viewers: the Judgment of Solomon and the Justice of Trajan. These two stories circulated widely in texts and images: magisterial epics and street ballads, serious political treatises and scurrilous scandal sheets, epic paintings and crude woodcuts. Both stories served as exemplary instances of wise judgment featuring model protagonists: "Solomon's judgement betweene the two harlots, maketh him renowned"; Trajan's "worthy deed ... shewed the true and perfect Iustice."[8] It is thus not surprising that the two stories sometimes appeared side-by-side. They flank the figure of Justice in Girolamo Mocetto's ceiling fresco (painted 1531).[9] John Trapp includes them together in his list of virtuous ruler-judges who listened to "the poor oppressed": "*Solomon* [heard] the two harlots [and] *Trajan*, the widow that would not be put off till another

[5] *Margarita philosophica* (manuscript), fol. 105r, 120v, 137v.

[6] Reisch, *Natural Philosophy Epitomised*, 16–17 (translation modified) (paraphrasing Augustine, *On the Trinity*, 9.c.3[3]).

[7] Sebastian Brandt, *Das Narren Schyiff* (Basel: John Bergmann, 1494), 186 (image sometimes attributed to Albrecht Dürer).

[8] John Speed, *The Genealogies Recorded in the Sacred Scriptures* (London: J. Beale, 1612), 1 Kings 3 (no signatures). Iñigo López de Mendoza, *The Prouerbes*, trans. Barnabe Googe (London: Richarde Watkins, 1579), fol. 44v.

[9] Musée Jacquemart-André, *Catalogue itinéraire* (Paris: n.p., 1913), 142 (sometimes attributed to Girolamo da Santacroce; see Jean Seznec, *The Survival of the Pagan Gods* [Princeton: Princeton University Press, 1953], 130).

time."[10] The names "Solomon" and "Trajan" were proverbial for justice: "*Iust* he was, a *Salomon*"; "Iust Queene! ... A she Traian! this!"[11]

To briefly summarize the Justice of Trajan (less familiar to modern audiences than to early modern ones): as the Roman Emperor Trajan is heading to war, a poor widow stops him on the road and begs him to avenge the murder of her son. Trajan tells her to wait until he returns. She protests that he may never return. He says that his successor will then give her justice. She tells him that another's justice cannot free him of his obligation: if each judge leaves justice to his successor, justice will never be done. Persuaded and moved by the widow's pleas, Trajan "does her justice." Although some versions specify the nature of this "justice"—Trajan immediately put the murderer to death—others leave it vague, giving rise to variants. Sometimes the murderer turns out to be Trajan's own son whose horse has trampled the widow's son: incorruptibly just, Trajan condemns his son to death or (in another version) replaces the widow's son with his own. In at least one version, the widow's son is actually a daughter who has been raped by one of Trajan's servants and must be avenged.[12] An important sequel often accompanied the story, buttressing Trajan's reputation as "the virtuous pagan": Saint Gregory was crossing Trajan's forum, remembered what Trajan did for the widow, and prayed fervently to God that Trajan be released from purgatory. God answered Gregory's prayers by bringing Trajan back to life, and the emperor became a devout Christian.

Together, the story and its sequel served to illustrate Trajan's virtue as a ruler-judge more generally: even when busy, "he did never ... growe negligent in the administration of Justice"; he sat "openly" at the city gate "to heare and determine matters of iustice," never "den[ying] audience" to those who "came to crave justice"; he appointed advocates to "defend the poore," setting aside a day in the week to hear their causes; he claimed "that for Princes to be Iusticers, it were right necessarie to be iust in their owne persons."[13] A famous anecdote—which often accompanied

[10] Trapp, *A Commentary* (London: Thomas Newberry and Joseph Barber, 1657), 142–43.

[11] John Bowle, *A Sermon Preached at Flitton* (London: Richard Woodroffe, 1615), sig. E3r; Ben Jonson, *The New Inne* (London: Thomas Alchorne, 1631), sig. D3r.

[12] Antonio de Guevara, *A Chronicle*, trans. Edward Hellowes (London: Ralphe Newberrie, 1577), 38.

[13] Guevara, *A Chronicle*, 38–39.

the story of the widow—stood for this proposition. When Trajan became emperor, he supposedly drew his sword before all assembled and declared "*Pro me si mereor in me*": use this sword for me, but against me if I deserve it.[14]

Justice as Forensic Comedy: Evidentiary Judgment Versus Penal Judgment in the Judgment of Solomon

The outsized sword in Justitia's hand references the swords that are so central to the two stories represented behind her, reminding viewers of the relationship between the allegorical figure and her narrative instantiations. The visual parallels draw still more attention to the relationship: for instance (to begin with the Solomon scene), both Justitia and Solomon wear floral crowns and beige robes with ermine trim and are seated under identical red canopies, holding their insignia of power upright in their right hands. The book and sword that Justitia holds are, of course, Solomonic icons, but they also specifically point to the story. As a symbol of wisdom, the book calls up the moment in 1 Kings 3:7–12 when God answered Solomon's prayer by giving him the wisdom to judge the case of the "harlots." As a symbol of judicial power, the sword calls up the moment in which Solomon ordered the living baby cut in two.

Echoes, of course, also call attention to differences: centrally here the fact that Solomon, unlike Justitia, is looking at the scene of law. In fact, the story—in early modern renderings—is precisely about using "the eyes of the body" as a basis for judgment, rather than expecting revelation "without mediation [from] the 'Father of lights.'" When Solomon cries to God that he is only "a lytyl Chylde" (in William Caxton's translation of the *Golden Legend*) and begs for the ability to "iuge thy people and dyscerne bytwene good & euyl," God gives him "an herte docyle & *taught* in Wysdome": that is, training in wise observation unswayed by unruly emotion. It is this, not a direct conduit to divine knowledge, that allows him to "dem[e] of ryghtfull domes" (pronounce correct judgments).[15]

[14] See, e.g. Fig. 2.5.

[15] Jacobus de Voragine, *Thus Endeth the Legende*..., trans. Caxton (London: Wynkyn de Worde, 1527), fol. 41v (emphasis added), hereafter cited in the text.

The story is thus what we might call an evidentiary parable, standing for judgment-as-knowledge (based on observation) rather than judgment-as-execution: for evidentiary judgment rather than penal judgment. The sword becomes a crucial figure in defining it as such. Signifying a godlike power to execute judgments, it is not merely a symbol but the exemplary icon of judgment-as-execution. It appears in the scene promising to serve as an instrument of legal violence. But instead of executing the violence it threatens, it turns out to be merely an evidentiary tool whose purpose is to reveal the truth. This transformation—from instrument of execution to instrument of knowledge—also involves a transformation of the sword from a thing with use-value to one with purely expressive value: a highly theatrical prop. Achieving its powerful effects purely through the realm of the imaginary, the sword thus also stands for the principle that theatricality without violence can in fact be highly legally efficacious. The image, transforming it from a regal sword into an ugly dagger, tellingly associates it with the most theatrical character in the scene: the executioner, who grimaces with villainous glee at the prospect of plunging it into the baby. In the image, it is Solomon's scepter that is parallel to Justitia's sword: a scepter that effectively revises her sword, turning it from an icon of rule-by-violence into an icon of rule-by-wisdom.

In early modern renderings of the story, the observation of emotion is key to knowledge. Caxton, like many, dwells on the physiology of internal feeling, which produces outward signs impossible to suppress: the true mother's "membres and bowelles were meued vpon her sone," and so she could not help crying out, "I beseche & praye the[e], my lorde [the] kynge gyue to her the chyld alyue & slee hym not" (fol. 41v). In a discussion of "violent presumptions" of guilt in his 1593 treatise on ecclesiastical law, jurist Richard Cosin similarly uses the story to illustrate how the judge may confidently treat the parties' visible emotion (here, "motherly pitie") as dispositive:

> [Solomon's] wisedome is ... highly commended, because he grounded his judgement ... upon the motherly pitie which he found in [the "true mother"], that would rather forgoe her naturall childe, then to see it dismembred and parted in twaine.[16]

[16] Richard Cosin, *An Apologie*, 2nd ed. (London: the Queen, 1593), Pt 2: 63–64 (parts separately paginated).

However, in the story, emotion is not in fact transparently legible. Rendering Solomon's court as a kind of stage with three actors, two baby-props, and an audience, the image stresses the fact that Solomon's judgment is the product not of direct and unmediated observation but of careful staging. The trial Solomon stages is a piece of forensic theater that takes the form of a "mousetrap" (to use Hamlet's phrase). Its aim, like Hamlet's mousetrap, is to deploy a (legal) fiction to shock the parties into emotional self-exposure.

The reason Solomon needs his mousetrap is precisely because courtroom emotion is not easily legible. Malefactors are often clever actors, adept at controlling their "membres and bowelles" to conceal their emotions. By making it hard to distinguish the true mother from the false, the Justitia image puts the viewer in the position of a judge who finds it difficult to read the emotions of the parties. It represents both mothers as beautiful women, expressing grace in their faces, figures, and clothing. One woman kneels as she begs for the baby's life, while the other presents her case. We can guess that the true mother is the one piously kneeling, hands pressed together in prayer: surely the artist would not have chosen that posture for the false mother. And yet, is not false piety a central early modern theme? We are precisely in Solomon's position, asking: which is the true mother, which is the false?

Caxton's phrasing—which casts legal truth and falsehood as "good & euyl"—reminds us that the evidentiary problem is not just juridical but theological, as the classic medieval typological interpretation of the story suggests. There, the true mother stands for Ecclesia (the Church) and the false mother for Synagoga (the Jewish synagogue)—representing the true and false religions—with Solomon standing for Christ (the "son of David"), who reveals the true religion through revelation. "That Solomon knew the true mother from the pity he saw in her and returned the infant to her," explains the *Bible moralisée*,

> signifies Jesus Christ who by his great wisdom and by the great pity he saw in her knew Holy Church as the true mother, and he gave her the living child—that is, good Christians, who live in good works. And the dead remained with Synagoga—these were Jews and infidels and heretics and all bad people.

Here, the true mother is at once the Church and Mary in the position of the Pietà: her "pity" is a form of revelation. A double image that represents the parallel accompanies this text: just as Solomon hands the living baby to the true mother (in the left-hand frame), so Jesus hands the living baby to Ecclesia (in the right-hand frame), reminding us of the difference between the Christian living spirit of the law and Jewish dead letter of the law (figured in the babies) (Fig. 2.2).[17]

It is not a surprise that the Justitia image recalls images of Ecclesia and Synagoga (both of whom are generally portrayed as beautiful women), nor that the executioner there resembles Christ's executioners in medieval portrayals of the Crucifixion, where they appear as grotesquely caricatured Jews (red hair, big noses, thick lips). If the Reformation replaced the conflict between Ecclesia and Synagoga with the conflict between Catholic and Protestant, the typologies that informed earlier versions of

Fig. 2.2 *Bible moralisée* (thirteenth century). Vienna Österreichische Nationalbibliothek, Cod. 2554, fol. 50r (details). Left: Solomon hands the living child to the true mother, while the false mother protests. Right: Jesus hands the living child to Ecclesia while Synagoga mourns (Courtesy of the Vienna Österreichische Nationalbibliothek)

[17] *Bible moralisée*, Vienna, Österreichische Nationalbibliothek, Cod. 2554, fol. 50a; quoted (with image) in Sara Lipton, *Images of Intolerance* (Berkeley: University of California Press, 1999), 84. The frames are arranged vertically rather than horizontally in the original.

the Judgment of Solomon continued to have purchased. The executioner remained identified with the Jews, the live baby with both the baby Jesus and the crucified Christ, and the story generally with blood libel stories. The false mother (like the Jews whom Synagoga represents) seeks the blood of the child, who figures the Christ-child destined for Crucifixion. The true mother's tragic acceptance of the sacrifice of her child ultimately brings about salvation. The child in the Judgment of Solomon is not, of course, actually killed (unlike that in early modern blood libel stories: Lope de Vega's *El niño inocente* [1594–1597], for instance, in which the Jews crucify the child and God promises resurrection).[18] But the baby's near-sacrifice, miraculous salvation, and restoration to the true mother figure a kind of resurrection. If the baby represents the Christ of the Nativity, Crucifixion, and Resurrection, Solomon represents the Christ of the Last Judgment: able to "dyscerne bytwene good & euyl"; penetrating falsehood as he "iuge[s] th[e] people." But he is a benevolent judge, representing not the sword but the book of life, enacting Christian judicial mercy: structurally through the suspension of the sword and juridically through the suspension of punishment in favor of restorative justice. The story is, in this sense, not a tragedy of legal knowledge (like *Oedipus* or *Hamlet*) but a comedy of legal knowledge. Here, judgment affects not merely restoration but—as in the divine comedy—salvation.

Justice as Forensic Tragedy: Penal Judgment Versus Evidentiary Judgment in the Justice of Trajan

If both scenes in the Justitia image reflect on the allegorical figure in the foreground, they also reflect on each other, as the visual parallels between the Solomon and Trajan scenes suggest. Both Solomon and Trajan are clad in beige and look down upon a woman dressed in red who kneels, hands clasped in supplication. (Theoretically, the widow should be in mourning, but she appears in red to emphasize the parallel.) In both scenes, a figure on the left gesticulates expressively, while a trio of spectators stands to the right of the judge. These visual similarities point to the stories' narrative and thematic similarities. The death of a child and the mother's demand for justice sets both stories in motion. In both, the grieving mother insists that the law take the life of another in exchange.

[18] See Félix Lope de Vega Carpio, *El niño inocente de la Guardia*, ed. Anthony Farrell (London: Támesis Books, 1985), 119–25.

In both, the virtuous mother's outcry leads the judge to recognize the justice of her claim and she emerges victorious. At the same time, the image highlights the differences between the two stories, most immediately in the contrast between the indoor, courtroom setting on the left and the outdoor, rustic setting on the right. Sartorial differences underscore the different classes the two images represent: the true mother's gorgeous red gown with its lavish purple sleeves becomes the simple red shift and wimple of the widow; the rich, fur-trimmed robes of Solomon's counselors become the short tunics and peaked caps of Trajan's spectators. Unlike Solomon (or Justitia, who sits so regally aloof), Trajan delivers justice "openly" to "the poore." These visual differences remind us of key differences in the class politics of the two stories. One features a clever royal judge as director, teaching rulers how to ferret out crime; the other features a poor but clever widow as director, teaching "the poor oppressed" how to demand justice. One serves as a warning to the common malefactor; the other serves as a warning to the ruler. One represents top-down judgment; the other represents bottom-up justice.

But the differences are also epistemological and ethical. If the Judgment of Solomon is an evidentiary parable celebrating judicial knowledge, the Justice of Trajan is a heavily didactic moral parable demanding judicial responsibility. In early modern treatments, the Justice of Trajan stands for four principles. First, judges must ensure justice for the poor and downtrodden: "they that be impotente shulde be defendid and holpyn in ther nede of them that be myghty."[19] Second, judges must not palm off their duty to justice on others: "thou art to receiue the rewarde [only] of thine owne doings," the widow tells Trajan, "the iustice of an other man [shall not] bee an excuse for thee."[20] Third, judges must not drag out justice: they must "do good, and short Iustice," without their common "delayes … and neglects."[21] Fourth, judges must "always [have] bowels of compassion, to heare the complaints of widdowes, orphans, afflicted and forlorne people, who endure all the torments of the world, to breake through the presse, to manifest their miseryes."[22]

[19] *Dialoges of Creatures Moralysed* ([Antwerp: Jan van Doesborch?] 1530), sig. X3v (Dialogue lxviii).

[20] López de Mendoza, *Prouerbes*, fol. 44v.

[21] Nicolas Caussin, *The Holy Court* (Paris: English College Press, 1626), 359.

[22] Caussin, *Holy Court*, 358.

In both stories, emotions (understood physiologically as "bowels") are key, but in the Justice of Trajan it is the judge who experiences emotion he cannot suppress: Trajan "was mouyd with pitie and descendid from his horse and auengid her cawse"; he was "touched with [the widow's] words," so he "thorowly satisfied the poore woman."[23] The widow is a cool legal reasoner whose logic sets off Trajan's emotions all-the-more starkly. She may briefly weep, but quickly sobers up, "tak[es] hold of [Trajan's] horse," and engages him in Socratic questioning (with a bit of Latin in the version Benjamin Hinton offers in his *Choice and Usefull Sermons* [1650]):

> Oh saith the Widow, but how if it happen that you never return? why then saith the Emperour I will leave it to my Successor…. [Y]ou are bound to do good in your own person, and what is that to you if another discharge that which is your duty? *num te liberabit aliena justitia?* will another mans justice excuse you?[24]

While the scene in the Justitia image portrays Trajan compassionately helping the poor "in [his] own person," it represents the third moral—the importance of not delaying justice—through its composite composition. The bottom half of the scene shows the widow pleading with Trajan for justice. The top half shows the outcome: the execution of her son's murderer. The composite emphasizes how swiftly Trajan acts: as in early modern recountings, essentially no time passes between judgment and execution. This apparent swiftness reminds us that the story is centrally about the relationship between time and justice. Trajan at first urges the widow "to rest content for a time."[25] But, as she points out, time is of the essence: justice cannot wait for him to return from the wars. In the story's *anagnorisis*, Trajan comes to realize that justice delayed is justice denied: it must be timely to be justice at all. There is in fact hardly a moment between the widow's accusation, Trajan's judgment, and its execution: no questions, no search for evidence, no trial. The image conveys the message: do not slow down for evidence, for justice brooks no delay. The

[23] *Dialoges*, sig. X4r (Dialogue lxviii); López de Mendoza, *Prouerbes*, fol. 44v.

[24] Benjamin Hinton, *Eighteene Choice and Usefull Sermons* (London: Humphrey Moseley, 1650), 56.

[25] Hinton, *Eighteene*, 56.

prominence of the hanging stresses the importance here of speed in judgment (judgment-as-execution quite literally). The accused is not allowed a defense: in the image—where the accused appears only as a hanged man, an effect of justice done—the accusation and execution are simultaneous.

In this, the image also highlights important contrasts between the two stories: not only between judgment-as-knowledge and judgment-as-execution but between civil justice and criminal justice, restoration and revenge, reprieve and execution, comedy and tragedy. This last difference comes into play in the parallel between the composition of the Justitia image and the standard composition of Last Judgment images: Christ-the-judge in the middle (where Justitia sits as judge); the reward of virtue on the heavenly side to Christ's right (where Solomon rewards the true mother); and the punishment of vice on the hellish side to Christ's left (where Trajan punishes the murderer). But something is not right. For in the Last Judgment, Christ-the-Judge surveys the scene from His tribunal, enacting divine justice. Here Justitia, so upright on her tribunal, looks away, divinely indifferent to the *divina commedia* that is law. The image seems to say: do not mistake Justice for God; He is omniscient; she (sadly) sees nothing.

Narratives of Justice in the Tudor-Stuart Political Imaginary

The Judgment of Solomon as Royalist Propaganda

While the two stories, standing for antithetical principles, engaged crucial early modern legal and political questions generally, they took on a more specific meaning in Tudor-Stuart England, serving there as pointed political parables in the fierce battles over religion, royal prerogative, and the people's rights.

Tudor monarchs had long identified themselves with Solomon.[26] Both Henry VII and Henry VIII were deemed "second Solomon[s]."[27] At

[26] For general discussions, see Victoria Brownlee, *Biblical Readings and Literary Writings in Early Modern England, 1558–1625* (Oxford: Oxford University Press, 2018), 49–78; and William Carroll Tate, "Solomon's Wisdom, Solomon's Folly: A Study in Early Stuart Iconography," diss. University of North Carolina at Chapel Hill, 1995.

[27] John N. King, *Tudor Royal Iconography: Literature and Art in an Age of Religious Crisis* (Princeton: Princeton University Press, 1989), 81.

the nine-year-old Edward VI's coronation pageant in 1547, "Truth" (with "Justice" by her side) announced that he was now the "yonge kynge Salomon."[28] In Hans Holbein's famous miniature of Henry VIII (c.1535), the king appears with the Queen of Sheba (a figure for the Church) kneeling submissively at his feet. The title page of the Coverdale Bible (1535) shows him in a similar posture, holding the Solomonic sword and book. A prayer book cover produced c.1540 portrays him in the Judgment of Solomon in a composition very like that in the Justitia image: enthroned with scepter, babies at his feet on the checkered floor, and true mother kneeling (Fig. 2.3).[29]

The Westminster School was clearly referencing this tradition when it staged the Latin play *Sapientia Solomonis*—the *Wisdom of Solomon*—for Elizabeth I and Princess Cecilia of Sweden in 1566.[30] The play identifies Elizabeth with both Solomon and the allegorical figure "Justitia," who appears onstage alongside Sapientia and Pax. "Blessed Solomon will see presently another ruler greatly blessed," declares the Prologue, "administering justice and the law to the people whom God gave her to rule over." Elizabeth is the "one judge … expert before all others": soon "like will see like; a queen will see a king.... Solomon with his wisdom will be here among us" (53). However, in the play itself, Solomon is baffled and irresolute rather than "expert": the "case is … perplexing," he declares, with "no evidence, much less positive proof"; so difficult to "say on which side the balance of justice lies" (89). The women confuse him, inviting his servant Marcolph's merciless mockery: "Fie, even a King is a mere laughing stock if he does not know that there is no faith in women, whose tongues belie their thoughts" (93). Any discomfort the two royal guests may have felt at hearing themselves called faithless liars would not have been assuaged by the appearance of the two women on stage: both of them "hooked-nos[e]" "harlots" engaged in a name-calling cat fight that

[28] Sydney Anglo, *Spectacle, Pageantry, and Early Tudor Policy*, 2nd ed. (Oxford: Clarendon Press, 1997), 293.

[29] Girdle prayer book cover, British Museum, 1894,0729.1. Available online: https://www.britishmuseum.org/collection/object/H_1894-0729-1, accessed 21 September 2023. On this and the other images of Henry VIII as Solomon, see King, *Tudor Royal Iconography*, 54–57, 81–88. The Holbein image is replicated in stained glass in the King's College Chapel.

[30] Sixt Birck, *Sapientia Solomonis*, ed. and trans. Elizabeth Rogers Payne (New Haven: Yale UP, 1938), hereafter cited in the text. See pp. 24–39 on the addition in English versions of compliments to Elizabeth, allegorical figures, and Marcolph's dialogue.

Fig. 2.3 Prayer book cover showing Henry VIII as Solomon in the Judgment of Solomon (c.1540). British Museum, 1894,0729.1 (© The Trustees of the British Museum)

fully justifies Marcolph's misogyny (83–87). If the performance hinted to the 32-year-old unmarried queen that she was like the true mother, so virtuous that she might end up childless, the identification was hardly a compliment.

In what was perhaps an attempt at recuperation of the story two years later, Elizabeth used it for the woodcut advertising her Great Lottery in 1567 (Fig. 2.4).[31]

The Judgment of Solomon might seem an odd choice for a lottery advertisement. However, it offered a corrective to the *Sapientia Solomonis* by identifying Elizabeth with the Solomon of her Tudor predecessors

Fig. 2.4 The Judgment of Solomon as a fairy tale pastoral in the advertisement for Elizabeth I's Great Lottery (1567). *A Very Rich Lotterie Generall* (London: Henrie Bynneman, 1567) (Detail from extra sheet following Folger Shakespeare Library, STC 8000 Bd. in STC 7758.3 Vol. 1 [flat]. Image number 43893)

[31] Included with lottery proclamation in some copies of *A Booke Containing All Such Proclamations as Were Published During the Raigne of the Late Queene Elizabeth* (London: Bonham Norton and John Bill, 1618) (vol. 1, no signatures, organized by year of reign). For additional references to Elizabeth as Solomon, see David Dean, 'Elizabeth's Lottery: Political Culture and State Formation in Early Modern England', *Journal of British Studies*, 50:3 (July 2011), 596 (and 592–98 on the lottery advertisement).

while implying that the lottery would not be rigged: Elizabeth would choose winners according to objective principles, as Solomon had when testing the women. The woodcut shows a bearded king who resembles a young, trim Henry VIII. But it is radically different from portraits of Henry as Solomon. Inset in a page displaying the lottery prizes, the woodcut draws the eye away from the shelves of cups, spoons, and coins to the world of fairy tale pastoral: a court set amidst rolling hills, peaked mountains, and fecundly flowering plants and fruits. The live baby looks like a rabbit about to be skinned after a sylvan hunt. The king holds a scepter that resembles a magic wand as if to say: the royal judge as fairy-king needs no evidentiary test, for he waves his wand and all is revealed.

Perhaps recalling the lottery woodcut, Spenser adapted the story in "The Legend of Artegall or Of Justice" in book 5 of *The Faerie Queene* (1596).[32] Here, an evil Knight named Sanglier has beheaded his own "Lady" and stolen that of a virtuous Squire, claiming that he is the rightful possessor of the living lady and that the headless one belongs to the Squire. Artegall—representing allegorical "Justice," Solomon, and Elizabeth all at once—determines to "cast about by sleight the truth thereout to straine." This "sleight" involves the staging of a test very like Solomon's. Artegall announces dramatically that he will share the lady between the two parties, giving half to each. Predictably, the Squire renounces his own share, proving his veracity. However, in a significant departure from the biblical story, Spenser tells us that Artegall had *already* "by signes perceiu[ed] plaine" that Sanglier was guilty. More omniscient than Solomon, he needs no sleight to look into the hearts of his subjects. It is surely not a coincidence that a year before Spenser published "Of Justice," Elizabeth had Robert Southwell hanged, drawn, and quartered for high treason. With no evidentiary function, Artegall's piece of legal theater serves only one purpose: it legitimizes Sanglier's spectacularly bloody punishment.

[32] Edmund Spenser, *The Fairie Queene*, ed. A. C. Hamilton, Hiroshi Yamashita, and Toshiyuki Suzuki, 2nd ed. (Harlow: Pearson, 2007), 507–15 (Bk 5, Canto 1; all quotes p. 514). Notably, Thomas Morton published his *Salomon* the same year with an image of Elizabeth and Solomon as "Reg. Pacis" and "Rex Pacis," holding up the royal coat of arms. *Salomon* (London: Robert Dexter, 1596), sig. A1v.

Trajan's Sword as Icon of Tyrannicide

The figure of Trajan offered dissenters (both Puritan and Catholic) an alternative to such proto-absolutist visions of justice. In Thomas Lodge's *A Margarite of America* (1596), the wise, old Arsinous cites Trajan in his reproaches to the Emperor Protomachus: "*Traiane* … was commended in Rome for hearing poore mens complaints," he cries. "[S]o art thou condemned … for shutting thy gates against all kind of sutors," leaving "the poore … to complaine," and "shutting thy eares lest thou heare those complaints that haue already deaffed the heauens for equitie."[33] Here, "equitie" denotes political equity generally, but more specifically the kind of judicial equity provided by the equity courts: royal courts established to bypass strict legality and offer relief according to the dictates of the judge's conscience. Since litigation fees were low in equity courts, even the poor could afford to bring cases there. In his *Looking Glasse for Princes and People* (1632), William Struther makes the point explicitly. Contrasting "righteous King[s]" like Trajan with Solomon, he notes that when Trajan refused to proceed "till hee did Iustice to an oppressed Widow," he was like "a Master of requeasts"—the judge of the equitable Court of Requests—who taketh the complaint in hand, and calling "Wisedome and Prudence to counsell, … doe[s] right according to the cause" rather than the strict letter of the law.[34]

Lodge's Arsinous points out to Protomachus that granting access to justice is not merely right: it is also prudent, since political loyalty depends on it. Rulers who "shut their gates against their subiects," he warns, "cause them not to open their hearts willingly to obey them," inviting rebellion.[35] Such political claims often came veiled in treatments of the Justice of Trajan as a parable of individual responsibility or spiritual responsibility to God. When the narrator of one of the moral dialogues performed in the radical utopian community of Little Gidding in 1631 recounts the Trajan story, she explains that "the Wisdome & Worth of [Trajan's] Action ought to be imitated by vs neuer putting off the doing

[33] Thomas Lodge, *A Margarite of America* (London: John Busbie, 1596), sig. F2v. Lodge converted to Catholicism around the time he wrote *A Margarite of America* and went into exile after James demanded the oath of allegiance in 1606.

[34] William Struther, *Looking Glasse for Princes and People* (Edinburgh: Andro Hart, 1632), 101.

[35] Lodge, *Margarite of America*, sig. F2v.

of right & iustice which wee are bound to performe."[36] The conversation soon turns obliquely to Charles I. "[O]ld stories mouc not so much" (another speaker declares): "our instances [should] bee of later times" (17). When she invokes "[t]he name of Charles," it "stilled not onely the tongues, but the thoughts of the whole Company" (24). This King Charles turns out to be Charles V (King of Spain and Holy Roman Emperor). But referred to as "Charles" throughout, and dominating the remainder of the dialogues, he clearly evokes his English namesake. Unlike Charles I (but very like Trajan), he appears as a model of "Iustice" (44): a king who once humbled himself before "a souldier of Base Ranke [and] baser condition" (26), who "restless[ly] [sought] Lawfull Counsell [to] Refor[m] corrupted manners & ... revnit[e] diuided opinions" (44), who eventually abdicated, giving up worldly for spiritual glory. "If Pietie & Iustice bee as seriously intended, Euery mans Condition may bee made as flourishing ... as Charles['s] was" (45),—as flourishing as Charles I's could be. A year after Charles's execution, we learn from Benjamin Hinton that when the widow asked Trajan rhetorically, "will another mans justice excuse you?" what she meant was: "Gods Commandements are given ... in the second person to every one, that every one might take them as spoken to himself, and so might performe them in his own person."[37] Everyone, even kings.

Paired with the story of the widow, Trajan's famous motto—"*Pro me si mereor in me*"—stood for the principle that the monarch was not above the law. In more radical terms, it stood for the people's right to tyrannicide. Writing in 1556 in exile from Marian England, John Ponet explained:

> The good emperour *Traianus*, ... minding to shewe, that he was not ordained to be a tiranne, ... and that ... he [was] subiecte to the lawes, toke a sweorde,... and saied: *Take this sweorde, use it for me against mine*

[36] A. M. Williams, ed., *Conversations at Little Gidding* (Cambridge: Cambridge University Press, 1970), 10 (hereafter cited in the text). For an analysis of the community's royalist-republican politics, see Debora Sugar, 'Laudian Feminism and the Household Republic of Little Gidding', *Journal of Medieval and Early Modern Studies*, 44:1 (Winter 2014), 69–94.

[37] Hinton, *Eighteene*, 56.

> *enemies…: and if I my self doo not iustly use it, than use it against me…. Iustice will, that princes be obedient [and] bounden to their owne lawes.*[38]

When George Buchanan argued for the right to tyrannicide in his *History of Scotland* (1582), he too cited the Trajan anecdote: "when he delivered a Sword to the Governour of a certain City, [Trajan] is reported to say, *Use it either for me, or against me, as I deserve.*"[39]

Buchanan served as tutor to the young James VI of Scotland—future James I of England—for roughly a decade. His *On the Law of Kingship* (1579), another defense of tyrannicide, provided the case for the prosecution of Mary Queen of Scots for treason and helped lead to her execution in 1587. It was almost certainly he who designed the coin issued for the coronation of thirteen-month-old King James in 1567 (Fig. 2.5).[40]

On one side were the words "*Iacobvs 6 Dei Gratia Rex Scotorum*" ("James the Sixth, by the Grace of God, King of Scots") with the Scottish royal arms. On the other was an image of a naked sword piercing a crown, encircled by Trajan's famous words, "*Pro me si mereor in me*," with a hand pointing ominously at the sword. The motto might seem a peculiar choice for a baby king: who wants to imagine a sword turned against a baby, even if he deserves it? But it helped to explain why baby James was being crowned in the first place when his mother was still alive. It also stood as a warning to the king, intended to accompany him from the cradle to the grave: wield the sword for justice or you will find it wielded against you.

The Entry of James VI into Edinburgh (1579): Two Swords, a Baby, and the Making of a King

On Friday, October 17, 1579 (the year Buchanan published *On the Law of Kingship*), thirteen-year-old King James VI arrived in full regalia at the

[38] John Ponet, *A Shorte Treatise of Politike Power* ([Strasbourg: W. Köpfel], 1556), sig.C6v–C7r. The Catholic Bishop of Winchester John White used the same anecdote against Elizabeth in his funeral oration for Mary Tudor in 1558. John Strype, *Ecclesiastical Memorials*, 3 vols. (Oxford: Oxford University Press, 1822), 3(2):542.

[39] Buchanan, *History of Scotland* (London: A. Churchil, 1690), 268–69 (Bk XX, pagination non-consecutive).

[40] See John Lindsay, *A View of the Coinage of Scotland* (Cork: Bolster, 1845), 52; and the copy in the British Museum (SSB,27.9) reproduced here, https://www.britishmuseum.org/collection/object/C_SSB-27-9, accessed 25 September 2023.

Fig. 2.5 Coin issued for the coronation of thirteen-month-old King James VI of Scotland in 1567, with a hand pointing toward the naked sword piercing the crown and Trajan's motto: "*Pro me si mereor in me*"; use this sword for me, but against me if I deserve it. British Museum, SSB,27.9 (© The Trustees of the British Museum)

West Port of Edinburgh for a triumphal entry marking his assumption of the duties of kingship. At the port, the town magistrates received him "under a pompous payle of purple velvot" and presented him with the first scene in the pageant:

> the wisdome of Solomon, as it is written in the thrid [*sic.*] chapter of the first buik of Kings: That is to say King Solomon was representit with the tua wemen that contendit for the young chylde. This done, they presented unto the King, the sworde for the one hand, and the scepter for the uther.[41]

[41] All quotes unless otherwise noted are from the eyewitness account in *The Historie and Life of King James the Sext*, ed. Thomas Thomson (Edinburgh: Bannatyne Club, 1825), 178–79. (For a discussion of the complicated textual history, see Thomson's introduction, I–XVIII.) I have supplemented *The Historie* with David Calderwood's more detailed early seventeenth-century version, reproduced in *The History of the Kirk of Scotland*, ed. Thomas Thomson, 8 vols. (Edinburgh: Wodrow Society, 1842–49), 3:458–59 (hereafter cited in the text as "Calderwood"). Calderwood was about four years old at the time of the events, but the additional details in his account are such that they must have been reported by an eyewitness. For discussion of Scottish royal entries generally, see

The choice of this subject for the pageant's opening established one of its central themes: Justice. At "the hous of Justice"—the "Old Tolbuith," which served as both courthouse and prison—"foure gallant vertewous ladeyis" greeted the king, among them the allegorical figure of "Justice." At the Kirk, James Lawson, a Senator of the College of Justice, gave a sermon on Psalm 2, verse 10: "O ye kings: be instructed, ye judges of the earth" (Calderwood 3:459). The presence of the town magistrates signified that the pageant would celebrate not just Justice but Justice realized through law.

The Solomon scene offered a thrilling spectacle: "*Solomon* with a Numerous Train, habited after the *Jewish* or (rather) the *Roman* manner"; two biblical "harlots" (probably performed by energetic boys) in a pitched battle over the baby; the action large and dramatic for the 300 officials and huge crowd of ordinary citizens in attendance.[42] The baby was almost certainly a real baby, as in the *Sapientia Solomonis* performance, where a woman was paid twelvepence to bring "her childe to the stage and there atten[d] upon it."[43] The boy king himself was part of the spectacle, facing the player king under the royal purple velvet canopy. Solomon must have appeared, in tableau, as a kind of adult projection of James: enlarged and mythically transformed into a biblical patriarch. The tableau seemed to suggest that James was about to take on the mantle of Solomon, following his royal forebears. But the symbolic analogy must also have highlighted the difference between the patriarch and the thirteen-year-old boy, closer in age to the baby on stage. James's first appearance in a royal spectacle had been his coronation as a baby. The baby on stage recalled James's past, the adult king his future.

The scene—a kind of *speculum principis* and emblem representing James's progress from royal cradle to throne—offered a microcosm in tableau of the procession as a whole, which moved from this scene, featuring a baby, to one with "a young boy," to one with a troupe of young "scollars," to the "cheif collegiall kirk," to a "genealogie of the Kings of Scotland" where "a nomber of trumpets ... cr[ied] with loud

Giovanna Guidicini, *Triumphal Entries and Festivals in Early Modern Scotland* (Turnhout: Brepols, 2020), especially 86, 191–92, 202, 246–47 (references to the Solomon scene).

[42] David Crawfurd, *Memoirs of the Affairs of Scotland* (London: Booksellers, 1706), 356; and Calderwood 3:458 on the crowd.

[43] Ruth Harriett Blackburn, *Biblical Drama Under the Tudors* (The Hague: Mouton, 1971), 144.

voyce, Wealfayre to the King."[44] At the same time, the Solomon scene was, transparently, a political allegory. A sword had figuratively hung over the head of baby James from the moment of his coronation, as violent struggles over the throne kept him barricaded in Stirling Castle. In saving the baby from the sword, the scene enacted James's reprieve: instead of being split in two by warring factions, he would be restored to his rightful place. It also called up the conflict between Mary Queen of Scots and Queen Elizabeth. In 1579, Mary had been Elizabeth's prisoner for over a decade, but to many in Scotland, they were engaged in an as-yet-undecided battle. It was a battle over (among other things) the English throne, which Mary had once claimed and which many Catholics thought was rightfully hers. Elizabeth was now 46 years old and James was a likely heir. So the two women were also, in a sense, battling over a child. For Catholics, it would have been obvious that Mary was the true mother and Elizabeth the false. Many Scots Protestants would have shared this view: certainly James himself (as his letters to Mary and Elizabeth show).[45] Elizabeth clearly did not like James: she would describe him a few years later as "[t]hat false Scotch urchin!"[46] If she could not have him alive, she would rather have him dead. Mary, on the other hand, seemed (like the true mother) willing to give up her claim to save her son. The religious struggles at the heart of English-Scottish politics added a theological undercurrent to the political allegory. Mary had long appeared to many as a type of the Virgin Mary (however un-virginal she may have been). As incipient Solomon, James was of course a prototype for Jesus: the living baby (Jesus) and the future Judge of Judges. So the true mother could represent, simultaneously, Queen Mary (mother of James) and the Virgin Mary (mother of Jesus), who must give up her child to save not just Him but humankind.

In this reading, the scene should have portrayed the discovery and victory of the true mother, as most representations of the story did. But to figure Mary vanquishing Elizabeth and snatching back the baby would have horrified not only Protestants but probably many Catholics, suggesting volatility and political chaos to come. It would certainly have

[44] On the *speculum principis*, see Guidicini, *Triumphal Entries*, 193–94.

[45] James I, *Letters of James VI & I*, ed. G. P. V. Akrigg (Berkeley: University of California Press, 1984), 44–51, 74–86 (she is his "natural mother" [82]).

[46] James I, *Letters*, 6.

been no compliment to James, whose hold on the throne was tenuous enough. There was only one solution. Do not give the baby to either mother. Instead, give it to James. At least that is how one eyewitness remembered it: the actors "presented the sword to the king *with the childe*" instead of the scepter.[47] Babies, of course, cry and are not always properly diapered, so the gesture courted comic disaster. But representing the defeat of *both* women, it might have seemed worth the risk: a young king in possession of the prize was now to replace the quarrelsome women who had preceded him on the throne.

The finale (whether with scepter or baby) achieved several things. It transferred authority from King Solomon to King James. It signified—through the figure of the sword—at once his legal authority and (rather heavy-handedly) his manhood. It shifted the focus from the true mother's victory to James's, implicitly sidelining Mary: what mattered was that James had emerged triumphant from the struggles over the throne and now possessed the insignia of royal power. And it took the focus off of Solomon's evidentiary test, shifting it onto the king's raw authority—signified by the sword—as the basis for judgment. The scene replaced judgment-as-knowledge with presumptive sovereign possession: authority that need not seek out evidence or even bother to demonstrate the truth of its judgments to the people (as Artegall does); power that was its own law.

However, when James took up the sword, some must also have thought of the coin with "James the Sixth, [only] *by the Grace of God*, King of Scots" on one side and Trajan's sword and motto on the other. The coin was still in wide circulation: reissued repeatedly, with a fresh issue in 1578, the year before the entry.[48] It was sufficiently memorable even decades later that John Williams, Bishop of Lincoln, used it in his funeral sermon for James (in 1625) as a metaphor for James's "aemulous *Posteritie*," forever with "*Traian['s]* ... engrauen."[49] As late as 1649, Milton referred to the coin in *The Tenure of Kings and Magistrates*, viewing it as prophetic:

[47] Calderwood 3:458 (emphasis added).

[48] See World of Coins, https://www.worldofcoins.eu/forum/index.php?topic=51128.0, accessed 30 August 2023.

[49] John Williams, *Great Britains Salomon* (London: John Bill, 1625), 61 (hereafter cited in the text).

> [T]hat very inscription stampt upon the first Coines at his Coronation, a naked sword in a hand with these words, *Si mereor in me, Against me, if I deserve*, [seem'd] to presage the sentence of Divine justice in this event upon his Son.[50]

Ten days before James's triumphal entry, the Edinburgh Council protested his appointment of a provost without their consent: a "breache of their privileges" (Calderwood 3:458). It is surely not a coincidence that James ordered another coin a few weeks after the entry, with "James the Sixth, ... King of Scots" on one side, and on the other the words "*Nemo me impvne lacesset*" replacing Trajan's motto: "No one shall hurt me with impunity."[51] As the actors handed him the sword, some spectators must have wondered. Would James be more like Trajan, as the sword on the coin had promised? Or would he be more like Solomon, whose sword may have represented wise judgment in youth but in age stood for autocracy and overtaxed manhood (those thousand wives and concubines...)?

In a session of Parliament that the still-new King James I of England attended in 1604, the Speaker of the House held up Trajan as a model of the subordination of the king to Parliament:

> Trajanus called his Senate his Father; for [the Senate] admonish[es] the King of Things profitable, and unprofitable, to him and [the] State,... [and] what is the Majesty, Prerogative, Greatness and Jurisdiction of a King, and what is the due Right and Liberty of Subjects; for they are the ... Judges between Force and Fear, Liberty and Servitude, the King and his People.[52]

But James had long before dissociated himself from identification with Trajan or the coin, which had come to represent the terrifying ghost of Buchanan, pointing his hand at the crown-piercing sword.[53] Instead, he appeared as Solomon: in Robert Wakeman's *Salomon's Exhaltation*

[50] Milton, P*olitical Writings*, ed. Martin Dzelzainis (Cambridge: Cambridge University Press, 1991), 25.

[51] Lindsay, *View of the Coinage*, 53–54.

[52] "Speaker's Speech to the King," 7 July 1604, *Journal of the House of Commons: Volume 1, 1547–1629*, British History Online, https://www.british-history.ac.uk/commons-jrnl/vol1/pp253-256, accessed 30 August 2023.

[53] On James's ongoing nightmares about Buchanan, see James I, *Letters*, 5, 42.

(1605), for instance, or Bishop Montagu's preface to James's *Works* in 1616. "*GOD* hath giuen vs a *Solomon*, [exalted] beyond all the *Kings* that euer were."[54]

The comparison with Solomon could sometimes convey a subtle warning along with homage. While James's reign is still "without any Eclipse or Shaddow," writes Montagu, he should learn from the example of Solomon, whose "vnchast life, ... immoderate excesse of *Women*, [and] weakest Posterity for Wisedome and Gouernment" led to "the fearefullest fall" of any king in history.[55] (At least no one had to worry about James indulging in the "immoderate excesse of *Women*.") Certainly, Sir John Harington identified James with this other Solomon in his famous description of the court masque representing Solomon and the Queen of Sheba performed for James and the King of Denmark in 1606. According to Harington, first the drunken Queen of Sheba fell "into his Danish Majesties lap [and] in his face," spraying food and drink about the room. Then King James

> got up and woud dance with [her] but [instead] fell down, [and so was] laid on a bed of state ... not a little defiled with the presents of the Queen which had been bestowed on his garments; such as wine, cream, jelly, beverage, cakes, spices, and other good matters.[56]

Defiled or not, James remained for his sycophants the exalted Solomon. He appears this way, for instance in Williams's funeral sermon, which identifies James as "*Great Britains Salomon*," the "*Booke* [and] Swor[d]" of "Christendome" (60). More surprisingly, Trajan appears in *Great Britains Salomon* too, resurrected but stripped of his historic political associations. The sermon (Williams explains) is a verbal effigy: "a *liuely Statue of King Salomon*" representing "our *Brittish Salomon*" but also representing Trajan, who "triumphed openly in the Citie of *Rome, In Imagine*, in a Liuely Statue, or Repraesentation" (35–36). Williams quotes 1 *Kings* 3 to remind us that this triple "Repraesentation" stands

[54] James I, *The Workes of the Most High and Mightie Prince* (London: Robert Barker and John Bill, 1616), sig. e2r–v.

[55] James I, *Workes*, sig. e2r–v.

[56] John Harington, *The Letters and Epigrams of Sir John Harington*, ed. Norman E. McClure (Philadelphia: University of Pennsylvania Press, 1930), 119–20.

for "IVSTICE": the "*Wisedome of God was in Him, ad faciendum iudicium*, to doe … *IVSTICE*" (54–55). The capital letters suggest that the allegorical figure of Justice has come to life in this "*liuely Statue*" that unites Solomon, Trajan, and James. But there is also a fourth figure present: a "*breathing Statue*" who "*walk't on foot* this day after the *Hearse*" and is a likeness of all three. It is the newly anointed King Charles I. Just as God

> hath made a liuely *Repraesentation* of the *Vertues of Salomon*, in the Person of King *Iames*: So hath he done a like *Repraesentation* of the *Vertues* of King *Iames*, in the Person of King *Charles* our Gratious *Soueraigne*. (75–76)

Buchanan's and Ponet's treatises, with their evocation of Trajan's sword as an emblem of tyrannicide, would eventually serve as foundational texts for the revolutionaries who executed Charles in 1649. On his way to the scaffold, Charles may have looked up at the ceiling of the Banqueting House where he had commissioned Rubens to paint his father as Solomon: engaged in the great scene of Judgment, and yet, like Justitia, magisterially oblivious to what was to come.

CHAPTER 3

Law of Nature in Inns of Court Drama

Doyeeta Majumder

On the Nature of the Law of Nature

The introduction to Thomas Hughes's *Misfortunes of Arthur* (first performed in 1587 at Gray's Inn, in London) enacts a mock verbal duel between the muses and a group of law students, where, tipping their hats to the role of imaginative literature in enriching the soil of jurisprudential knowledge, the students are finally forced to acknowledge:

> With Muses still we entercourse allowe,
> T'enrich our state with all there forreine freight. (95–96)

Among all the interdiscursive literary productions of sixteenth-century England, the crossroads between 'law and literature' is signalled with the most remarkable vividness in the dramatic productions of the Inns of Court. This chapter seeks to isolate one particular strand of jurisprudential thought—the law of nature—and to trace the trajectory of its development in the following plays produced by the Inns of Court:

D. Majumder (✉)
Jadavpur University, Kolkata, India
e-mail: doyeeta@gmail.com; doyeeta.majumder@jadavpuruniversity.in

S. Mukherji and D. Roberts (eds.), *Literature and the Legal Imaginary*, Crossroads of Knowledge in Early Modern Literature 4,
https://doi.org/10.1007/978-3-031-74093-0_3

Thomas Norton and Thomas Sackville's *Gorboduc* (1561, Inner Temple), Gascoigne and Kinwelmersh's *Jocasta* (1566, Gray's Inn), *Gismond of Salerne* (1567–1568, Inner Temple), and Thomas Hughes's *Misfortunes of Arthur*, along with the interlude *Horestes* (1567), written by John Pykeringe, a former member of the Inns.[1]

The law of nature was a dense and loaded concept throughout the medieval and early modern period, with an Aristotelian-Thomist foundation which kept accruing other layers as jurists, political philosophers, and polemicists, all staked claim to the idea at every moment of jurisdictional or ideological conflict. In effect it remained an interpretive battlefield, a realm of exceptionality constantly invoked by interested parties to legitimize their point of view.[2] This chapter argues that the theatrical productions of the Inns of Courts use the representations of natural law to re-evaluate common law's own controversial relationship with natural law as well as with competing jurisdictions of positive law, notably that of the Chancery. In his account of the canonical literary uses of the philosophical *topoi* of natural law R. S. White argues persuasively that the sixteenth century marked a crucial shift away from the Thomist definition of natural law as an instinctive impulse propelling rational creatures towards virtuous action, and towards the more restricted, sceptical, seventeenth-century understanding of natural law as the instinct of self-preservation alone.[3] This chapter posits that the drama of the Inns of Court registers this turn from medieval notions of natural law, based on conscience and reason, and foreshadows the association between natural human proclivities and a tendency towards strife and violence—an entente consolidated by Thomas Hobbes' *Leviathan* (1651). In so doing, it will attempt to untangle the intermeshing of the universally poetic and the specifically legal manifestations of the law of nature in a group of texts which limn the margins of the 'literary' in the sixteenth century.

[1] All quotations from the Inns-of-Court tragedies are from *Early English Classical Tragedies*, ed. John W. Cunliffe (Oxford: Clarendon Press, 1912). Quotations from *Horestes* are from Marie Axton, ed., *Three Tudor Classical Interludes* (Cambridge: D. S. Brewer, 1982).

[2] Frederick Pollock, 'The History of the Law of Nature: A Preliminary Study', *Journal of the Society of Comparative Legislation*, 2:3 (1900), 418–33.

[3] R. S. White, *Natural Law in English Renaissance Literature* (Cambridge: Cambridge University Press, 1996), 1–13. White's monograph is an in-depth study of the literary uses of the philosophical notion of natural law in the Renaissance.

In the realm of philosophy, the idea of universal principles of natural justice dates back to Aristotle. Subsequently developed by Cicero and Seneca, it continued to be of crucial significance in Stoic, scholastic, and, later on, humanist discussions of philosophy. The juridical tradition developed parallel to this as the Justinian code enshrined the importance of natural law in civil jurisprudence, defining it as the law that is common to all members of the natural world—rational or not. Six centuries after Justinian, Gratian's *Decretum* (1150), one of the key texts of medieval canon law, 'based all justice on natural law' and 'identified it with divine law', defining natural law as that 'by which everyone is commanded to do to another what he wishes to be done to himself, and is forbidden to do to another what he is unwilling to have done to himself'.[4] Another century later, Thomas Aquinas' *Summa Theologica* amalgamated the pre-Christian notions of natural justice with the divine revelation by way of 'reason', claiming that 'participation of the eternal law in the rational creature is called the natural law'.[5] Aquinas's natural law was an immutable principle engraved in the hearts of men which relentlessly propelled them towards virtuous action and provided the framework which underpinned the corpus of positive law.[6] This view of natural law seemed to suggest a skewed equation between natural and positive law, which axiomatically upheld the historic and moral antecedence of the former.

The English jurisprudential tradition, with its body of custom-based common law, and its somewhat contentious relationship with Roman civil law and Church-administered canon law, presents a complex story of the development of natural law. Asserting the uniqueness of custom-based

[4] S. Kuttner, 'Natural Law and Canon Law', in Edward F. Barrett, ed., *Natural Law Institute Proceedings*, vol. 3 (Indiana: University of Notre Dame, 1950), 95, 99.

[5] Thomas Aquinas, *Summa Theologica*, trans. Fathers of the English Dominican Province (New York: Benziger Bros., 1947), Part 1 of Part 2, Q 91, Article 6. https://dhspriory.org/thomas/summa/FS/FS091.html#FSQ91OUTP1.

[6] *Summa* is perhaps the most influential statement of natural law as synderesis or conscience, a culmination of the scholarship and philosophical explorations of a number of writers before Aquinas. For a detailed and nuanced account of this, see Robert A. Greene, 'Natural Law, Synderesis, and the Moral Sense', *Journal of the History of Ideas*, 58:2 (1997), 173–98. Aquinas establishes an unbreakable connection between rationality and the law of nature, and distinguishes it as 'law of reason', separate from the other natural laws and impulses which govern irrational creatures and the objects and phenomena of nature. This latter sense of natural law re-emerges forcefully in the seventeenth century as the discourses of 'new science' acquire momentum.

English law, while simultaneously acknowledging the ideological superiority of natural law, became a tightrope act. The trickiest conundrum was that natural law was, by definition, both immutable and unwritten. Implicit in this very idea there was a radical antinomianism. In a bid to control this antinomian impulse jurist after jurist—beginning from the earliest, Henry of Bracton (*c.* 1210–1268), right up to William Blackstone (1723–1780), the father of modern English jurisprudence—tried to assimilate the elusive notion of *jus naturale* into the foundational basis of the positive law of the kingdom.[7]

Although it was a particular product of the Wars of the Roses, John Fortescue's treatise *De Natura Legis Naturae* (1461–1463) became a major influence on most sixteenth-century legal treatises and marks a crucial moment in this narrative.[8] Building on Gratian's conflation of divine law and natural law, and Aquinas's idea of conscience and reason-based natural law as anterior to positive law, Fortescue declares:

> This Law of Nature sprang from God alone, is subject to His Law alone, and under Him, and with Him, governs the whole world; whence it comes that all other laws are its servants, so that there is not a law on earth put forth by man which obeys not the commands of nature's law. (Chapt. XXIX)

This attempt to establish the superiority of natural law was made with the aim of demolishing the Yorkist claim to the throne. Fortescue's argument was that the 'natural' inferiority of women meant that both the female and male descendants of the female line should be excluded from succession to the English throne.[9] But although his text was the product of the political turbulence of the Wars of the Roses, it had much wider ramifications, and

[7] See Henry of Bracton, *On the Laws and Customs of England*, ed. George E. Woodbine and trans. Samuel E. Thorne, 4 vols. (Cambridge, MA: Belknap Press of Harvard University Press, 1968), II, p. 26 (available the Harvard Law School Library's *Bracton Online* Project: http://amesfoundation.law.harvard.edu/cgi-bin/brac-hilite.cgi?Unframed+English+2+26+nature); *The Student's Blackstone*, ed. Robert Malcolm Kerr (London: John Murray, 1877), 7–8.

[8] All quotations from *The Works of Sir John Fortescue…Collected and Arranged by Thomas (Fortescue) Lord Cleremont* (London, 1869).

[9] The Yorkist claim to the throne was derived via Anne of Mortimer, a descendant of Lionel of Antwerp, who was the second son of Edward III, and who was therefore senior to John of Gaunt, who was the third son of Edward III, and who was the father of the

in particular, had the effect of consolidating the practice of invoking the 'law of nature' as the first and last word in any legal or jurisdictional debate.

As Frederick Pollock's comprehensive account of the history of natural law points out, in England, Chancery law, the Law Merchant, and common law, all traced their points of origin, in theory, to the law of nature. The sixteenth century witnessed an unprecedented rise in the fortunes of the common law courts, accompanied by bitter jurisdictional rivalries between various courts administering different branches of positive law, all of which staked ideological claims to the touchstone of 'natural law'.[10] Natural law (a term often used interchangeably with divine law) acquired the status of a quasi-magical formula and became the single most important legitimating factor in sixteenth-century legal polemics. Christopher St German's *Doctor and Student*, the most influential legal treatise written in the first half of the sixteenth century, extended Aquinas's argument by making the law of nature prior even to the law of God—which, after all, was revealed at a certain point of time in human history, whereas the law of nature is co-extensive with human history:

> The law of nature specially considered, which is also called the law of reason, pertaineth only to creatures reasonable...And as to the ordering of the deeds of man, it is preferred before the law of God, and it is written in the heart of every man...And all other laws, as well the laws of God as to the acts of men, as other, be grounded thereupon.[11]

Later in the treatise, in a rhetorical *tour de force*, he makes English common law synonymous with law of nature. Thus, according to the Student, English common law and statute law are nothing but 'law of reason, secondary particular...because the reason in that case is derived

first Lancastrian king, Henry IV. See Paul E. Gill, 'Politics and Propaganda in Fifteenth-Century England: The Polemical Writings of Sir John Fortescue', *Speculum*, 46:2 (1971), 333–47.

[10] Christopher Brooks, *Law, Politics and Society in Early Modern England* (Cambridge: Cambridge University Press, 2008), 1, 8–9.

[11] Christopher St German, *Doctor and Student*, revised and corrected by William Muchall (Cincinnati: Robert Clarke, 1874), 5.

of such a law that is only holden for law in this realm, and in none other realm'.[12]

However, one problem that kept resurfacing in these treatises was the question of who should have the right of way when man-made laws seem to run counter to the principles of natural justice. St German, like Fortescue before him, writes:

> Nor it is not to be understood of a law made by man commanding or prohibiting any thing to be done that is against the law of reason or the law of God. For if any law made by him, bind any person to any thing that is against the said laws, it is no law, but a corruption, and manifest error.[13]

But in practice things were not that simple. English common law was governed by peculiar technical formalities which were unintelligible to anyone outside of the legal profession—a far cry from the law supposedly written on the hearts of every rational creature. Throughout the sixteenth century, as far as actual litigation was concerned, the law of nature was not evoked very often in the Court of Common Pleas. The trainee lawyers at the Inns of Court too would have encountered the idea only vaguely and tangentially, unless personal interest drove them to explore it further.[14] Natural law was much more directly evoked in rival courts, such as the Chancery. In light of this, the repeated, nearly obsessive invocation of natural law in the entertainments of the Inns of Court becomes something of a puzzle. What follows will attempt to prove that, through a dramatization of the questions of natural law, the aspiring common lawyers of the Inns of Court probed the shifting and dynamic relationship between the law of nature and the law of men, while emphatically claiming an underpinning of natural law for common law, in order to negotiate the jurisdictional rivalries which divided the various kinds of legal operation in early modern England.

All four tragedies written and produced by members of the Inns—*Gorboduc*, *Jocasta*, *Gismond of Salerne*, and *Misfortunes of Arthur*—along with the interlude *Horestes*, present to us controversial renderings of the

[12] St German, *Doctor and Student*, 13.

[13] St German, *Doctor and Student*, 53.

[14] R. H. Helmholz, *Natural Law in Court: A History of Legal Theory in Practice* (Cambridge, MA: Harvard University Press, 2015), 84–90.

law of nature which are symptomatic of the anxieties of common law *vis-a-vis* natural law. In different ways, each of these plays, produced by young men trained in the mechanics of positive law, imaginatively explores the possibilities of a head-on collision between natural justice and positive law and the outcomes thereof. In each case this conflict ruptures the fabric of familial relationships, as natural law invades the jurisdiction of positive law in the context of either sexual misdemeanour or homicide within the family, i.e. incest, or adultery, or kin-murder, or sometimes a combination of all three.

Sex and Murder in the Family

Orestes and his deeds figured prominently in the most important treatises of forensic rhetoric of the time. The mythical tale, with its competing and contradictory claims to natural law and justice, was the foremost example of the various ways in which a 'cause' could be effectively presented in a court of law, typifying an 'issue of law' as opposed to an 'issue of fact', i.e. the fact that Orestes had killed his mother was never disputed, what was disputed was whether his action was legally and morally justifiable.[15] John Pykeringe's play, *Horestes*, comprises a series of forensic orations (much in the style of classical rhetoric manuals)[16] in which he attempts to persuade various other characters (Idumeus, Councell, Menelaus, Nature, etc.) that he was essentially lawful and just in choosing to commit matricide in order to avenge his father's murder.

This adaptation of the Oresteian myth would have had a distinct topical resonance because it was performed in the immediate wake of Mary Stuart's deposition from the Scottish throne on the grounds that she had committed adultery and murdered her husband.[17] The focus of the

[15] See *Ad Herennium*, trans. Harry Caplan (Cambridge, MA: Harvard University Press, 1954), 1.x.17; *De Inventione*, in Charles Duke Yonge trans. and ed. *The Orations of Marcus Tullius Cicero* (London: George Bell and Sons, 1888), 1.xiii,18.

[16] The case of Orestes was cited in a number of classical manuals of rhetoric as an exemplum of an 'issue of law', and the justifications uttered by Horestes within the play echo these classical texts rather closely. See [Cicero] *Rhetorica Ad Herennium*, trans. Harry Caplan (Cambridge, MA: Harvard University Press, 1954), 1.x.17; Cicero, *De Inventione*, in Charles Duke Yonge trans. and ed. *The Orations of Marcus Tullius Cicero* (London: George Bell and Sons, 1888), 1.xiii.18.

[17] J. E. Phillips, 'A Revaulation of *Horestes* (1567)', *Huntington Library Quarterly*, 18:3 (1955), 227–44.

play is the conflict between a son's natural desire to avenge his father's death and the fundamental unnaturalness of matricide. Dramaturgically, the play is a hybrid that recasts a classical theme into the formal accoutrements of a morality play. Thus, the prime mover of the play is 'Vyce', who pretends to be a divine agent and incites Horestes to exact revenge upon his adulteress, murderess mother. The allegorical form also allows the personification of natural law as Dame Nature, rendering the conflict between positive justice and the law of nature vividly theatrical.

Dame Nature, alone among Horestes' interlocutors, remains unconvinced by his rhetoric, instead advising the revenge-crazed Horestes to refrain from the heinous crime, to pause and think of his mother, to consider 'what payne for the she toke' (412), and tells him 'from mothers bloud thou must thy hands refrain' (415). In response, Horestes invokes both the 'law of gods and man' (422) to support the justice of his cause, but Nature deems his chosen path to be the path of 'cruell tyraney' (431). Horestes turns to classical authorities and quotes Pythagoras to argue that 'lo, no tyraney to be / When that justyse is mynestryd as lawe and godes decree' (432–33). The laws of men, the dictates of authority and custom, effectively the whole machinery of positive law, urge Horestes to do what 'cruell beasts that raung in the fields' would recoil from. Despite the otherwise haphazard construction of the plot, the exchange between Horestes and Nature displays a remarkable sophistication, in that it resists being reduced to a simple binary between natural and positive law: while denouncing Horestes' desire for vengeance as monstrous, Nature herself acknowledges the wicked unnaturalness of Clytemnestra's actions, and as a son desiring justice for his father's death, Horestes is seen to be well within his natural rights, which in turn contradicts the unnaturalness of his revenge. Well-versed in the technique of arguing *in utram que partem*, Pykeringe forces us to consider the contradictions implicit in the different principles of natural law itself. In the end Nature leaves the scene, refusing to grant her benediction to Horestes, and thereby creating a sense of deep discomfiture regarding the ethics of the protagonist's endeavour in the minds of the audience.[18]

[18] Karen Robertson genders the two bodies of law at odds in this play: law of nature which is inclined towards mercy is seen as maternal and feminine, whereas revenge is dictated by paternal, positive law. 'The Body Natural of a Queen: Mary, James, "Horestes"', *Renaissance and Reformation*, 14:1 (1990), 30.

Horestes does, of course, later on, succeed in overcoming both his own hesitation and society's collective moral scruples. He murders Clytemnestra and Egisthus, and conquers 'Mycoene citie'. Menelaus, though initially critical of Horestes' actions, finally relents and gives him his daughter Hermione's hand in marriage, thus providing the play with a conventional ending which seems to ultimately endorse Horestes' revenge. The title which was given to the play when it was printed—*A Newe Enterlude of Vice conteyning the History of Horestes with the cruell revengement of his Fathers death upon his one naturall Mother*—sits uneasily with this happy conclusion and keeps alerting the audience/reader to the inherent unnaturalness of Horestes' 'cruell revengement' upon his 'naturall mother' and to the fact that Horestes' claims of divine legitimacy for his actions are based on nothing but Vyce's confidence trick. Consequently, despite Horestes's apparent success, the debate between natural law and positive law remains strikingly open-ended.

Primogeniture and Fratricide

The allegorical nature of the *Horestes*' dramaturgy allows the playwright to endow the abstract sophistries surrounding the concept of natural law with a corporeal concreteness which is, by and large, absent from the more rigorously Senecan plays produced by the Inns. However, all four of these plays depict bloodshed or illicit sexual liaisons within close kinship groups, and, albeit with varying degrees of urgency, each invokes principles of natural justice or law in order to counter the fiat of positive law.

In *Gorboduc*, this conflict is presented in the very first act as the collision between primogeniture and an older model of partible inheritance, in which each finds justification in 'nature'.[19] King Gorboduc declares his wish to divide his kingdom equally between his sons, Ferrex and Porrex. The elder son, Ferrex, sees this contravention of primogeniture as a violation of both natural *and* positive law. He tells his companion Hermon

[19] Like *Horestes*, *Gorboduc*, and indeed also *Jocasta*, and *Misfortunes*, have been linked with the controversies surrounding Mary Stuart, her deposition, Elizabeth's reluctance to execute her, and to the collective Elizabethan anxiety regarding 'the succession question'. While topical political allusions cannot be divorced from legal debates, for pragmatic reasons I have chosen to focus specifically on the use of law of nature in questions pertaining to royal succession in general and to other kinds of inheritance custom.

that the kingdom, by 'law and nature should remayne to me' (II, i, 4). However, Gorboduc himself, and Philander, one of his advisors, see the man-made custom of primogeniture as an aberration against nature and the cause of internecine violence in kingdoms:

> And suche an egalnesse hath nature made,
> Betwene the brethren of one fathers seede,
> As an vnkindly wrong it seemes to bee,
> To throwe the brother subject vnder feete
> Of him, whose peere he is by course of kinde,
> And nature that did make this egalnesse,
> Ofte so repineth at so great a wrong,
> That ofte she rayseth vp a grudginge griefe,
> In yonger brethren at the elders state :
> Wherby both townes and kingdomes haue ben rased. (I, ii, 181–90)

In *Gorboduc*'s words, we find an echo of Tudor humanist Thomas Starkey's assertion that brothers 'but even as they be of nature without difference brought forth, so without difference they equally succeed in their inheritance left to their family'.[20] Starkey's treatise argued that English common law had strayed from the principles of natural law, and that one of the customs in dire need of reform was the unnatural practice of exclusive primogeniture. In matters of inheritance, primogeniture was fast becoming the norm among the largest landowning families and indeed, by the seventeenth century, had permeated down at least to the gentry, but the custom was still far from being universal.[21] As Amy Erickson points out, strict adherence to primogeniture was upheld by common law courts only and pertained mostly to real estate, but there were other bodies of law administering inheritances of other kinds. Inheritance of movable property was governed by canon law courts, which 'advocated a form of community property within marriage and the equal division of parental wealth among all children'. The Chancery, too, ameliorated the harsh decisions of common law courts based on appeals

[20] Thomas Starkey, *A Dialogue Between Reginald Pole and Thomas Lupset*, ed. Kathleen M. Burton (London: Chatto and Windus, 1948), 108.

[21] Michelle M. Dowd, *The Dynamics of Inheritance on the Shakespearean Stage* (Cambridge: Cambridge University Press, 2015), 34–35.

to equity and 'natural justice', and was particularly effective in the cases of female litigants.[22]

Admittedly, succession to the throne was not entirely the same as inheriting landed property. By the sixteenth century, the custom of dynastic male primogeniture had become the determining principle of royal succession in England, but the presence of an heirless, unmarried, female monarch made things unpredictable. In the previous century, Fortescue's treatise had argued that the only way to settle a disputed succession was to follow the law of nature, as manifested in the narrowest form of male primogeniture. However, the reign of two successive female monarchs proved that in the sixteenth century, the law of succession had moved beyond the presumed 'natural' inferiority of women. The body politic of England rendered the 'natural' weaknesses of the female body null and void. Later in the century, towards the end of Elizabeth's reign, Robert Parson's *A Conference about the Next Succession to the Crown of England* (1594), asserts that 'the next propinquitie or ancetry of blood alone' could not be taken as 'sufficient to be admitted to a crowne'.[23] Parson, like Fortescue, is driven by a specific polemical project: his argument is directed against the right of James VI of Scotland, Elizabeth's 'natural' heir, to succeed to the English throne. Nevertheless, he puts forward a robust case in favour of following positive laws and parliamentary statutes instead of natural law as far as royal succession is concerned. Though the treatise post-dates the plays discussed here, it is perhaps not far-fetched to infer that these debates pervaded the reign of Elizabeth and that the issue was far from being decisively settled.

In *Gorboduc*, however, it is in fact the 'natural' division of the kingdom between these two equal peers, against the dictates of custom and positive law, that results in civil war and bloodshed. The two brothers display none of the natural affection Gorboduc sanguinely expects of them and begin plotting against each other as soon as they come to power. The hot-headed Hermon assures Ferrex that sovereignty is exempt both from the laws of nature and the laws of God:

[22] Amy Louise Erickson, *Women and Property in Early Modern England* (London: Routledge, 1995), 5.

[23] Robert Parsons (attrib.), *A conference about the next succession to the crowne of Ingland diuided into two partes* (London, 1594), sig. [*1]^{v} (unpaginated) (available via http://name.umdl.umich.edu/A09097.0001.001).

> But if the feare of Goddes, and secrete grudge
> Of natures law, repining at the fact,
> Withholde your courage from so great attempt:
> Know ye, that lust of kingdomes hath no law.
> The Goddes do beare and well allow in kinges,
> The thinges they abhorre in rascall routes. (II, i, 140–45)

Eventually, Ferrex is killed by Porrex and, after three acts have elapsed, Gorboduc is compelled to resume the duties of the sovereign. In Porrex's judgement scene in the fourth act, the even-handed debate on the law of nature is pushed to a point of crisis. In presiding over the trial, Gorboduc is in the impossible position of being, at once, the supreme judge in the kingdom, the father of the victim, and the father of the perpetrator. In this vital scene, the law of nature, in its specific manifestation of the law of kind, is appealed to both by Porrex and Gorboduc.

> Porrex, if we so far should swerve from kind,
> And from those bounds which law of Nature sets
> As thou hast done by vile and wretched deed
> In cruel murder of thy brother's life,
> Our present hand could stay no longer time,
> But straight should bathe this blade in blood of thee
> As just revenge of thy detested crime.
> No; we should not offend the law of kind
> If now this sword of ours did slay thee here:
> For thou hast murdered him whose heinous death
> Even Nature's force doth move us to revenge
> By blood again; But Justice forceth us
> To measure Death for Death, thy due desert,
> Yet since thou art our childe, and sith as yet
> In this hard case what word thou canst allege
> For thy defense, by us hath not been heard
> We are content to say our will for that
> Which justice bids us presently to work:
> And give thee leave to use thy speech at full
> If ought thou have to lay for thine excuse. (IV, ii, 15–34)

On the one hand, the law of the state embodied in 'Justice' and the law of kind embodied in 'nature' both enjoin him to pronounce a death sentence on his son—who is a fratricide and the killer of Gorboduc's son. But, on the other hand, that very same law of 'kind' compels Gorboduc, as a father, to 'stay' his sovereign 'will'. I have argued elsewhere that this scene is a perfect enactment of the dialectic of the two bodies of the king, a legal fiction that was often invoked by common lawyers, most notably by Edmund Plowden in his *Reports*.[24] However, the scene can be read not just as the conflict between the king's two bodies, but between two kinds of legal imagination. Using the ambivalence of Senecan rhetoric and *in utram que partem* techniques, Norton and Sackville, like Pykeringe, carefully avoid a reductive adversarial equation between natural law and state administered, positive law. Instead, what is held up for scrutiny is a complex double binary between natural and positive law, on the one hand, and the often self-contradictory claims of natural law on the other. Gorboduc is not entirely sure whether or not he would at all 'offend the law of kind', since '[e]ven Nature's force' moves him to avenge Ferrex, and yet that revenge would in turn compound the crimes against nature.

A third claim to the 'law of kind' is staked by Porrex himself, who argues that, far from having 'swerved' from the law of kind, his actions have resulted from an adherence to the highest law of nature—the impulse of self-preservation. Porrex says it was in fact Ferrex who, through his treacherous plotting against his own brother, '[t]he law of kinde and trouth thus rent in twaine' (118). At this point, in murdering Ferrex, Porrex has but followed the law of nature:

> Euen nature moued me than to holde my life
> More deare to me than his, and bad this hand,
> Since by his life my death must nedes ensue,
> And by his death my life to be preserued,
> To shed his bloud, and seeke my safetie so. (125–29)

Porrex's understanding of the law of nature is distinctly Hobbesian—it enshrines the desire to advance oneself as the highest natural good,

[24] Doyeeta Majumder, 'Absolutism Without Tyranny in *Gorboduc*: The Changing Poetics of Tudor Political Drama', *Renaissance Studies*, 32:2 (2018), 201–8. On the conflict between the king's two bodies, Plowden writes that though Agamemnon knew it was his duty as a king to sacrifice his beloved daughter Iphigenia, he was still torn 'for albeyt he was a kinge and ought to do as seemely was for that estate, yet in the kinge there was a father (sayth the poete) and in his body pollitické there was a body naturall'. *'A Treatise of the two Bodies of the king, vis. natural and politic...The whole intending to prove the title of Mary Quene of Scotts to the succession of the crown of England and that the Scots are not out of the allegience of England'*, Oxford, Bodleian Library, MS Don. c. 43, pp. 22–23.

while Gorboduc's view is more amenable to the dictates of reason and conscience.[25] The debate, however, is not permitted a resolution. In an act of cataclysmic unnatural violence, Porrex is murdered by his own mother Videna.[26] The play ends with a final iteration of crimes against nature as the subjects of the kingdom rise up in arms and kill the king and queen, leaving the kingdom vulnerable and acephalous.

This story of unnatural fraternal strife resulting in a political disaster is continued in *Jocasta*, but in this case, the act of fratricide is presented as an inevitable consequence of a prior unnatural act of incest. An adaptation of Sophocles' Theban plays, *Jocasta* dramatizes the war between Eteocles and Polynices, the two sons of the eponymous protagonist Jocasta, who tries unsuccessfully to intercede between them, appealing time and again to the laws of natural fraternal affection. But the unnaturalness of their very existence, repeatedly referred to by Jocasta herself, casts its ominous shadow and predetermines the course of their actions (I, i, 145). The first transgression occurs when Laius, hearing the prophecy that his son would murder him and marry Jocasta, and 'forgetting lawes of natures loue' (I, i, 46), decides to abandon the infant Oedipus. The cyclical desecration of the law of nature, once unleashed, cannot be contained. That the 'unnaturall fruite' (I, i, 145) of her and Oedipus' union would never become the comfort of their late years is a poignant truth that Jocasta seems to know from the very beginning. Despite this, as a hapless mother bound to her unnatural incest-born sons by the law of nature, she appeals to that very law to make peace between them:

> yet as a pitifull mother
> Whom nature binds to loue hir louing sonnes,
> And to prouide the best for their auaile,
> I haue thought good by prayers to entreate
> The two brethren (nay rather cruel foes)
> A while to staie their fierce and furious fight. (I, i, 190–95)

[25] Marking a radical departure from the classical and medieval tradition of natural law, Thomas Hobbes posits that *lex naturae* primarily indicates the precept 'by which a man is forbidden to do, that, which is destructive of his life, or taketh away the means of preserving the same' (*Leviathan*, Part 1, XIV, 3). For a detailed account see J. C. A. Gaskin's Introduction to *Leviathan* (Oxford: Oxford University Press, 1996), xxxii–vi.

[26] See Karen L. Raber, 'Murderous Mothers and the Family/State Analogy in Classical and Renaissance Drama', *Comparative Literature Studies*, 37:3 (2000), 298–320.

As in *Gorboduc*, the bone of contention in *Jocasta* is sovereignty and the division of a state between two brothers, but instead of the territorial partition which is agreed in *Gorboduc*, Eteocles and Polynices agree upon a policy of 'timesharing' in which they will rule the city for alternate years. However, when Eteocles finishes his year, rather handing power over to Polynices, he instead banishes him. All this happens before the start of the play. The play begins at the point when an enraged Polynices, intent on revenge and aided by the army of his father-in-law, is laying siege to his own native city. Even though Polynices is the unpatriotic aggressor, the chorus and Antigone seem to be far more favourably disposed towards him than Eteocles—who appears as a power-hungry tyrant. Jocasta pleads with Eteocles to cast aside 'vaine ambition', by which

> loue and amitie destroyde,
> It breakes the lawes and common concord beates (II, i, 407–8)

She then turns to examples from the natural world in order to convince Eteocles that the law of nature makes the sharing of sovereignty between peers obligatory:

> If then the dayes and nightes to serue our turne
> Content themselues to yeld each other place,
> Well oughtest thou with waightie dome to graunt
> Thy brothers right to rule the reigne with thee,
> Which heauens ordeyned common to you both. (II, i, 430–35)

But all her appeals to natural reason and justice are in vain, as Eteocles' 'lust for kingdoms' (to borrow an apt phrase from *Gorboduc*) overrules the dictates of 'natural' fraternal affection. As the brothers go to war, the chorus laments:

> Where are the lawes of nature nowe become?
> Can fleshe of fleshe, alas can bloud of bloud,
> So far forget it selfe, as slay it selfe? (IV, i, Chorus: 13–15)

The relentless invocation of the laws of natural fraternal affection in *Jocasta* was not just a naively sentimental theatrical device, but bore a specific legal resonance, particularly for common lawyers of the mid-1560s. In 1565, in what was one of the very few common law cases which explicitly appealed to natural law contra common law procedure, natural affection between brothers was declared to take precedence over statute and custom. In the case of Sharington v. Strotton, in Plowden's *Reports*, Andrew Baynton had made an indenture naming his brother Edward and his wife Agnes (the defendants) as his heirs for the use of a thirty-acre plot of land, but the plaintiffs, who claimed rights to the land by means of an earlier deed, argued that a mere indenture was not sufficient to transfer the use of an estate to another person. According to the common law, this required a contract.[27] Unusually for a common law case, it was decided that even in the absence of the specific customary documentation required to pass the use from one person to another, if the parties concerned are brothers, 'brotherly love which he bore to his brothers is sufficient consideration to raise the uses in the land' (309–10). The report presents a concrete, practical instance of the way in which principles of natural law were co-opted into positive law, arguing that 'those who descend from one same parentage, are joined nearest in blood, are by nature joined in love' (306) and that the law works accordingly. Thus, a younger brother entering his father's property after his death will not be seen as committing a trespass against his older brother, because the law presumes not enmity, but love between brothers. Going back to the natural justice foundations of common law, Plowden says:

> [T]he founders of our law did not make laws to countenance things against nature, which are monstrous and seldom happen, but to licence things which are consistent with nature and often happen. (306)

The case was decided a year before the performance of *Jocasta*, and it is entirely likely that the playwrights were familiar with it. Sharington v. Strotton presents a crucial example of the incursion of the claims of 'natural' familial love into the domain of legal technicalities of inheritance and property, an incursion that is dramatized with dexterity in the plays. In *Jocasta*, fraternal strife, resulting in the death of the brothers and in Jocasta's suicide, is seen to be contrary not just to the law of nature, but also to customary, positive law, since that which 'often happens' in nature inevitably also acquires the force of custom.

[27] All quotations from 'Sharington v. Strotton', in *The Commentaries or Reports of Edmund Plowden* (London: S. Brooke, 1816), Part 1, 297a–309a.

Incest, Filicide, Civil Discord

Gismond of Salerne, a play which is based on a tale from Boccaccio, is roughly contemporaneous with *Jocasta*. It is the shortest of the four plays discussed here and it presents an erotic construction of the adversarial relationship between nature and custom. It shows that unlike fraternal affection, which is accepted and assimilated within the structure of common law, sexual desire, especially female desire, persists as the inextricable thorn in the side of patriarchal positive law. The play depicts Tancred's obsessive and unnatural affection for his widowed daughter Gismond, which results ultimately in her death and his. Tancred forbids his daughter to remarry, and when he finds her with her lover, he has him executed and presents Gismond with her lover's heart. The sovereign's command is binding on Gismond, but, as her aunt Lucrece comments, the command is a distinct contravention of the 'course of kinde' (II, ii, 22) which would inevitably propel a youthful and beautiful woman towards love and companionship. In Tancred's unnatural decree, connotations of incest are clearly present, although in the play they were toned down for reasons of modesty because the play was performed in the presence of two of the Queen's ladies in waiting.[28] However, the references to natural law notwithstanding, the play does not engage head-on with questions of juridical or political import, or explore fully the veiled references to the unnaturalness of incest.

It is in the last extant tragedy produced by the Inns of Court, Thomas Hughes's *Misfortunes of Arthur*, written two decades after the other plays, that incest and filicide are re-invoked in the context of natural law. Richard McCabe argues that as the family is seen as the microcosm of the state, '[p]erversions in the sexual politics of the family provide ready analogies for corruptions in the power politics of the state'.[29] Thus the violation of natural law in the royal family results in violent discord within close kinship groups throughout England—a pattern shared by these Inns-of-Court plays in which the political fallout of incest is, invariably, civil war. In *Misfortunes*, fraternal discord is replaced by filial violence, as Mordred, the product of an incestuous union between Arthur and his

[28] Cunliffe, *Early English Classical Tragedies*, lxxxviii.

[29] Richard McCabe, *Incest, Drama and Nature's Law, 1550–1700* (Cambridge: Cambridge University Press, 1993), 25.

twin sister Anne, usurps Arthur's throne and becomes Guinevere's adulterous lover. Arthur comes back after his French expeditions, lays siege against his own capital and, despite his paternal misgivings about committing the gravest sin against the law of nature, finally fights with Mordred and kills him. The realm is beset with chaos and internal bloodshed, as:

> The brethren broach their bloud: the Sire his Sonnes,
> The Sonne againe would proue by too much Wrath,
> That he, whom thus he slew, was not his Sire.
> No blood nor kinne can swage their irefull moodes.
> No forreine foe they seeke, nor care to finde:
> The Brytaines bloud is sought on euery side. (IV, ii, 170–75)

In a neat turn of phrase, kinship becomes emblematic of both nature and nation. *Misfortunes*, like *Jocasta*, perfectly illustrates McCabe's thesis, as this national crisis is seen to be the culmination of a series of unnatural crimes, beginning, as the ghost of the Duke of Cornwall reminds us, with Uther Pendragon's seduction of his wife. The playwright 'conjoins his dominant concerns of political strife and civil upheaval with an emphasis on the perversion of sexual experience (or the inversion of the natural order of things)'.[30] Arthur and his sister were the products of this original, unnatural, and ill-fated union, and they in turn compounded this transgression with incest and produced Mordred. Arthur, like Jocasta, is filled with regret as he rules his own 'incestuous life' and Mordred's 'wicked birth' (V, i, 121).

Incest becomes a recurring concern in these plays not because it violates 'nature', but because of a collective social anxiety that incest might in fact be more natural than we tend to think—an anxiety that is manifested in positive law's repeated attempts to criminalize incest. In the chiastic obverse of the natural being established as the customary and legal, as in the case of fraternal love, incest is a peculiar instance of a custom-based legal prohibition being elided into natural revulsion. McCabe argues that incest could not be deemed 'unnatural' in the way intercourse between two species was unnatural; instead, incest presents a

[30] Christopher J. Crosbie, 'Sexuality, Corruption, and the Body Politic: The Paradoxical Tribute of "The Misfortunes of Arthur" to Elizabeth I', *Arthuriana*, 9:3 (1999), 68–80 (71).

case wherein 'custom is nature'. Thus, those who declaim incest as unnatural 'react against its violation with the full force of social conditioning'.[31] Common lawyers display a pragmatic understanding of this fact, underscored by an anxiety regarding this indeterminacy between nature and custom. In fact, in Sharington v. Strotton, Plowden uneasily acknowledges the powerful affinity that exists between people connected by blood and cites this 'natural' affinity as the reason why marriage between close relatives is forbidden. Intensifying this natural love by adding to it the love that exists between spouses is needless and might lead to an undesirable kind of excess, whereas marrying outside kinship groups is how 'love is propagated and increased'. Hence the 'divine policy' forbidding endogamy was justified and, even if not strictly 'natural', it acquired the force of nature.

Apart from incest, *Misfortunes* is replete with echoes of the earlier plays. Mordred, like Eteocles and Herman, displays an irrationally strong desire for sovereignty that holds the claims of filial affection in abeyance. When reminded of the bonds of natural affection, Mordred replies

> Come sonne, come sire, I first preferre my selfe.
> And since a wrong must be, then it excels,
> When t'is to gaine a Crowne. I hate a peere,
> I loath, I yrke, I doe detest a head.
> B'it Nature, be it Reason, be it Pride,
> I loue to rule. (I, iv, 110–15)

Arthur, on the other hand, is unable until nearly the end of the play to claim back what was lawfully his own, arguing that among all bonds of kinship, the filial bond is the highest and most sacrosanct.

> Great is the loue, which nature doth inforce
> From kin to kin, but most from sire to sonne. (III, i, 41–42)

He is urged by his counsellors to eschew the path of leniency and enforce the lawful punishment on his traitorous and usurping son, but the conflict between the political body of the sovereign and the natural body of the father intervenes.

> Ah too seuere, farre from a Fathers minde.

[31] McCabe, 21.

Compassion is as fit for Kings as wrath.
Lawes must not lowre. Rule oft admitteth ruthe.
So hate, as if there were yet cause to loue:
Take not their Hues as foes, which may be friends.
To spoile my sonne were to dispoile my selfe: (III, i, 84–89)

Redolent with echoes of the judgement scene in *Gorboduc*, this speech is also a reference to the legal idea of equity. Arthur expresses a desire to ameliorate the word of the law to admit the compassionate exception hidden in the rule of every positive law, which was the very definition of equitable law that was adjudicated in the Court of the Chancery, and claimed closer kin with the idea of natural law. By the sixteenth century, common law had become beset with rigid technicalities which cleaved it from the principles of natural justice. *Misfortunes* itself mounts a stringent attack on the rigidity of common law in the exchange between the muses and the law students, where the former reminds the latter that the precise 'formes of pleading' in common law were 'More bound to words then is the Poets lore' (Introduction, 28–31).[32] The perceived chasm between common law and nature's law is also reflected in Thomas Starkey's *Dialogue*, which argued in favour of Roman civil law because its 'rules [were] more convenient to the order of nature than they be in this barbarous tongue Old French, which now serveth to no purpose else'.[33]

However, the self-critique of the 'unnatural' practices of positive law in *Misfortunes* conceals a claim to natural justice that was more often seen as the domain of the equitable jurisdiction of Chancery. With its roots in Aristotelian *epieikeia* and Latin-Christian *aequitas*, equity refers to the power of the individual judge to interpret the letter of the law according to the needs of the individual case in order to ameliorate the injustice that the rigidity of the law might inflict.[34] In England, by the sixteenth century, equity had become a separate body of law, distinct

[32] On writs and procedure, see Sir John Baker, *The Oxford History of the Laws of England: Volume VI, 1483–1558* (Oxford: Oxford University Press, 2003), 323–24.

[33] Starkey, *A Dialogue*, 173. 'Starkey advocated the substitution of the Roman Law for the English common law because he did not feel that the common law was a sufficiently pure statement of divine and natural law.'—Stuart E. Prall, 'The Development of Equity in Tudor England', *The American Journal of Legal History*, 8 (1964), 1–19 (8).

[34] For a concise account of 'equity' and its relationship with Parliamentary sovereignty, see Prall, 'Development of Equity', 1–19.

from the common law and often represented as a corrective to the excessively technical procedures of the common law. With its direct link to conscience, equitable law claimed a closer propinquity to the principles of natural reason and justice, from which common law was perceived to have strayed. Thus, for Fortescue, natural law is synonymous with natural equity. St German, although a common lawyer seeking to subsume equity within the overarching structure of positive law, concedes that the conscientious operation of equity intervenes when positive law seems to go against the natural law:

> …epieikeia; the which is no other thing but an exception of the law of God, or the law of reason, from the general rules of the law of men, when they by reason of their generality, would in any particular case judge against the law of God or the law of reason: the which exception is secretly understood in every general rule of every positive law.[35]

Later treatises, such as William West's *Symboleography* and William Perkins' *Discourse on Conscience*, continue to emphasize the connection between equity and natural law.[36] However, this very emphasis on natural law became the eye of the storm of rivalry between the common law courts and Chancery, a rivalry which was one of the defining features of sixteenth-century litigation in England. Helmholz argues that, in crucial matters of inheritance, '[n]atural law principles seem to have figured to a greater degree' in the Chancery,[37] implying that at times Chancery also acted as an appellate court for matters settled in the Court of Common Pleas.[38] Thus common lawyers often took umbrage at what they perceived as the 'overly aggressive application of natural law principles in the Chancery'.[39] In the context of this ongoing quarrel between the two bodies of legal operation about who could rightfully claim to

[35] St German, *Doctor and Student*, 45.

[36] Mark Fortier, *Culture of Equity in Early Modern England* (New York: Routledge, 2016), 41, 68.

[37] Helmholz, *Natural Law*, 104.

[38] Because an action could only be commenced in the Court of Common Pleas through predetermined writs, there were certain cases which could not be fit into these writs and could claim remedy only at Chancery. Erickson for instance points out the preponderance of femme covert litigants in Chancery. *Women and Property*, 114–25.

[39] Helmholz, *Natural Law*, 99.

be the 'proper interpreters' of natural law,[40] the repeated invocation of natural law in the plays produced by common lawyers could be interpreted as an insidious jurisdictional claim, an attempt to recover the once vital but now lost affinity between common law and the laws of nature and, simultaneously, to curb Chancery's exclusive monopolization of the *lex naturae*.

Conclusion

However, despite this bid to reestablish the diminishing links between common law and the law of nature, collectively the plays exhibit a lack of faith in the efficacy of the idea of *lex naturae*. Each of the plays discussed here registers this growing scepticism as, time and again, natural law reveals its own fractures and admits defeat at the hands of human greed, ambition, and the man-made laws of positive justice. This is symbolic of the systematic erosion of the values of natural justice, based on the synderesis (i.e. the instinct towards virtue possessed by all humans) that was taking place throughout the later decades of the sixteenth century, as well as the rising tide of legal positivism.

Even as Hugo Grotius's monumental *De Iure Belli ac Pacis* (1625) emphasized the importance of natural law in the law of nations—a branch of jurisprudence which had become crucially important with the commencement of what is euphemistically called Europe's 'Age of Discovery'—in other spheres of legal operation, the ideological primacy of natural law was shifting. A century after St German, John Selden gives voice to the impracticability of a Thomist conception of law of nature that is simultaneously instinctive and binding:

> I cannot fancy to myself what the law of nature means, but the law of God. How should I know I ought not to steal, I ought not to commit adultery, unless somebody had told me so? Surely 'tis because I have been told so, 'Tis not because I think I ought not to do them, nor because you think I ought not; if so, our minds might change: whence then comes the restraint?[41]

[40] Ibid.

[41] *Table Talk of John Selden*, ed. Samuel Harvey Reynolds (Oxford: Clarendon Press, 1892), 101.

In response to King James's assertion of his superior natural reason, Sir Edward Coke wrote that the fortunes of Englishmen 'are not to be decided by naturall reason but by the artificiall reason and judgment of Law'.[42] In philosophy, this scepticism towards natural law is expressed by Montaigne, in the realm of political science the influence of Machiavelli leads to a tectonic shift away from a fundamental belief in human beings' ontological propensity for virtue. The watershed moment comes with Thomas Hobbes's *Leviathan*, which, while retaining the category of 'natural law', radically alters both its connotations and the vocabulary of conscience and instinctive virtue traditionally associated with it.[43] The seemingly frivolous entertainments staged by unruly law students seem to have anticipated this transformation with remarkable clairvoyance.

[42] *Selected Writings and Speeches of Sir Edward Coke*, 3 vols., ed. Steve Sheppard (Indiana: Liberty Fund, 2003), Vol. 1: 481. Though it is important to note that Coke does pay lip service to the conventional praises of natural law elsewhere.

[43] For an account of the connections between Selden, Grotius, and Hobbes, and Hobbesian legal positivism, see Perez Zagorin, *Hobbes and the Law of Nature* (New Jersey: Princeton University Press, 2009), 18–20, 42–54. For a comparative evaluation St German's and Hobbes's understanding of equity (based partly on their different conceptions of natural law), see Sharon K. Dobbins, 'Equity: The Court of Conscience or the King's Command, the Dialogues of St. German and Hobbes Compared', *Journal of Law and Religion*, 9:1 (1991), 113–49.

CHAPTER 4

Escalus' Dream: Re-imagining Shakespeare's States

Richard K. Sherwin

> A discussion of character is not only about the kind of self produced in a particular kind of society but about the kind of moral understandings and moral commitments that are possible.[1]

> The character, or tone, of a society depends on what the society regards as most respectable or most worthy of admiration.[2]

[1] James Davison Hunter, *The Death of Character* (New York: Basic Books, 2000), 8.
[2] Leo Strauss, *Natural Rights and History* (Chicago: University of Chicago Press, 1965), 137.

R. K. Sherwin (✉)
New York Law School, New York, NY, USA
e-mail: richard.sherwin@nyls.edu

S. Mukherji and D. Roberts (eds.), *Literature and the Legal Imaginary*, Crossroads of Knowledge in Early Modern Literature 4,
https://doi.org/10.1007/978-3-031-74093-0_4

Introduction: Sovereignty and Its Vicissitudes

In this chapter, I contend that Shakespeare's *Measure for Measure* serves as a brilliant case study in the entangled vicissitudes of sovereignty and character. As in a sacred wood, where an Amazon Queen falls in love with an ass (as is Titania's fate in *A Midsummer Night's Dream*), when sovereignty is in spin anything can happen. In the fictional Vienna of *Measure*, turbulence prevails. From the hyper-moral and hyper-legalistic rigidity of Angelo, the Duke's substitute sovereign, to the bawdy irreverence of Lucio, the Duke's trickster double, to the indomitable life force of Barnardine—divergent micro-climates are breaking out all over town, emanating from one character to the next.[3] Which will rule the other?

Law wants authority. My theme lies in the ambiguity of that phrase. Law desires authority in order not simply to be obeyed, but to be accepted as legitimate. Legitimacy makes law more than a gunman writ large, to use H. L. A. Hart's apt formulation.[4] But the source of law's legitimate authority lies beyond it. Law wants to be self-founding, but if shared fundamental values or beliefs are necessary to legitimate law's power, rendering it worthy of acceptance, they must arise extra-legally. As Harold Berman has written: "Law – in all societies – derives its authority from something outside itself."[5] Or as Jacques Derrida more recently put it: "The positing or establishing of law or right are exceptional and are in themselves neither legal nor properly juridical."[6] Law desires what it lacks, but it wants more than it can bear. There is a law's paradox in a nutshell.

If the source of authority that legitimates law lies beyond it, which is to say, if law's sovereignty arises from the potentially violent intercession of a transcendent (simultaneously antinomian and constitutive) authority

[3] According to Paul Roquet: "[A]tmospheres are involved whenever something is being staged." Paul Roquet, *Ambient Media: Japanese Atmospheres of Self* (Minneapolis: University of Minnesota Press, 2016), 17. In a similar vein, Watsuji Tetsuro uses the word "Fudo" to denote "not only the external, natural climate and geographic features of a region," but also to refer to "an internalized nature, infused with a cosmological and spiritual *Lebenswelt*." John Breen and Mark Teeuwen, *Shinto in History: Ways of the Kami* (Surry: Curzon Press, 2000), 33.

[4] H. L. A. Hart, *The Concept of Law* (Oxford: Clarendon Press, 1979), 6, 80.

[5] Harold J. Berman, *Law and Revolution* (Cambridge, MA: Harvard University Press, 1983), 16.

[6] Jacques Derrida, *The Beast & the Sovereign*, Vol. 1 (Chicago: University of Chicago Press, 2009), 49.

that may either affirm or suspend ordinary rules, including those that determine what makes legal rules valid in the first place, then sovereignty and the sacred need to be thought together.[7] Indeed, the function of the sacred in the social order is to perform transcendence. The sacred clears a space for claims of sovereign authority by disrupting extant norms and conventions, including principles of utility and exchange.[8] But it also fills the gap thus created by providing a compelling basis to reaffirm existing (or identify alternative) foundational beliefs and values that legitimate the law's authority.[9] In an endless dialectic of destabilization and regeneration, sovereignty and the sacred serve as correlative forces of legal, political, and social bonding.

Thinking of sovereignty in terms of the sacred also invites us to consider anew the phenomenon of identity formation. Law clings to rules to stabilize a preferred normative reality. But in order to sustain that reality rules alone never suffice. In the absence of normative commitment—the belief necessary to constitute or revitalize acceptance of law's authority as legitimate—legal rules tend to float free, prey to caprice and tyranny. In the perennial legal and political contest between meaning and power, character is decisive. Character is the dark matter of law.

Meanings rise or fall in conjunction with the sort of character most fit to sustain them. Lacking the self-reflexive capacity to at least periodically affirm or revise the meaning of shared core values, character devolves into a narcissistic jumble of will and desire. Recurrent public performances of normative consensus renew law's sovereignty by identifying those shared values and beliefs that are deemed most sacred.[10] Public assent identifies (and identifies with) shared norms that provide the binding power of society. In this sense, we may say that the spirit (or

[7] Robert Yelle, *Sovereignty and the Sacred* (Chicago: University of Chicago Press, 2019), 8. As Wallace Stevens wrote, "A violent order is disorder; and a great disorder is an order. These two things are one" Wallace Stevens, *Selected Poems* (New York: Alfred A. Knopf, 2009), 124.

[8] Robert Yelle, *Sovereignty and the Sacred*, 20.

[9] Leo Strauss, *Natural Right and History*, 15 ("Transcendence is not a preserve of revealed religion. In a very important sense it was implied in the original meaning of political philosophy as the quest for the natural or best political order").

[10] As Justice Sonia Sotomayor put it in her dissenting opinion in *Trump v. Hawaii*: "Our Constitution demands, and our country deserves, a Judiciary willing to hold the coordinate branches to account when they defy our most sacred legal commitments." https://www.nytimes.com/2019/02/15/us/politics/national-emergency-trump.html.

daimon[11]) that animates and binds character within, animates and sustains the bond of law's sovereignty without.[12] This kind of bonding occurs in social rituals of investiture or in the course of constitutional conventions or mass assemblies[13] in which, as Emile Durkheim classically described it, collective "effervescence" sets society up as a sacred or transcendent reality.[14]

The source and nature of the core values that establish law's sovereignty are most vividly displayed during times of political crisis, such as the French Revolution of 1789, or the American Civil War (1861–1865). When consensus on shared meanings breaks down, violence—both for and against the state that has been clouded by illegitimacy—increasingly threatens to trump civil discourse. How meanings are made (and unmade) in politics and culture thus serves as a vital resource

[11] In Plato's *Phaedrus*, the *daimon* is the spirit or value or ideal with which we identify (or love) most, the one that rules our character. Plato, *The Collected Dialogues*, eds. Edith Hamilton and Huntington Cairns (Princeton: Princeton University Press, 1969), 494, 498 ("So does each lover live after the manner of the god in whose company he once was, honoring him and copying him so far as may be." [Ibid., 252.c.8–9]). Closer to our own time, Simone Weil has written: "What is sacred in a human being is the impersonal in him." Simone Weil, *Selected Essays 1934–1943* (Eugene, OR: Wipf & Stock, 1962), 13. See also Philip Rieff, *Fellow Teachers* (New York: Delta Publishing, 1973), 49 ("Only cultureless societies can exist without presiding presences. No presence can preside when all are subject to abandonments quick as their adoptions. Our passionate truths are so provisional, they move so quickly with the electrified times, that none can prepare us to receive them deeply into ourselves, as character").

[12] See Emile Durkheim, *The Elementary Forms of the Religious Life* (New York: The Free Press, 1915), 240 ("Society cannot exist except in and through individual consciousness"). Eric Santner describes this collective performance as our "libidinal bond with society." Eric L. Santner, *The Royal Remains* (Chicago: University of Chicago Press, 2011), 123. As Hermia implies in Shakespeare's *A Midsummer Night's Dream*, the "soul's consent" is the source of sovereignty. William Shakespeare, *The Complete Works*, eds. Stephen Orgel and A. R. Braunmuller (New York: Penguin, 2002), 259 [*MSND*, I.1.82].

[13] See Judith Butler, *Notes Toward a Performative Theory of Assembly* (Cambridge, Harvard University Press, 2015), 160 ("[B]y freedom of assembly the nation-state protects precisely that right that could, if collectively exercised, bring down the state itself"). See also Emile Durkheim, *Sociology and Philosophy* (New York: The Free Press, 1974), 92 (noting that social ideals "could not survive if they were not periodically revived…[through] religious or secular feasts and ceremonies"). It is not an idle detail that in *Measure for Measure* Shakespeare stages the Duke's return to power before the citizenry outside the city gates. See Shakespeare, *The Complete Works*, 556 (*Measure for Measure* ['*MfM*'], IV.3.130–32) Sovereignty is enacted in a state of exception—a liminal state betwixt and between conventional order and its originary (extra-legal) source.

[14] See Emile Durkheim, *The Elementary Forms of the Religious Life*, 241, 244.

for understanding law's sovereignty and how its source and content change over time. Texts, images, and public performances of various kinds provide important insights into who or what counts as an authorized (or tainted) bearer of the sacred. Sovereign is the one or the many—King or Parliament or People[15]—who most effectively wield the name or image or character ideal that best captures the shared sacral source underpinning law's authority.[16]

The felt need to grasp the authoritative source and nature of shared core values shifts our attention away from Carl Schmitt's authoritarian understanding of sovereignty as the exercise of executive will alone.[17] The singular wisdom of liberal jurisprudence consists in never taking the shared foundational act of legitimation for granted.[18] Such an acknowledgment requires an inner as well as an external discursive capacity to live openly and self-reflexively with the uncertainty and concomitant anxiety that attend law's paradox. This emphasis within the liberal paradigm upon normative reflexivity invites closer scrutiny of the political, cultural, historical, and psychological conditions under which sovereignty is understood and sustained.

For Shakespeare, we might say, "character is polity." Properties of law and politics arise from modalities of character manifest in a given character's discourse and action. In *Measure*, these performances simultaneously enact diverse rhetorical, emotional, and political realities. Along the way, especially in pursuit of the question as to how far the delegation of legitimate authority may extend, we encounter the limit of substitution and, by extension, the fallacy of legally proclaimed equivalence. The limit

[15] See Dieter Grimm, *Sovereignty: The Origin and Future of a Political and Legal Concept* (New York: Columbia University Press, 2009), 21.

[16] The meaning of sovereignty is rooted in history and culture. In aboriginal cultures, for example, the source of sovereignty has been be traced to ancestral lands. See Joanne Barker, 'For Whom Sovereignty Matters', in *Sovereignty Matters* (Lincoln: University of Nebraska Press, 2005) and Kilipaka Kawaihonu Nahil Pae Ontai, 'A Spiritual Definition of Sovereignty from a Kanaka Maoli Perspective', ibid., 154 (using the native term '*ea*' ["Life, breath…Spirit"] to denote sovereignty).

[17] See Carl Schmitt, *Political Theology* (Chicago: University of Chicago Press, 1985 [1922]), 5; Giorgio Agamben, *Homo Sacer: Sovereign Power and Bare Life* (Stanford: Stanford University Press, 1998), 19.

[18] See Bruce Ackerman, *Social Justice in the Liberal State* (New Haven: Yale University Press, 1980), 324 ("It is only when people forget the meaning of the question of legitimacy that the liberal spirit will have been dealt a mortal blow").

lies in the sublime singularity of each other. This is what we witness when the Duke's sovereign power breaks against the impregnable resistance of Barnardine's refusal to die when the state commands it. We see it as well at the end of the play when the Duke's power seems to break again, this time against Isabella's unyielding silence in response to his repeated proposals of marriage. Yet, the play's lessons in the vicissitudes of sovereignty and character remain paradoxical. For it is precisely the extra-legal surplus, manifest in the *daimonic* force of "unassimilable" characters like Barnardine and Isabella,[19] that delimited law wants for itself, for the sake of its legitimacy. What are we to make of sovereignty caught in the crucible of law's paradox?

As within, so without. For every Hobbesian citizen ideal, reflecting a characteristic brutishness within that models a reciprocally severe sovereign force without, alternative character ideals beckon, reflecting alternative political possibilities. Characters such as Prospero and Lear, for example, each of whom, after great personal suffering, come to appreciate the precarity of sovereign power along with the elusive virtues of humility and mercy.[20] As a political matter, these ideals contrast sharply with the totalizing power of Hobbes' Leviathan (or absolute state). They propound an order based on tolerance, empathy, and compassion—attributes of character upon which social justice in a liberal democratic state crucially depends.

Cultivating the cognitive and prudential skills necessary to achieve a more temperate and lasting balance among the extremes of our nature requires keen emotional attunement as well as rhetorical and political sophistication. We need to recognize the changing emotional weather that different characters generate and its implications for the political climate of the republic at large. A polity that operates within a register of suspicion or license, for example, has its own norms and practices, its own

[19] A. D. Nuttall, *The Stoic in Love* (New York: Barnes & Noble Books, 1989), 20.

[20] King Lear irrationally cuts off Cordelia, the daughter he loves most, when, upon being asked to convert her own paternal love into words, she refuses to do so: "I cannot heave my heart into my mouth." Shakespeare, *The Complete Works 1489* (*King Lear*, I.1.80–81). When the storm of his rage against her finally subsides, Lear perceives the error of his ways and seeks reconciliation with Cordelia: "I'll kneel down and ask of thee forgiveness." Ibid., 1563 (*King Lear*, V.3.10–11). For his part, Prospero, after long years of isolated exile, having at last rendered helpless before him his fraternal foe, meets cruel political and personal betrayal with these words: "I do forgive thy rankest fault." Ibid., 758 (*The Tempest*, V.1.131–32).

forms of life, just as a polity operating on the basis of trust and belief enjoys forms of life of its own.

Language provides a key source of insight here. For example, when words are twisted and opaque, as when, at the outset of *Measure*, the Duke conceals his true intention to remain concealed in Vienna (the better to surveil his subjects from the shadows), the light of any possible transcendent source of sovereign authority appears distant and dim. And when opacity gives way to parody, as when the Duke's language in the last scene of the play seems to mock equity amidst a mad cascade of serial pardons—comically culminating in the act of falsely bearing a head (an "offence that pardons itself"[21])—the Duke's authority seems on the verge of collapsing in an empty vapor of words.

Conversely, when Isabella, on behalf of Mariana, Angelo's forsaken betrothed, selflessly assails as excessive the Duke's imposition of a capital sentence upon Angelo, Isabella's words achieve, at least momentarily, a luminous moral clarity. Putting aside her own grievance against Angelo for having unjustly ordered her brother's death, Isabella selflessly and empathically performs what equity requires. And even when characters catch a glimpse of their own moral deceits (as when Angelo, discerning the crack in his alleged moral virtuosity, says of Isabella's virtuous allure, "O cunning enemy, that to catch a saint, With saints dost bait thy hook,"[22]), their words betray an inner moral precarity that may unsettle us all. We recognize this is so even when self-deception remains caught in a character's blind spot, as when Isabella's "prone and speechless dialect" yields to moral passion with words aflame with unseemly sensuous delight (preferring rather to bear "the impression of keen whips as rubies," and to "strip myself to death, as to a bed that longing have been sick for"[23] than to yield up her virginity to Angelo's coercive demands). Is it any wonder, after sharing with Angelo her fantasy of flagellation while longing to couple naked abed with death, that Isabella would later concede there might be something to the temptation she posed? Witness her protestation at Angelo's trial that "[a] due sincerity did govern his deeds till he did look on me."[24]

[21] Ibid., 564 (*MfM*, V.1.532).

[22] Ibid., 542 (*MfM*, II.2.179).

[23] Ibid., 544 (*MfM*, II.4.99–102).

[24] Ibid., 563 (*MfM,* V.1.444–46).

These characters are veritable powder kegs waiting to go off—a portentous tribute to Freud's Vienna centuries hence. But what are the lessons in law and politics amid the deliberate deceptions, opaque self-deceits, and critical insights they bear? One possibility is this: polities that are unable to consciously work through the entangled fates of self and state sovereignty are likely to remain caught in endless oscillation between untamed desire on the one hand, and supercilious morality on the other. It would seem that humility, empathy, and grace must somehow be worked into the political and legal dialectic of order and justice. If the paradox of law's excess and lack can never be resolved, but may be prudently managed, these are the qualities of self and collective governance that are needed most.

Ever fearful of the people's sovereign power, the withholding of which would ensure the collapse of legitimate authority, the Duke seeks to win popular acceptance through strategic concealment and deceit. In the end, however, these Machiavellian stratagems rebound against him. Despite his best efforts to effect political and legal change, the conditions underlying the state's oscillation between licentious anarchy and hyper-moral tyranny persist. As a result, legitimacy and the political and social stability that it allows lie beyond the Duke's grasp. The political and legal impasses that set the play in motion seem likely to continue so long as an authentic (sacral) source of sovereignty, along with the qualities of character that render it bearable, remains untapped, unspoken, and unperformed by public acclamation.

That is the instruction in civic republicanism that *Measure* provides. In what follows, I offer a fuller defense of this claim.

Performing Subjunctivity

Measure for Measure has been called many things: a comedy, a tragedy, perhaps even a farce. It may well be all of those things. But most important for the purposes of the present analysis is what I shall call its ***subjunctivity***. A subjunctive narrative in this sense remains inconclusive until its audience acts to complete it. For example, in the Epilogue to *The Tempest*, Prospero, standing alone on stage, beseeches the audience to "release me from my bands with the help of your good hands.

Gentle breath of yours my sails must fill, or else my project fails…"[25] By their concluding act of approbation, the audience sets Prospero free—just as Prospero sets Ariel free upon the completion of that good spirit's assigned tasks. The audience's emulation of Prospero's emancipatory act sets a collective seal of approval upon the play's shared objectives: liberation and mercy. It is as if the play cannot close until the audience enacts the moral charge that lies at its heart.

Subjunctivity, then, is a performative formula for collective affirmation. It stages the ethical by asking: how shall we actualize the available range of possible selves and possible states? In what emotional bandwidth, in the name of what character ideal, shall we participate in political discourse and action? Political freedom, in practice, attains meaning through a process of trial and error. What does it feel like to try on a particular character, or action, or discourse in a given situation? Do we like who we become—both individually and collectively? By providing an opportunity for this kind of experimental political and characterological praxis, *Measure* teaches viewers who become willing participants in the drama before them that by freely exercising their political imagination as citizens they may arrive at a better understanding of the state's proper nature and function.

Subjunctivity in this sense provides a deep defense of the essentially rhetorical, which is to say, contingently agonistic and ultimately precarious nature of liberal democratic culture, a form of life that crowns precarity in freedom. To be sure, freedom may be a creative or a destructive force in society. In any event, when inadequately regulated, freedom fails[26]—devolving into licentiousness or tyranny. This is the essential paradox of law and character that lies at the heart of *Measure for Measure*.

The play begins and ends seemingly frozen in social and political disarray, vacillating between the disorder of unconstrained desire on the one hand, and the tyranny of moral intemperance and legal rigidity on the other—with no clear indication of whether positive political change could possibly break the deadlock. As it turns out, the resolution of this entrenched dilemma lies not in the plot but in the method of its unfolding. By making us aware of the cultural and psychological resources

[25] Ibid., 761 (*The Tempest*, Epi, 9–12).

[26] See, for example, Richard K. Sherwin, 'Anti-speech Acts and the First Amendment', *Harvard Law and Policy Review*, 16:2 (2022).

needed to properly understand the social, political, and legal conditions that perpetuate such untenable extremes, the play directs us beyond incessant strife and violence by pointing beyond *Measure* itself. The play must be completed subjunctively by those who witness it. The real action lies ahead.

Agonistic Culture and the Proto-Liberal State

The opening lines of *Measure for Measure* may provide the play's key, but upon reflection their cryptic nature only deepens: "Of government the properties to unfold would seem in me t'affect speech and discourse, since I am put to know that your own science exceeds, in that, the lists of all advice my strength can give you."[27]

The Duke speaks these words to Escalus, his chief political advisor. Their gist is plain enough: since Escalus's "own science" exceeds "all advice" the Duke might provide, it would seem but an affectation on the Duke's part (both artificial and presumptuous) to sermonize on the subject of governance.

Of course, as we will soon learn, the Duke's *modus operandi* as Vienna's ruler is ripe with affectation and artifice. Indeed, his very reference to the "properties" of government suggests an approach to politics that aligns with theater. This association arises not simply from his choice of the word "properties" which invokes the props or stage properties that plays typically engage, but also from the performative context in which these words are spoken. After all, it is the unproven Angelo, not tried and true Escalus, whom the Duke has selected, without forewarning or counsel, to stand in the Duke's place during his proposed absence. "Old Escalus" remains "secondary."[28] Even Angelo begs the Duke for a greater test of his character and worthiness of such a commission. As ensuing events will show, however, it is not confidence in Angelo's character, but rather suspicion of his flaws that guides the Duke's calculated choice.

Duplicity, it seems, is the rule of the day. The Duke may praise Angelo's virtues and Escalus's wisdom, but in practice neither amount to much. Notwithstanding Escalus's unparalleled knowledge of affairs of state, it is ducal "strength" alone that prevails. Once the executive decision to

[27] Shakespeare, *The Complete Works*, 532 (*MfM*, I.1.3–7).

[28] Ibid., 533 (*MfM*, I.2.46).

appoint Angelo has been made "no more remains"[29]—not counsel, nor even discussion. It but remains for Escalus to obey what the Duke has decreed.

Practically, if not rhetorically, Angelo's professed virtues fare no better, for notwithstanding his assertions to the contrary, the Duke has selected Angelo not for a soul that "seems good" but rather for one that will predictably implode under the pressure of his new office. In appointing Angelo the Duke sets in motion a political play that will, if his strategies work as intended, not only rid Vienna of the disorder that has plagued the city due to toothless law enforcement, but also heap blame upon Angelo, his expungable substitute, for the insufferable harshness of law's renewed efficacy under Angelo's rule.

While claiming an aversion to "staging" his own virtues before the people's eyes[30] apparently that is precisely what the Duke has in mind. Angelo's anticipated fall into the disgrace of moral intemperance will allow the Duke to swoop in and rescue the good people of Vienna from Angelo's sanctimonious rigidity and hypocritical abuse of power. By staging a well-timed return the Duke will appear to expunge intemperance from above and below, at once repulsing both tyranny and domestic licentiousness.

If governance is but a play of power gilded by misleading rhetoric, as the Duke's words and subsequent deeds suggest, we can expect little of real substance (or veracity) to come of political "speech and discourse." But while the play the Duke stages never directly challenges his Machiavellian motives, it does call into question the Duke's opening proposition: Do the properties of government necessarily unfold from the sovereign ruler's will alone, or might the constitutive power of a broad range of speech and discourse remain more politically potent than the Duke imagines?

Clever as they may be, the Duke's manipulative stratagems ultimately do not resolve the political crisis that prompts them. In the play's final scene—set amidst a mad flurry of ducal pardons and a pall of uncertainty that arises from Isabella's ambiguous silence in response to his repeated proposals of marriage—the Duke's authority (and the law's) seems no

[29] Ibid., 532 (*MfM*, 1.1.7).

[30] Ibid., 533 (*MfM*, I.2.68–69).

more secure than at the play's outset when the Duke's calculated staging of Angelo began.

From this apparent relapse into political impasse it seems reasonable to conclude that so long as the Duke fails to alter his shadowy ways (in both speech and action) the political problems he faces are likely to persist. In matters of ethics and politics, it would seem that the pre-Socratic philosopher Heraclitus was onto something when he said: "*Ethos anthropos daimon*" ("Character is fate"[31]). Indeed, the paradoxical reciprocity between character and fate, or between the power of constitutive rhetoric and political or legal reality, resounds not only within Heraclitus's famous dictum but also within the opening lines of *Measure* itself.

Consider again the play's opening words: "Of government the properties to unfold would seem in me t'affect speech and discourse." As with Heraclitus's dictum, we cannot but be alert to the contronymic aspect of Shakespeare's word choice. Contronyms paradoxically assert simultaneously opposed propositions. For example, in Heraclitus's saying, is character fate because character determines fate? Or is character fate because fate masters character? One interpretation propounds freedom, the other necessity. Likewise in *Measure's* opening lines, do the properties of government as embodied in the sovereign shape speech and discourse? Or might speech and discourse shape the properties of government that the sovereign then comes to embody? The former propounds tyranny, the latter leaves open a broad array of political possibilities.

Seen from one angle, we appear to be constituted by the way we are governed. Thus, for example, governance characterized by surveillance and deceit makes us puppets of hidden or disguised state power. Yet, seen from a different perspective, if speech and discourse shape the properties of government, then it is by our rhetorical or expressive choices that we may constitute preferred forms of self and state governance. The Duke's Machiavellian schemes may eat our soul and dominate our spirit one leader and one citizen at a time,[32] or come to be repudiated along

[31] Also translated as: "Man's character is his *daimon*" (G. S. Kirk and J. E. Raven, *The Presocratic Philosophers* [Cambridge: University of Cambridge Press, 1957], 213), and "A man's character is his guardian divinity" (Philip Wheelwright, *Heraclitus* [New York: Atheneum, 1968], 68).

[32] In an effort to make sense of how amoral political leaders corrupt those around them, former United States FBI Director James Comey had this to say about President Donald Trump's effect on his Attorney General (William Barr): "Mr. Trump makes everyone a

with the quality of being-among-others that such strategies of deceit and manipulation model and encourage. The latter prospect is where Barnardine's inexorable life force and resistant agency, like Isabella's empathic capacity for self-reflexive change, come into play. Both constitute forms of resistance and grace that affirmatively guide the citizenry's choice of emotional and characterological ideals in the service of imagining sovereignty anew.

In this analysis, *Measure* invites us to try on and assess a variety of linked political and personal identities. In so doing, it trains us in the overlapping vicissitudes and responsibilities of political and personal freedom. This is the fruit of performing character and politics in the Shakespearean atmosphere of early modernity. Everything depends on how the properties of government unfold: by whose agency are discrete forms of governance made manifest, constituting what kind of character, in what preferred or imposed expressive and performative register?

Against this interpretive context, consider once more what we see as the curtain rises over Shakespeare's Vienna, where the law has grown slack and the populace is doing as it pleases. For years, rules prohibiting prostitution and fornication before marriage have gone unenforced. Bawdy houses have proliferated along with the diseases they spread. The Duke faces a dilemma: if he does nothing, general licentiousness will only increase, leading to more civil disorder and disrespect for law. But if he suddenly clamps down on freedoms the people have grown used to, he risks provoking their ire. ("'Twould be my tyranny to strike and gall them."[33]) So he comes up with a shrewd solution. He will announce to the people that he is taking a leave of absence. In his place, he appoints Angelo as fully empowered, but—unnervingly—tasked with putting teeth back in the law. If the populace comes to resent Angelo as a tyrant, the Duke can simply step in and relieve him of his duties. Having staged himself as the city's savior, the Duke will have garnered all the benefits of restored order leaving disgraced Angelo to pay the price for having revived the violence of law's deterrence.

co-conspirator to his preferred set of facts, or delusions... You use his language, praise his leadership, tout his commitment to values. And then you are lost. He has eaten your soul." Go to: https://www.rollingstone.com/politics/politics-news/james-comey-william-barr-trump-eat-their-souls-829902/.

[33] Shakespeare, *The Complete Works*, 536 (*MfM*, I.3.36).

The Duke's ingenious plan begins on track. In his first official act as head of state, Angelo condemns to death a man named Claudio for the offense of fornicating with and impregnating Juliet. At first glance, this test case for law's renewed vigor seems extraordinarily ill chosen. Claudio, it turns out, was for all intents and purposes married to Juliet. Their mutual love and commitment are never questioned. They but lacked the "outward order" of a proper dowry. To treat this technical violation of the law as a capital offense seems wildly disproportionate. Not even the short-lived and historically anomalous Adultery Act of 1650 went this far: it made *adultery*, not fornication, a capital offense.[34] But what if the wild disproportion of Claudio's sentence is precisely the point Angelo wishes to make?

As cultural anthropologists David Graeber and Marshall Sahlins have written, the more monstrous and violent the law seems, the greater the king's perceived proximity to a godlike sovereignty.[35] Claudio himself expresses a cognate sense of the irrationality of law's sovereign power. For example, after being sentenced he says: "Thus can the demi-god, Authority, make us pay down for our offence by weight The words of heaven; on whom it will, it will, On whom it will not, so; yet, still 'tis just."[36] Likewise, Escalus, the Duke's chief counsel, reflects on the role of caprice in law's domain: "Some rise by sin, and some by virtue fall."[37]

If Angelo's assigned task were to renew the populace's sense of awe, the monstrous or godlike irrationality that attends the sacred origin of law's legitimacy, we might be tempted to attribute to him a modicum of success.[38] But in *Measure*, it is not awe that triumphs. Angelo's tyrannical abuse of power may breed a collective sense of fear, but when fear mixes with political mistrust and resentment, sovereign authority falls

[34] Under the Act, the crime of fornication carried a sentence of three months in prison. See Johanna Rickman, *Love, Lust, and License in Early Modern England: Illicit Sex and the Nobility* (London and New York: Routledge Taylor & Francis, 2008), 23. As Rickman notes: "The act of 1650 was only in effect for about a decade and the burden of proof was so heavy that it was only rarely enforced." Ibid., 24.

[35] David Graeber and Marshall Sahlins, *On Kings* (Chicago: University of Chicago Press, 2017), 5, 12.

[36] Shakespeare, *The Complete Works*, 534 (*MfM*, I.2.121–22).

[37] Ibid., 538 (*MfM*, II.1.38).

[38] As the Duke puts it: "For terror not to use – in time the rod more mocked than feared – so our decrees." Ibid., 532 (*MfM*, I.1.27–28).

from heavenly grace. Angelo's intemperate and ultimately self-interested rule—as reflected, for example, in his willingness to abuse political power (offering to pardon Isabella's brother in exchange for her virginity)—is not the stuff heavenly awe is made of. The consequences of deceit and intemperance are manifest throughout the remainder of the play. We see this occur outwardly, for example, in grossly disproportionate sentencing and other acts of irrationality and corruption that are the hallmark of tyranny, and inwardly, as the hidden mysteries and frailties of character continually lead to gross errors in judgment.

But what if one could choose from among discrete character types? In what political mood, brought on or held fast by what character ideal, might political states flourish or fail? From Isabella's "prone and speechless dialect" to Barnardine's mostly mute assertion of vitally embodied existence, character attunes those with whom it interacts with the expressive and emotional norms that constitute the local weather (or mood or emotional tone) in which that character operates. It is in this sense that we may read *Measure* as a political and legal mystery play, posing the question: how do we recognize and respond to the varying signs and entangled vicissitudes of character and sovereignty?

Character Is Polity

In order to ensure the legitimacy of the law's sovereignty, the body politic must be ready to respond when faced with the question: who is a proper bearer of the sacred? Consider the Duke, who has taken to the shadows (as Lucio, his libertine counterpart, puts it). He has chosen to exercise power by Machiavellian plots and deceits such as covert surveillance and disguise. He constantly manipulates others, somewhat like a trickster. As Lucio puts it, "[i]t was a mad fantastical trick of him to steal from the state."[39] Yet, who is he really? Escalus tells us that the Duke, "above all other strifes, contended especially to know himself."[40] It is unclear, however, how well he succeeds in that quest. Indeed, it often seems as if it is only through his vicarious enjoyment of what *others* experience that the Duke can taste experience at all.

[39] Ibid., 549 (*MfM*, III.2.88–89).

[40] Ibid., 551 (*MfM*, IV.1.222–23).

Testing the character of others and provoking a range of moral and intimate emotional responses may be the Duke's way of addressing a sense of emptiness that craves the animus of lived experience. Is it his internal fragmentation, the perturbations of his inner incoherence, that we witness when, disguised as a friar, the Duke counsels Claudio to make peace with death? Could it be that the Duke is speaking to, or perhaps *about* himself when he says, "Thou art not thyself, for thou exist on many a thousand grains that issue out of dust"?[41] The Duke's frightening image of dispersed, dis-en-souled emptiness is hardly a source of solace. Cut off from grace, devoid of the influx of love that illuminates "the dust you seldom see" (to cite a memorable Leonard Cohen lyric[42]), the Duke seems to lack access to any unifying spirit (or *daimon*) that could make material grains cohere. In this respect, the Duke appears to embody sovereignty in its nihilistic register—as a force of disruption issuing from a state of empty suspension.[43] Nihilism makes it easy to yield life to death. One's own life, and others'. Such is the logic of the death of life as endless death, a death that cannot die. As Gillian Rose puts it: "Death as nothing is pure violence beyond representation."[44]

This is the Duke's world: all plot, and no meaning; dust without spirit. As the Duke tells Escalus: "There is scarce truth enough alive to make societies secure."[45] That's what it's like when law's meaning and law's violence split apart.[46] In such a state, public law oscillates between tyranny, amidst devious plots and manoeuvers in the service of naked

[41] Ibid., 546 (*MfM*, III.1.19–21).

[42] Leonard Cohen, "Love Itself" ("In streams of light I clearly saw the dust you seldom see, out of which the nameless makes a name for one like me"). Go to: https://songmeanings.com/songs/view/3530822107858574779/.

[43] See Robert Yelle, *Sovereignty and the Sacred*, 18 ("The antinomianism that is associated with the sovereign is ambivalent, not merely because it can lead to either the founding or the overthrow of polity…but also because of what such antinomianism suggests about the nature of sovereignty. The chaos and violence that attend such states of exception…[are] expressions of the singularity of the sovereign, of the manner in which she or he transcends and potentially transgresses any regular order").

[44] Gillian Rose, *Mourning Becomes the Law* (Cambridge: Cambridge University Press, 1997), 132.

[45] Shakespeare, *The Complete Works*, 551 (*MfM*, IV.1.216–18).

[46] See Richard K. Sherwin, 'Law in the Flesh: Tracing Legitimation's Origin to "The Act of Killing"', *No Foundations: An Interdisciplinary Journal of Law and Justice*, No. 11 (June 2014). http://nofoundations.com/issues/NoFo11Sherwin.pdf.

power, and anarchy, in the service of untamed desire. This is the state of affairs in which *Measure* begins and ends—the outward display perhaps of the Duke's fraught internal state.

The varieties of character and the various forms of discourse and action that discrete characters play out not only generate and operate within dominant fields of power. They also point to and comment on *subordinated* semantic fields, *suppressed* cognitive and emotional registers—ways of knowing and speaking, feeling and judging, acting and imagining that operate on the margins of a dominant text or action. Such alternative registers tell us that the locus of sovereignty may vary and shift. Consider, for example, how Juliet's calm and radiant joy eloquently counters (and critically comments on) the conventional view of her pregnancy as illicit: "I do repent me as it is an evil And take the shame with joy."[47]

Or consider that other memorable minor character, Barnardine. Barnardine has been condemned to death, but due to a lack of firm evidence, he has been languishing in prison for nearly a decade. He is "[a] man that apprehends death no more dreadfully but as a drunken sleep: careless, reckless, and fearless of what past, present, or to come: insensible of mortality and desperately mortal."[48] When Barnardine's head is at last called for, he replies: "I am not fitted for't… I swear I will not die today for any man's persuasion."[49] Hearing this, the Duke concludes that to execute a man so "unmeet for death" "were damnable."[50] So Barnardine lives on. He puts himself, in that symbolic moment, beyond the reach of law's violence.

Unlike the Duke, Barnardine is a man firmly ensouled in his own flesh. In him we witness the life force laid bare. His resistance displays a sense of sovereignty directly opposed to the Duke's voracious emptiness. Rather than reflecting the sacred in the valence of disruption, Barnardine seems to vitalize the sacred as uncanny excess. Like Antigone, who resisted King Creon's will in the name of sacred burial rites more ancient and lasting than mere positive law, Barnardine lays claim to a similarly extra-legal (*daimonic*, perhaps chthonic) authority in his mostly mute opposition to the Duke's destabilizing nihilism.

[47] Shakespeare, *The Complete Works*, 543 (*MfM*, II.4.35–36).

[48] Ibid., 554 (*MfM*, IV.3.140–43).

[49] Ibid., 555 (*MfM*, IV.3.42–43).

[50] Ibid., 555 (*MfM*, IV.3.66–67).

For her part, Isabella enacts a sacral bearing of another kind—the kind one negotiates within oneself. Consider in this regard Isabella's display of empathy near the end of the play. Notwithstanding Angelo's gross abuse of power by unjustly seeking the execution of her brother Claudio, even after falsely promising to save Claudio's life in exchange for Isabella's virginity, Isabella nevertheless pleads for Angelo before the Duke. She does this not for herself, but for Mariana, Angelo's abandoned fiancé. Isabella's earlier moral certainty ("More than our brother is our chastity"[51]), even in the face of Claudio's existential suffering ("Death is a fearful thing," he tells her[52]), yields now to an ethical register that evinces a more complex, fluid, and empathic form of knowing and judging. Epiphanic grace, rather than the strict dictates of abstract moral law with its calculable equivalents, seems to motivate Isabella's ethical demotion of self in the service of another.

Barnardine and Isabella, like the sacral forces they bear, are inimitable, singular, which is to say, without substitute or equal measure. Their disparate acts of resistance contest the conventional binary of law versus disorder which appears inadequate to meet the uncertain, highly circumstantial demands of justice as equity. The ultimately untenable rigidity of equal measure justice, like the Duke's static vision of human behavior as something that can be predictably anticipated and controlled, finds its limit here. The precarity of self it seems is a two-way street: it may implode under pressure or ascend inexplicably to higher states of moral awareness and responsibility. Traveling the different roads along which precarity leads brings into view different sources of the sacred and, by extension, differences in the nature of sovereignty itself.

Along one path lies mercy and the possibility of redemption, along another, tyranny and death. The dramatic clash among actual and possible selves in the play's world confronts us not only with a complex range of multiple cognitive and affective registers, but also with the realization that we harbor within ourselves that very complexity. We come to see that this clash constitutes the rhetorical play of law and politics alike. It sounds both the risk and the promise that human freedom holds out. In its darker register, freedom invites disorder and existential anguish. This is the note that echoes in Angelo's words when he confronts his own moral depravity,

[51] Ibid., 544 (*MfM*, II.4.64–65).

[52] Ibid., 547 (*MfM*, III.1.116).

"What art thou, Angelo?"[53] We hear it as well in the Duke's nihilist vision of life dispersed as dust, a sentiment Pascal famously expressed when he wrote: "The eternal silence of these infinite spaces fills me with dread."[54]

But the promise of freedom also models emancipatory possibility, the kind that lies at the heart of Italian Renaissance culture.[55] When Barnadine defies the power of the state ("I swear I will not die today for any man's persuasion"[56]) it is as if we can discern in the supercharged vitality of his indomitable will echoes of Pico della Mirandola's humanist credo: "To man it is allowed to be whatever he chooses to be!"[57] As if in asking *who have I been? who am I now?* and *who might I become?* one sets in motion a power to realize not only possible selves, but actual worlds.[58] In this respect, *Measure* lays bare a deep antinomy seeded in modernity from the outset: a vision of the human condition framed by the ecstasy of a radically emancipated will to power, on the one hand, and the anguish of moral deracination from occluding the sacred, on the other.

[53] Ibid., 542 (*MfM*, II.3.172).

[54] Blaise Pascal, *Pensées* (London: Penguin, 1995), 66. See also ibid., 19 ("When I consider… the infinite immensity of spaces of which I know nothing and which know nothing of me, I take fright and am amazed to be here rather than there, now rather than then"). See also Giuseppe Mazzotta, *Cosmopoiesis: The Renaissance Experiment* (Toronto: University of Toronto, 2001), 74 (noting that Shakespeare sees "unreality lying at the heart of making and as the outcome of making" and that as he "connects making, freedom, and magic, making is the mask of non-being, or nothing"). On Mazzotta's analysis, Prospero's farewell to his art at the close of *The Tempest* reveals "the pursuit of nothing as the essence of the fascination the modern world holds for making." Ibid., 75.

[55] See ibid., 74 ("The primacy the Renaissance gives to *vita activa* tells us we are free to the extent that we invent ourselves"). See also Ernesto Grassi, *Renaissance Humanism* (Binghamton, NY: Medieval & Renaissance Texts & Studies, 1988), 119, and Paul Oskar Kristeller, *Renaissance Thought and the Arts* (Princeton: Princeton University Press, 1980), 108 ("Thus the dignity of man is no longer conceived in terms of [man's] universality, but in terms of his liberty").

[56] Shakespeare, *The Complete Works*, 555 (*MfM*, II.4.3.59–60).

[57] Go to https://users.manchester.edu/Facstaff/SSNaragon/Online/texts/316/Pico,%20Oration.pdf.

[58] See Michael Allen Gillespie, *Nihilism Before Nietzsche* (Chicago: University of Chicago Press, 1996), xxiii ("Nihilism is not the result of liberalism but of a strain of modern thought that is largely at odds with liberalism, which sees man not as a limited and imperfect being who 'muddles through,' but as a superhuman being who can create the world anew through the application of his infinite will").

Recognizing the need for humility and vigilance in the face of moral grandiosity and self-deceit, without abandoning openness to the unpredictable mystery of grace (within) and the public acclamation of shared transcendent values (in society at large), responds to the most pressing political and legal challenges associated with the onset of modernity. The rise of natural rights jurisprudence, with its at least tacit assertion of transcendent knowledge,[59] in uneasy conjunction with liberalism's precarity-conscious paradigm for a duly constrained state,[60] may be viewed from the vantage of this historic predicament. Oscillating between the stark polarities of executive will ("an order backed by threats"[61]) and moral obligation (an extra-legal authority rooted in the sacred), the law's sovereign authority seems caught in a perpetual crisis of legitimation.[62]

Seen in this light, it should prove less surprising for a play that anatomizes the vicissitudes of character and sovereignty in early modernity to open and close with scenes of paradoxical impasse, as *Measure for Measure* does.[63] The lessons of politics studied as a matter of science and rhetorical craft alone are insufficient guides to judgment. The properties of government also unfold constitutively and reciprocally through exemplary character development and mutually attuned discursive exchange. "Character is polity"—but whether this is a formula for tyranny ("the governor forges the governed") or freedom ("citizens may publicly acclaim what is sovereign") depends on choices made from above and below, within and without.

[59] See, for example, Leo Strauss, *Natural Right and History*, 24 ("[T]here cannot be natural right if human thought is not capable of acquiring genuine, universally valid, final knowledge").

[60] See Bruce Ackerman, *Social Justice in the Liberal State*, 4 (citing as the first principle of liberal theory the need to test in collective public dialogue the basis for legitimizing political power: "No form of power is immune from the question of legitimacy").

[61] H. L. A. Hart, *The Concept of Law*, 6.

[62] See Jurgen Habermas, *Legitimation Crisis* (Boston: Beacon Press, 1975).

[63] Impasse also should prove unsurprising in association with the play's repudiation of the logic of equivalence. See Sarah Kofman, 'Beyond Aporia?', in Andrew Benjamin, ed., *Post-structuralist Classics* (London: Routledge, 1983), 27 ("Aporia, which breaks with the logic of identity, and which pertains to the logic of the intermediary, is an untranslatable term"). Authority as the originary lack, an already always absent presence, is, of course, a central theme in Derridean deconstructivism, traceable perhaps to this early modern Shakespearean enactment.

By *Measure's* end, we learn that the fate of the choices that have been made is "what's yet behind"[64]—which paradoxically may want to mean what lies ahead (open to future possibilities, behind palace doors, in joyful conjugal union), but may actually mean trapped in the past, ensnared in the same dogged cycle of untempered power and desire. It depends on what precisely the Duke is alluding to in the play's final lines as "meet".

If Isabella's fateful consummation of the Duke's proposal of marriage remains blind to choice, then "what's yet behind" implicates (and perhaps replicates) the kind of illicit fornication that has plagued Vienna and driven the play's plot from the outset—from Claudio's non-formalized marriage to Julia, to Angelo's coercive seduction of Isabel, to his actual (albeit unwitting) consummation of wedlock with Mariana. What sort of *Eros* will sovereignty channel and represent: wilful sexual desire or a desire to transcend the limits of self by creatively and self-reflexively imagining new ways of living and thinking in community together?[65]

Impasse is a suitable condition for subjunctivity: some additional action or external force is required to relieve the perplexity it provokes. But not Machiavellian calculation; plots like the Duke's cannot produce a stable order, only more plots. Something more is required. What makes intercourse (public or private) legitimate is consent. And what governs consent is trust—a collective investment of shared beliefs and values sufficient to authorize the exercise of power.

Rhetorical opacity as a result of either deliberate deception or self-deceit is but one of the ways consent may be thwarted. Illiberal discourse emanates like perturbed and perturbing microclimates from the characters who perform it. Conversely, the discourse of liberal democracy takes the precarity of governance (including self-governance) as the proper point of law's departure and limit. Precarity, it turns out, serves as a precondition to preserving singularities within an ecology of tolerance, respect, and empathy. The kind of political prudence this requires will never be mastered by the mechanics of abstract rules and rigid moral formulas ("head for head," "measure for measure"), much less by the shadowy deceits of surveillance and disguised manipulation.

64 Shakespeare, *The Complete Works*, 564 (*MfM*, V.1.530–31) ("So bring us to our palace, where we'll show what's yet behind that's meet you all should know").

65 See Andrea Nye, "The Hidden Host: Irigaray and Diotima at Plato's Symposium," 56 (describing Diotima's understanding of *Eros* as a movement "beyond individual life into the lives of others" in discourses that serve as "interchanges that initiate social order").

A just balance must be struck between what law lacks and what it craves: unassimilable spirit (or *daimon*) within, extra-legal excess (transcendent significance) without. Whether the sovereignty (that's "yet behind") will be violently disruptive in its onset and coercive in its rule, or bound to an ethics of equity in conjunction with the accidents of grace and the obligations of shared transcendent values, depends on the properties of government, character, and discourse that unfold.

Measure for Measure suggests that the more attuned we become to singularity and complexity, the more informed and self-reflexive our choices may be. By identifying and assaying various characters, the play identifies diverse forms of political and legal knowledge and practice and, by extension, possible sources of self and state sovereignty—the extra-legal beliefs and values we hold most sacred. This insight provides a path to meaningful freedom in the development of self and political governance alike. At the same time, however, the shadow cast by humanist freedom remains. In shadows and grace, the entangled vicissitudes of secular power and sacred meaning recapitulate law's paradox.

Conclusion: *Eudaimonic States*

Law and theater, like law and literature, and indeed like law and the humanities more generally, share a common reliance upon the performance of competing imaginaries. To experiment with different cognitive and affective registers, projecting divergent socio-political and legal realities is to engage in a pedagogic and ultimately an ethical practice. It presupposes a nimble imagination and a willingness to learn from its exercise. As Isabella put it in her effort to move Angelo to save her brother's life: "If he had been as you, and you as he, you would have slipped like him, but he like you would not have been so stern."[66] Angelo's terrible (albeit predictable and much regretted) fall and Isabella's grace-kissed transformation (from moral rigidity to empathic dexterity) attest to the wisdom of these words.

[66] Ibid., 541 (*MfM*, II.2.64–66). See Julia Reinhard Lupton, *Citizen-Saints: Shakespeare and Political Theology* (Chicago: University of Chicago Press, 2005), 157 (describing "the theater of citizenship" as a public place "whose legal, ritual, economic, and social realities undergo continual exchange and typological refunctioning in response to those represented on the stage").

Empathy, reciprocity, mercy: these are the fruits of existential uncertainty self-reflexively grasped in the midst of life's vicissitudes. We are all to some extent wounded, morally broken, or at risk of becoming so, hidden from ourselves, yet capable of grace and redemptive transformation. That is why we must remain attentive to alternative epistemological registers and imaginary states: left unchecked, the discrete limitations of a given way of knowing or feeling or speaking risks overwhelming its virtues. For example, moral certainty, indifferent to the precarity of self and circumstance, as readily becomes tyrannical as unchecked license. The extremes of our nature call out for a prudent allocation of power among discrete forms of knowledge and discourse so that their collective strengths may check and balance their respective weaknesses.[67]

Thinking about thinking, feeling, and judging mitigates the quick seductiveness of flawed persuasion. That is what dramatic asides, dissents, and other reports from the margins are for. Political freedom in this sense aspires to harmonize the conflicting sacral forces of violence and meaning, disruption and regeneration, nihilism and grace. These opposing registers—as enacted by the Duke's disruptive agency, on the one hand, and Isabella's and Barnardine's regenerative agency on the other—constitute the strife of sovereignty within which the binding, unbinding, and rebinding of the state perpetually play out. Thus do we ask, by what *daimon* do we live, bound to what sacred or transcendent source of law's sovereignty?

Had the Duke succeeded in knowing himself and others better, would he have learned to turn away from the dark corners of deceit and manipulation (deploying "craft against vice"[68])? Would he have attended more carefully to Escalus's wise counsel on "the nature of our people, our city's institutions, and the terms for common justice?"[69] Would his proposal of marriage to Isabella have then become worthier of her consent than her silence? The Duke seems incapable of any of these things. It is as if his being blocked from instruction by the *daimon* condemns him to the twinned characterological and political impasses with which *Measure* begins and ends.

[67] See Richard K. Sherwin, 'Dialects and Dominance', *University of Pennsylvania Law Review*, 136:3 (January 1988), 729–849.

[68] Shakespeare, *The Complete Works*, 548 (*MfM*, III.2.239).

[69] Ibid., 532 (*MfM*, I.1.9–11).

Like the Duke's hollow instrumentalism, opaque to the accidents of grace but not the arrogance of control that strategic calculation holds out, Angelo's intolerant and defective moral rigidity also stands in stark contrast to the *daimonic* dimension of Barnardine's and Isabella's disparate forms of resistance. As Angelo wistfully realizes, "Once our grace we have forgot, nothing goes right."[70] By guiding us to more fully appreciate the consequences of failing to attend to what the *daimon* asks of us, *Measure for Measure* invites us to consider alternative sovereign imaginaries based on sources of characterological ideals that cultivate and sustain *Eudaimonia* (the good life).

By casting its audience into a subjunctive register the play stokes our creative capacity to deliberately assimilate and, in so doing, test out a range of possible inner and outer states. The Duke may remain incapable of change, but those of us who witness the staging of such political and personal impasses may, upon due reflection, come to discern their cause and cure. Political judgment and action may be shaped and informed by such insights. Such are the cultural and political conditions necessary for prudent judgment and meaningful freedom.

But how might an advisor like Escalus more effectively have met the challenge the play's subjunctive posture presents? By what prudent counsel might he have helped the Duke to know himself and the nature of sovereignty better, prompting wiser speech and discourse? We may begin our response by imagining...

Coda: Escalus' Dream

It is the evening after the Duke's surprise return to Vienna. Escalus has retreated to his chamber with a heavy heart. The escalating fervor of the Duke's bizarre pardons, followed by the shock of his sudden proposal to Isabella, weigh upon Escalus like a fever. When sleep at last relieves his distress, a dream comes to him. He will recount it to the Duke the next morning in these words:

> I saw a great wheel turning and turning. And on the circumference of that wheel sat many people, as if it were a great stage.

[70] Ibid., 557 (*MfM*, IV.4.31–32).

> I saw Angelo, and Isabella, and Lucio, and others as well. And when one of them pointed toward the north star, it was as if the weather of the world took its properties from the climate their character brought forth. So that, when his turn north came round, all things became Angelo's hollow righteousness, but when it was Lucio's turn, all things turned licentious and bawdy. And so it went, dizzying and topsy-turvy!
> And then you stood, and joined each in turn, as if taking their proper measure and scope. And it seemed to me my Lord as if your majesty contained multitudes, each a sovereign soul, indivisible and incommensurable, unassimilable in its force and mystery, each a possible future, a sovereign self and state waiting to be staged, yet together, an ensemble, held in a single drama.
> Whether this was my dream, or I was but a living shadow in yours, I cannot now say. Yet, upon waking, my heart told me there are sacred boundaries no sovereign may cross even by the keenest of strategies of will or desire, for the source from which sovereignty flows is at once its origin and limit— a sacred good that by consensus publicly acclaimed sovereign states exist to promote and secure.

Escalus then grew silent, leaving the Duke deep in thought. At last, having completed his musing, the Duke looked up and spoke, pronouncing his words with great deliberation, as if each were being uttered for the first time: "Of government the properties to unfold would seem in me t'affect speech and discourse…"[71]

Acknowledgements I wish to express my sincere thanks to Subha Mukherji, Camilla Temple, and Dunstan Roberts for their instructive engagement with this essay. Professor Mukherji's luminous insights and intellectual generosity during my spring 2018, Visiting Fellowship at Fitzwilliam College, Cambridge deepened my encounter with Shakespeare's genius. I am grateful as well for the feedback I received in response to an earlier version of this work at the conference on "Law and Poetics in Early Modern England and Beyond" (July 2–4, 2018), an event hosted by the project *Crossroads of Knowledge in Early Modern England: the Place of Literature*, based (in part) in the *Centre for Research in the Arts, Social Sciences and Humanities ("CRASSH")* where I enjoyed the great privilege of serving during the Lent and Easter terms of 2018, as Senior Visiting Scholar. Errors in the text are mine alone.

[71] Ibid., 532 (*MfM*, I.1.3–4).

Bibliography

Agamben, Giorgio. *Homo Sacer: Sovereign Power and Bare Life*. Stanford: Stanford University Press, 1998.

Berman, Harold J. *Law and Revolution*. Cambridge, MA: Harvard University Press, 1983.

Breen, John and Teeuwen, Mark. *Shinto in History: Ways of the Kami*. Surry: Curzon Press, 2000.

Bruner, Jerome. *Actual Minds, Possible Worlds*. Cambridge, MA: Harvard University Press, 1986.

Butler, Judith. *Notes Toward a Performative Theory of Assembly*. Cambridge: Harvard University Press, 2015.

Cover, Robert. 'Nomos and Narrative'. In *Narrative, Violence, and the Law*, edited by Martha Minow, Michael Ryan, and Austin Sarat. Ann Arbor: University of Michigan Press, 1995.

Derrida, Jacques. *The Beast & the Sovereign*. Vol. 1. Chicago: University of Chicago Press, 2009.

Durkheim, Emile. *The Elementary Forms of the Religious Life*. New York: The Free Press, 1915.

Durkheim, Emile. *Sociology and Philosophy*. New York: The Free Press, 1974.

Gillespie, Michael Allen. *Nihilism Before Nietzsche*. Chicago: University of Chicago Press, 1996.

Graeber, David and Sahlins, Marshall. *On Kings*. Chicago: University of Chicago Press, 2017.

Grassi, Ernesto. *Renaissance Humanism*. Binghamton, NY: Medieval & Renaissance Texts & Studies, 1988.

Grimm, Dieter. *Sovereignty: The Origin and Future of a Political and Legal Concept*, translated by Belinda Cooper. New York: Columbia University Press, 2009.

Habermas, Jurgen. *Legitimation Crisis*. Boston: Beacon Press, 1975.

Hart, H. L. A. *The Concept of Law*. Oxford: Clarendon Press, 1979.

Hunter, James Davison. *The Death of Character*. New York: Basic Books, 2000.

Kirk, G. S. and Raven, J. E. *The Presocratic Philosophers*. Cambridge: University of Cambridge Press, 1957.

Kofman, Sarah. 'Beyond Aporia?'. In *Post-structuralist Classics*, edited by Andrew Benjamin. London: Routledge, 1983.

Kristeller, Paul Oskar. *Renaissance Thought and the Arts*. Princeton: Princeton University Press1980.

Lupton, Julia Reinhard. *Citizen-Saints: Shakespeare and Political Theology*. Chicago: University of Chicago Press, 2005.

Mazzotta, Giuseppe. *Cosmopoiesis: The Renaissance Experiment*. Toronto: University of Toronto, 2001.

Nuttall, A. D. *The Stoic in Love*. New York: Barnes & Noble Books, 1989.

Nye, Andrea. 'The Hidden Host: Irigaray and Diotima at Plato's Symposium'. *Hypatia*, Vol. 3, No. 3, pp. 45–61 (Winter 1989).
Pascal, Blaise. *Pensées*. London: Penguin, 1995 [1670].
Plato. *The Collected Dialogues*, edited by Edith Hamilton and Huntington Cairns. Princeton: Princeton University Press, 1969.
Rickman, Johanna. *Love, Lust, and License in Early Modern England: Illicit Sex and the Nobility.* London & New York: Routledge Taylor & Francis, 2008.
Rieff, Philip. *Fellow Teachers*. New York: Delta Publishing, 1973.
Roquet, Paul. *Ambient Media: Japanese Atmospheres of Self*. Minneapolis: University of Minnesota Press, 2016.
Rose, Gillian. *Mourning Becomes the Law*. Cambridge: Cambridge University Press, 1997.
Santner, Eric L. *The Royal Remains.* Chicago: University of Chicago Press, 2011.
Schmitt, Carl. *Political Theology*, translated by George Schwab. Chicago: University of Chicago Press, 1985 [1922].
Sherwin, Richard K. 'Dialects and Dominance'. *University of Pennsylvania Law Review*, Vol. 136, No. 3, pp. 729–849 (January 1988).
Sherwin, Richard K. *When Law Goes Pop*. Chicago: University of Chicago Press, 2000.
Sherwin, Richard K. 'Law in the Flesh: Tracing Legitimation's Origin to "The Act of Killing"'. *No Foundations: An Interdisciplinary Journal of Law and Justice*, No. 11 (June 2014).
Sherwin, Richard K. 'Anti-speech Acts and the First Amendment'. *Harvard Law and Policy Review*, Vol. 16, No. 2 (2022).
Stevens, Wallace. *Selected Poems*. New York: Alfred A. Knopf, 2009.
Strauss, Leo. *Natural Right and History*. Chicago: University of Chicago Press, 1965.
Weil, Simone. *Selected Essays 1934–1943.* Eugene, OR: Wipf & Stock, 1962.
Wheelwright, Philip. *Heraclitus.* New York: Atheneum, 1968.
Yelle, Robert. *Sovereignty and the Sacred*. Chicago: University of Chicago Press, 2019.

PART III

Text, Knowledge, Hermeneutics

CHAPTER 5

The Letter and the Spirit: Portia's Case

Regina Schwartz

Nietzsche is not our most balanced reader of Christian thought—to put it mildly—but I open with him to highlight the power of biblical hermeneutics. In *Daybreak*, he writes:

> Again and again they say, 'I am right, for it is written and–' then follows an interpretation of such impudent arbitrariness that a philologist who hears it is caught between rage and laughter and asks himself: is it possible? Is this honourable? Is it even decent? – How much dishonesty in this matter is still practised [...] how the Bible is pummelled and punched [...] But after all, what can one expect from the effects of a religion which in the centuries of its foundation perpetrated that unheard-of philological farce concerning the Old Testament? I mean the attempt to pull the Old Testament: I mean the attempt to pull the Old Testament from under the feet of the Jews with

R. Schwartz (✉)
Northwestern University, Evanston, IL, USA
e-mail: rsreginamara@gmail.com

S. Mukherji and D. Roberts (eds.), *Literature and the Legal Imaginary*, Crossroads of Knowledge in Early Modern Literature 4,
https://doi.org/10.1007/978-3-031-74093-0_5

> the assertion it contained nothing but Christian teaching and *belonged* to the Christians as the *true* people of Israel, the Jews being only usurpers.[1]

Nietzsche goes on to describe Christian exegesis:

> And then there followed a fury of interpretation and construction that cannot possibly be associated with a good conscience: however much Jewish scholars protested, the Old Testament was supposed to speak of Christ and only of Christ, and especially of his Cross; wherever a piece of wood, a rod, a ladder, a twig, a tree, a willow, a staff is mentioned, it is supposed to be a prophetic allusion to the wood of the Cross; even the erection of the […] brazen serpent, even Moses spreading his arms in prayer, *even* the spits on which the Passover lamb was roasted – all allusions to the cross and as it were preludes to it! Has anyone who asserted this ever *believed* it?[2]

Indeed, this may have been what Saint Paul believed, and it surely is what exegetes from Origen to the Reformation believed. What is at stake in interpreting this way? Not some dry academic exercise, but, according to Nietzsche, even "the church did not shrink from enriching the text of the Septuagint […] For they were conducting a *war*."[3] Nietzsche makes dramatic the insight that a hermeneutic principle not only harbors power, but even violence, and this obtains not only in scriptural interpretation, but in law courts.

Attending to the question of interpretation, I will be trying to tease out some of the relations between theology and law through the phrase "letter and spirit," a phrase which was used most notably by Paul in II Corinthians 3:6, where he says "the letter kills but the Spirit giveth life."[4] This formulation became the proof-text for over 1200 years, from Origen to Luther, for grounding biblical hermeneutics. The "letter" signifies scripture and the "spirit" signifies how to interpret it. Then, from Luther onwards (and sometimes before him), the same phrase became the key to Pauline theology on the Law: for Luther, the "letter" means the law

[1] Friedrich Nietzsche, *Daybreak: Thoughts on the Prejudices of Morality*, ed. Maudemarie Clark and Brian Leiter, trans. R. J. Hollingdale (Cambridge: Cambridge University Press, 1997), 49.

[2] Ibid., 49–50.

[3] Ibid., 50.

[4] All biblical quotations are from the New King James Version.

and the "spirit" means faith. More recently—perhaps from the late nineteenth century onwards—a new phase of controversy has been reached, in which new questions are being asked about what Paul thinks about the law: questions about works and righteousness, faith and spirit, Judaism and Christianity. But that is not all. Ever since E. P. Sanders' work in the 1970s on the first-century Jewish Palestinians, the whole question of Paul on the Law has been radically revised; Judaism in Paul's day is now understood as covenanted, and obedience to the covenant is only a necessary condition for entering the covenant rather than being sufficient by itself. Now the gift of the covenant, its spirit, is understood to be as much a part of Judaism as Christianity.[5]

In an essay in the *Jewish Quarterly Review* in 1892, Moritz Güdemann writes that in Judaism at the time of the birth of Christianity,

> men did not hesitate to sacrifice a letter here and there, when the object was to find a home in the Torah for some religious idea, and to shelter it under its sacred authority. This fact, which ought not to cause surprise, [...] perhaps gave rise to the legend that when the first Tables of the Covenant were broken the letters flew into the air (*Pesachim*, 87b). Whatever view may be taken of the matter, so much is certain, that this legend could only have arisen and spread among those to whom the letter was no *rocher de bronze*. [...] What can this Hagadah mean [...] but that it is not the letter of the Bible but the spirit that is of value? [...] The history of biblical exegesis from the oldest times furnishes irrefutable proofs of this fact. How could the *jus talionis* (Exodus xxi. 24 *seq.*) have been set aside, how could the operations of the year of release (Deut. xv. 2) have been annulled, if the letter and not the spirit of the Torah had been clung to?[6]

The phrase "spirit of the law," *ruach mishpat*, is rabbinic, having no direct Greek or Roman forebears. Then, too, the compelling question arises of the relation of this phrase to law, to jurisprudence, and particularly to

[5] E. P. Sanders, *Paul and Palestinian Judaism* (New York: Fortress Press, 1977).

[6] M. Güdemann, 'Spirit and Letter in Judaism and Christianity', *Jewish Quarterly Review*, 4 (1892), 345–56 (350, 352). See also Boaz Cohen, 'Note on Letter and Spirit in the New Testament', *The Harvard Theological Review*, 47:3 (July 1954), 197–203; Stephen Westerholm, ''Letter' and 'Spirit': The Foundation of Pauline Ethics', *New Testament Studies*, 30:2 (April 1984), 229–48; Heiko Obermann, 'Biblical Exegesis: The Literal and Spiritual Sense of the Scripture', in *Forerunners of the Reformation: The Shape of Late Medieval Thought* (New York: Holt, Rinehart and Winston, 1966), 281–96.

equity, which often sees itself as following the spirit of the law, in the sense of the intention, instead of the letter, the rule.

Clearly, the phrase "the letter kills and the spirit giveth life" in II Corinthians 3 is a difficult and contested one, but if there is a modern consensus, from the Reformation to Sanders, it is that Paul means that the letter is the Old Testament law, which "kills" because it makes demands which cannot be rendered and/or kills because it makes demands per se, thereby provoking legalistic "works-righteousness" instead of faith. In contrast, the spirit alludes to the new gospel which offers the life of faith through the power of the Spirit. However, from Origen until the Reformation there was no such consensus. Instead, there were competing interpretations, and they boiled down to these two (as Gerhard Ebeling summarizes):

> In the ancient Church and in the Middle Ages the understanding of Spirit and letter gravitated into the interpretation of the antithesis as a hermeneutical principle (the distinction between a literal and spiritual sense of Scripture) on the one hand, and as an economy of salvation contract (the distinction between the law and the Spirit, the Old Testament and the New Testament) on the other.[7]

This means that the modern consensus not only ignores the existence of two very different meanings, but it has reversed the dominant interpretation. For from Origen through to Luther, the hermeneutical principle prevailed: the Bible was to be interpreted spiritually and allegorically. Until the Reformation, exegetes would have had no quarrel with the scene in Jerome Lawrence and Robert E. Lee's play *Inherit the Wind* (1951)—which focuses on the trial of a teacher who taught evolution instead of creationism—in which the lawyer for the defense, who is intended to resemble Clarence Darrow, asks his fundamentalist witness, "what is a day? When God blessed the first day, he had not yet created the Sun. So could a Day in Genesis have been thirty hours! Or a month! Or

[7] Gerhard Ebeling, 'Geist und Buchstabe', in *Die Religion in Geschichte und Gegenwart: Handwörterbuch für Theologie und Religionswissenschaft*, 7 vols. (Tübingen: Mohr, 1957–1965), II, pp. 1290–96 (1292).
Cited in Scott Hafemann, *Paul, Moses, and the History of Israel: The Letter/Spirit Contrast and the Argument from Scripture in 2 Corinthians 3* (Tübingen: J.C.B. Mohr, 1995), 2. For a fuller discussion of this history of the Pauline formula, see Hafemann, *passim*.

a year! Or a hundred years! Or ten million years!"[8] The prevailing understanding for over twelve hundred years was that Paul was teaching how to read Scripture: don't be over-literal or you will miss the real meaning.

Aquinas encoded the familiar fourfold method: Like all church fathers and most scholastics, he thinks that there is a basic literal sense which is what is directly referred to. Then this thing referred to, in nature or history, has an allegorical sense which points to Christ (in consequence, every single word of the Old Testament/Hebrew Bible does this); an ethical sense which refers to how we should live our lives; and an anagogical sense which points to the eschaton. The literal terms of the ritual law only applied in the Old Testament time. The literal terms of the ethical and natural and political law are valid for all times. Allegorically, this moral and political law points to Christ and so to charity and mercy and reconciliation beyond command.

But with the Reformation, the allegorical interpretation associated with Origen does not just diminish; it is explicitly rejected. Calvin wrote, without mincing his words, that in the Second Epistle of Paul to the Corinthians, "nothing could have been further from Paul's mind! [than how to read scripture]."[9] Now II Cor. 3:6 was no longer used as a proof-text to justify a hermeneutical procedure that included literal and allegorical meanings of scripture, but instead became a proof-text for the distinction between the Law and Gospel, the dead letter and the faith that lives. So, in 1886, F. W. Farrar said that the foundations of Origen's use of II Cor. 3:6 for an exegetical method are "built upon the sand."[10] Again, viewed from the Reformation perspective, the letter/Law kills because it demands a sinless perfection which cannot be attained and/or because it produces a deluded self-confidence in the attempt to do so. In contrast, the Spirit-gospel lives because it calls for a justification by grace through faith alone, made possible by the crucifixion of Christ.

[8] Jerome Lawrence and Robert E. Lee, *Inherit the Wind* (New York: Random House, 1951), Act II, scene ii (pp. 97–98).

[9] In *The Second Epistle of Paul the Apostle to the Corinthians and the Epistles to Timothy, Titus and Philemon, Calvin's New Testament Commentaries*, trans. T. A. Smail, ed. David W. Torrance and Thomas F. Torrance (Edinburgh: Oliver and Boyd, 1964), 42. Cited in Hafemann, 6n19.

[10] F. W. Farrar, *History of Interpretation: Eight Lectures Preached Before the University of Oxford in the Year 1885* (London: Macmillan, 1886), 201. Cited in Hafemann, 7.

What happened to this 1200-year emphasis on hermeneutics? Did it just disappear, go underground? I am of the persuasion that cultural forms tend to linger, even if transformed. Classical deities become Christian saints, classical rhetoric becomes scriptural hermeneutics, and sacred rituals transform into secular ones: now the national anthem is sung at sporting events. This principle of biblical hermeneutics moved quietly, without fanfare, into that of law. It did so via Jean Gerson's debt to the medieval tradition, including to Aquinas, and then through Christopher St German's well-known debt to Gerson in *The Doctor and the Student*, which in turn had such influence in England.[11] During the Reformation, through the backdoor, the Catholic medieval tradition of reading for the intention of the law, and not just its letter, joined forces with the classical tradition, in which Aristotle's discussion of the concept of *epieikeia* (decency, fairness, equity) played a paramount role.[12] A key expression of his thought on this topic is to be found in his *Nicomachean Ethics*:

> [T]he equitable is just, and better than one kind of justice—not better than absolute justice, but better than the error that arises from the absoluteness of the statement. And this is the nature of the equitable, a correction of law where it is defective owing to its universality. In fact this is the reason why all things are not determined by law, namely, that about some things it is impossible to lay down a law, so that a decree is needed. For when the thing is indefinite the rule also is indefinite, like the leaden rule used in making the Lesbian moulding; the rule adapts itself to the shape of the stone and is not rigid, and so too the decree is adapted to the facts. It is plain, then, what the equitable is, and that it is just and is better than one kind of justice.[13]

In an influential discussion of this passage, Noel Dermot O'Donoghue characterizes *epieikeia* as a "law beyond the law" which brings much

[11] Christopher Saint German, *The Doctor and the Student*, ed. T. F. T. Plucknett and J. L. Barton (London: Selden Society, 1974). J. A. Guy explores St German's debt for the concept of equity to Jean Gerson. Guy asserts that "it is Gerson who unquestionably dictates the formulation" of St German's discussion of equity in *The Doctor and Student*. See Guy, *Christopher St German on Chancery and Statute* (London: Selden, 1985), 72.

[12] Paul even refers to the *epieikeias* of Christ, alluding to his gentle forbearance (II Cor. 10:1).

[13] Aristotle, *Nicomachean Ethics*, trans. W. D. Ross (Oxford: Clarendon Press, 2009), 1137b20–35 (Book 5, Chapter 10; p. 99).

needed flexibility to the written law and, in doing so, brings it closer to the higher (and unattainable) standard of absolute justice.[14] Its function was, he suggests, meant to be governed by the Aristotelian virtue of *gnomé* (or "good judgement"), in a relationship whereby "*gnomé* belongs to the head and *epieikeia* to the heart."[15] When the two capacities are used together, it becomes possible to decide *when* to go beyond the law.

Aristotle takes great pains to avoid the implication that the mechanical application of law may result in injustice. Indeed, by definition, such application of law is always legally just. The conflict between the law's generality and the varied, fact-specific situations to which the law is applied may at times not allow us to "speak correctly in universal terms," or may in some respects "[miss] the mark" or result in a "shortcoming." Still, the law "is none the less correct; for the error is not in the law nor in the legislator but in the nature of the thing."[16] Accordingly, while the strict application of law is just, it may not always be equitable. Equity then supplements positive law, as a principle of construction, extending the lawgiving or legislative function to the person or body responsible for its application.[17] Here is Gerson's formulation in *The Regulae Morales*: "Equity is justice [which] having weighed all the particular circumstances is tempered with the sweetness of mercy."[18] St German defines equity as "a [ryghtwysenes] that consideryth all the pertyculer cyrcumstaunces of the dede/ the whiche also is temperyd with the swetnes of mercye. And [suche an equytye] must alway be obseruyd in euery lawe of man/ and in euery generall rewle therof/ & that knewe he wel that sayd thus. Lawes

[14] Noel Dermot O'Donoghue, 'The Law Beyond the Law', *American Journal of Jurisprudence*, 18 (1973), 151–64. O'Donoghue's study is discussed in Gary Watt, *Equity Stirring: The Story of Justice Beyond Law* (Oxford: Hart Publishing, 2009), 19 (and see also 27–28).

[15] O'Donoghue, 'The Law Beyond the Law', 154.

[16] Aristotle, *Nicomachean Ethics*, 1137b15–20 (Book 5; Chapter 10; p. 99). See also Watt, *Equity Stirring*, 8–9, 199.

[17] Thomas C. Bilello, 'Accomplished with What She Lacks: Law, Equity, and Portia's Con.', *Law and Literature*, 16:1 (Spring 2004), 11–32.

[18] Jean Gerson, *Œuvres complètes*, ed. Palémon Glorieux, 10 vols. (Paris, New York: Desclée, 1960–1973), IX, pp. 95–96. The translation given here is from Alistair Fox and John Guy, *Reassessing the Henrician Age: Humanism, Politics and Reform, 1500–1550* (Oxford: Basil Blackwell, 1986), 183–84.

couet to be rewlyd by equytye. And the wyse man sayth: be not ouer moch ryghtwyse for the extreme ryghtwysense is extreme wrongc."[19]

While the Reformation denied the hermeneutic legacy of Paul's allusion to the letter and the spirit, it was carried forward through Aquinas, Gerson, Sir John Fortescue and St German in the realm of law, where interpreting according the intent, the spirit of the law, the *aequis*, *epieikeia*, for the common good and the promotion of divine law, were intermixed. Here, in law, the hermeneutics of literalism being a dead letter was to have far reaching effects on so many lives. How does it sound to join the classical tradition of *epieikeia* to the Pauline theology of the dead letter and living spirit? Aquinas saw *epieikeia* as part of the arrangement that secured the common good in a universe ordered by divine law. He writes:

> But this is done by the Holy Spirit who perfects man inwardly with a good habit, so that from love he avoids evil, as if the divine law had commanded. Consequently, he is called free not as though he is not subject to the divine law, but because he is inclined by a good habit to do what the divine law ordains.[20]

In Gerson, all valid laws are accompanied by exceptions derived from the higher laws of God; the intention of the legislators is rooted in the eternal and immutable rules of divine law. This led to a general appeal to the law's spirit: "a monastic superior invoking *epikiea* could be seen as being 'as it were a living law tempering dead laws'."[21] Similarly, in his *De natura legis naturae*, Fortescue wrote that the king has absolute power not to do away with complete law, but so that he might better fulfill the law of his kingdom: "For oftentimes the written law lies as it were dead under a covering of words."[22]

[19] Saint German, *The Doctor and the Student*, 95, 97.

[20] Aquinas Thomas, *Commentary on the Letters of Saint Paul to the Corinthians*, trans. F. R. Larcher, B. Mortensen, and D. Keating, ed. J. Mortensen and E. Alarcón (Lander, WY: Aquinas Institute for the Study of Sacred Doctrine, 2012), 445.

[21] Gerson, *Œuvres*, VI, 144. Cited (and translated) in Alan Cromartie, '*Epieikeia* and Conscience', in Lorna Hutson *Oxford Handbook of English Law and Literature 1500–1700* (Oxford: Oxford University Press, 2017), 327.

[22] John Fortescue, *Works*, ed. and trans. Thomas Fortescue, 2 vols. (London: Printed for Private Distribution, 1869), II, p. 215. Discussed in Alan Cromartie, 328.

Now, when we distinguish the letter of the *law* from the spirit of the law, we typically refer to the distinction between a narrow application of rules—the letter—and an effort to reconstruct the intention behind those laws and to apply them to a specific circumstance—the spirit. And so the phrase from Paul can seem almost synonymous with the impulses of equity in law. Almost, for Paul writes so radically in II Cor. 3 that the letter *killeth* but the spirit *giveth life.*

When we tease out the distinction between the biblical and classical legacies on the question of the literal application of the law and the spiritual meaning, a difference emerges. For Aristotle, as Watt carefully shows, does not understand the application of the law as unjust—the letter does not kill, it just does not always suffice. And that difference—that, for Paul, a literal application of the law can violate justice, can kill—is one of the results of the infusion of the Pauline formula into equity.

What does Paul mean by this invocation of the extremes of life and death, by such a radical formulation? If he is interpreting the old covenant as the dead letter, how can the law elsewhere be endorsed? And law is not just endorsed, but embraced fully; as Christ says, not one jot or iota shall be transgressed but All will be fulfilled. Let us turn to the textual context for help. II Corinthians 3 is truly a confusing text. (While we advise our students not to mix metaphors, Paul seems to have missed that lesson.) He begins speaking of epistles, epistles of commendation from the Corinthians or to the Corinthians, and claims that "you are our epistles written in our hearts, not in ink but by the spirit, not tablets of stone but on tablets of flesh, that is, of the heart" (alluding to Jeremiah 31:31 where the covenant is written on the heart). If Paul wants to contrast the new covenant with the old and say the old is a dead letter, why does he open his address with an explicit quotation from the Old Testament about how God is writing the covenant on the heart and not on stone tablets? You will recall that when Shylock the Jewish moneylender, in Shakespeare's *The Merchant of Venice*, wants to take a pound of flesh from the Christian merchant Antonio, he wants to take his heart—so while the drama is teasing out the implications of the letter and the spirit, the flesh and faith, Shylock does not seem to grasp the difference. For this literalist, the heart is materialist.

But to return to Paul, in II Corinthians he turns from epistles, from letters, to "the letter": the letter kills and the spirit gives life. The Ministry of death is engraved on stones. And then he switches to the face of Moses, to his glory, and the veil, so if we read the law with a veil, we are blinded.

> ...unlike Moses, who put a veil over his face so that the children of Israel could not look steadily at the end of what was passing away. But their minds were blinded. For until this day the same veil remains unlifted in the reading of the Old Testament, because the veil is taken away in Christ. But even to this day, when Moses is read, a veil lies on their heart. Nevertheless when one turns to the Lord, the veil is taken away. (II Cor. 3:13–16)

The chapter concludes with the image of the mirror: "Now the Lord is the Spirit; and where the Spirit of the Lord is, there is liberty. But we all, with unveiled face, beholding as in a mirror the glory of the Lord, are being transformed into the same image from glory to glory, just as by the Spirit of the Lord" (II Cor. 3:17–18). Another way to describe this rush of metaphors is as an exquisite symphony in which letters, the letter, ink, stone, flesh, heart, face, veil, mirror and glory come together to produce a thrilling movement from flesh to spirit, from death to life, from blindness to sight, from darkness to light, from veiled to unveiled, from ignorance to the glory of the Lord. In the end, he wraps together word, veil, sight, light, face and heart: "But we have renounced the hidden things of shame, not walking in craftiness nor handling the word of God deceitfully, but by manifestation of the truth commending ourselves to every man's conscience in the sight of God [...] For it is the God who commanded light to shine out of darkness, who has shone in our hearts to give the light of the knowledge of the glory of God in the face of Jesus Christ" (II Cor. 4:2, 6). (For the adept writer, mixing metaphors works brilliantly.) Clearly, much more is being offered here than the advice to consider the intention of the lawgiver. But we must qualify that, for the lawgiver is understood to be God and God's intention is what is being spelled out. What is that? Let us attend again to the context of II Corinthians 3. God's intention is delineated as forgiveness. "Now whom you forgive anything, I also forgive. For if indeed I have forgiven anything, I have forgiven that one for your sakes in the presence of Christ" (II Cor. 2:10). The sight of divine glory is the apprehension of forgiveness, the law of love. Jesus is wonderfully clear on this. In expounding upon the law, he is in dialogue with a Hebrew legal mind, who tauntingly asks him what the law is. "And behold, a lawyer stood up to put him to the test, saying, 'Teacher, what shall I do to inherit eternal life?'" (Luke, 10:25) He is doubtless trying to capture him as disobedient to the law: "What is written in the Law? What is your reading of it?" (Luke, 10:26) But Jesus is not only obedient to the letter of the law, quoting the love command of Leviticus: "You shall love the Lord your God with all your heart [...] and love the neighbor as yourself" (Matthew, 22:37, 39). He is obedient to its spirit, for when he is asked "and who is my neighbor?" he offers the example of the saving care of the compassionate Samaritan over the legalistic priest and the Levite.

What is added, when the Pauline formulation inflects the classical *epieikeia*, is first—negatively—a deep suspicion of the adequacy of rules, so deep that they alone cannot achieve justice; and secondly, an explicit kind of moral sense—call it love, mercy, forgiveness. Justice cannot be the cold application of rules without tending to this understanding of the good as the telos. There is also the dark shadow of Nietzsche, that the other will be persecuted when the law is seen through a blinding veil.

All these are at play in *The Merchant of Venice*. To begin, this explains why, in the play, justice is explicitly contrasted to mercy. It is worth honing in on what Portia says *before* her famous "Quality of Mercy is not strained" speech. First, she wants to establish what must be done legally, according to the letter of the law, the letter of the bond.

> Portia asks Antonio, "Do you confess the bond?"
> Antonio responds, "I do."
> Portia responds, "Then must the Jew be merciful". (IV.i.182–84)

With law failing to be truly just, with it being death-dealing instead of life-giving, we must resort to mercy. This exchange is unintelligible without the Pauline formula.

But Shylock, bound to the letter of the law, the literalism of his bond, asks "On what compulsion must I? Tell me that?" (IV.i.185). He gets a big speech from her about the value of mercy and is utterly unmoved. He responds, "I crave the law, the penalty and forfeit of my bond" (IV.i.206–7). That bond in *The Merchant of Venice*, that "merry".

(I.iii.146) bond—rather, that sealed and notarized contract, hence one subject to the strictest application of the law—offers the chance to investigate not just the inadequacy of rules, but the downright injustice of the letter of the law, the inhumanity of it. "There is no power in Venice can alter a decree established" (IV.i.218–19). Necessity, the language of "must," recurs: "this strict court of Venice must needs give sentence against the Merchant there" (IV.i.204). The Duke finds the contract unjust but feels compelled to honor it, else "let the danger light upon your charter and your city's freedom," as Shylock argues (IV.i.38–39).

"Twill be recorded for a precedent" (IV.i.220). In this play, both the hermeneutic and the theological understanding of "the letter killeth and the spirit maketh live" are operative, joined seamlessly in the improbable plot. For to obey the letter of the law, to interpret the bond legalistically, without regard to justice, is death-dealing. Literally, the letter killeth.[23]

If a play during the Reformation predictably depicts Jews as legalistic and death-dealing, surely a notion Calvin would endorse, what it says about Portia is more surprising.[24] Portia should be Pauline. She should be upholding a spiritual interpretation of the law, and when she speaks of the quality of mercy as generous, not strained, we think she will follow through with such mercy. But when her speech does not work, she takes a different tack. Unwilling to enforce the murder of Antonio, she looks for another way to save him, and her solution is chilling: "as thou urgest justice, be assured / Thou shalt have justice, more than thou desirest" (IV.i.317). While she is disguised—veiled before the law?—she reads more literally than Shylock,

> Portia: This bond doth give thee here no jot of blood,
> The words expressly are "a pound of flesh":
> Take then thy bond, take thou thy pound of flesh,
> But in the cutting it, if thou dost shed
> One drop of Christian blood, thy lands and goods
> Are (by the laws of Venice) confiscate
> Unto the state of Venice. (IV.i.307–13)

Her emphasis on quantity casts her down deeply into the Reformation understanding of the quantitative failing of the law: it kills because no one can perform it all.

> Portia: Therefore prepare thee to cut off the flesh,
> Shed thou no blood, nor cut thou less nor more
> But just a pound of flesh: if thou tak'st more

[23] Is it an accident that the trial scene begins with a letter of commendation as II Cor. 3 does?

[24] Here I depart from a great deal of criticism on the *Merchant of Venice* that endorses Portia and equates her "mercy" with the superiority of Christian charity to Jewish law. On law and equity in *The Merchant of Venice*, see Thomas Bilello's fine discussion, 'Accomplished with What She Lacks: Law, Equity, and Portia's Con', *Law and Literature*, 16:1 (2004), 11–32.

Or less than a just pound, be it but so much
As makes it light or heavy in the substance,
Or the division of the twentieth part
Of one poor scruple, nay if the scale do turn
But in the estimation of a hair,
Thou diest, and all thy goods are confiscate. (IV.i.325–33)

This travesty of justice based on measurement reverberates: so much of the law is based on measure, on imagined just proportions for punitive repayment. Aristotle even described the judge as a measurer, the one who divides equally: "Now the judge restores equality; it is as though there were a line divided into unequal parts, and he took away that by which the greater segment exceeds the half, and added it to the smaller segment. And when the whole has been equally divided, then they say they have 'their own'—i.e. when they have got what is equal."[25]

Indeed, the etymology of the judge is one who bisects: "It is for this reason also that it is called just (*dikaion*), because it is a division into two equal parts (*dikha*), just as if one were to call it *dikhaion*; and the judge (*dikastēs*) is one who bisects (*dikhastēs*)."[26] If this sounds like a cold definition of a judge, it is. The preoccupation with just measure has endured: in the iconography, justice is holding scales.

> This understanding of justice presupposes that goods can be measured, exchanged in proportion, and that such exchange is the basis of social intercourse; moreover, these goods are finite. Indeed, the most sought commodities, like honor or wealth, are in scarce supply. Not only are goods measurable, so are acts, so that it is possible to create a price for injury and require compensation for it. A deep debt to this understanding of justice, stressing measurement and proportionality, is evident throughout legal systems with economic models of justice. Furthermore, most ideas of fairness in political and ethical thought rely on an understanding of some proportional distribution.[27]

[25] Aristotle, *Nicomachean Ethics*, 1132a25–30 (Book 5; Chapter 4; p. 87).

[26] Ibid., 1132a30–35.

[27] Here I am quoting from Regina Schwartz, *Loving Justice, Living Shakespeare* (Oxford: Oxford University Press, 2016), 10–11. See also chapter IV, "The Economics of Love," which further explores Shakespeare's critique of contractual justice in *The Merchant of Venice*.

And then the qualitative critique of the law follows, for this performance of the law is itself misguided as Portia does not love the neighbor, welcome the stranger, or care for the widowed, fully violating the substantive commands of the law so upheld by Jesus: to love God and love the neighbor. When we keep in focus that the letter kills, the result of Portia's hyperliteralism comes as no surprise—the conclusion is that Shylock must die. Reading the Alien Statute literally becomes the instrument of her vengeance as well as the bond. Seeing the trial scene within the context of II Cor. 3, "The letter kills and the spirit maketh live," casts both Shylock and Portia as hermeneutic literalists, veiled readers, and theological death-dealers. The Jew and the Christian are not contrasted; rather, when Portia imitates Shylock, she bests him at his embrace of the letter of the law. This likeness, it seems to me, is anticipated in Shylock's "hath not a Jew eyes" speech: if we are wronged, do we not learn from you Christians how to seek revenge? Only she does it better.

But having rescued Antonio, how is the play going to rescue Portia? On the one hand, she reads the bond for Shylock's intent—to kill—and mercy disavows this interpretation. On the other, she will encounter the letter and the spirit problem again with the other plot, the ring episode: in the play, the ring Portia gives to Bassanio stands for fidelity; to lose it is to be unfaithful. But then she reveals that another interpretation is necessary, moves away from literalism to an allegorical sense of the ring: it signified fidelity, but that fidelity stands for fidelity to charity, and the ring was given in charity to someone charitable, so not only was a life saved, but their love also. Her husband says it signified his gratitude that his friend was saved. Here is an unforeseen interpretation, a moral one, like the anagogical ones from the middle ages, and an eschatological one, as Antonio was saved by love. The literal meaning of the ring, infidelity, would have killed Portia and Bassanio's love. In *The Merchant of Venice*, the concluding ring plot—not the well-known bond plot—is asked to carry the burden of the living Spirit.

If we were to assume that this conjoining of hermeneutics and theology were unique to Shakespeare, however, we should look again. Since the publication of E. P. Sanders' book on Paul and the Palestinians, contemporary debate about what Paul thinks about Law has heated up. In brief, the hermeneutic principle has come back in favor, now joined to the theological meaning. Paul thinks, many say, that reading the Law right, with the hermeneutic lens of the promise of Christ, will be life-giving, but reading it without that promise—i.e., veiled, will deal death. Reading and salvation come together. So, after all, scriptural hermeneutics and a theology of salvation are not so far apart: the difference between the letter and the spirit, the historical and the allegorical sense, can be understood as precisely the distinction between the old covenant and the new. There is in one sense an opposition between the two testaments: one way then, another way now. But the second does not destroy the first. In fulfilling it, it gives it new life and transfigures it. In a word, it changes its letter into spirit.

For Henri de Lubac, who wrote magisterially on the fourfold sense of scripture, "this Pauline understanding of allegory is and must be rooted in the concrete historical fact of the Incarnation. Christ's life, death and resurrection initiates the New Covenant in history. In Christ, the eternal and the spiritual penetrate the temporal and corporeal. Because of this, the spiritual truth of the gospel penetrates the literal and historical sense of the Old Testament. The specifically Christian sense of allegory, then, is defined not by method, but by content – not by methodology, but by theology: it grows out of the conviction that Christ is revealed in the events related in Scripture. The moral […] dimension of the fourfold sense can only follow from the allegorical sense: it generates a specifically Christian moral response."[28] Finally, the anagogical sense points toward the eschatological and eternal realities of the Kingdom of God in its glory, which can only follow after the Christian's moral life. "Together, the four senses thus present a vision of salvation history and of the individual soul's place within it. One can readily see, then, how de Lubac concludes that this fourfold sense offers more than a method for reading; it offers a theological hermeneutic for both scripture and life, both a theology of Scripture and a Christian spirituality."[29]

Both this hermeneutic and theological understanding actually makes the wedding of the Pauline letter and spirit with *epieikeia* and equity even easier, for to refer to Gary Watt again, for Aristotle, *epieikiea* was more an ethical disposition than a recommendation for how to practice law. Watt: "Later, as jurists looked back to Aristotle, they tended to overlook the fact that his legal illustrations of *epieikeia* were not intended to be read as reports of contemporary legal practice, but rather to illustrate

[28] Kevin L. Hughes, 'The "Fourfold Sense": De Lubac, Blondel and Contemporary Theology', *The Heythrop Journal*, 42 (2001), 451–62 (455).

[29] Hughes, 'The "Fourfold Sense"', 455.

the equitable character which Aristotle considered an ethical aspiration." Interpreting spiritually was interpreting ethically, both for the classical ancients, and for Augustine and his followers. I quote Eden: "For the exegete who reads Scripture spiritually—that is, for the *voluntas*, or intention—discovers that, with the same economy characteristic of the best pagan literature, all its parts accommodate the whole; and the whole or general intention of the divine *scriptor* is the promotion of *caritas* and the eradication of *cupiditas*. [...] *Caritas*, in other words, is the *summa* of all scriptural teaching [...] *caritas* represents the Christianization of *aequitas*, or equity. Like equity, charity corrects the rigidity of the law. [...] Like equity, charity accommodates human weakness, not only measuring any single event against the quality of our lives as a whole but also pitying and pardoning our errors."[30]

I began by pointing out how very different interpreting "the letter kills but the spirit giveth life" is as a principle of reading from a dictum of theology. The first says we should not be too literal when we read, but think about intention, think about the end of the good, the spirit of charity. The second says the old law kills and has been superseded by the New One; Christianity has trumped Judaism, which is far inferior. And while the former prevailed for 1200 years, the latter took hold at the Reformation and largely held until quite recently. But what about *The Merchant of Venice*? It is remarkably synthetic, for it includes both the hermeneutic question of the dangers of literalism as well as the question of the relative merits of Judaism and Christianity. Seen as an extended gloss on Paul's verse, the play brings to the fore both of these two meanings, and relates one to the other, for with the Jew insisting on the literal enforcement of his contract, he intends to kill: the letter kills—and when the Christian response to urge forgiveness is not taken up, and Portia turns to hyper literalism, she too threatens to kill (and this particular feature was not in the sources of the play). The play does not reserve literalism to Jews, in this way, but to any veiled against the truth of scripture, the centrality of the law of love. If the letter kills, then Portia's recourse to literalism is not a clever use of a quibble, it imperils her soul.

What then do we make of that other meaning, the supersession of Christianity over Judaism? Antonio's hatefulness, Shylock's defense of his humanity, Jessica's running away with a Christian, and the question of

[30] Kathy Eden, *Hermeneutics and the Rhetorical Tradition* (New Haven: Yale University Press, 2005), 57–58.

the conversion of Shylock—as an act of mercy (to save him) or punitive (to defeat his vengeance with further vengeance)—are all implicated. I don't think we can separate the two meanings to approach this question: for if the Christian embraces the letter of the law that killeth, then the Christian Spirit is not prevailing. The spirit that giveth life would be not only reading the proper intent, one aimed toward the good, but also one that is directed by divine love. It is hard to imagine that Shakespeare writes a forced conversion as redemptive: it is not one of heart, nor of the spirit.

All of these issues are very much alive today, in practice and in theory.

First, the theory: Speaking of the command not to kill, Charles Taylor writes in *The Language Animal* that "it would be a highly impoverished moral code which only included such purely external observance, where the 'spirit' in which one acts is irrelevant. Morality can't consist simply in forbidding or enjoining such objectively identifiable patterns of action."[31] He goes on, and this description sounds remarkably like equity: "And in fact, it [morality] can't rely simply on rules or principles of whatever sort. Human beings, and their needs and situations, are too diverse; we cannot define how we ought to treat them exclusively in terms of codes. At some point what the code prescribes will bear too heavily, even inhumanly, on some people, as when justice needs to be tempered with mercy, or some principle of equal treatment needs to take account of special needs, so that a valid general rule requires that we make reasonable accommodation."[32]

Next, the practice: In the United States, Attorney General Jeff Sessions was claiming to follow the letter of the law when he arrested migrants at the border, forcibly taking their children from their parents and putting them in cages. He even cited Paul to justify himself, leaning on his injunction that we should obey the authorities (Romans 13:1). But he ignored the next verse—that we are obligated to welcome strangers. And the United Methodist Congregation responded with a letter signed by 600 clergy, that he got both his hermeneutics and ethics wrong, dead wrong.

[31] Charles Taylor, *The Language Animal: The Full Shape of the Human Linguistic Capacity* (Cambridge, MA: Harvard University Press, 2016), 202.

[32] Ibid., 202.

CHAPTER 6

Configuring God as Law: Richard Hooker's Poetics of Law

Torrance Kirby

Richard Hooker was born in April 1554 at Heavitree near Exeter in Devonshire; he died at Bishopsbourne, Kent, on All Souls' Day, 2 November 1600. He was educated at Exeter Grammar School and Corpus Christi College, Oxford, where he matriculated in 1569. His tutor was John Rainolds, later President of Corpus Christi and one of the translators of the Authorized Version of the Bible. Hooker gained a BA and was admitted a 'disciple' of Corpus Christi in 1573. In 1577 he proceeded MA, was elected a full fellow in 1579, and was appointed deputy lecturer to Thomas Kingsmill, the Regius Professor of Hebrew. Hooker delivered the Hebrew lecture for the remainder of his time at Oxford. So Hooker began his academic career as a biblical scholar, and this was to be definitive. On 17 March 1585, by Letters Patent from the Crown, and under the patronage of John Whitgift, Archbishop of Canterbury, Hooker was appointed Master of the Temple Church at the Inns of

T. Kirby (✉)
McGill University, Montreal, PQ, Canada
e-mail: torrance.kirby@mcgill.ca

S. Mukherji and D. Roberts (eds.), *Literature and the Legal Imaginary*, Crossroads of Knowledge in Early Modern Literature 4,
https://doi.org/10.1007/978-3-031-74093-0_6

Court where he shared the pulpit with the disciplinarian Puritan divine Walter Travers. Before a congregation of the English judges and barristers in the Temple Church these two engaged in a theological controversy which was to occupy Hooker for the rest of his short life (he died in 1600, not having reached the age of 50). The polemics of this pulpit exchange served as a stimulus to Hooker's composition of the *Ecclesiasticall Politie*.[1] Richard Hooker's contribution to the theology of the English Reformation emerges in the context of the polemics surrounding the implementation of the constitutional provisions of the Elizabethan Settlement of 1559. His apologetic strategy in his great treatise *Of the Lawes of Ecclesiasticall Politie* (1593) is largely governed by his 'sapiential' approach.[2] Hooker's wisdom theology provides the matrix within which he develops his figural reading of Holy Scripture. What is particularly noteworthy in this approach is his combining Christian Neoplatonic metaphysics with Reformed biblical hermeneutics.[3] Hooker's integration of a Reformed theological perspective with his inheritance of an ancient philosophical tradition is the hallmark of his unique contribution to the later development of Anglican exegesis, liturgics, and devotion. This essay will focus principally on Hooker's subtle and intricate configuration of God as 'law' in the first book of his treatise:

> In sundry the workes both of art and also of nature, where that which hath greatest force in the very things we see, is notwithstanding it selfe oftentimes not seene. The statelinesse of houses, the goodlines of trees, when we behold them delighteth the eye; but that foundation which beareth up the one, that root which ministreth unto the other nourishment and life, is in the bosome of the earth concealed: and if there be at any time occasion to search into it, such labour is then more necessary then pleasant both to them which undertake it, and for the lookers on. In like maner the use and

[1] Richard Hooker, *Of the Lavves of Ecclesiasticall Politie: Eyght Bookes* (London: By Iohn Windet, dwelling at the signe of the Crosse keyes neere Powles Wharffe, and are there to be soulde, 1593).

[2] See Torrance Kirby, 'The 'sundrie waies of Wisdom': Richard Hooker on the Authority of Scripture and Reason', in Kevin Killeen, ed., *Oxford Handbook of the Early Modern Bible* (Oxford: Oxford University Press, 2015), 164–75. This volume of essays was awarded the Roland H. Bainton Prize (Reference Works), by the Council of the Sixteenth-Century Society and Conference.

[3] See also Torrance Kirby, 'Richard Hooker as Biblical Interpreter', in Oda Wischmeyer, ed., *Handbuch der Bibelhermeneutiken* (Berlin: De Gruyter, 2016), 395–407.

> benefite of good lawes, all that live under them may enjoy with delight and comfort, albeit the groundes and first originall causes from whence they have sprong be unknowne, as to the greatest part of men they are.[4]

Hooker commences his discussion of the origin of law—'that lawe which giveth life unto all the rest'[5]—with an appeal to two vivid metaphors, one artificial and another natural, a constructed foundation and a nourishing root. As his argument unfolds, it becomes clear that his aim in his treatise is to show that the Elizabethan religious and constitutional settlement of 1559—the 'stately house', as it were, of the established Church and the 'goodly tree' of the flourishing Commonwealth—is based upon 'good lawes' whose ultimate source is altogether hidden from view—'in the bosome of the earth concealed', according to the metaphor. Is this subterranean root or foundation in any way knowable? The metaphor serves to introduce an extended analysis of the origin of law. He goes on to identify this veiled 'first original cause' of good laws as that 'lawe whereby the Eternall himselfe doth worke'.[6] Hooker defines law in general as 'that which doth assigne unto each thing the kinde, that which doth moderate the force and power, that which does appoint the forme and measure of working'.[7] He goes on to affirm that the highest 'measure of working' in the divine activity is on the ground that 'only the workes and operations of God have him both for their worker, and for the lawe whereby they are wrought. The being of God' he maintains 'is a kinde of lawe to his working: for that perfection which God is, geveth perfection to that he doth ... God therefore is a law both to himselfe, and to all other things besides'.[8] This identity of worker, the work done, and

[4] *Of the Lawes of Ecclesiasticall Politie*, I.1.2; in The Folger Library Edition of the Works of Richard Hooker, gen. ed. W. Speed Hill, 7 vols. (Cambridge, MA: Belknap Press of Harvard University Press, 1977–98), vol. 1, ed. W. Speed Hill, p. 57, ll. 4–16. All references to the *Lawes* below cite book, chapter, and section followed by the volume, page, and line numbers found in the Folger edition.

[5] *Lawes*, I.1.3; 1:58.13–14.

[6] *Lawes*, I.1.3; 1:58.15.

[7] *Lawes*, I.2.1; 1:58.26–29.

[8] *Lawes*, I.2.2; 1:59.3–6; 60.17–18. On the character of sapiential theology and its employment by Hooker, see Rowan Williams, 'Hooker: Philosopher, Anglican, Contemporary', in A. S. McGrade, ed., *Richard Hooker and the Construction of Christian Community (RHCCC)* (Tempe, AZ: Medieval and Renaissance Texts and Studies, vol. 165, 1997), 369–75.

the activity of working anchor the assertion of his metaphorical speech in a non–metaphorical affirmative proposition, namely that God in himself is essentially law. As Thomas Aquinas puts this: 'the end of the Divine government is God Himself, and His law is not distinct from Himself'.[9]

Hooker's reputation of being a Thomist harks back to his Disciplinarian Puritan opponents' accusation of his promoting 'Romish doctrine' and 'the darknesse of schoole learning', chiefly on the ground of his theological claims concerning the capacity of the human faculties of intellect and will with respect to the workings of both nature and grace. This, at least, was the charge levelled against Hooker by the anonymous author(s) of *A Christian Letter of Certaine English Protestantes* (1599), the only attack on the *Lawes* to have been published in Hooker's own lifetime. Possibly composed by Andrew Willet (as suggested by John Booty), these critics of Hooker professed themselves 'unfayned favourers of the present state of religion, authorized and professed in England' and in their tract proceeded to compare Hooker's writings with the doctrine of the *Articles of Religion* in a highly unfavourable light. They impugn his theology as incompatible with the basic tenets of a Reformed doctrine: 'it seemed unto us that covertlie and underhand you did bende all your skill and force against the present state of our English Church: and by colour of defending the discipline and governement thereof, to make questionable and bring in contempt the doctrine and faith itselfe'.[10] Hooker's stance on major soteriological questions, faith and works, the freedom of the will, the sacraments, and the doctrine of the church are all challenged as deviating in a medieval scholastic direction away from received norms of orthodoxy, as articulated by both the traditional formularies of the Church of England and by such respected continental magisterial reformers as Luther, Calvin, Bullinger, and Vermigli. The stakes were high: which party could claim adherence to recognized standards of Reformed orthodoxy?

In the peroration to his exposition of the nature of law and its generic division into various derivative kinds found at the end of the first book of

[9] Thomas Aquinas, *Summa Theologica*, trans. Fathers of the English Dominican Province (New York: Benziger Bros, 1947), Ia IIæ q.91. art.1. Cited hereafter as *ST*.

[10] *A Christian Letter*, in the *Folger Library Edition of Hooker's Works*, ed. John Booty (Cambridge: MA: Harvard University Press, 1982), vol. 4:7.11,12,19,20. See Booty's introduction to this text.

his treatise *Of the Lawes*, Hooker summarizes this argument in a striking passage evocative of the hymns to Holy Wisdom in the scriptures:

> Of lawe there can be no lesse acknowledged, than that her seate is the bosome of God, her voyce the harmony of the world, all things in heaven and earth doe her homage, the very least as feeling her care, and the greatest as not exempted from her power, butoth Angels and men and creatures of what condition so ever, though ech in different sort and maner, yet all with uniforme consent, admiring her as the mother of their peace and joy.[11]

As Rowan Williams has observed, Hooker's use of the feminine pronoun in explicit reference to law 'would alert any scripturally literate reader to the parallel with the divine *Sophia*'—and indeed, what Hooker claims on behalf of Law the sapiential books of Proverbs, Job, and the Wisdom of Solomon affirm of the very Wisdom of God[12]: 'The LORD possessed me in the beginning of his way, before his works of old. I was set up from everlasting, from the beginning, or ever the earth was'.[13] 'Wisdom reacheth from one end to another mightily, and *sweetly* doth she order all things'.[14]

For Hooker the sapiential theologian, then, it is because God *is* his own Wisdom that he may also affirm that God in himself *is* law,

> a law both to himselfe, and to all other things besides ... All those things which are done by him, have some ende for which they are done: and the

[11] *Lawes*, I.16.8; 1:142.8–14.

[12] *Lawes*, I.2.5; 1:62.2–6. Rowan Williams, 'Hooker,' in *RHCCC*, 370. Proverbs 8:22–31; Job 28; Wisdom 6:12–9:18; and see also Rom. 11:33.

[13] Prov. 8:22, 23.

[14] Wisdom 8:1. In the Vulgate: adtingit enim a fine usque ad finem fortiter et disponit omnia suaviter / διοικεῖ τὰ πάντα χρηστῶς in LXX. See also the Advent antiphon 'O Sapientia', retained in the Almanack of the *Book of Common Prayer* (1559)—quoted by Hooker in *Lawes* I.2.3; 1:60.27–61.6. David Neelands has shown that this passage, favoured by Richard Hooker, is frequently quoted in Aquinas's writings, especially in the *Summa Theologica*, e.g. in discussions of divine government (Ia, q.103. art.8), grace (Ia IIæ q.110. art.2), charity (IIa IIæ q.23. art.2), the temptation of Adam and Eve (IIa IIæ q.165. art.1), Christ's miracles (IIIa q.44. art.4), the passion of Christ (IIIa q.46. art.9), and the manifestation of the Resurrection (IIIa q.55. art.6). See Neelands's essay on 'Predestination', in Torrance Kirby, ed., *A Companion to Richard Hooker* (Leiden and Boston: E.J. Brill, 2009), 209.

> ende for which they are done, is a reason of his will to do them ... They erre therefore who thinke that of the will of God to do this or that, there is no reason besides his will.[15]

This claim bears comparison with Aquinas for whom 'the end of the Divine government is God Himself, and His law is not distinct from Himself'.[16]

Are such claims that God *is* his Wisdom, and consequently that 'God *is* law' mere metaphors? Are these figures of speech, comparable to the 'stately house' or 'flourishing tree'? Or, alternatively, can definitive, literal propositions about the divine nature be justifiably formed? There is perhaps something just a tiny bit transgressive about comparing God to a basement or a root, although it is clear enough that such images imply an 'intuitive perception of similarity in dissimilars'—and as Aristotle says 'it is a great thing to be a master of metaphor'.[17] The similarity of God to a basement is concealment from view. To propose that God is in some sense 'law' or 'wisdom' is not on the same footing, so to speak. In Q. 13 of the *Prima Pars* of the *Summa Theologica*, on 'The Names of God', Aquinas asks in Article 3 whether all names applied to God must need be metaphorical, or whether some can be applied in a literal sense. He argues that 'true affirmative propositions can be formed about God'. This assertion depends upon drawing a distinction between signification 'in reality', what it is in itself, and what is for us (*pro nobis*) 'in idea'. God as considered 'in Himself', is altogether one and simple, yet 'our intellect knows Him by different conceptions because it cannot see Him as He is in Himself (*in se*)'. Hence diverse names are ascribed to God: God is One, Good, Infinite, Just, and so on. While it is possible to affirm diverse essential qualities or predicates, our intellect knows that in reality one and the same simple object corresponds to its conceptions. Therefore, the plurality of predicate and subject, in Hooker's case 'Law' and 'God',

[15] *Lawes*, I.2.5; 1:60.17–18, 20–23; 61.18–19. Compare Aquinas, *ST*, Ia IIæ q.91. art.1: 'The law implies order to the end actively, in so far as it directs certain things to the end; but not passively—that is to say, the law itself is not ordained to the end—except accidentally, in a governor whose end is extrinsic to him, and to which end his law must needs be ordained. But the end of the Divine government is God Himself, and His law is not distinct from Himself. Wherefore the eternal law is not ordained to another end.'

[16] *ST*, Ia IIæ q.91. art.1.

[17] Aristotle, *Poetics*, 22 (1459a5).

represents the plurality of idea; nonetheless, for the intellect (*pro nobis*) this plurality represents 'unity by composition', that is by predication.[18]

For Hooker the primordial Wisdom is the law 'which God hath eternallie purposed himselfe in all his works to observe';[19] this law is the 'highest welspring and fountaine'—a Plotinian image—of all species of law.[20] Hooker agrees with Aquinas when he speaks of the radical simplicity of God in himself when he states that God is 'one, or rather verie *Onenesse*, and meere unitie, having nothing but it selfe in it selfe, and not consisting (as all things do besides God) of many things'.[21] Of the divine simplicity, says Hooker,

> our soundest knowledge is to know that we know him not as in deed he is, neither can know him: and our safest eloquence concerning him is our silence, when we confesse without confession that his glory is inexplicable, his greatnes above our capacitie to reach. He is above, and we upon earth, therefore it behoveth our wordes to be warie and fewe.[22]

As 'first originall cause', the first eternal law has 'her seate in the bosome of God'. Simultaneously, this original 'Eternal Law' in its unity contains within itself a plurality of multiple derivative species of law—as 'ofspringe of God, [all things which God hath made] are *in him* as effectes in theire highest cause, he likewise actuallie is *in them*, thassistance and influence of his deitie is *theire life*'.[23] And so it is with original law and its diverse derivative laws. Hooker proceeds to distinguish between a 'First' and a 'Second' Eternal Law.[24] The latter is the ordering 'voyce' of the divine Wisdom, law as God's utterance proceeding from the ineffable unity of

18 *ST*, Ia pars, q. 13, art. 12.

19 *Lawes*, I.3.1; 1:63.7.

20 In his essay concerning the Beautiful, Plotinus remarks: 'But if you accurately distinguish the intelligible objects you will call the beautiful the receptacle of ideas; but the good itself, which is superior, the fountain and principle of the beautiful; or, you may place the first beautiful and the good in the same principle, independent of the beauty which there subsists.' *Ennead*, 1.6; see also 5.8. Plotinus (204/5–270 AD) was a Hellenistic philosopher who lived in Alexandria, Egypt, and is generally regarded as the founding figure of the Neoplatonic school of thought.

21 *Lawes*, I.2.2; 1:59.20–22.

22 *Lawes*, I.2.2; 1:59.15–19.

23 *Lawes*, V.56.5; 2:237.23–25.

24 *Lawes*, I.3.1; 1:63.6–64.3.

the first eternal law and comprising within it all derivative species of law which 'participate' the eternal law as discrete emanations ordered dispositive in hierarchical 'procession', while the first eternal law is the original, self-constituting divine source as it remains ineffably simple, at unity within itself—as God's 'verie Onenesse'.[25]

> By law eternall the learned for the most part do understand the order, not which God hath eternallie purposed himselfe in all his works to observe, but rather that which with himselfe he has set downe as expedient to be kept by all his creatures, according to the severall condition wherwith he hath indued them ... All things therfore, which are as they ought to be, are conformed unto to *this second law eternall*, and even those things which to this eternall law are not conformable, are notwithstanding in some sort ordered by *the first eternall lawe*.[26]

It is the *Second Eternall Lawe* whose 'voyce is the harmony of the world' as distinct from that prior law whose place is in the 'divine bosome'. The *Second Eternal Lawe* 'doth not worke infinitely but correspondently unto that end for which it worketh, even al things *chrestos* (χρηστῶς), in most decent and comely sort'.[27] Hooker's account of the Eternal Law as simultaneously unity in radical simplicity and participation of that unity by a multiplicity of derivative forms of law recapitulates the ontology of causality set out by Proclus in his *Elements of Theology* whereby 'every effect remains in its cause, proceeds from it, and reverts upon it'.[28] For

[25] *Lawes*, I.2.2; 1:59.14–15.

[26] *Lawes*, I.3.1; 1:63.6–10, 26–29.

[27] *Lawes*, I.2.3; 1:60.27–61.6. 'If therfore it be demanded, why God having power and habilitie infinite, th'effects notwithstanding of that power are all so limited as we see they are: the reason hereof is the end which he hath proposed, and the law whereby his wisdome hath stinted th'effects of his power in such sort, that it doth not worke infinitely but correspondently unto that end for which it worketh, even al things *χρηστῶς*, in most decent and comely sort, *all things in measure, number, and waight*.'

[28] Proclus, *The Elements of Theology*, ed. E. R. Dodds, 2nd edn. (Oxford: Clarendon Press, 1963), 38–39; proposition 35. Cited hereafter *ET*. Proclus Lycæus, called 'Diadochus' (i.e. the 'Successor' of Plato as head of the Academy in Athens), was a Greek Neoplatonic philosopher. He set forth one of the most elaborate and fully developed systems of Neoplatonism. He stands near the end of the classical development of philosophy and influenced Western medieval philosophy profoundly. It is said that Proclus's *Elements* initiates the scholastic tradition of theology as 'science'.

Proclus the totality of reality beneath the One or the Good itself is structured by *monē* (μονή) [remaining or abiding], *prohodos* (πρόοδος) [going out procession], and *epistrophē* (ἐπιστροφή) [return or conversion]. All reality is in the One, proceeds from it, and returns, is converted back towards its source when it achieves its proper good. In Hooker's formulation, this double motion of procession or emanation and return (*exitus/redditus*) is remarkably similar: 'every effect doth after a sort conteine, at least wise resemble the cause from which it proceedeth: all things in the worlde are saide in some sort to seeke the highest, and to covet more or lesse the participation of God himselfe'.[29] Hooker anchors his elaborate exposition and defence of the Elizabethan religious settlement in a metaphysical theory of law which itself assumes a Neoplatonic ontology of 'participation' in the Proclean tradition:

> All thinges are therefore pertakers of God, they are his ofspringe, his influence is in them, and the personall wisdome of God is for that verie cause said to excell in nimblenes or agilitie, to pearce into all intellectuall pure and subtile spirites, to goe through all, and to reach unto everie thinge which is. . . All thinges which God in theire times and seasons hath brought forth were eternallie and before all times in God as a worke unbegunne is in the artificer which afterward bringeth it unto effect. Therefore whatsoever wee doe behold now in this present world, it was inwrapped within the bowells of divine mercie, written in the booke of eternall wisdom, and held in the handes of omnipotent power, the first foundations of the world beinge as yeat unlaide.[30]

Hooker's apophatic emphasis on law as it is written in 'the booke of eternall wisdom', having 'her seat in the bosome of God', raises doubt about whether God can be named literally as either Wisdom or Law. The extraordinary metaphor of 'the bowels of divine mercie' intimates that creation may be viewed as tantamount to a divine excretion. Is it possible to speak significantly about the first eternal law? Or is Hooker confined to solely figurative language. After all, of God's 'verie Onenesse', says Hooker, 'we confesse without confession that his glory is inexplicable, his greatnes above our capacitie and reach'.[31] And as Pseudo-Dionysius

[29] *Lawes*, I.5.2; 1:73.7–10.

[30] *Lawes*, V.56.5; 2: 236.26–31, 237.15–22.

[31] *Lawes*, I.2.2; 1:59.17–19.

the Areopagite asserts in *On the Divine Names*, 'Of Him there is neither name, nor can one be found of Him'.[32] Ambrose of Milan, on the other hand, maintains ambivalently that 'some names there are which express evidently the property of the divinity, and some which express the clear truth of the divine majesty, but others there are which are applied to God metaphorically by way of similitude'.[33] Aquinas asks whether all names are applied to God solely in a metaphorical sense or whether any can be applied literally: 'the names of creatures are applied to God metaphorically, as when we say, God is a stone, or a lion, or the like'. After some discussion Aquinas eventually concludes that some names of God can be applied in an affirmative, literal sense:

> There are some names which signify these perfections flowing from God to creatures in such a way that the imperfect way in which creatures receive the divine perfection is part of the very signification of the name itself as 'stone' signifies a material being, and names of this kind can be applied to God only in a metaphorical sense. Other names, however, express these perfections absolutely, without any such mode of participation being part of their signification as the words 'being,' 'good,' 'living,' and the like, and such names can be literally applied to God.[34]

Law and Wisdom are such names as express an essential property of the divinity. 'The perfect unity of God requires that what are manifold and divided in others should exist in Him simply and unitedly. Thus it comes about that He is one in reality, and yet multiple in idea, because our intellect apprehends Him in a manifold manner, as things represent Him'.[35] And so it is with the Wisdom of God read out, as it were, in the manifold species of law.

[32] Pseudo-Dionysius the Areopagite, *De Divinis Nominibus*, I.5 (*Patrologia Græca*, 3, 593). Quoted by Aquinas, *Summa Theologica*, Ia, q.13, art.1. Dionysius was a Christian Neoplatonist who wrote in the late fifth or early sixth century and 'baptised' Pagan Neoplatonism from Plotinus to Proclus, but especially that of Proclus, into the service of Christian theology.

[33] Ambrose, *De Fide*, II, Prol. (*Patrologia Latina*, 16.583). Quoted by Aquinas, *ST*, Ia, q.13, art.3. Aurelius Ambrosius (c. 340–397) was Bishop of Milan, and—with Augustine, Jerome, and Gregory the Great—one of the four great Latin Fathers of the Church.

[34] *ST*, Ia, q.13, art.3, reply 1.

[35] *ST*, Ia, q.13, art.4, reply 3.

According to Hooker, the second eternal law, whose 'voyce is the harmony of the world', comprises the manifold divine order as 'kept by all [God's] creatures, according to the severall condition wherwith he hath indued them'.[36] This law has a variety of 'names' depending on the different orders of creatures subject to the one divine government. The two principal derivative *genera* of the second eternal law are (1) the natural law and (2) the revealed law of the scriptures, the latter sometimes termed by Hooker the 'divine law'—not to be confused with the eternal law itself. The entire system of the laws comprised within this second eternal law thus expresses the Proclean twofold motion of creative procession from (*proodos*) and return to (*epistrophē*) the original unity of the eternal law as expressed by this primary distinction between the natural and the revealed orders of law. Each of these two primary *genera*—Natural Law and divinely Revealed Law—is further participated by multiple derivative and dependent forms. The natural law, by way of a further procession, comprises in turn subordinate species of law which govern irrational natural agents as well as rational; the law governing the rational creatures is distinguished further into the 'law cœlestial', which orders the angels, and the 'law of reason', sometimes identified simply as the 'natural law' per se, which orders rational humankind. All of these sub-species represent the outward unfolding or *processio ad extra* of the second eternal law: 'reaching from one end to the other mightily'.

> Now that law which as it is laid up in the bosome of God, they call *æternall*, receyveth according unto the different kinds of things which are subject unto it different and sundry kinds of names. That part of it which ordereth naturall agents, we call usually *natures* law: that which Angels doe clearely behold, and without any swarving observe is a law *cælestiall* and heavenly: the law of *reason* that which bindeth creatures reasonable in this world, and with which by reason they may most plainly perceive themselves bound; that which bindeth them, and is not knowen but by speciall revelation from God, *Divine* law; *humane* lawe that which out of the law either of reason or of God, men probablie gathering to be expedient, they make it a law.[37]

[36] *Lawes*, I.3.1; 1:63.9–10.

[37] *Lawes*, I.3.1; 1:63.14–29.

On the converse side of the second eternal law, the law of God's special revelation, the revealed law of the scriptures, presupposes the disorder introduced into the cosmos by the Fall and is provided in order to secure the final restoration or 'return' of the creation to its original condition of unity under and within the primordial first eternal law. Hooker's distinction between these two *summa genera* of natural law and divinely revealed law corresponds to the cosmic logic of procession and return but also reflects the epistemological distinction of a twofold knowledge of God (*duplex cognitio Dei*), namely by the light of supernatural revelation and by the natural light of reason: in addition to the 'Book of the Eternal Wisdom' there are the 'Book of Nature' and the 'Book of Scripture', three books corresponding to three genres of Law. There are, moreover, composite species of law—such as human positive law and the law of nations, for example—which derive from a conscious, pragmatic reflection upon the general principles contained in the natural law. These additional derivative species of law are viewed by Hooker (here following Augustine) as a consequence of human sin, presupposing the Fall, and, like the divine law, they also constitute a corrective to the disorder introduced by Adam's disobedience. Augustine speaks of such law as a remedy of sin (*remedium peccati*).[38] Throughout this complex legal discourse, Hooker presents the human creature as the *imago dei* at the focal point of the cosmic drama of procession from and return to the original fount of order established in the divine simplicity of the first eternal law.[39]

As intellectual natures mortals share the desire of the angels for an infinite good in which alone such a nature can be finally satisfied. 'Then are we happie therfore when fully we injoy God, as an object wherein the powers of our soules are satisfied with everlasting delight: so that although we be men, yet by being unto God united we live as it were the life of God'.[40] Yet, 'of such perfection capable we are not in this life. For while we are in the world, subject we are unto sundry imperfections, griefs of body, defectes of minde, yea the best thinges we do

[38] For the use of coercive positive law as a *remedium peccati*, *see* Augustine, *De civitate Dei*, Bk XIX.

[39] On the theme of the 'cosmic drama', see C. A. Patrides, *The Grand Design of God: The Literary Form of the Christian View of History* (London: Routledge and Kegan Paul, 1972).

[40] *Lawes*, I.11.2; 1:112.17–20.

are painefull ...'.[41] The predicament of the human condition is to be of a mixed nature, partaking of both an intellectual nature shared by the angels and the physical shared by the irrational 'necessary agents'. For Hooker, there can be no natural overcoming of this hiatus between a 'natural' desire for divine perfection and a complete natural incapacity to achieve that end desired. While the desire for *theosis* is a natural desire—'so that nature even in this life doth plainly claime and call for a more divine perfection'[42]—nonetheless

> the light of nature is never able to finde out any way of obtayning the reward of blisse, but by performing exactly the duties and workes of righteousnes. From salvation therefore and life all flesh being excluded this way, behold how the wisedome of God hath revealed a way mysticall and supernaturall, a way directing unto the same ende of life by a course which groundeth it selfe upon the guiltines of sinne, and through sinne desert of condemnation and death.[43]

The '*exitus-redditus*' structure of this generic division of law in Book I of the *Ecclesiasticall Politie* shows that Hooker has read Aquinas on law very closely, as indeed numerous scholars have noted.[44] Hooker's distinction between the first and second eternal laws constitutes, nonetheless, a highly significant departure from the Thomist scholastic model. The effect of the distinction between these two aspects of the eternal law is simultaneously to widen and to decrease the distance between the creator-lawgiver and the created cosmos.

In addition, the distance between the two principal aspects of the second eternal law—that is to say between the Natural Law and the divinely Revealed Law—is most pronounced in Hooker's account of soteriology. The final 'return' to God of all creation can only be by 'a way

[41] *Lawes*, I.11.2; 1:112.24–113.1.

[42] *Lawes*, I.11.4; 1:115.23–24.

[43] *Lawes*, I.11.5, 6; 1:118.11–18.

[44] *Summa Theologica*, Ia IIae, qq.90–108. See Peter Munz, *The Place of Hooker in the History of Thought* (London: Routledge and Kegan Paul, 1952; repr. New York, NY: Greenwood Press, 1970), 49–57; Alessandro Passerin d'Entrèves, *The Medieval Contribution to Political Thought: Thomas Aquinas, Marsilius of Padua, Richard Hooker* (New York: The Humanities Press, 1959), esp. chaps. 5 and 6; and John S. Marshall, *Hooker and the Anglican Tradition: An Historical and Theological Study of Hooker's Ecclesiastical Polity* (Sewanee, TN: University of the South Press, 1963).

mysticall and supernaturall'. In *Notes toward a fragment on Predestination*, a manuscript in the library of Trinity College, Dublin, Hooker distinguishes between two species of the divine governance—a *duplex gubernatio Dei*:

> Government is that work of God whereby he *sustains created things* and disposes all things *to the end which he naturally* chooses, that is *the greatest good* which, *given* the law *of creation*, can be elicited. For, given the law of creation <is the rule of all> it was not fitting that creation be violated through those things which follow from creation. So God does nothing by his government which offends against that which he has framed and ratified by the very act of creation. The government of God is: general over all; special over rational creatures. There are two forms of government: that which would have been, had free creation not lost its way; that which is now when it has lost its way.[45]

This passage reveals the soteriological principle underlying the generic division of laws. On one side are laws governing the order of an unfallen Creation. Among these laws, Hooker includes the law of nature in so far as it governs irrational and non-voluntary natural agents. This again is a significant departure from the usual, more restricted sense of Natural Law as an 'intellectual habit' of the soul, that is to say, the *summa ratio* as it is present and known to rational creatures.[46]

[45] John Booty's translation of Hooker's original Latin notes in the *Folger Library Edition of Hooker's Works* 4: 86.28–87.12: "Gubernatio est ea Dei operatio qua res creatas sustentat disponitque omnia in finem ab ipso naturaliter expetitum id est maximum bonum quod posita creationis lege potest elici. Etenim posita creationis lex <est regula omnium> per ea quae secuta sunt creationem violare non decuit. Nihil itaque operatur Deuos [sic] gubernando contra id quod creando fixum ratumque habuit. Gubernatio Dei: Generale super omnia; Speciale super creaturas rationales. Gubernationis duplex modus: Qui fuisset si creatura libera non exorbitasset; Qui nunc est cum exorbitarit." Cp. Aquinas, *ST*, 1a, q.20, art.2; q.49, art.2, and q.103, art.7.

[46] See, for example, Aquinas's discussion of the definition of natural law in *ST*, 1a2ae q.94, art.1; also, Cicero, *De Legibus*, 1.4; and Gratian, *Decretum*, Part I, Distinct. 1: 'Natural law is that which is contained in the Law and the Gospel whereby everyone is commanded to do to another that which he would have done to himself.' Hooker cites Gratian's definition at *Lawes*, I.12.1; 1:119.30–120.1. For further discussion of the significance of this distinction see Torrance Kirby, 'Richard Hooker's Theory of Natural Law in the Context of Reformation Theology', *Sixteenth Century Journal*, 30:3 (1999), 681–703.

To conclude, for Hooker, the form of law 'to be kept by all creatures according to their several conditions' is comprised of three *summa genera*—the eternal law, the natural law, and the divine law—where the latter two species are understood as comprehended within the first, and yet nonetheless distinct both in their operation and in our knowledge of them. Together these *summa genera* constitute a comprehensive division of the many diverse 'kinds' of law. To understand their derivation from the original unity of the first eternal law is to gain critical insight into the underlying ontological assumptions of Hooker's argument, and moreover provides a vital instrument for interpreting the manner of Hooker's reconciliation of Neoplatonic ontology of participation with a Reformed soteriology. Viewed from the standpoint of their divine principle of origin—i.e. in the first eternal law where 'the being of God is a law to his working'—these three *summa genera* of law may be considered as simply one. The predication of law to God is not metaphorical for Hooker. Law is a perfection of the divine being and can consequently be affirmed literally so long as we understand that what God is 'in reality' is not to be confused with what he is 'in idea'. Our intellect apprehends God in the manifold manner of the expression of the voice of his Wisdom. Viewed from below, as it were, that is from the standpoint of mortal finitude, the original unity takes on the aspect of articulated multiplicity of kinds which nonetheless all 'participate' and 'proceed from' the undivided unity that is their common source.[47] This account of the simultaneous unity and diversity of law in its multiple species lies at the very heart of Hooker's vision of law as an expression of the divine governance:

> Who the guide of nature but only the God of nature? *In him we live, move, and are.* Those things which nature is said to do, are by divine arte performed, using nature as an instrument: nor is there any such arte or knowledge divine in nature her selfe working, but in the guide of natures worke.[48]

Hooker begins with metaphors of 'the nature of law in general'—law as the root of a flourishing tree, law as the foundation of a stately house, law

[47] On the concept of the *procession* of the forms of law, see, for example, I.3.4; 1:68.6–8: '...the naturall generation and processe of all things receyveth order of proceeding from the settled stabilitie of divine understanding.'

[48] *Lawes*, I.3.4; 1:67.16–20.

as a wellspring or fountain, all hidden 'in the bosome of the earth'—and proceeds to identify these underlying, hidden sources with the primordial Wisdom of God. This Wisdom is in turn presented metaphorically as hidden 'in the bosome of God' and the 'bowels of the divine mercie', and manifest in the 'voyce' of cosmic harmony. In effect, when we mix these metaphors, what is 'hidden in the bosome of the earth' is in actuality 'hidden in the bosome of God'. The conclusion for Hooker is that God, in some literal sense, is Law. His law is not distinct from himself, and therefore it becomes possible to move beyond metaphor to a more literal affirmation. This predication must be interpreted cautiously—it is composite in form, but refers the theological understanding to an essential simplicity, the ineffable unity and simplicity of all law in the divine self-regulating activity: 'the being of God is a kinde of law to his workinge' and on this working a manifold diversity of laws depends.

CHAPTER 7

The Common Consent of Words: An Aristotelian Element of Hobbesian Legal Rhetoric

Charles McNamara

Studies of Thomas Hobbes often divide his scholarly output into two halves: the first half defined by his humanist training and the second defined by his turn toward what many would call a scientific approach. At the fulcrum point of this intellectual biography, so the story goes, lies Hobbes' epiphanic encounter in 1630 with Euclid's *Elements*, a text that inspired him to abandon the methods of humanism for the demonstrative certainty of geometry, applied to his new *scientia civilis*, or "civil science."[1] What, then, to make of a peculiar entry in the Register of the Company of Stationers of London from 1636 to 1637: "A briefe of the

C. McNamara (✉)
Department of Classical and Near Eastern Religions and Cultures, University of Minnesota, Minneapolis, MN, USA
e-mail: mcnamarc@umn.edu

[1] To take one example of this account, Leo Strauss writes, "Hobbes was over forty when he 'discovered' Euclid's *Elements*, and not until after that did he begin to take a serious interest in natural science. The 'discovery' of Euclid was beyond doubt an epoch

S. Mukherji and D. Roberts (eds.), *Literature and the Legal Imaginary*, Crossroads of Knowledge in Early Modern Literature 4,
https://doi.org/10.1007/978-3-031-74093-0_7

art of Rhetorique, conteyninge in substance, all that Aristotle hath written in his three Bookes of that subject by T:H:"? According to Ioannis Evrigenis, this English translation is itself also the work of Hobbes' hand; that is, Hobbes is the "T:H:" listed in the catalog, compiled at a time "eight years into [Hobbes'] scientific phase."[2] But as Evrigenis notes, the *Briefe* "has an awkward place in accounts of Hobbes's intellectual development[, for] commentators have found it difficult to fit it into the neat story of Hobbes's turn to science, and have rejected it, passed it by, or considered it a byproduct of Hobbes's tutorial duties."[3] What would the charm of rhetoric and the pleasantries of persuasion have to do with Hobbes' new civil science rooted in the demonstrative rigor of geometric methods?

Some scholars have embraced the *Briefe* as Hobbes' own writing and have argued for his enduring attraction to Aristotelian rhetoric, still finding traces of this pillar of ancient oratory in Hobbes' later works. Taking a particular interest in the Aristotelian roots of Hobbes' theory of the passions, Leo Strauss contends that "it would be difficult to find another classical work whose importance for Hobbes's political philosophy can be compared with that of the *Rhetoric*."[4] According to Strauss' analysis, Hobbes relies on this ancient forebear when he enumerates honorable and dishonorable deeds, sketches the psychology of pity and envy, and proposes categories of good and pleasant activities.[5] More recently, Timothy Raylor has argued that Hobbes' later attention to

in his life; everything he thought and wrote after that is modified by this happening" (*Political Philosophy of Hobbes: Its Basis and Its Genesis*, trans. Elsa M. Sinclair [Chicago: University of Chicago Press, 1952], 29). Timothy Raylor emphasizes that "the implication of the anecdote—that Hobbes had not previously encountered, or at least reflected on Euclid—is, of course, drawn for rhetorical effect" (*Philosophy, Rhetoric, and Thomas Hobbes* [Oxford: Oxford University Press, 2018], 127).

[2] Ioannis D. Evrigenis, *Images of Anarchy* (Cambridge: Cambridge University Press, 2014), 46.

[3] Evrigenis, *Images of Anarchy*, 47.

[4] Strauss, *Political Philosophy of Hobbes*, 35.

[5] For a helpful comparison of Aristotle's text with relevant sections of *Elements of Law*, *De Homine*, and *Leviathan*, see Strauss, *Political Philosophy of Hobbes*, 36–41. Hobbes was not indiscriminate, however, in his admiration for Aristotle's works, and he turned his back on the Aristotelian teachings of politics and ethics from his earlier education. In Strauss' view, this persistent interest in Aristotelian notions of the passions amounts to "the last remnants of the Aristotelianism of his youth" (42).

rhetoric "only appears shifting or inconsistent if we start from the assumption that he was in his early career committed to a Ciceronian-humanist understanding of rhetoric as a moral art with philosophical pretensions and civic responsibilities."[6] Indeed, Hobbes himself gave the impression that he found something valuable in Aristotle's text, for he once remarked, according to John Aubrey's biography, that "Aristotle was the worst teacher that ever was, the worst Politician and Ethick ... but his *Rhetorique* ... was rare."[7]

Even if Strauss, Raylor, and others have found ample evidence for Aristotelian views of the passions and human psychology in Hobbes' later political writings, other scholars have cast doubt on his authorship of this Aristotelian epitome. Karl Schuhmann rejects the possibility of Hobbes' involvement on the grounds that "the translator of the *Briefe*, apparently by lack of acquaintance with Aristotle's original, sometimes misunderstood the exact meaning of certain words and phrases," adding that the errant author who in fact wrote it "adds a few remarks that are not in line with what is known to be Hobbes's thought."[8] Quentin Skinner shares these suspicions. Although his seminal book *Reason and Rhetoric in the Philosophy of Hobbes* takes the *Briefe* as a genuine work, his more recent *Hobbes and Republican Liberty* expresses support for Schuhmann's position.[9] Despite these two skeptical views on the origins of the *Briefe*, many

[6] Raylor, *Philosophy, Rhetoric, and Thomas Hobbes*, 275. Also taking the *Briefe* to be an authentic work of Hobbes' hand, Victoria Kahn concurs that his "conversion to Euclid clearly did not preclude a continued interest in the uses of rhetoric" (*The Trouble with Literature* [Oxford: Oxford University Press, 2020], 39).

[7] John Harwood, ed., *The Rhetorics of Thomas Hobbes and Bernard Lamy* (Carbondale, IL: Southern Illinois University Press, 2009), 2. Karl Schuhmann also highlights Hobbes' attested admiration for Aristotle's text. "Skinner leaves us in the dark," he explains, "as why Hobbes always, and notwithstanding his later outspoken aversion to rhetoric, considered Aristotle's *Rhetoric* as 'rare'; i.e. why he continued to hold it in high regard, and why he had used it in the way it was used more generally throughout the Renaissance, namely as the best manual for introducing a pupil to ethics" ('Skinner's Hobbes', *British Journal for the History of Philosophy*, 6:1 (1998), 115–25 (118–19)). This selective admiration for Aristotle's *Rhetoric* departs from his earlier humanist phase, for Hobbes notes in the letter to readers of his 1629 translation of Thucydides that "Homer in poesy, Aristotle in philosophy, Demosthenes in eloquence, and others of the ancients in other knowledge, do still maintain their primacy."

[8] Schuhmann, 'Skinner's Hobbes', 118.

[9] For a brief account of this shift, see Quentin Skinner, *Hobbes and Republican Liberty* (Cambridge: Cambridge University Press, 2008), 5, especially note 20.

scholars remain committed to Hobbes' authorship, including Evrigenis and Raylor as well as John Harwood and Thomas Sorell.[10]

The persistent controversy surrounding the *Briefe* may just be attributable to the idea that, as Evrigenis suggests, "the *Briefe* is an idiosyncratic summary of Aristotle's *Rhetoric*, not simply a presentation of Hobbes's own views."[11] There is, however, a more significant kinship between the *Briefe* and Hobbes' later thought than previously acknowledged, and in this essay, I argue that the *Briefe* introduces models of argumentation that Hobbes will rely on in his later political writings, especially as those models bear on the origins and knowledge of civil law.[12] The author of the *Briefe* sets forth literary methods for working with the "common opinions" of one's audience—strategies of persuasion that exhibit striking parallels to the methods of grounding *scientia civilis* in Hobbes' *Elements of Law*, specifically in its interest in eliminating controversy through rhetorical encounters. In his *De Cive*, another emblematic work of his later period, Hobbes continues to rely on the notions of "common opinion" in his putatively scientific study of civil law, and he tightly couples the possibility of political knowledge with the "common consent of men" that arises through linguistic consistency. With such compelling parallels available, there is no need for the rhetorical tactics of the *Briefe* to be crudely shoehorned in alongside the unquestionably genuine later works of Hobbes. We might even find that its

[10] See especially Raylor, *Philosophy, Rhetoric, and Thomas Hobbes*, 281–91, for an extended critique of Schuhmann's skepticism of Hobbes' authorship of the *Briefe*. Adding some small measure of doubt, Tom Sorell writes that Hobbes is "apparently" responsible for the *Briefe* ('Hobbes's Unaristotelian Political Rhetoric', *Philosophy & Rhetoric*, 23:2 (1990), 96–108 (96)).

[11] Evrigenis, *Images of Anarchy*, 48n13. This "idiosyncratic" character of the *Briefe* presents problems for some positive accounts of Hobbes' authorship. To take one example, Karl Schuhmann and Quentin Skinner search for clean correspondence between the *Briefe* and the Aristotelian original, and while "Skinner is no doubt right in affirming that the definitions of the passions in the *Elements of Law* echo those of Aristotle's *Rhetoric* [, ...] detailed study makes it clear that these definitions are by no means 'virtual quotations from his own translation of Aristotle's text', i.e. from the *Briefe*" (Schuhmann, 'Skinner's Hobbes', 118n8). For a discussion of the relationship between Hobbes and Aristotle's political thought, see Schuhmann's 'Hobbes and Aristotle's *Politics*', in Gianfranco Borrelli, ed., *Thomas Hobbes: Le Ragioni Del Moderno Tra Teologia e Politica* (Naples: Morano, 1990), 97–127.

[12] My study addresses some of the epistemological questions underlying Hobbes' writings that Timothy Raylor sets aside in his own recent account of Hobbes' enduring commitment to rhetorical methods (*Philosophy, Rhetoric, and Thomas Hobbes*, 15).

discussions about controversy, persuasion, and the decisive importance of shared language are central to Hobbes' later treatments of *scientia civilis*.

The *Briefe* on "Common Opinion"

Before turning to the undisputed works of Hobbes, it will be helpful to look at some qualities of the *Briefe* itself, especially where its structure and language suggest that its author makes careful choices in rendering Aristotle's Greek. Following Aristotle's structure, the *Briefe* is separated into three books, each of which approximately mirrors the chapters of the Greek original: the author of the *Briefe* has fifteen chapters in Book One, where Aristotle has sixteen, but the author has twenty-eight in Book Two, where Aristotle has twenty-six. There are both deletions and additions, abbreviations and expansions. In the second chapter of the *Briefe*, we get a sense of the shortenings. There the author explains that "Proofes, are in Rhetorique, either Examples, or Enthymemes; as in Logicke, Inductions, or Syllogismes. For an Example is a short Induction, and an Enthymeme a short Syllogisme; out of which are left as superfluous, that which is supposed to be necessarily understood by the hearer; to avoid prolixity, and not to consume the time of publique businesse needlesly."[13] As John Harwood notes in his edition of the *Briefe*, where Chapter 2 of the English translation occupies hardly half of a page of text, the author "has omitted ... the three *pisteis* (*ethos*, *pathos*, and *logos*) as well as the nature of rhetorical inference."[14]

Despite these omissions, however, the author of the *Briefe* nevertheless follows Aristotle's *Rhetoric* quite closely when he offers his own definitions of the example and the enthymeme, the building blocks of inductive and syllogistic forms of reasoning, respectively. Aristotle's corresponding text reads as follows:

> The enthymeme and the example are concerned with things which may, generally speaking, be other than they are, the example being a kind of

[13] Harwood, *The Rhetorics of Thomas Hobbes and Bernard Lamy*, 40. For citations of the text of the *Briefe* itself, I provide page numbers for Harwood's edition.

[14] Harwood, *The Rhetorics of Thomas Hobbes and Bernard Lamy*, 40n3. The Loeb translation of Aristotle's second chapter, by contrast, fills nearly ten full pages of English text. See John Freese, ed. and trans., *The "Art" of Rhetoric* (Cambridge, MA: Harvard University Press, 1926).

> induction and the enthymeme a kind of syllogism, and deduced from few premises, often fewer than the regular syllogism; for if any one of these is well known, there is no need to mention it, for the hearer can add it himself.[15]

Like Aristotle, the author of the *Briefe* maintains the primary separation of the example and the enthymeme, and in the case of the enthymeme, he relays Aristotle's advice to keep one's arguments short.[16] When one's audience is deeply familiar with premises, he reminds readers, there is no need to "consume the time of publique businesse needlesly." Perhaps appropriately, then, the author has left out much of the original Aristotelian material on the three kinds of persuasion not because he disagrees with it, but simply because he knows his readers have all slogged through Aristotle's *pisteis* enough to rattle off *logos*, *pathos*, and *ethos* in their sleep.

But we should recall that the approach in the *Briefe* is not merely to excise what is familiar—there are additions and repetitions as well. We get a sense of those expansions in the following chapter of the *Briefe*, which the author titles "Of the severall kinds of Orations: and of the Principles of Rhetorique." Here he again follows the structure of Aristotle's work, whose third chapter similarly introduces the categories of deliberative, forensic, and epideictic rhetoric, but the *Briefe*, straying from the Greek, includes another passage that has no clear antecedent in the corresponding chapter of the original *Rhetoric*. In his later epitome, the author explicitly defines the goal of persuasion in a way that Aristotle's original chapter does not, drawing a distinction between the techniques of "Logicke" and "Rhetorique"[17]:

[15] ἀναγκαῖον τό τε ἐνθύμημα εἶναι καὶ τὸ παράδειγμα περί τε τῶν ἐνδεχομένων ὡς τὰ πολλὰ ἔχειν ἄλλως, τὸ μὲν παράδειγμα ἐπαγωγὴν τὸ δ' ἐνθύμημα συλλογισμόν, καὶ ἐξ ὀλίγων τε καὶ πολλάκις ἐλαττόνων ἢ ἐξ ὧν ὁ πρῶτος συλλογισμός· ἐὰν γὰρ ᾖ τι τούτων γνώριμον, οὐδὲ δεῖ λέγειν· αὐτὸς γὰρ τοῦτο προστίθησιν ὁ ἀκροατής, 1357a13–19. Translations of Aristotle's *Rhetoric* are adapted from Freese's Loeb translation.

[16] Scholars often define the enthymeme as an abbreviated syllogism, but this concision-focused rendering is just one of many competing definitions, as argued in James Fredal, 'Is the Enthymeme a Syllogism?', *Philosophy & Rhetoric*, 51:1 (2018), 24–49.

[17] Harwood, too, notes this difference in his edition of the *Briefe*, where he calls the added sentence "an important interpretation of the function of rhetoric" (*The Rhetorics of Thomas Hobbes and Bernard Lamy*, 41n5).

> The Principles of Rhetorique out of which Enthymemes are to be drawne; are the common opinions that men have concerning Profitable, and Unprofitable; Just, and Unjust, Honourable and Dishonourable; which are the points in the severall kinds of Orations questionable. For as in Logicke, where certaine and infallible knowledge is the scope of our proofe, the Principles must be all infallible truthes: so in Rhetorique the Principles must be common opinions, such as the Judge is already possessed with: because the end of Rhetorique is victory, which consists in having gotten beleefe.[18]

In his *Reason and Rhetoric*, Quentin Skinner observes that there is "nothing in Aristotle corresponding to [the *Briefe*'s] sneering conclusion … that rhetoricians are only interested in victory and not in truth."[19] This insistence on victory as rhetoric's aim, however, is not the only addition we find in this section of the *Briefe*, for the passage doubly underscores the importance of "common opinions" as the tools of enthymematic proof, an emphasis which is absent from the Greek's third chapter. This turn toward "common opinion" anticipates the remainder of the first book of the *Briefe*: of the thirteen chapters left in Book One, five of them document the "common opinions" of topics such as good and evil, pleasure, and injury.

Given the prominent repetition of this phrase throughout the *Briefe*, we should consider possible technical meanings of "common opinion" in Aristotelian rhetorical practice more broadly. As the headings of the later chapters in Book One attest, these "common opinions" could be understood as the "colours" or *loci communes* of rhetoric, and indeed there is good evidence in the *Briefe* itself to support such an equivalence.[20] In the titles of Chapters 6 and 7, the author even makes explicit the overlap in terminology: "Of the Colours, or common opinions concerning Good and Evill." This notion of the "colours of rhetoric" as common but

[18] Harwood, *The Rhetorics of Thomas Hobbes and Bernard Lamy*, 41.

[19] Quentin Skinner, *Reason and Rhetoric in the Philosophy of Hobbes* (Cambridge: Cambridge University Press, 1996), 257. Timothy Raylor, however, contends that "it is not entirely accurate to suggest that there is nothing in Aristotle corresponding" to this claim, for Hobbes is not merely interested "in winning at all costs"; instead, Hobbes believes that "the aim of rhetoric is to establish conviction in a given audience" (*Philosophy, Rhetoric, and Thomas Hobbes*, 170).

[20] For one suggestion that "common opinions" here stands as a translation of *loci communes*, see Skinner, *Reason and Rhetoric in the Philosophy of Hobbes*, 115–16.

perhaps erroneous beliefs can be found, moreover, in other writings of Hobbes' era, including Francis Bacon's 1597 *Of the Colours of Good and Evill*, where Bacon cautions in his preface to be on guard against such beliefs, "showing in what cases they hold, and in what they deceive."[21]

Turning back to the *Briefe*'s third chapter, however, we find a second mention of "common opinions" that define such beliefs particularly as those "such as the Judge is already possessed with," rather than commonplaces more generally.[22] This second account of "common opinion," linked to one's specific audience, does not have a clear counterpart in Aristotle's third chapter. But in Chapter 2 of the original Greek, where Aristotle defines the abbreviated nature of the enthymeme, he also notes the importance of building arguments from the shared ideas and premises of one's hearers. In that earlier chapter of the *Rhetoric*, we find a plausible antecedent for the translation's comments on "common opinion," particularly regarding the availability of these opinions to the case's judge:

> It is possible to draw conclusions and inferences partly from what has been previously demonstrated syllogistically, partly from what has not, which however needs demonstration, because it is not *endoxon*. The first of these methods is necessarily difficult to follow owing to its length, for the judge is supposed to be a simple person; the second will obtain little credence because it does not depend upon what is either *homologoumenon* or *endoxon*.[23]

The corresponding section in Chapter 3 of the *Briefe* does not exactly parallel Aristotle's concerns here—Aristotle's second chapter makes no mention of the difference between rhetoric and logic—but we do find some echoes of the emphasis on the judge's ready possession of an argument's premises. The *Briefe*, then, seems to have transported some of the

[21] Brian Vickers reports, moreover, that Bacon "shows what might be called ethical realism, readily conceding that an unscrupulous orator can abuse his persuasive skills to evil ends" ('Bacon and Rhetoric', in *The Cambridge Companion to Bacon* (Cambridge: Cambridge University Press, 1996), 200–231 (211)).

[22] At least in Aristotle's context, these judges are "not professional specialists but mere citizens—'simple persons'" (Raylor, *Philosophy, Rhetoric, and Thomas Hobbes*, 168).

[23] ἐνδέχεται δὲ συλλογίζεσθαι καὶ συνάγειν τὰ μὲν ἐκ συλλελογισμένων πρότερον, τὰ δ' ἐξ ἀσυλλογίστων μέν, δεομένων δὲ συλλογισμοῦ διὰ τὸ μὴ εἶναι ἔνδοξα, ἀνάγκη δὲ τούτων τὸ μὲν μὴ εἶναι εὐεπακολούθητον διὰ τὸ μῆκος (ὁ γὰρ κριτὴς ὑπόκειται εἶναι ἁπλοῦς), τὰ δὲ μὴ πιθανὰ διὰ τὸ μὴ ἐξ ὁμολογουμένων εἶναι μηδ' ἐνδόξων, 1357a7–13.

material from Aristotle's second chapter to the epitome's third, an easy migration from one page to the next. Just as the third chapter of the *Briefe* demands that the rhetorician work from "common opinions," Aristotle's second chapter similarly underscores the sort of material (rather than the length of material) that characterizes enthymematic proof: *endoxa* and *homologoumena*, the "reputable" and "agreed upon," respectively.[24]

Having viewed Aristotle's comments on the judge's available beliefs, we might consider the *Briefe*'s phrase "common opinion" as a conflation or catch-all for the *endoxon* and *homologoumenon*. We could even add *loci* or *topoi* as possible ancient antecedents, following Bacon. The author of the *Briefe* takes a different approach, however. Rather than belabor the distinctions among all these terms, he simply treats the material of rhetorical proof as a simplified notion of ideas shared among one's audience, whatever is "common" and (perhaps even more significantly) whatever is mere "opinion" rather than firm, unimpeachable knowledge.[25] The *Briefe*, then, cautions that an enthymeme should avoid building upon material that is unfamiliar, unintuitive, or otherwise "less known." Its premises may be omitted or shortened, but crucially, these premises must be widely believed.

Given that the author of the *Briefe* maintains a persistent interest in "common opinions" throughout the remainder of his text, I am

[24] In 'On *Endoxa* in Aristotle's *Topics*', *Rheinisches Museum Für Philologie*, 158:3 (2015), 225–46, Tobias Reinhardt resists the prevalent understanding of *endoxa* in Aristotle as commonly held opinions. Timothy Raylor's recent study of Hobbes' *Briefe* itself shows the difficulty of pinning down a simple definition of *endoxa*, for he refers to them as "beliefs the audience already holds" (*Philosophy, Rhetoric, and Thomas Hobbes*, 177) but also as "authoritative opinion[s]" (221). Raylor points to a passage of *De Cive* (10.11) where Hobbes himself appears to adopt the former definition, where speakers begin not "from true Principles, but from vulgar received opinions, which, for the most part, are erroneous" (*non procedunt tamen a principiis veris, sed ab ἐνδόξοις, a id est, opinionibus iam vulgo receptis, quae maxima ex parte erroneae esse solent*) (*Philosophy, Rhetoric, and Thomas Hobbes*, 178–79). For a treatment of the various types of material used in enthymematic proofs, including *topoi* and other ancient categories of belief, see Brad McAdon, 'Probabilities, Signs, Necessary Signs, Idia, and Topoi: The Confusing Discussion of Materials for Enthymemes in the *Rhetoric*', *Philosophy and Rhetoric*, 36:3 (2003), 223–48.

[25] A later discussion of judicial oratory (3.16) affirms the questionable validity of "common opinions," too, since the author of the *Briefe* explains how one should not "endeavour to proove every thing by Enthymeme lest like some Philosophers, he collect what is knowne, from what is lesse knowne" (Harwood, *The Rhetorics of Thomas Hobbes and Bernard Lamy*, 125).

happy to agree with Skinner when he explains how Aristotle's original text teaches an art that "is essentially that of learning to manipulate a rhetorical form of syllogism, the so-called enthymeme, in which the premises are merely probable and the point of deploying them is to arouse emotion as well as to furnish proofs."[26] This Aristotelian approach, Skinner continues, "stands in marked contrast with the outlook of the Roman theorists and their Renaissance followers, few of whom exhibit any serious interest in this predominantly psychological theme."[27] Eschewing formulaic methods of excision and compression, the author of the *Briefe*, so these passages indicate, is attuned to rhetoric's interest in an audience, one whose cognitive characteristics are key to producing agreement or, in the author's words, achieving "victory."

The Rhetorical Character of Hobbesian Legal *Scientia*

That the author of the *Briefe* understands rhetorical proof through the lens of Aristotelian psychology rather than formulaic, abbreviated structures calls for a recalibration of the anti-Aristotelian position to which Hobbes is often thought to adhere. In other words, we should reconsider rejections of Hobbes' authorship of the *Briefe* that stem from a rigid view of the rhetorical syllogism as a concise argumentative template. To take one example of these rejections, Tom Sorell argues that Hobbes' moral and political works "do not make use of the enthymeme" whose characteristic quality is "that it leaves much unstated, gaining its brevity from omission."[28] But as William Grimaldi reminds us in his commentary on Aristotle's original text, the Aristotelian "enthymeme and the syllogism can be, and often are, the same in form-structure—i.e., two premisses and a conclusion. [...] But in the content and character of its statements, the enthymeme will usually differ from other types of syllogism."[29] If Hobbes elsewhere seems not to use the abbreviated syllogism of Roman

[26] Skinner, *Reason and Rhetoric in the Philosophy of Hobbes*, 36.

[27] Skinner, *Reason and Rhetoric in the Philosophy of Hobbes*, 37.

[28] Sorell, 'Hobbes's Unaristotelian Political Rhetoric', 104.

[29] William M. A. Grimaldi, S.J., *Aristotle, Rhetoric: A Commentary* (New York: Fordham University Press, 1980), 1.48.

textbooks, we might nevertheless still find reason for his interest in the methods of Aristotle's *Rhetoric*.[30]

In this second section, I argue that, whether or not Hobbes was the author of the *Briefe*, Aristotle's *Rhetoric* would certainly have been highly relevant to him as he developed his later political and philosophical thought in works like the *Elements of Law*.[31] Just as we see in the *Briefe*, these later works of Hobbes also take an interest in "common opinions," but with a special twist. As we shall find first in Hobbes' discussion of "infallible" truths in the *Elements*, his approach to his new civil science and his ideal of communicating knowledge is similarly grounded in achieving a kind of victory and expanding the reach of "common opinion," where his ideal of "victory" is unanimity—common belief taken to its logical extreme.

Published just two years after the *Briefe*, the *Elements* also examines, among other topics, language and its capacity for persuasion. I focus my attention first on Chapter 13 of Hobbes' text, entitled "How by Language Men Work Upon Each Other's Minds," where Hobbes explains the difference between "teaching" and "persuasion"[32]:

> The first use of language, is the expression of our conceptions, that is, the begetting in another the same conceptions that we have in ourselves; and this is called teaching; wherein if the conceptions of him that teacheth continually accompany his words, beginning at something from experience, then it begetteth the like evidence in the hearer that understandeth them, and maketh him know something, which he is therefore said to learn. But if there be not such evidence, then such teaching is called persuasion,

[30] Harwood, *The Rhetorics of Thomas Hobbes and Bernard Lamy*, 2.

[31] Recent scholarship sees these two late works as representative of Hobbes' scientific method, but to varying degrees. Karl Schuhmann, describing Skinner's perspective, explains how some see "only the *Elements of Law* and *De Cive* [as representatives of] the phase of pure science in Hobbes, as opposed to (the use of) rhetoric" ('Skinner's Hobbes', 121). For his part, Schuhmann sees the *Elements* and *Leviathan* as "natural candidates for a high dose of eloquence, for these were works written for a public which did not claim citizenship in the republic of letters" ('Skinner's Hobbes', 121–22). Of course, one might even see the title of Hobbes' *Elements of Law* as an approving nod to the Euclidean tradition.

[32] Numbering and text of Hobbes' *Elements of Law* are taken from Ferdinand Tönnies, ed., *The Elements of Law, Natural and Political* (London: Cass, 1969).

> and begetteth no more in the hearer, than what is in the speaker, bare opinion.[33]

While Hobbes' central concern here is not the division of "rhetoric" and "logic," he nevertheless suggests a distinction similar to what we have already seen in the *Briefe*: when speech aligns with perspicuous conceptual evidence, more grounded and assured conclusions are produced in one's audience. But when we lack this clear evidence, we are left with what Hobbes calls "persuasion." The final sentence in this passage, moreover, suggests that the "persuasion" of the *Elements* and the "rhetoric" of the *Briefe* are close cousins, since they both operate on the standard of "opinion," whether "common" or "bare." On a surface reading, at least, we might position "teaching" and "persuasion" as parallel terms to "logic" and "rhetoric," with persuasion and rhetoric not meeting the standards of evidence with which we make "maketh the hearer know something."[34]

In the following paragraph, Hobbes hardens the separation of these two practices:

> The infallible sign of teaching exactly, and without error, is this: that no man hath ever taught the contrary; not that few, how few soever, if any. For commonly truth is on the side of the few, rather than of the multitude; but when in opinions and questions considered and discussed by many, it happeneth that not any one of the men that so discuss them differ from another, then it may be justly inferred, they know what they teach, and that otherwise they do not. [...] There is therefore a great deal of difference between teaching and persuading; the signs of this being controversy; the sign of the former, no controversy.[35]

[33] *Elements of Law*, 1.13.2.

[34] Skinner sees here that Hobbes revives "the Socratic objection that the techniques of teaching and persuading are irreconcilable" (*Reason and Rhetoric in the Philosophy of Hobbes*, 275). A key lexicographical and philosophical point—and one beyond the scope of this essay—is Hobbes' understanding of "evidence," a word that spans matters of scientific demonstration, legal proof, and rhetorical persuasion. For one treatment of *evidentia* and *enargeia* in Aristotelian rhetorical frameworks, see Kathy Eden, *Poetic and Legal Fiction in the Aristotelian Tradition* (Princeton, NJ: Princeton University Press, 1986), 62–111.

[35] *Elements of Law*, 1.13.3. See also *Elements* 1.1.1, where Hobbes writes that "seeing that true knowledge begetteth not doubt nor controversy, but knowledge; it is manifest from the present controversies, that they which have heretofore written thereof, have not well understood their own subject."

At least in its first clauses, this paragraph suggests that "teaching exactly" is not an eventual elimination of controversy through the correction of one's interlocutors. Rather, one can only "teach" knowledge that is fundamentally incompatible with controversy: no one "ever" teaches the contrary position. Hobbes emphasizes that knowledge can be found where "not anyone of the men that so discuss ... differ from another," and combined with the temporal aspect suggested by "ever," Hobbes' notion of teaching concerns knowledge which is readily apparent to all, assented to by all, at all times. Elsewhere in the same paragraph, Hobbes provides examples of such uncontroversial matters, including "portraying of the face of the earth," the "foresight of the course of heaven," and other facts rooted in "measuring distances, planes, and solids of all sorts."[36] Concluding that it was "never heard of, that there was any controversy" concerning these geometrical topics, Hobbes again hints that controversy is something that either exists or does not and that one cannot simply eliminate preexisting controversy as a method of generating new knowledge.

Similarly radical separation of incontrovertible knowledge and controversial opinion can be found elsewhere in the *Elements*, for example in the Epistle Dedicatory. There Hobbes emphasizes again his preference for geometric methods over humanist debate, for those who "have written of justice and policy in general, do all invade each other, and themselves, with contradiction." As a remedy, he calls for a kind of Cartesian demolition of previous assumptions and a careful construction of wholly new and unquestionably sturdy epistemic edifices, "which hitherto have been built in the air." Not looking merely to repair an Aristotelian cloud castle, Hobbes wants to start anew, building upon the firmest foundations.

Despite the *Elements*' call for a fundamentally new kind of *scientia civilis*, free from controversy, it also shows that this epistemic project is no solitary meditation which is immune to moments of interpersonal disagreement. The knowledge at which the *Elements* aims is still the

[36] Here Hobbes' plan is "to compare directly the approach and results in geometry with the approach and results of classical political philosophy," and ultimately "Hobbes's great ambition was to make civil philosophy as useful as the natural philosophy being developed by his contemporaries, and to accomplish this by the same method, namely, the method of geometry" (John W. Danford, 'The Problem of Language in Hobbes's Political Science', *The Journal of Politics*, 42:1 (1980), 102–34 (106–7)).

product of rhetorical encounters, where one needs to wrest agreement from interlocutors who themselves might not assent to one's reasoning[37]:

> [I]f reasoning aright I win not consent (which may very easily happen) from them that being confident of their own knowledge weigh not what is said, the fault is not mine but theirs. For as it is my part to show my reasons, so it is theirs to bring attention.[38]

Even in his purified methodology, Hobbes still finds that he must "win consent," a phrase that recalls the "victory" of the *Briefe*. The failure to convince, which "may very easily happen," stems not from some literary obscurity of Hobbes' own words but instead from the misplaced confidence of the listener, who fails to "bring attention" to the arguments at hand.

Turning back to Chapter 13 of the *Elements*, we should reconsider our preliminary reading of "teaching" and "persuasion" as fundamentally incompatible practices. As the first chapter of the *Elements* shows, even geometric demonstration can meet with disagreement, and Hobbes' absolutist claim that it was "never heard of, that there was any controversy" concerning demonstrable knowledge deserves some softening. Our listeners might simply find us boring or otherwise not worthy of attention. Despite Chapter 13's suggestion of an unbridgeable gap between teaching and persuasion, Hobbes also hints that knowledge might morph from a true belief "on the side of the few" to widespread, uncontroversial knowledge of all.[39] "Teaching exactly," then, aims at unanimity without automatically enjoying it. Like "persuasion," this Hobbesian notion of teaching also relies on expanding shared beliefs—one needs to "win

[37] Here Hobbes acknowledges the difficulty of a project where scientific knowledge still "must be communicated in language" (Raylor, *Philosophy, Rhetoric, and Thomas Hobbes*, 253).

[38] *Elements of Law* 1.1.3. Hobbes' caveat here raises the interesting problem of the expectations one can reasonably hold with regard to an interlocutor's so-called "epistemic virtues." For a recent exploration of this topic, see Abrol Fairweather and Carlos Montemayor, *Knowledge, Dexterity, and Attention: A Theory of Epistemic Agency* (Cambridge: Cambridge University Press, 2017).

[39] As a possible example, John Danford explains how in the Epistle Dedicatory of *De Corpore* Hobbes "credits Copernicus with the founding of astronomy" because he took an ancient "hypothesis [...] which he did not invent" and transformed it into knowledge ('The Problem of Language in Hobbes's Political Science', 104).

consent." The "victory" at which rhetoric aims, if carried far enough, might even arrive at the kind of firm, unanimous knowledge that the *Elements* desires.[40]

The Limits of Legal Knowledge in *De Cive*

To be sure, "teaching" or propagating knowledge might be an altogether rare achievement. In *De Cive*, Hobbes contends that one "who relies 'on opinions that are already commonly received' is relying on opinions 'which for the greatest part are usually erroneous.'"[41] We must not, therefore, optimistically conclude that Hobbes sees rhetoric as an unconditionally capable method for acquiring knowledge. In the following discussion, I show how *De Cive* limits the kind of *scientia* Hobbes thinks we might arrive at through rhetoric, a method rooted in and limited by linguistic communication. Reaffirming the place of Aristotelian rhetorical thought in his discussion of civil law—but finding no place for it in divine law—Hobbes underscores how we can hope to find *scientia* of human legal affairs but not of the affairs of God.[42]

De Cive is divided into three sections, the second of which (titled *Imperium* or "Empire") turns in its final chapter to the topic of laws, both divine and civil. Contrasting the heavenly source of divine law with the constructed origins of civil law, Hobbes remarks that some people "confound Law, and Covenant, who conceive the Lawes to be nothing

[40] Taking another approach to this kinship between geometry and rhetoric, Victoria Kahn underscores how what "impressed Hobbes about geometry was the fact that it offered certain knowledge because we construct the objects of investigation ourselves," and in this methodology "Hobbes immediately saw the relevance [...] to politics" (*The Trouble with Literature*, 38). What Kahn calls in the same discussion "maker's knowledge" would serve as the aim of both geometrical proof and political persuasion, for both activities "claim that we can only truly know what we make ourselves."

[41] Skinner, *Reason and Rhetoric in the Philosophy of Hobbes*, 265. Skinner cites Hobbes' criticism of rhetorical victory at *De Cive* 10.11: Eloquence's "end (as all the Masters of Rhetorick teach us) is not truth (except by chance) but victory, and whose property is not to inform, but to allure." Compare this separation of rhetorical "victory" from the methods of logic in *Briefe* 1.3.

[42] An investigation of Hobbes' notion of truth is outside the scope of this article. For one relevant discussion, see Dorothea Krook, 'Thomas Hobbes's Doctrine of Meaning and Truth', *Philosophy*, 31:116 (1956), 3–22.

else but certain *homologēmata* (ὁμολογήματα), or forms of living, determined by the common consent of men (*communi consensu hominum*)."[43] We have already seen how the Aristotelian term *homologoumena* likely grounds (at least in part) the phrase "common opinion" in the *Briefe*, and here Hobbes similarly begins his studies of "common consent" by citing the rhetorical doctrines of his Peripatetic predecessor. After suggesting that some people conflate the notions of "law and covenant," Hobbes points to a Pseudo-Aristotelian definition of the law as "a speech limited according to the common consent (*kath' homologian*) of the City, declaring every thing that we ought to doe."[44]

As Hobbes bemoans in this discussion of civil law, however, it is an error to identify these *homologēmata*—these covenants—with laws of all kinds. Divine law, Hobbes writes in the same paragraph, does not arise from the Peripatetic *homologēmata* of human agreements but comes instead from God: "it is manifest that the Divine Lawes sprang not from the consent of men (*consensu hominum*)."[45] The reappearance of the Greek root *homolog*—in the citation of Pseudo-Aristotle and Hobbes' interest in the role of "consent" in civil laws, moreover, suggest that an investigation of civil laws bears some relationship to the rubrics of persuasion and rhetoric, while divine laws, by contrast, do not.

This division between the *homologēmata* of Aristotelian rhetoric and those divine laws that "sprang not from the consent of men" anticipates a later discussion in *De Cive* on the distinction between "knowledge" and "opinion," terms which echo Hobbes' earlier treatment of persuasion and teaching in the *Elements*. In a chapter of *De Cive*'s third section

[43] *Legem cum pacto confundunt ii, qui leges putant nihil aliud esse quam ὁμολογήματα, siue formulas vivendi, communi consensu hominum determinatas*, *De Cive* 14.2. Citations of the Latin and English versions of *De Cive* are taken from Howard Warrender, ed., *De Cive: The Latin Version* (Oxford: Clarendon Press, 1983) and Howard Warrender, ed., *De Cive: The English Version* (Oxford: Clarendon Press, 1983).

[44] *De Cive* 14.2. Here Hobbes quotes in Greek the Pseudo-Aristotelian *Rhetoric to Alexander* by Anaximenes: ὁ νόμος ἐστὶν ὡς ἁπλῶς εἰπεῖν λόγος ὡρισμένος καθ' ὁμολογίαν κοινὴν πόλεως, μηνύων πῶς δεῖ πράττειν ἕκαστα (pr.5.1). In the sixteenth century, Piero Vettori argued against the genuine Aristotelian authorship of the *Rhetoric to Alexander*, but Hobbes here seems to have cited the text as a source of Aristotle's own legal theory.

[45] *Manifestum enim est, leges Diuinas non esse ortas a consensu hominum*, *De Cive* 14.2.

on *Religio*, Hobbes returns to the topic of the sources of religious knowledge, but here he is concerned less with the particular topic of divine law, and more with the broader definitions of "thinking" and "knowing":

> Now the Propositions which we receive for truth, we alwaies grant for some reasons of our owne, and these are deriv'd either from the Proposition it selfe, or from the person propounding. They are deriv'd from the Proposition it selfe, by calling to minde what things those words which make up the Proposition doe by common consent (*communi consensu*) usually signifie: if so, then the assent which we give is called knowledge, or Science (*scire*). But if we cannot remember what is certainly understood by those words, but sometimes one thing, sometimes another seeme to be apprehended by us, then we are said to thinke (*opinari*).[46]

Hobbes again argues that our words, whose meaning we take from "common consent," determine whether our thinking avoids controversy and rises to the standard of "knowledge or science." If, however, we encounter controversy, perhaps through faulty memory where language means "sometimes one thing, sometimes another," then we do not know what is "certainly understood by those words" and "we are said to thinke," merely to opine. And crucially, while linguistic *consensus* earlier underlies rhetorical *homologēmata* in *De Cive* 14.2, here it stands as the foundation of true knowledge.

Building upon this discussion of "common consent," Hobbes looks not only to Aristotle but also to Plato to reinforce his idea from the *Elements* that scientific knowledge requires the broadest *consensus* among interlocutors. Such unanimity, however, fractures and disintegrates when "vulgar use" assigns additional meanings to words, introducing literary ambiguity and eliminating agreement:

> And to know truth is the same thing as to remember that it was made by our selves in the common use of words. Neither was it rashly, or unadvisedly said by Plato of old, that knowledge was memory. But it happens

[46] *Propositiones autem quas pro veris recipimus; concedimus semper propter aliquas rationes nostras. Eae vero derivantur vel ab ipsa propositione, vel a persona proponentis. Derivantur autem ab ipsa propositione revocando in memoriam, quibus rebus significandis, nomina ex quibus propositio conflatur communi consensu usurpantur; quod si fiat, assensus quem praebemus dicitur Scire. Si vero recordari non possimus, quid cerro per ea nomina intelligendum sit, sed modo hoc videtur, modo illud, tum dicimur opinari, De Cive* 18.4.

> sometimes, that words although they have a certaine, and defin'd signification by constitution, yet by vulgar use either to adorne, or deceive, they are so wrested from their owne significations.[47]

Hobbes later complains, moreover, that this knowledge of the truth by memory is difficult to acquire, since "there are many words which have no proper, determin'd, and every where the same signification."[48] Knowledge, thus, degrades in the presence of controversy, ambiguity, or even forgetfulness.

Hobbes' worry about the "vulgar use either to adorn or deceive" underscores that literary craft, while it may win consensus, might just as well be used to produce uncertainty. And as Hobbes laments earlier in *De Cive*, rhetoricians might strive for the goal of mere "victory," not truth—the goal of eloquence, he remarks, "(as all the Masters of Rhetorick teach us) is not truth (except by chance) but victory."[49] But his later works suggest that Hobbes also wants to recalibrate the methods of consensus-building into a literary art that lights upon the truth intentionally, not by accident, where one might achieve *scientia* of "civil laws" or *homologēmata* by winning over any and all interlocutors through the "common consent" of words. Rhetoric, at least for civil science, could be a cause of confusion as well as its best remedy.

[47] *& veritatem scire, idem quod esse eam a nobismetipsis, ipsa nominum usurpatione factam meminisse. Neque temere olim a Platone dictum est scientiam esse memoriam. Accidit autem interdum, ut voces, etsi certam & ex constituto definitam habeant significationem, usu tamen vulgari, ad ornandum vel etiam fallendum particulari studio a propriis significationibus ita divellantur*, *De Cive* 18.4. For a discussion of the links among "certain," "constitution," and "consensus" in ancient and early modern rhetorical writings, see Charles McNamara, '*Certum atque Confessum*: Lorenzo Valla on the Forensics of Certainty', *Rhetorica: A Journal of the History of Rhetoric*, 36:3 (2018), 244–68. For Hobbes' interest in memory as a source of knowledge, see also *Elements* 1.1.2: "intending not to take any principle upon trust, but only to put men in mind of what they know already, or may know by their own experience, I have to err the less."

[48] *Accidit quoque plurimas voces nullam habere propriam sive determinatam & eandem ubique significationem*, *De Cive* 18.4. Hobbes may have inserted this reference to Platonic *anamnesis* as part of his well-known turn to geometric methods. For one account of Hobbes' broader relationship to Plato, see Strauss, *Political Philosophy of Hobbes*, 138–65.

[49] *Neque est hoc hominis, sed ipsius eloquentiae vitium, cuius finis, ut magistri rhetoricae omnes docent, non veritas est, nisi per accidens, sed victoria*, *De Cive* 10.11.

Conclusion

In these later scientific works—*Elements* and *De Cive*—Hobbes emphasizes how controversy itself is a sign of imperfect forms of knowledge. These disagreements allow one only to "think" or "opine" but not to "know"; to "persuade" but not to "teach." But as we first noticed in the *Briefe*, Aristotelian rhetoric is more than a matter of shortening one's proofs. It is, fundamentally, a practice that builds upon common opinions and aims to make them more common—to generate consensus and propagate conviction. Or in the words of the author of the *Briefe*, to arrive at victory. This kind of rhetorical victory, it turns out, is not unrelated to the discovery and acquisition of Hobbes' *scientia civilis*. As *De Cive* shows, Hobbesian *scientia* (as opposed to mere opinion) is defined by its lack of controversy, when the common consent of words extends to all interlocutors. These verbal agreements—*homologoumena* or *homologēmata*, literally "things said together"—underlie civil laws and the *Briefe*'s rhetorical syllogisms alike.

The later works of Hobbes, then, as much as we may see them as anti-rhetorical, nevertheless associate legal knowledge with Aristotelian rhetorical concepts. *Scientia civilis* takes its inspiration not simply from the logical cogency of Euclid but also from the *homologoumena* of Aristotle, for resolving controversy can be achieved either through a mathematician's demonstrative proof or an orator's literary speech. By eliminating conflict, Hobbes suggests, we might transform our various opinions into one settled fact—we simply need common opinions to become the commonest knowledge. This understanding of his "civil science," moreover, should urge us to reconsider Hobbes' possible role in producing an abbreviated text on Aristotelian strategies for achieving argumentative "victory." While I do not claim to have settled once and for all the authorship of the *Briefe* or to have arrived at some kind of unanimously understood knowledge of its place in Hobbesian thought, I hope at least to have persuaded some readers that a summary of Aristotelian rhetorical methods is rather at home alongside the *Elements of Law* and *De Cive*. These texts, themselves in agreement on the role of *homologoumena* in grounding civil science, all seem to speak with one voice.

PART IV

Play and Pleasure

CHAPTER 8

Doublings: Comedy, Office, Law

Peter Goodrich

Law is classically a melancholic science. It identifies most with the figure of a weeping Heraclitus, and endeavours at least to govern, if not to stop, the flux and fugacity of time. The saturnine gravitas of the juridical is leavened with the portent of posterity, the *longue durée* of the legal forms and formulae which for common lawyers are the symbolæographics of the art. The law also, however, collapses under the weight of its collection and the scale of its monuments. The permanence at which its repetitious modalities aim is, if we allow the observation, simultaneously structural and ridiculous, two-faced, bifurcated. The more sombre and Heraclitic the ceremonies, the greater the formality and weight of juridical enunciation, and the more evident the phantasmatic qualities of the rites. The sacral is also visibly satirical of everyday life, implicitly parodic in its hierophantic gestures, and in its saturnine modality. It can be seen as a mood, a mask of emotions, a cloak for laughter and the absurd, which follow upon the coattails of judicial costumes and their sumptuary elevations. The jurist is present only in his mask, his *momon* in early French diction

P. Goodrich (✉)
Cardozo School of Law, New York, NY, USA
e-mail: goodrich@yu.edu

S. Mukherji and D. Roberts (eds.), *Literature and the Legal Imaginary*, Crossroads of Knowledge in Early Modern Literature 4,
https://doi.org/10.1007/978-3-031-74093-0_8

being the visage that has to be worn to play the game of law, with all that such implies by way of duplications.[1] For law, the stage is set precisely by an inaugural doubling, a bipolarity of affect, a parting of conjoint ways that offers not simply a choice but the equiparation of ritual and risible; *scintillae iuris* play upon law as *au jus*, a rule and a culinary concoction, just as the sages of the early modern tradition tottered in mood between *melancholia juridica* and *ius ridiculus*.[2]

There is a doubling—I am at it already—that unsettles the saturnine complacency of meaning by altering the sense and the affect of its reference. Doubling dissipates, if only momentarily—a thought, a glimpse—the certainty of designation and the univocality of ostentation. Comedy, in this play of ambiguity, threatens an eruption of laughter, a bursting out from ennui, and a shake-up of familiarity. This, however unpopular it may be with agelasts, cachinnataphobes, risists, ridists, and the anti-jocastic in their entirety, is my theme. Comedy, humour and, of course, also theatre, crack things up, shake both diaphragm and wit, change physical equilibrium, bend the realist nose, and generate a morphosis, a transport in how we know. It is the titular character, specifically Ambidexter Ignoramus, who is shown to utter the words '*currat lex*' (the law runs its course), as he is presented in his study, surrounded by his law books and manuscripts, on the frontispiece illustration of George Ruggle's *Ignoramus* (first performed 1615, first published 1630), an academic farce in Latin on common-law lawyers and legal jargon. This is a point of incisive satire that was aimed, four hundred years ago, at the fog-bound wits of Cambridge University, and seems as good a place as

[1] Gilles d'Aurigny, *Le Cinquante deuxiesme arrest d'amour, avec ses ordonnances sur le fait des masques* ([Paris]: Jean Cheradame, 1528), sig. b2^{r} (unpaginated): "Et n'entend-on par ce les priver d'aller en mommon." Frédéric Godefroy, *Lexique de l'ancien Français* (Paris: Champion, 2000), s.v. momon. Thanks to Valérie Hayaert for the first reference. Momon also referenced pleasure and specifically dice playing, a world of hedonistic histrionics and performance. For elaboration in relation to the dialogues of Etienne Forcadel, *Sphaera legalis* (1549), see the excellent and exhaustive Anne Teissier-Ensminger, *Fabuleuse juridicité. Sur la littérarisation des genres juridiques* (Paris: Classiques Garnier, 2015), 401 et seq.

[2] Charles Darling borrows from Horace – *est operae pretium duplicis pernoscere juris naturam*, see *Scintillae Juris* (London: Davis and Sons, 1879), preface (unpaginated). *Sensus legis ridiculus* is taken from the introduction to Antonio de Nebrija, [no diphthong—*Aenigmata*] *Ænigmata iuris civilis* ([Salamanca]: [Juan de Porras], 1506); reproduced in 'Ex observationibus […] in libros iuris civilis', in *Vocabularium utriusque iuris* (Venice: Zalterium, 1612), fol. 392^{v}.

any to start.[3] The lawyers, for Ruggle, were a jumped-up class, a babblative crowd whose air of Latinity and esoteric law French was a cover for nebulous arguments and self-interested practices. The Inns of Court were a site of *rabulae forenses* or a form of public raving: Quixotic figures tilting at linguistic windmills on the plains of juridical parchment.

In establishing the early modern law of comedic knowledge, the saturnalian doubling of law, both in the juxtaposition of word and image, and in the complementary antinomy of *gravitas* and *levitas*, the jurist Andreas Alciatus proposes the classical form of the emblem in his groundbreaking *Emblematum liber* (1531). A festive invention, a saturnalian device introduced by his publisher, the visual emblem was the doubling, though never merely a duplication, of law in an image. The maxims that the emblemata realized in the form of the woodcut were manifestations of legal and other theological, moral, and political norms that were enacted in their figurative portrayal. The visualization of *ratio scripta* was comedic both in the sense of being theatrical and in being humorous. The emblem took the law from the passive page, the *litera mortua* of scriptural decree, and put it into life as an animated propaedeutic and active expression of oikonomic governance. Doubling, thus, actively instigates a trajectory and argument which in the case of the *emblemata* sought to drag legality from its sepulchral and solemn hideouts into view and into life. The encounter is staged most directly by the emblem *In vitam humanam*, as it appears in the 1536 edition (sig. N7^{v}) (Fig. 8.1).

The two figures, Democritus on the right, in place of honour, and Heraclitus on the left, *sinistra*, in second place, are set opposite each other. Democritus, he whom Robert Burton has reciting to pillars and

[3] George Ruggle [1630] (London: Payne, 1787)—mistakenly called 'R. Ruggles' in Robert Codrington in his 1662 translation of Ruggle's Latin play, and by Edward Ravenscroft in his 1678 translation. The Latin play saw at least ten editions between 1630 and 1787. The 1630 edition (London: T.H., 1630) has a frontispiece showing the figure of Ignoramus issuing, in a banderole, the words 'Currat Lex'. The fool, jester, or clown, it is implied, will weigh the law in novel forms. Ignoramus (literally, we know not), a proper name invented by Ruggle, is hard to translate because of the pun on Petrus Ramus and his *Logike*, but also because the term has an early modern juristic meaning, being written on any Bill of Prosecution that was deemed inadequate and implies a suspension of law, meaning that the fool views less law as the best approach to juristic ills. See Thomas Blount, *Glossographia* (London: Thomas Newcombe, 1656), s.v. *ignoramus*—explaining that when an Inquest judged evidence of a crime too weak or defective for a Presentment (an indictment) then it inscribed ignoramus upon the Bill of Attaint and this forever stopped further pleading.

Fig. 8.1 *In vitam humanam*, from Andrea Alciato, *Livret des emblemes* (1536) (With permission of the University of Glasgow Archives and Special Collections)

declaiming to trees for want of auditors, is here the more active, gesticulating, holding his head, adorned with something close to a clown's hat.[4] The hands raised to the head are chironomic indigitations of exuberance and bemusement at the surreal state of the world. Heraclitus, by contrast, is supine, stooped, and limp, with downcast eyes, his left hand interestingly making the chirosophical gesture of closure or ending, an inverted exordium or retraction which John Bulwer notes as *suspicionem et odium*

[4] Robert Burton, *The Anatomy of Melancholy* [1638] (New York: Tudor Publishing Company, 1938), 16: "To this end I write, like them, saith Lucius, that recite to trees, and declaim to pillars, for want of auditors ...".

noto.[5] The refusal to give the hand, the fingers making an uninviting claw, 'is a sign of enmity' to world and laughter alike. The antinomy is important, on the spectrum one might say, because of the propensity to suppress one element and elevate the other in the juxtaposition. It can be seen even more clearly in a later version of the same emblem from 1584 in which Heraclitus is not only looking down and away from the exuberant Democritus but also has his fingers stopping up his ears, while his books fall to the ground.[6] Laughter seems to impugn both the sagacity and the seriousness of sorrow and has to be held at bay (Fig. 8.2).

The antipathy is to the viscera of ludic affect, to the feeling body as an active corporeality, and to the doubling that it threatens. Hostility to humour in the form of the insignificance attributed to *rem levem* or light-hearted things dates back, of course, at least to Roman law and the ban on jokes recorded in the introduction to the *Digest*, and indeed the interdiction of any commentary on the laws.[7] Theatre was prohibited and, along with it, *artem ludicram*, games, and trials by combat were all subject to strict administrative governance that both limited access and exiled such activities to *dies nec fasti*, or non-law days. I will not repeat that history here, but it is the frame through which I will apprehend and view the visual comedy of doubling and its resistance to dismissal. It is the parity of the dual figures, the equality of affects and dispositions, the equivalence of differences that is most distinctive and extreme. A further example can be taken from Johann Theodor de Bry's 1627 emblem book, *Proscenium vitæ humanæ* (Fig. 8.3).[8] The image of Democritus and Heraclitus shows the duo, each of identical height and features, standing in exactly parallel dispositions, although while Heraclitus weeps and avoids the world, Democritus' left hand reaches out and almost touches the crucifex globe. The motto is explicitly to the point that the pair are of

[5] John Bulwer, *Chirologia or the Naturall Language of the Hand composed of the speaking motions, and discoursing gestures thereof. Whereunto is added Chironomia: or, the Art of Manuall Rhetoricke* (1656), 154 (fig. v).

[6] Andrea Alciato, *Emblemata* (Paris: Richer, 1584), cli.

[7] *The Digest of Justinian*, ed. Theodor Mommsen, Paul Krueger, and Alan Watson, trans. Alan Watson (Philadelphia: University of Pennsylvania Press, 1985). For making jokes a crime (*iniuria est ludos exercere*), see pp. liii–liv; for the prohibition (in *De Conceptione digestorum*) of commentaries and interpretations of the written law, see pp. xlvii–xlviii.

[8] Johann Theodor de Bry, *Proscenium vitæ humanæ sive emblematum secularium* (Frankfurt: Wilhelm Fitzer, 1627).

Fig. 8.2 *In vitam humanam*, from Andrea Alciato, *Emblemata* (1584) (With permission of the University of Glasgow Archives and Special Collections)

equal dignity and, in its early modern meaning, office. They are to be addressed together and, as the accompanying verse has it, *par est sapientia utrique* (each part is equally wise). This two-faced or twofold quality of the image is coda and key to the diversionary, subversive, and potentially upending or transformative character of the comedic. Law, to be blunt, is to all appearances no friend to comedy and its *usus modernus* enjoys an active forgetting of this particular *duplicem sententiam* and, along with it, of Horace's fine protocol of juristic invention- that it is necessary to learn law at least twice, to examine it multiple times (*duplicis pernoscere juris naturam*).[9] Soup and law, *au jus* and *jus non scripta*, the trackless path of decisions, are, equally, concoctions from plural sources, cooked up, one could say of common law, by Sir Edward Coke. For the jurist the reference is to *duplex jus* as the estimable Judge Darling pronounces in the opening to his *Scintillae iuris*,[10] and thereby evidences both the persistence and the liminal, minor and marginal character of what I will term *officium ludicræ*—the office of play and of humouring the norm. There is within the tradition, as Del Mar extrapolates elegantly in this volume, a lengthy traversal of ludic themes, and learning games, as well as revels and moots that play the law. It could be argued that the great mythic source of common law, *tempus ex mente* or time out of mind, is in fact, *mens cum affectu,* wisdom with emotion, or the affective reasoning of justice and casuistic decision.[11]

Lost in the annals of common law, to take one example, there is the early modern English jurist John Selden's history of the insular jurisdiction under the title *Jani Anglorum facies altera* (1610), the multiple faces or many doublings of the English Janus. The Latin of the title tells us immediately that this sense of two-facedness, of disparate directions, is enfolded in the European tradition and mirrors the civilian themes of *ius commune*. Whether applauded or impugned, whether scoffed at or embraced, the fickleness of the fundamental, the levity of lawyering, *serio-ludere*, is close to the origin of the early modern sagaciousness of common law as a tradition that self-consciously utilized theatre, playbook, and staging of scenes to persuade the populace of the verity of the verdict and the commonality of common law. As a tradition explicitly tied to the *lex terrae*, to the itinerant and ambulant jurisprudence of the earth, it is the feet of the English Janus which should be our first object, whose proper representation could indeed be taken from a comedic civilian depiction of *ius commune* in Jacobus Bornitius' *Emblematum Ethico-Politicorum*.[12]

[9] Horace, *Satires*, Loeb Classical Library, trans. H. Rushton Fairclough (Cambridge, MA: Harvard University Press, 1926), Book 2, Ode 4.

[10] Darling, *Scintillae Juris*, 7.

[11] A theme Del Mar also pursues in 'Emotion Experiments in Legal Thought', *Critical Analysis of Law*, 5:2 (2018), 178–195. For an expansive exploration of the elements of the theatrical, see Julie Stone Peters, *Law as Performance* (Oxford: Oxford University Press, 2022).

[12] Jacobus Bornitius, *Emblematum Ethico-Politicorum* (Heidelberg: Bourgeat, 1664), emblem 45 (sig. M1^{r}).

Fig. 8.3 *Democritus et Heracletus*, from Johann Theodor de Bry, *Proscenium vitæ humanæ* (1627) (Courtesy of Herzog August Bibliothek)

A quill held between the toes, an inkpot beside a page, inscribes for the armless legal figure. The comic *sententiae* and emblems that flourished in the early modern era form the unacknowledged office of multiplying what Sir Edward Coke, chef, cook and part-time comedian of common law, practised artfully as the proliferation of sesquipedalian meanings, and the reasoning of revels (Fig. 8.4). These are the early form and advocacy of what Watt, in this volume, skillfully extrapolates in terms of rainbow meanings from the more recent legal philosophy of the unjustly overlooked or insouciantly forgotten Owen Barfield. This reference, and emblematic image, is to comedy that walks, that writes, that juggles the quill, and dances on the page. Comedy, as in the jurisliterary figure of the *stultifera navis*, is marked, as Foucault notably traces, by movement, the winds of chance, the favours of *Fortuna*.[13]

Serio-ludere was from early on a foolosophical tradition and practice, changing, multiplying, enfolding meanings so as to achieve that morphosis which, like laughter, transforms the collective body that is termed thought. It is *duplex ius*, an act of doubling which I will pick up again in the well-known figure of Sebastian Brant's clown blindfolding *Justitia* as a woodcut accompanying the satirical excoriation of lawyers in *The Ship of Fools*.[14] The figure is much commented on, so I will briefly extract the pertinent parameters of the comedic. *Justitia* is in her proper form, sword pointing upward and to the right, 'dexter chief', while her left hand holds the scales in perfect equipoise. Her fingers, index and thumb, clasp the balance in the indigitated mode of suspension without intervention, as Valérie Hayaert has recently described and meticulously detailed.[15] *Justitia* is not influencing the proper measure. Behind her, surprisingly, is the figure of the clown wearing a foolosophical cap with bells, a reminder perhaps of things human but also a doubling, a second figure, lips pursed, a lyre behind him and, with a proleptic reference to

[13] Michel Foucault, *History of Madness* (London: Routledge, 2006 edn): "but there was more: water brought its own dark symbolic charge, carrying away, but purifying too. Navigation brought man face to face with the uncertainty of destiny." Erasmus, *In Praise of Folly*, also pursues this dance of madness, the folly in the façade of reason.

[14] Sebastian Brant, *The Ship of Fools*, trans. William Gillis [1494] (London: Folio Society, 1971).

[15] Valérie Hayaert, 'Lady Justice's Fingers: Gesture and Allegory', in Hayaert, *Lady Justice: An Anatomy of Allegory* (Edinburgh: Edinburgh University Press, 2023).

Fig. 8.4 *Consuetudo est altera natura*, from Jacobus Bornitius, *Emblemata ethico-politica* (1664) (Hathi Trust, public domain)

Rabelais no doubt, two caltrops (i.e. sharp prongs or spikes sticking up to impede attackers) on the floor to his side.[16]

Two scales of justice, two caltrops, two figures bound together by their differences. The fool is standing, justice is seated; she is in the feminine, the fool is in all likelihood in the masculine; she wears a crown, he wears a dunce's cap; she is decorated with arms and armed with the law of balance, he moves to the music of chance and the flow of fortune.

[16] I am aware that the poem depicts these as 'heckles', combs used for processing wool or flax, but these have also a secondary meaning that we inherit in 'to heckle' and 'hecklers', one who throws barbs or speaks ill of others. Visually, however, the point is that the upturned heckles are caltrops, spikes to wound any who endeavour to approach. My thanks to Valérie Hayaert for clarifying this point by disagreeing with me.

She is serious and he is ludic. Enough, however, of doubling. It is their proximity and jointure that is significant, their double face. The fool is dressing *Justitia*, playing a sumptuary role and adding to her habit with the comedy of a blindfold. The point is that the fool, the mortal, *in vitam humanam*, is dressing the sovereign figure of fairness, protecting her with further clothes, and adding a mask, while on the floor caltrops protect the enthroned figure. Justice is being protected by the human, the fool, and while the clown may appear secondary, he is necessary and adds the complement of comedy, and the harmony of the musical, to the awe and especially the effect of justice. To the necessity of protection and the complementarity of these symbolically plural figures, we can add the foundational character of comedy, of the fundamental place of the fool as the mark of time and flow of *Fortuna* and of the Fates. The comedic figure reminds justice of law, of the temporal in the spiritual and in essence also plays the role of Nietzsche's monkey holding the coat tails of the human. The blindfold is here a humorous form of mask and one that suggests strongly the theatrical quality of the comedic, of the image and of its referent. If *Justitia* is divine, and represents an unbounded totality, law is human and constrained and appears here in the image of the fool.

The doublings could be extended but text should give precedence to images, it should give way to the power of symbols. So, allow me another example from later in the tradition, a satire of exquisite proportions, Johann Flitner's 1620 Latin adaptation of the sixteenth-century German satirical poet Thomas Murner's *Die Schelmenzunft* (1512) in the form of an emblem book, entitled *Nebulo Nebulonum* (or, A Fog of Frauds).[17] The blindfold attributed to our sartorial fool is a mask, a sign of play which signals the theatrical character of all of the temporal domains of knowledge, and particularly of theology and law, combined in the figure of justice. Flitner is etymologically a nebulosity away from *flitter*, meaning bangle, glitter, décor and from which the English 'to flit' derives. Flitner flits, he doubles and doubles again, the nebulous squared, fog thickened, in his satirical images which begin with the elaborate title page (Fig. 8.5). *In ludo veritas*, many a truth in jest, the title suggests, and on either side of the inscribed tableau the Roman divinities *Fraus* and *Nequitia*. Just as the flitter's work is 'jocoserious', ludically lawful, the divinities depicted are suitably enigmatic. *Fraus* is most immediately

[17] Johann Flitner, *Nebulo nebulonum; hoc est, iocoseria modernæ nequitiæ censura* (Frankfurt: Jacob de Zetter, 1620).

fraud but in the ambivalent sense that any image is *veritas falsa*, both the objective appearance, the reality of what is seen and, simultaneously, the unhappy necessity of not being what it represents. It is in this sense that *Fraus* is also Mercury's helper, a Hermes or hermeneut, a masker who helps to transmit the messages of our various sovereigns and laws, represented in part by the dog, a figure of loyalty and law, at her feet. *Fraus* is thus shown as a theatrical figure, holding a mask, about to put on her *persona* for the specific performance of the satire of scoundrels, fraudsters, defilers, drifters, and other pessimists of the polity.

Nequitia, at the other end of the tableau, is at one level a figure of lewdness, inebriation, and the dissolute, standing barely clothed, a hound at her side devouring a Paschal lamb. She is also, however, a figure of levity and lightness, corporeal sensibilities, earthly love, and visceral affects. The contrast is between an actress who is selling wares, playing her part, persuading and purveying, and the less self-conscious but no less theatrical dame iniquity, she of hidden motives and self-interested pursuit of earthly pleasures. Neither is in any singular sense a figure of evil or mere wantonness but the striking feature of the frontispiece is that it presents a defence of the theatrical, and is clearly in favour of the comedic. Our righthand divinity is doffing her mask, confessing her play, admitting that she too, authorial figure, symbol of the plenitude of meaning, is a thespian, a dramatist commenting upon the comedy of all social roles and legal acts. It is not masks or maskers that are to be criticized; it is, rather, the nebulous uses to which they are put that are the object of Flitner's often hilarious critique.

There is no escape from comedy, no *exeunt* of the social, just the choice of the mask that one will wear, the role to be played, the outcome sought. Thus Guillaume de la Perrière, the famous emblematist of the French Renaissance, presents masks as choices, as *dramatis personae* to elect from and between, in his early work, *Le Thëatre des bons engins* (the first vernacular emblem book). *Fraus* is here the interpreter, a multiple figure wearing, I will inopinately opine, the top right of Perrière's quadruple choices of fairly ordinary masks, unnecessary to reproduce here.[18] The accompanying verse, blankly translated, is quite explicit:

[18] Guillaume Perrière, *Le Thëatre des bons engins* (Toulouse: Janot, 1540), emblem VI (sig. B3^{v}).

Fig. 8.5 Title page, from Johann Flitner, *Nebulo nebulonum* (1620) (Hathi Trust, public domain)

> There are none that do not at present use a mask. Everyone wishes to play and paint their face. All desire to portray themselves under the guise of beauty and dulcet language, making it a marvel that this power is not everywhere abused. For each of us will paint our face and fabricate its use.[19]

Thomas Combe in his early seventeenth-century translation of Perrière is more positive, ending his versification as follows:

> Now be they used in earnest of the best,
> And of such maskers there abound such store,
> That you shall find but few in any place,
> That carry not sometime a double face.[20]

Certainly, the mask can betray or conceal, and it can be fearsome as well as comic, but it is the social, who we are and the part we play as common legal subjects, as political beings that cannot go without *personae*, the legal forms of social being and recognition. The emblem in this respect is always a representation of figures of law, a symbolæographic exercise in which the game of the social is evidenced as precisely that, a theatrical skrim upon which an impermanent being sketches the comedy of its days. The emblem is in this sense an exercise in self-recognition, the comedic—both enacted and humorous—image of social forms. And who can resist laughing? The Dutch satirist Jacob Cats shows a divine hand holding a mask in mid-air to the terror of children, pre-legal beings who scamper away (Fig. 8.6). The interesting feature here is that there is nothing behind the mask, it is all and only *frons*, or front without residue or remainder. That is the joke, in the sense that the children run in fear from a façade—they have failed to insist on seeing what is behind, the rear of this *persona* and in a comedic sense the moon or ass that has made asses of them.[21] They are fools fooled by the foolosophical façade of an impermanent appearance. At the same time, however, Cats cites Seneca to the effect that 'we know that everything is of an equal levity' and that we

[19] Ibid., emblem VI (sig. B4^{r}).

[20] Thomas Combe, *The Theatre of Fine Devices* (London: Field, 1614), emblem VI (sig. B1^{r}).

[21] Jacob Cats with the opening motto *Deus nobis hæc otia fecit* (Our Lord devised these quips) on the title page of his *Silenus Aclibiadis, sive Proteus, vitæ humanæ ideam* (Middelburg: Iohannis Hellenij, 1618).

wear diverse faces, making exteriority a mutable and multiple habiliment of painted cloth and visage.

Returning to Flitner's frontispiece of *Fraus* we can note that here the mask is off, and the comedy of performance is made visible, the ambiguity of face and figure alike displayed. This doubling of the visage, *frons* and frontispiece, and of *Fraus* and *Nequitia* too, can leave us in no doubt as to the mutability of face and *facies altera* or backface, the noseless cheeks. Comedy is also comic because it shows what is hidden, it acts out the double face, and in doing so plays with the variability and plasticity of appearances. To know the mask is to see things as they are and Flitner, translating Murner's text into Latin, rails against the inconstancy of the evil doer, the fraudster and tortfeasor: 'And he's treacherous, like a chameleon, going from white face (*facias*) to black, and from black to pitch'.[22] It is not fraud to wear a mask, though it is evil to change *persona* so as to escape recognition. It is rather that we are bound to occupy our *persona*, to be true to our face, or as Flitner has it, we should call a pig a pig, evil evil, and the worthless worthless. The fraudster has neither mask nor face, lacks singularity of vizard, and so also individuation, and thus is invisible, a non-referent, without designation or meaningful manifestation.

Starting with a critique of theology, a quacking priest is portrayed holding a duck, an unusual mask, with at least a double meaning (Fig. 8.7). Birds, including ducks, are signs of freedom, of the spirit in flight and bird catchers are ridiculed as miserable tellurian tykes. The preacher is acting out the opposite of any proper role of interior insight and celestial conusance. Constraining liberty of speculation, this miscreant bird-catcher is also preaching in cerulean fashion, like a duck, quacking in this version of the emblem to open space, without auditors, melancholically spreading hot air abroad. The castigation is a strong one, dismissing the ignorant, contentious, and vapid preachers, the peddlers of insignificance, as rabid dogs (*rabidi canes*) running amok in the polity, 'filling the temples, the schools, the courts, the public sphere, with tumult and

[22] Flitner, *Nebulo*, sig. [*3]^{v} ('Ad Momum'): "Subdolique Chamæleontis inftar / Ex albo facias nigrum colore / Cum tamen pice nigrior nigella". Note the percipient dedication to Momum, to masks and play.

INVERTE, ET AVERTES. 53

XXVI.

Plutarch, in Moralib.

V*T pueris cum terrentur perſonis, damus eas in manus, & verſatas oſtendimus inanes, vt diſcant non timere; ita conveniet adhibitâ ratione res ſpecie terrificas excutere, vt, cum viderimus non eſſe quod apparet, contemnamus.*

Sen. de Tranq. S*Ciamus omnia æquè levia eſſe, extrinſecus diverſas facies habentia, introrſus pariter vana.*

G 3 *Ontcleên,*

Fig. 8.6 *Inverte, et avertes*, from Jacob Cats, *Silenus Alcibiadis* (1620) (Hathi Trust, public domain)

division, and vexing the kingdom'.[23] These are not, he continues, proselytizers of the sacred, but wolves who wreak havoc upon the populus and desire only the break-up of community. The mask, in other words, is the sign of community, of social cohesion, and belonging, the first *insignum* of place and role. To borrow from Horace's definition, he should be *emunctæ naris*, or of clean and straight nose.[24] A duck's bill is not an adequate proboscis and yet it is for the sake of the bill that the lawyer bends their nose whichever way the wind blows in the 1634 edition of *Nebulo nebulonum* (Fig. 8.8).

Ius cereum or law's wax nose, Flitner's chameleon conk, bending for money, is the second object of the treatise's scourge of scoundrels. The lawyer twists, distorts, rolls, and reformulates as his fees dictate. The nose twitches like that of another symbol of nefarious multiplication and nebulous persuasion, *cuniculus*, the rabbit, but by etymological extension *cunnus*, *cuniculus* and *cunnilingus*, to add the obvious sexual sense of play, the double of doubling, to the sniffing of the opening purse that the lawyer portends. To give you a further sense of the satirical screed of bawling and rambling lawyers, 'they are ministers of fraud (*ministrant fraudibus*)' and they love to '[t]wist the tapper of the law, twitch, and turn it around [and] gloss Digest, Decretals, Codex, Novella, law, rubric, and textbook; and then soon go over and unwind them again a second time, and a third time'.[25] In a similar vein:

> [the advocate] invents the laws and glosses, whatever laws there are get forged and refashioned; or the victim's testimony strays evasively. Or they fraudulently postpone proceedings, so they have more [time to] craft perversions of the law. Glosses, thus, establish the authority to subvert the law's meaning and the intention of a legislator. Here are the most important skills of an advocate: cry loudly, be audacious, and in litigation, secretly devour the prey.[26]

[23] Flitner, *Nebulo nebulonum*, 13: "vexant regna, solicitant bella, diruunt ecclesias, rabidi canes, non sacri præcones, non homines, sed lupi …"

[24] Horace, *Satires* I.4. Antonio de Jorio, *Gesture in Naples and Gesture in Classical Antiquity* [1832] (Indiana University Press: Bloomington, 2000) at 96 makes the same point.

[25] Flitner, *Nebulo nebulonum*, 16 (Ode III): "Horum ministrant fraudibus / Digesta, Decretalia, / Codex, Novellæ, Rubrica, Dein glossa, lex, paragraphus / Libellus atque …"

[26] Flitner, *Nebulo nebulonum*, 25.

Fig. 8.7 *Hic de cæruleis prædicat anatibus*, from Johann Flitner, *Nebulo nebulonum* (1664) (Hathi Trust, public domain)

Pretending to noble birth, the lawyers 'have the understanding of stones, the judgement of wood, the forgiveness of iron, the friendship of panthers, the pride of bulls, and the ravenous voracity of dissolute minotaurs'.[27] The advocate is hiding his role as a player, the theatre of the *leges actiones*, behind the opaque and occlusive folds of the text and the comedy of the chameleon, a mask that is no more than a veil of recondite words, the argot of the babblative art. My interest is in the pre- and post-textual aspects of the critique, the other facet of the image, which is that

[27] Flitner, *Nebulo nebulonum*, 23–24: "in quæstionibus statuæ, ad intelligendum saxei, ad iudicandum lignei, ad ignofcendum ferrei, ad amicitias pardi, ad facetias urfi, ad fallendum vulpes, ad superbiendum tauri, ad consumendum minotauri."

Fig. 8.8 *Hic garriendo literas perforat*, from Johann Flitner, *Nebulo nebulonum* (1634) (Courtesy of Herzog August Bibliothek)

the lawyer has turned his pliable proboscis away from the perforations of the text.

The drive through, beyond and away from the text and the casuistic cavillations of legal hermeneutics, the call to life, laughter, and action that jettisons the dead letters and desiccated parchment of law, finds diverse avenues of exploration. The risible qualities of the *ars bablativa*, and the unnecessary restraints of the archaic texts, the rote and rituals of legal instruments, are even more evident in the earlier depiction of the flexiphilic forensic orator which first appeared in the 1620 edition of *Nebulo* (Fig. 8.9). His head among the *nebulæ*, the lawyer is holding a text that is not simply perforated but disintegrating, tearing asunder. Moving forward, the rambling and nonsensical advocate appears to be looking through the *litera*, passing beyond, unconstrained or unconcerned with the inscriptions as anything other than suggestions for a plurality and enfolding of actions. This is peripatetic imposture, to borrow from Flitner, but it is also visibly a break-out from the prison house of the text, a drive from *litera mortua* to *anima lex*. The advocate is portrayed in nature, outside the city, external to the social, reminding us again of Horace's dictum that the law of nature is not *simplex*, but *duplex*. This is most obviously evident not only in the complicated fact of the image as a signification in its own right, but also in the active quality of the depiction, indicative as it is of the triplex stages of the theatre of law and its trinitarian jurisdictions of divinity, nature and temporality. Comedy takes to the stage, it acts and enacts and in the performance doubles and redoubles, showing the theatre of justice and law to be a play of masks and affects, *ludicra seriis miscere*, as Ernst Curtius reminds us.[28] Central to this shift is the transition from text to image, from linear to depicted which is most apparent in the stride of the flexiloquatious advocate looking through and beyond the page to the image of nature and its invisible tellurian law. The point is that the comedy activates, the image moves and transforms. The comedy that in common law terms duplicates and reduplicates is both serious and theatrical, playing as it does upon the enacted character of law, its human qualities, its aspirations to justice. The key lies in the visual depiction breaking into the text so as to portray an image breaking out of the text. The figurative form, the portrayal of the lawyer reading a dissolving text, looking through the page, is a call to action, an incitation

[28] Ernst Curtius, *European Literature and the Latin Middle Ages* (London: Routledge, 1979), 429.

to move beyond the deadening scriptural instrument, to leave the book of black letters, and join the dominion of images, the realm of the living, the doubling of the text in the materiality of its referent. This is the moment of invention, of image as imagination, the instance of engendering and entering both nature and the *socius*. It is relevant to note here that the image is a gendered concept, then and now, and for our purposes we can understand it best as a development from the *querelle des femmes* and nascent affect theory. The *ius imaginum* is the law of persons, of *personae*, masks, and masquers and comedically enough it is also the lure and allure of the feminine, intimating, as Hayaert puts it, the 'enticement' of justice as a woman.[29]

Let us look at an engraving from 1534 by an anonymous German artist, 'H.C.' (Fig. 8.10). *Justitia* and *Fortuna* are joined in a single figure, both humanising and eroticizing the virtues. Justice stands atop a rolling globe, Fortuna's wheel, and holds in her right hand the sword and scales, while in her left she clings to the sails that move her at the whim of the winds of chance. The depiction fuses the symbolic attributes of *Justitia* and *Fortuna* and in keeping with Brandt's earlier and more direct portrayal, the artist shows the risks of judgement: that the human and temporal are the media of the fool, and that the mode of the comedian always plays a part and has its place in the practice of law. More than that, however, there is the striking physicality of *Iustitia*, the scantily veiled breasts, the muscular thighs and calves. She is in part the imposing figure of justice, and in part, though better clad than in most emblems, the naked form of *Fortuna*. There is something strongly sensual in the depiction, an eroticism that mixes awe and attraction, that motivates the image of the flesh, paradoxically and therefore comically, to make certain that the carnal and amative quality of justice, the feminine in the *formulae*, is not forgotten.

The theme is too vast artistically and emblematically intricate to take up in detail, but some examples can provide an opening. De Bry, again in his remarkable *Proscenium vitæ humanæ*, starts with an emblem of *Iudicium Extremum* in which Moses born aloft on clouds, naked from the waist upward, dispenses judgements which angels and devils enforce upon a tremulous populace below. That is the visual precursor to the emblem

[29] Valérie Hayaert, 'In the Orbit of Lady Justice', in Samuel Mareel, ed., *Call for Justice: Art and Law in the Low Countries 1450–1650* (Antwerp: Hannibal, 2018), 23–39 (23).

16 NEBVL. NEBVLON.

Hic garriendo literas perforat.

Capicius, Calcaneus,
Zuccardus & Giphanius
Donellus atque Boßius,
Capolla, Farinacius,
Connanus atque Accursius,
Corasius, Costalius,

Cra

ODA III. 17

Crauetta, Couarruuias,
Forcatulus, Marsilius,
Maranta, Natta, Mantica,
Mornæus atq; Mozzius,
Mudæus & Muscornius,
Pagninus, Oldendorpius,
Pinellus atq; Scipio,
Sichardus & Sigonius,
Negusantius, Sonsbecius,
Et quis retexat singulos?
Contentiosa millies
Vocantur in certamina,
Tot sensa, quot Capitolia:
Tot iura, quot volumina.
Affirmat hoc Corasius:
Idem negat Costalius.
Idem Maranta comprobat:
Idem Maranta reprobat.
Non contimere me queo,
Quin quid noui recenseam,
Quod forte nuper accidit.
Gnatum educabat rusticus,
Quem liberalioribus
Fors manciparat artibus.
Hic cum progreßu temporis
In iure sic profecerat,
Vt iuris vtriuslibet
Doctor creatus publice
Laudem referret maximam.
Noui parentes gaudii

B Hic

Fig. 8.9 *Hic garriendo literas perforat,* from Johann Flitner, *Nebulo nebulonum* (1664) (Hathi Trust, public domain)

Iustitiæ languor in which an indomitable horse with a globe on its head is shown bucking *Iustitia* off its back (Fig. 8.11).[30] Justice herself is leaning back in disarray, about to be thrown to the ground, seemingly off the edge of a cliff. The chaos of human life, the ebb and flow of foolishness, and the insanity of the world, all combine to toss the large and imposing, all too physical figure off her transport in a humorously undignified way, scales flying, sword dropping, mouth open: 'the world', the verse ends, 'does not accept the bonds of justice and law'. By the same token, however, this very visceral *Iustitia* joins the world and in doing so

[30] De Bry, *Proscenium vitæ humanæ*, 10—*Non recipit mundus vincula Iustitia.*

Fig. 8.10 *Allegory of Fortuna and Justitia*, Anonymous (1534) (Courtesy of the Metropolitan Museum of Art, public domain)

provides an antidote to the *hieros* and hierarchy of the extreme judgement of Moses.

To the physicality of De Bry's engraving can be added an expansive tradition of *Justitia* kissing *Pax* and sometimes, as in Hendrick Goltzius' *Iustitia et Prudentia*, the eros of the image is inescapable (Fig. 8.12). Two naked figures mingle bodies, fluids, and breath, and this is certainly a depiction that would attract attention and convey an erotic charge that can also be seen in the various figures of *Iustitia* naked or more often bare-breasted, in emblems, in murals, in paintings and sculptures. The mottoes and descriptions of the depictions seldom reference the comedic and erotic dimension of the femininity of *Iustitia*, but rather reference details, as with Goltzius' engraving of *Iustitia* in Fig. 8.11 where a bare-breasted and seemingly fair justice holds the scales in even equilibrium,

Fig. 8.11 *Iustitiæ languor*, from Johann Theodor de Bry, *Proscenium vitæ humanæ* (1627) (Hathi Trust, public domain)

and the inscription reads that the scales alone judge and no other weight or measure intervenes, one could say, to corrupt the chaste virtue of justice as beauty, which is poorly translated as fairness in modern jurisprudence.[31] Look closer and comedically enough there is a face on her stomach, a sign of lust, want, and greed. The belly is the site of voraciousness and carnality, of consuming desire, and again undoes any easy, single (or monotheistic?) interpretation of the depiction. The incarnadine and voluptuous character of *Justitia* as the physical and frequently bare-breasted figure of fairness and measure transcending law is somehow unspoken, a duplication too far and yet, as in Lucas Cranach's portrayal

[31] Goltzius "Aequa judicii suspendo singula lance / Nec me divitie, nec me data munera flectunt" (I suspend my judgments to the only force of a levelled scales / Richnesses and presents do not bend me).

Fig. 8.12 *Iustitia et Prudentia*, Hendrick Goltzius (Courtesy of the Rijksmuseum, Amsterdam)

of 'Justitia' (1537) as a thinly veiled female nude with scales and a sword, it provides a most striking feature of this paradoxically sexualized representation of a virtue that is supposedly free of carnal drives or affective influences beyond the cause itself.

The theme could easily be expanded but suffice to use one more substantive example. Raphael's 'Allegory of Justice' (Fig. 8.13) can make the point again, as here a fair-faced *Justitia* looks at the scales which are held in a carefully balanced fashion, all suggestion of undue pressure chironomically avoided.[32] That said, the right breast is bared to the viewer, symbolizing mercy and the milk of nurture of which the Psalmist speaks, but it is also naked and erogenous. Then to the right her hand

[32] Hayaert, *Lady Justice*, 106 et seq. on the 'immense care and learning' which was expended on depicting the chironomic principles, or in Bulwer, *Chirologia* (London, 1644), 157 et seq., the dactylogy, of honest weighing or ponderation.

is lightly clasping the thick and extensive neck of an ostrich. The touch seems light, the neck too wide for her fingers to encompass but it is nonetheless phallic for all of that excess of breadth and of length. The final comedy of the image is thus that of the histrion, an erotic theatre that aims to mingle with and arouse the audience, to goad to action by making justice corporeal, present, desirable, and in proffering her as affective, makes her effective. Come with me, beckons the finger of a substantial and muscular marching *Justitia*, scantily clad, seemingly naked breasted in the anonymous figure from the mid-sixteenth century (Fig. 8.14). 'Come on', she seems to signal, 'enough with others, I am for you', the raised finger pointing perhaps to the absence of the gods and the haptic pleasures and haecceity of the flesh, here and now. As Antonio de Jorio might have put it, *ostendit digitum impudicum*, a beckoning, a call to follow, that echoes the ethical injunction to attend to our desire.[33]

In the second edition of *Angliæ notitia*, Edward Chamberlayne lists the King's servants above the stairs. These include a hydrographer and a cosmographer. There is also a scenographer or 'master of prospects' and a master of cockfighting. A sound suite or following already, but there is more. There is a master of revels 'to order all things concerning comedies', then 17 male comedians and eight female.[34] It is not just that there is play, *divina commedia* as it were, but that it is comedic, doubling and doubling over. Play enacts and laughter changes. *Mens emblematica*, the theatre of the book, is also the spirit of comedy, and the *leges actiones* are necessarily also *leges togatorum*, matters that the jurist should view in their symbolic and satirical, customary and comedic forms. These are revels, rebellious and ridiculous in their turns and levels. If we return to Perrière and his *Theâtre des bons engins*, the title itself references theatrical machinery, props and *pegma* or other modes of bringing actors onto the stage. It expresses explicitly, in the language of the time, that theatre is a device for virtuous tricks, expedient ruses, white lies, a mode of deceit

[33] Hayaert, *Lady Justice* (118), interprets the indigitation or digital ostentation as a threatening deictic gesture, to which I simply add reference to the inimitable and older Andrea de Jorio, *Gesture in Naples and Gesture in Classical Antiquity*, trans. Adam Kendon (Bloomington, IN: Indiana University Press, 2000), whose schemata allow an interpretative as well as digital extension to include the erotic valences of the image for the present age.

[34] Edward Chamberlayne, *Angliæ notitia, or The present state of England: together with divers reflections upon the antient state thereof* (London: John Martyn, 1669), 193, 195.

Fig. 8.13 *Justitia*, Maratti, Royal Collection (Courtesy of the Royal Collection Trust. © His Majesty King Charles III 2024)

Fig. 8.14 Anonymous drawing attributed to Lambert Lombard (© The Trustees of the British Museum)

that makes the social work.[35] The better translation of the title would in fact be *Machinery of Good Governance*.

The engines are mechanical devices, motors of social persuasion, calls to action that are layered with comedy, not least in the duplication of structures but also in their humour and the exercise of the *officium ludicrae*. The function of the office is that of changing moods, physical and mental states, and most importantly transforming somnolence and complacency into action. Democritus is a necessary figure, and I will hazard that if one were to revise the four levels of meaning that hermeneutic exegesis traditionally relays, then between the moral and the anagogic or spiritual levels of the text should be the intervening level of what the humanist Nebrija, in *Aenigmata iuris*, as adverted earlier, terms *sensus ridiculus*.[36] That is not a dismissive or diminutive tier of textuality but rather a necessary recognition of another and active dimension of meaning that early modern humanistic lawyers understood and manipulated to significant if sometimes understated effect. The democritic is democratic, an anarchic and transformative incitation to change, shaking up the pectoral and the political, challenging complacency and admitting that it is hedonism, the work of the gay scientist that will most likely be embodied and that will live on.[37] She who laughs lasts. I will end with a final image, again from Perrière's *Foolosophy*, again of Democritus, the figure that stands over the comedic level of interpretation and meaning[38] (Fig. 8.15). The wheel of fortune joins the image of justice and truth, as before, but here it is the winged satyr time that approaches Democritus who stands high as if on a pedestal. Time wishes to find his daughter truth and a laughing Democritus, dressed as a lawyer, points to a well in which Truth is hiding. She is, as Gary Watt has lengthily elaborated, feminine and naked.[39] The elongated and lustful hand of the law reaches

[35] Godefroy, *Lexique de l'ancien Français*, s.v. *engin*.

[36] On the levels of the text as conceived in Christian exegesis, see Henri de Lubac, *Medieval Exegesis: Volume 1: The Four Senses of Scripture* (Edinburgh: T&T Clark, 1998), ch.1.

[37] I borrow here from Nietzsche's epistemology of the *gaya scienza*. See Friederich Nietzsche, *The Joyful Wisdom (La Gaya Scienza)*, trans. Thomas Common (Edinburgh: T.N. Foulis, 1910).

[38] Guillaume Perrière (Lyon: Bonhomme, 1553), 48.

[39] Reference is to that fine and exhibitionist work, Gary Watt, *Law, Dress and the Naked Truth* (London: Bloomsbury, 2013), esp. 43–47.

Fig. 8.15 *Democritus, Time and Fortune*, Guillaume Perrière, *Morosophie* (1553) (With permission of the University of Glasgow Archives and Special Collections)

towards the uncovered female form that looks suspiciously like *Fortuna*: bare chance, pure luck, the poetry of change, hidden in a well, breaking the repression barrier as it were, the affective cause, as an expression lodged in the comedy of how things are.

Reprising, doubling the opening theme, suggests a law of attraction, and appeal of opposites, in which *ludi* and *leges,* two parallel *artes*, shadows of each other, are entangled in common sway and pursuit. As Huizinga famously expounded, play is intrinsic to law, and is indeed the defining feature of the legal jurisdiction and of its procedures. The separate stage, excised from the quotidian and social, creates a jurisdiction, a field, a garden, and latterly a court in which the game will be played, the trial held, and a winner and a loser will emerge from the comediographic enterprise. For Del Mar as well, the element of play is intrinsic to the creation of law and lawyers. Focusing upon the theatrical dimensions of training in the Inns of Court, the point is made that it is precisely the evacuation from the real that allows the bolts and moots, cupboard judgements, revels, and other didactic rites of passage to imagine interpreting laws, deciding absurd hypothetical cases, in novel ways. Play allows access to other disciplines and possibilities of invention. Play corporealizes and adds both enthusiasm and wit to judgement. It allows access to the phantasmata and other affects that precede thought. The ludic, *ars ludicra*, is generative of law, internal and external to the drive of decision. As a double to law's identity, law *a comicis* brings the body and the unconscious into the process, into the *legis actio* which is also the incalculable moment of judgement, of liturgical and legal *effectus*. To make law requires stepping outside of the legal, leaving the jurisdiction to return and revise, reform and revitalize, inhabit and enliven a tradition of dead letters. Play takes law outside itself, so as to return covertly in novel ludic guise, as a principle of change, of moving the jurist along, of acknowledging the uncertainty of the human condition and the comedy of conflict at the core of law.

CHAPTER 9

Ludic Legal Pedagogy: Mooting in Early Modern England

Maksymilian Del Mar

Introduction

The argument of the chapter is that modelling knowledge as play can help illuminate the culture of legal knowledge in late medieval and early modern England. A focus on play foregrounds three elements: a sense of active engagement in practices of doing or making; the anchoring of

A version of this essay was delivered at a conference on 'Law and Poetics in Early Modern England and Beyond', at the University of Cambridge, 2–4 July 2018. I am especially grateful for comments and questions, raised at the conference, from Subha Mukherji, Rachel Holmes, Kathy Eden, Andrew Zurcher, Sebastian Sobecki, Julie Stone-Peters, Gary Watt, Lorna Hutson and Richard Sherwin. In addition, a number of friends and colleagues have helped me, by sharing resources, reading earlier drafts or simply encouraging me in this endeavour. I thank, in particular, John Baker, Roger Cotterrell, Karen Cunningham, Paul du Plessis, David Foster, Michael Lobban, Simon Stern, Peter Mack and Quentin Skinner. In addition, Subha Mukherji, Dunstan Roberts and Camilla Temple provided very helpful comments and edits on earlier drafts, for which I am most grateful. All errors are of course my own.

S. Mukherji and D. Roberts (eds.), *Literature and the Legal Imaginary*, Crossroads of Knowledge in Early Modern Literature 4,
https://doi.org/10.1007/978-3-031-74093-0_9

that activity in affective, sensory and embodied experience and a further grounding of that activity in interaction and community.[1] The playful dimensions of knowledge are not, however, always easy to discern. To help bring them into view, I focus in this paper on pedagogical practices, and in particular on mooting. One of the most significant aspects of an English lawyer's knowledge in this period was oral pleading in the Court of Common Pleas.[2] This court was the most important court of civil litigation in England in the late medieval and early modern periods. Those with an exclusive licence to plead in that court were known as 'serjeants', and to become a serjeant—certainly from the late fourteenth century—one had to study at one of the Inns of Court. There, by engaging extensively, and over many years, in the pedagogical practice of mooting,

M. Del Mar (✉)
Department of Law, Queen Mary University of London, London, UK
e-mail: maks.delmar@qmul.ac.uk

[1] Play itself is of course a contested concept with its own complex history: e.g. for play in Ancient Greece, see Stephen E. Kidd, *Play and Aesthetics in Ancient Greece* (Cambridge: Cambridge University Press, 2019); for the medieval period, see Johan Huizinga, *Homo ludens: A Study of the Play-Element in Culture* (London: Routledge and Kegan Paul, 1949), which includes a chapter on law, and Mary Carruthers, *The Experience of Beauty in the Middle Ages* (Oxford: Oxford University Press, 2013) and for the early modern period, see Joel Altman, *Tudor Play of Mind: Rhetorical Inquiry and the Development of Elizabethan Drama* (Berkeley: California University Press, 1978) and more recently Bret Rothstein, 'Early Modern Play: Three Perspectives', *Renaissance Quarterly*, 71:3 (2018), 1036–46. Play also becomes crucial, though in a different way, during the enlightenment for Immanuel Kant and Adam Smith, and then the Romantics: see, e.g. Wolfgang Iser, *The Fictive and the Imaginary: Charting Literary Anthropology* (Baltimore: Johns Hopkins University Press, 1993). I model play here in a particular, and no doubt also anachronistic, way. What is crucial for my argument is that I do not understand play (or pleasure) to operate outside law, but very much within it: put another way, legal knowledge and legal reasoning are, and have to be to an extent, playful (e.g., in order to remain appropriately sensitive to the circumstantial complexity that law deals with) and pleasurable (because pleasure both motivates epistemic inquiry and encourages us to collaborate epistemically). In short, the opposition between play and pleasure on the one side and law and knowledge on the other is a false one. For other attempts in this volume at seeing play and pleasure as part of law, see Watt (where wordplay is shown to be vital to the active knowledge of legal language) and Goodrich (where comedy is argued to have an important function in the exercise of legal office).

[2] Medieval and early modern common law was an intensely oral practice and much of its later written poetics still contains many traces of many centuries of oral exchange. For a demonstration within this volume of the importance of orality to legal culture, see the chapter by Hayaert.

one rose through the ranks, learning the art of pleading. By examining mooting, we can better appreciate the playful dimensions of pleading, and, or so this chapter argues, better understand the kind of knowledge pleading required.

Early modern moots were playful in many ways. For example, moot problems withheld facts that required speculative filling-in, including the generation and maintenance of possible actions and their ethical and political consequences. They also required students to explore issues in the borderlands of the law, where thorny ethical and political issues often arose, and thus where delicate ethical and political judgement was needed. Such glimpses into the ways in which the moots offered training in ludic legal knowledge enable us to see pleading as the affective, sensory, embodied and communal experience of making ethical and political insight.[3] By being exposed to mooting, and, more broadly, to the pedagogical culture of the Inns of Court, future serjeants acquired an ability to participate in a highly inventive and interactive art, which fine-tuned judgement by grounding it in the emotions, the senses and interpersonal dynamics.

Playing to Learn in the Inns of Court

Before we turn to the moots themselves, some context is needed, especially regarding the pedagogical culture—and the many varieties of play—which existed in the late medieval and early modern Inns of Court. Although there is evidence of groups of lawyers living and learning together prior to the fourteenth century,[4] the general consensus amongst legal historians is that it was with the emergence of the Inns of Court in the early-to-mid fourteenth century that common law education began to acquire the distinctiveness that was to flourish over the next few centuries.

[3] For another take, in this volume, on the affective, sensory and embodied aspects of legal knowing, see Peters. As Peters shows, both texts and images (and of various kinds, including emblems) offer evidence of the intense debate over what kinds of emotions or postures/gestures were important for good judgement. The emotional and embodied performance of authority and virtue (e.g., prudence) also plays an important role in Sherwin's chapter and his discussion of law and politics in *Measure for Measure*.

[4] See Paul Brand, 'Courtroom and Schoolroom: The Education of Lawyers in England Prior to 1400', *Historical Research*, 60 (1987), 147–65; and John Baker, *Collected Essays in English Legal History* (Cambridge: Cambridge University Press, 2014), chapters 7 and 16.

Prior to the mid-fourteenth century, the education of aspiring serjeants was based more on apprenticeship with a master, including listening and taking notes from within the 'crib', which was added to the Common Bench at Westminster in 1291.[5] The actual practising group of serjeants in this early period (prior to the establishment of the Inns) was very small—about thirty in the late thirteenth century.[6] The numbers, certainly of aspiring students, soon grew with the increasing availability of legal education at the Inns, though in truth serjeants throughout this period were always a small, elite group. Of course, the education of canon and civil lawyers—as distinct from common lawyers—was much more advanced, but concentrated at the Universities of Oxford and Cambridge, and not in London.[7] For common lawyers, London had distinct advantages, such as 'allow[ing] its students to support themselves while studying through work as attorneys', and giving them 'privileged access to the courts and to their leading personnel', thereby also keeping the students '*au courant* with the latest decisions, something which neither Oxford nor Cambridge could offer'.[8]

For all the professional advantages of being in London, however, most of the young gentlemen—for they were largely, though not exclusively, the sons of wealthy English and Scottish families—who flocked to the Inns of Court, were not destined for legal practice. Instead, they were there because there was hardly a better institution at which to meet and socialise with other young gentlemen, many of whom would, in due course, take up important positions in the government and administration of the realm. As John Baker puts it, 'More than half the members of Lincoln's Inn make no appearance in the records beyond their admission,

[5] See Paul Brand, 'Legal Education in England Before the Inns of Court', in Jonathan Bush and Alain Wijffels, eds., *Learning the Law: Teaching and the Transmission of Law in England, 1150–1900* (London: The Hambledon Press, 1999), 51–84.

[6] Ibid., 61.

[7] See also John Baker, 'Oral Instruction in Land Law and Conveyancing', in Bush and Wijffels, eds., *Learning the Law*, 157–73; and James Brundage, 'The Canon Law Curriculum in Medieval Cambridge', in Bush and Wijffels, eds., *Learning the Law*, 175–90.

[8] Brand, 'Legal Education in England before the Inns of Court', 83.

and it seems probable that no more than a third of the resident membership of the inns were following the law'.[9] Rather, the Inns were the place where 'they joined in work and play, learned the names which would matter to them, dined and prayed together, displayed their wealth or their talent—whichever was more conspicuous—talked of law and much else, drank, diced, and misbehaved'.[10] Most of the students came to one of the four Inns of Court—Lincoln's Inn, Inner Temple, Middle Temple and Gray's Inn—after two years at one of the nine Inns of Chancery. A few may have gone to university, though often only for a year and without taking a degree. The overwhelming majority, however, had received little if any classical education beyond grammar school.

The Chancery Inns would have exposed the students—also called 'apprentices'—to a range of social and educational activities that they would then engage in more intensively when they progressed to the Inns. Thus, for instance, at the Christmas revels at Clifford Inn in 1482, there were performances of 'selected songs, choice music, majestical masques, stately stage-play, bountiful banquettings, dicing, dancing, and many other rare invented court-like pastimes' and even some 'oratory speeches whereby was unfolded the brave wits and ingenuous capacity of sundry persons'.[11] A few years later, in 1487, the Christmas celebrations at Clifford's Inn involved 'mummeryes…martial stratagems, heroicall inventions in matters of honour and armes, and other wyttye devices there acted and contrived'.[12] In addition to these various performances, there were also moots, though these were less complex than the moots that the students would encounter at the Inns of Court.[13]

When the students advanced to the Inns of Court, then, they had already socialised together and had been initiated into particular kinds of play, with their own distinct communal and interactive dynamics. The newly arrived students were called 'inner barristers', and they remained so for another five or six years, until they qualified to argue in moots, were called to the 'utter bar', and thus became 'utter barristers'. After a

[9] John Baker, *The Oxford History of the Laws of England, 1483–1558* (Oxford: Oxford University Press, 2003), 462.

[10] Ibid., 462.

[11] Ibid., 456, quoting from a report of the period.

[12] Ibid., 456n94.

[13] Ibid., 458.

further ten to twelve years, they were called to 'read'—that is, to deliver lectures on a well-known statute. This would allow them to sit on the bench to judge moots: hence the term 'benchers'. Out of those benchers, some were invited (as Thomas More would be) to deliver a 'second reading', and it is from these selected few that serjeants were chosen to plead before the Court of Common Pleas. From there they could aim, one day, to become a judge, for judges were picked only from the pool of serjeants.

The forms of learning in the Inns included bolting, reading and mooting. Bolting (from 'bolter', meaning one who sieves or sifts things),[14] 'consisted of conversational arguments upon cases and questions put to [a student] by a Bencher and two Utter Barristers sitting as his judges in private'.[15] Readings, in turn, were important learning occasions, especially when a famous judge, serjeant or bencher delivered them. They would begin with an exposition of the statute by the reader, including commentary, but would then involve the audience of students by way of disputation. This involvement was enabled by the practice of cases being 'put as law' by the reader followed by those present—benchers, barristers, serjeants and judges—being invited to challenge the cases for argument. Significantly, the cases were not always directly related to the reading—that gap, too, offered a space for interactive experiments.[16]

Edward Waterhouse, in his *Fortescutus Illustratus* (1663), describes just how collaborative these disputative elements of readings could be:

> ...one of the younger utter barristers rehearseth one question propounded by the reader, and doth by way of argument labour to prove the reader's opinion to be against the law; and after him the rest of the utter barristers and readers one after another in their ancienties do declare their opinions and judgments in the same; and then the reader who did put the case endeavoureth himself to confute objections laid against him, and to confirm his own opinion; after whom the judges and serjeants, if any be present, declare their opinions; and after they have done the youngest utter

[14] For comparison, the term moot comes from the Anglo-Saxon 'mot', meaning meeting: see Adwin Wigfall Green, *The Inns of Court and Early English Drama* (New Haven: Yale University Press, 1931), 40.

[15] Kenneth Charlton, 'Liberal Education and the Inns of Court in the Sixteenth Century', *British Journal of Educational Studies*, 9:1 (1960), 25–38 (28).

[16] See Baker, *The Oxford History of the Laws of England, 1483–1558*, 464–65.

barrister again rehearseth another case, which is ordered as the other was. Thus the reading ends for that day....[17]

Discussions of the cases connected to the readings also continued after dinner—not only at the table of the reader, but also at the other tables. The process was intensively social, and intertwined with other convivial occasions, such as eating together.[18] Indeed, we might conceive of the readings as their own form of play.[19]

However, not all communal learning was as structured as the readings. The Christmas revels were a famous, if not infamous, aspect of cultural and educational life at the Inns. Perhaps originally meant to be convivial entertainment for Inns—members who could not return to their country homes and stayed back over the Christmas vacation, they became, over time, extraordinary spectacles, reaching remarkable proportions of extravagance during the reign of Elizabeth I. Lasting for several weeks, and involving feasts, dance and theatre, often in the form of masques, they included, as guests, members of the royal court and sometimes even the monarch. Governance of the Inns was inverted during the revels, with junior members taking on the role of administering their respective Inns. A leader, or a Prince, was elected and wielded power over the next few weeks.[20] The festivities included 'elaborate emblazoning of the Prince's titles, a detailed description of the responsibilities of court officers, a conferring of 'knighthoods', a declaration of laws and edicts for the Prince's realm, an arraignment of a criminal with his incarceration in 'the

[17] Edward Waterhouse, *Fortescutus Illustratus, or A Commentary on that Nervous Treatise, De Laudibus Legum Angliae* (London: Thomas Dicas, 1663), 545.

[18] See also Peter Goodrich, 'Eating Law: Commons, Common Land, Common Law', *The Journal of Legal History*, 12 (1991), 246–67.

[19] For more on the readings in this period, see Margaret McGlynn, 'Teaching the Law in a Time of Change: The Royal Prerogative and the Statute of Uses', in Bush and Wijffels, eds., *Learning the Law*, 211–25; M. C. Mirow, 'The Ascent of the Readings: Some Evidence from Readings on Wills', in idem, 227–54; and Wilfred R. Prest, 'Readers' Dinners and the Culture of the Early Modern Inns of Court', in Jayne Archer, Elizabeth Goldring and Sarah Knight, eds., *The Intellectual and Cultural World of the Early Modern Inns of Court* (Manchester: Manchester University Press, 2011), 107–23.

[20] See Paul Raffield, 'The Elizabethan Rhetoric of Signs: Representations of *Res Publica* at the Early Modern Inns of Court', *Law, Culture and the Humanities*, 7:2 (2010), 244–63 (247).

tower' (that is, the stocks) and many long orations on a variety of 'subjects'. The revels ended when the Prince 'died', usually with a banquet on Candlemas Night, February 2.[21]

As Paul Raffield says, the masques, in particular, demonstrated 'an interest in examining alternative forms of governance and their applicability to the English constitution'.[22] They would often present an image of an ideal polis, set in a pastoral atmosphere, such as Arcadia or Olympus. Variously dressed up and masked—in green velvet or green satin (as, say, forest rangers), or as animals or birds—the participants would perform rituals or enact scenarios, such as hunting scenes.[23] In addition to the masques, various other kinds of comic sketches would be performed during the course of the revels.[24] Future lawyers, or at least future legally trained men of the realm, could try their hand—or rather, their voice and their body—at playing a role they might go on to play in their later career (as indeed maybe of them in fact did). Riotously fun occasions, they also had a serious dimension. This chapter sees the revels generally (with their inverted governance structure), and especially the masques, as an alternative form of play, which, through its peculiar kind of collaborative composition, allowed for the generation and exploration of an alternative set of ethical and political norms and values for the realm.[25]

The Inns were also places of reading, writing and performance for a variety of other literary forms. According to Jessica Winston, in her recent *Lawyers at Play: Literature, Law and Politics at the Early Modern Inns of Court*, which examines the relations between law, literature and drama in the sixteenth century, it was around the 1560s that 'a large literary network first coalesced around the legal societies'.[26] Winston's specific

[21] Philip J. Finkelpearl, *John Marston of the Middle Temple* (Cambridge, MA: Harvard University Press, 1969), 35–36, 38. See also Edward Berry, 'Thomas More and the Legal Imagination', *Studies in Philology*, 106:3 (2009), 316–40 (321).

[22] Raffield, 'The Elizabethan Rhetoric of Signs', 249.

[23] See ibid., 250; see also Green, *The Inns of Court and Early English Drama*, 15–16.

[24] See Green, *The Inns of Court and Early English Drama*; and Desmond Bland, 'Interludes in Fifteenth-Century Revels at Furnival's Inn', *Review of English Studies*, 3 (1952), 263–68.

[25] See further the essays collected in *The Intellectual and Cultural World of the Early Modern Inns of Court*, eds. Archer, Goldring and Knight.

[26] Jessica Winston, *Lawyers at Play: Literature, Law, and Politics at the Early Modern Inns of Court, 1558–1581* (Oxford: Oxford University Press, 2016), 5.

focus is on how 'literary activities help to raise the status of early modern legal men and the common law' (Winston 2016, 12), but she makes a point of acknowledging that such a focus is one aspect of a broader relationship between literary and legal forms at the Inns of Court.[27]

It is here that we can also relate, as Winston does, to the broader literary experiments in the Inns of Court, with mooting. For Winston, 'there is an important connection between the legal exercises – which were known as moots and preoccupied with property law – and *Gorboduc*, and likewise between the point-by-point combative nature of arguments in the moots and the vituperative back-and-forth of satirical epigrams and poetry in the 1590s'.[28] *Gorboduc* was a play written by two young lawyers, Thomas Norton and Thomas Sackville, and it, along with some other examples, some of them written by members of the Inns and some performed in and by the members of the Inns, are said to have been influenced by the moots.[29] *Gorboduc*, for instance, has been said to have been clearly influenced by the mooting 'technique of arguing on both sides of an issue',[30] which was itself a common technique of humanist education (*in utrumque partem*).[31] As Doyeeta Majumder elaborates, the 'play

[27] See also Michelle O'Callaghan, *The English Wits: Literature and Sociability in Early Modern England* (Cambridge: Cambridge University Press, 2009); Lorna Hutson, *The Invention of Suspicion: Law and Mimesis in Shakespeare and Renaissance Drama* (Oxford: Oxford University Press, 2007); Luke Wilson, *Theatres of Intention: Drama and Law in Early Modern England* (Stanford: Stanford University Press, 2000) and Karen Cunningham, *Imaginary Betrayals: Subjectivity and the Discourses of Treason in Early Modern England* (Philadelphia: University of Pennsylvania Press, 2002). Within this volume, Majumder shows how important sixteenth-century drama (including *Gorboduc*) in the Inns of Court was to exploring the tensions and connections between natural law and common law.

[28] Winston, *Lawyers at Play*, 11.

[29] The examples include George Gascoigne and Francis Kinwelmersh's *Jocasta* (Gray's Inn, 1565–1567), *Gismond of Salerne* (?1566), and *The Misfortunes of Arthur* (Gray's Inn at Greenwich, 1588), as well as Shakespeare's *Measure for Measure*. See Winston, *Lawyers at Play*, 11.

[30] Doyeeta Majumder, 'Absolutism Without Tyranny in *Gorboduc*: The Changing Poetics of Tudor Political Drama', *Renaissance Studies*, 32:2 (2017), 201–18 (213).

[31] Majumder also argues that the 'technique of arguing on both sides of an issue coupled with the equivocal *sententiae* of Senecan drama underlie the play's formal and thematic radicalness. Together they enabled the young lawyers Norton and Sackville [who were also trained in mooting] to craft a new poetics of political drama' (Majumder, 'Absolutism Without Tyranny in *Gorboduc*', 204). For an extended account of the emergence of a 'political poeisis' in this period (with *Gorboduc* as its inaugural dramatic instance), see

presents to us a hypothetical case of absolutism pertaining to a single extreme fictitious situation, and forces us to re-examine the connections between morally neutral absolutism and active tyranny, without offering direct commentary on either'.[32]

The moots, then, were intimately related to the play of literary genres in the Inns. We might ask: what exactly was it about mooting that so fired the imagination of the dramatists of the period? According to Karen Cunningham, writing in particular about *Measure for Measure*, and calling it 'an instance of a dramatic moot',[33] common law was figured by the moots 'not as a self-interpreting code that could be "applied" to particular cases… but as a prompt for speculating, for imagining challenges to its operations and disasters befalling the citizens it organises'.[34] Mooting, one might say, provided a model of what drama could be—not the making of statements, but the asking of questions and the exploration of issues via concrete fictive narratives.[35] We shall see in a moment in what ways exactly mooting might be characterised precisely as offering such prompts for speculation, or triggers of imagining.

Mooting, then, did not operate in a vacuum at the Inns of Court. On the contrary, it was part of a network of mutually influencing varieties of play. Cultural life at the Inns, thus, offered many opportunities for learning-by-playing, and can only be separated out from education at the Inns at our peril. It is far more productive to think about how they related with and influenced each other—to consider the relations and continuities between the putting of cases in readings and the masques, revels and drama, and how they located a student within a vibrant environment fizzing with an active, performative mode of learning. Though there are of course important differences of form and process amongst all

Victoria Kahn, *The Future of Illusion: Political Theology and Early Modern Texts* (Chicago: Chicago University Press, 2014). For more on the relations between humanist education and theatre in this period, see Kent Cartwright, *Theatre and Humanism: English Drama in the Sixteenth Century* (Cambridge: Cambridge University Press, 1999).

32 Majumder 'Absolutism Without Tyranny in *Gorboduc*', 213.

33 Karen Cunningham, 'Opening Doubts upon the Law: *Measure for Measure*', in Richard Dutton and Kean Howard, eds., *A Companion to Shakespeare's Works: Volume IV: The Poems, Problem Comedies, Late Plays* (Oxford: Blackwell, 2003), 316–32 (318). On *Measure for Measure*, see also Sherwin in this volume.

34 Cunningham, 'Opening Doubts upon the Law', 317.

35 See also Altman, *Tudor Play of Mind*; and Subha Mukherji, *Law and Representation in Early Modern Drama* (Cambridge: Cambridge University Press, 2006).

these modes of playing and learning, they must also be seen to be part of the holistic experience of active, interactive and communal making—a process that was not merely fun and games, but designed at the same time to generate and explore an alternative set of ethical and political norms and values for the realm.

Mooting as Playing

The most commonly cited source of the origin of moots as a form of common law learning is that of disputation.[36] Legal disputation was said to have been 'established in the second quarter of the 12th century with the questions of Bulgarus (d. 1166)'.[37] As Baker and Thorne tell us, the 'essential structure' of a legal disputation consisted of '1) The *casus*, or problem; 2) the *quaestio*, whether general or specific, arising from the problem; 3) the *disputatio*, consisting of arguments *pro* and *contra*; 4) the *solutio*, sometimes called the *determinatio* or *responsio*, expressing any authoritative answer or ruling given by the teacher'.[38]

Disputation can also be thought of as a mode of embodied play. In his exemplary account of the medieval culture of disputation, Alex Novikoff characterises disputation as a 'dialogue of voices', full of hypothesis and conditional belief, and situates this art in the culture of the period—as for instance in the genre of debate poems or jeu-parti, a sung debate in which two or more singers argued for and against a given question—and in musical practices—such as the 'simultaneous vertical combinations of pitches in performance'.[39] It would be fascinating to trace further this 'medieval dialogic imagination' and thus to inquire into the cultural history of these playful and interactive modes of learning through to

[36] I refer to 'mooting' as the specific form of learning exercises in the Inns of Court, and use 'disputation' as the more general term referring to debate, often in pedagogical contexts.

[37] John Baker and Samuel Thorne, 'Introduction', in *Readings and Moots at the Inns of Court: Volume II* (London: Selden Society, 1990), xv–lxxvi (xvi–xvii).

[38] Baker and Thorne, 'Introduction', in *Readings and Moots at the Inns of Court*, xvii.

[39] See Alex Novikoff, *The Medieval Culture of Disputation: Pedagogy, Practice, and Performance* (Philadelphia: University of Pennsylvania Press, 2013), 139, 147, 148, 151.

the moots.[40] Such a project would profit from paying attention to the many different expressions of dialogical or agonistic dynamics in medieval and early modern literature, underwritten as all this was by the rhetorical tradition of arguing on both sides of a question.[41] This rhetorical tradition itself has many interesting connections to pretend or playful combat: 'stasis', for instance, once referred to a stance in battle, and joining the issue (which was also the object of pleading) was once called 'pugna', meaning fistfight or battle.[42] There is certainly a fascinating history to be told here—combining law with aesthetics, theology and much else besides—under the guise of spectacles of playful battle or dramas of pretend combat.

For present purposes, what is important to see is that already by the early-to-mid fourteenth century, something like the moots had come into existence. Certainly, by the 1380s or 1390s, we have evidence of complex moots, which may in fact have been in use all the way back to the 1340s. Baker and Thorne have described the process of what was being looked for in these early moots as follows:

> In each case [from the collection of moots in the 1380s and 1390s], the first part of the exercise was to make a choice of writ and of parties to the action. The mooters drew the writ verbatim, in Latin… The parties were given names at this stage, as were any other persons and places mention in the writ. Names were also made up for the pleadings, if necessary… The choice of writ was the first occasion of discussion, since the defendant could advance a tentative plea in abatement; this happened in three of the cases. The pleadings then followed the usual course, and were designed to raise all the questions secreted in the moot problem. …this might necessitate separate pleas as to different parts of the demand, each raising a different

[40] For an overview of disputation techniques from antiquity to the early modern period, with attention also to law, see Olga Weijers, *In Search of the Truth: A History of Disputation Techniques from Antiquity to Early Modern Times* (Turnhout: Brepols, 2013); see also Hermann Kantorowicz, 'The Quaestiones Disputatae of the Glossators', *Tijdschrift voor Rechtsgeschiedenis*, 16:1 (1939), 1–67; and James Brundage, 'A Twelfth Century Oxford Disputation Concerning the Privileges of the Knights Hospitallers', *Medieval Studies*, 24:1 (1962), 153–60.

[41] See, for example, Jody Enders, *Rhetoric and the Origins of Medieval Drama* (Ithaca: Cornell University Press, 1992); and Altman, *Tudor Play of Mind*.

[42] See Hanns Hohmann, 'The Dynamics of Stasis: Classical Rhetorical Theory and Modern Legal Argumentation', *American Journal of Jurisprudence*, 34:1 (1989), 171–97 (171).

> aspect of the case. Exceptions were taken to pleadings which were considered questionable. These exceptions were fully argued, and if a plea was ruled bad the party went on to plead something else. The rulings were made (with reasons) by 'the court', which was evidently taken to represent the Common Pleas.[43]

The kinds of question these moots posed were less abstract points of law than they were tasks in framing 'an issue in a legally acceptable form'.[44] They are likely to have considered novel, unlikely, exaggerated or fictional questions, such as: 'how to try bigamy in an appeal brought against a clerk by the bishop and archbishop' or 'whether a woman justice of the peace could send her own husband to goal' or 'how a person could be a villein every other day of his life and a free man on alternate days'.[45]

These questions might have resembled the form that problems in legal practice took at the time, but not their substance. The questions of moot problems allowed the students to operate in the borderlands of the law. For instance, the emphasis in the moots on 'deraignment' (which we shall see in a moment in the moot I shall discuss) was, say Baker and Thorne, 'out of all proportion to any practical repercussions of this rare procedure in early Tudor times, but entirely justified in terms of its troublesome theoretical consequences'.[46] The point was less to teach the rules, and more to teach 'a method, a cast of mind'.[47] The questions were chosen 'to stretch the mind'.[48] This is a clear example of how playfulness may be more accentuated or visible in a pedagogical practice.

The moots of this period, as noted above, and as we shall see in the example below, were very complex. Some occupied the students for weeks, and some even for entire vacations. The moot called 'Le Virge'

[43] Baker and Thorne, 'Introduction', in *Readings and Moots at the Inns of Court*, xlix.

[44] Ibid., xlix.

[45] Ibid., lxxii.

[46] Ibid., lxxiii.

[47] Ibid., lxxii.

[48] Ibid., lxxii. Although the substance of the questions in the moots may have been in the borderlands of law, exploring these questions meant that the mooting discussion became directly helpful when these matters did come up, rarely as they did, in practice. In this respect, as Baker has pointed out on many occasions, early modern common law was to some extent the creature of the Inns of Court' (Baker, *The Oxford History of the Laws of England, 1483–1558*, 445–46). Discussions in the moots were at the coal-face of law-making in this period.

(or the Rod) 'occupied the whole of the autumn vacation of 1529 in the Inner Temple'; another case, that of 'Isaac and Jacob', occupied the entire autumn vacation of 1533.[49] Further, the moots were organised around the social rite of dining together. Most moots took place every evening after supper, during term and the vacations. Certain post-supper moots involved a surprise, with the case 'laid upon the cellar support' and 'none was to look into it upon pain of expulsion'.[50] Some moots, then, were designed for maximum spontaneity and improvisation. Others, which extended over long periods of time, were less immediately unpremeditated, though they were also complex enough to preclude complete predictability about the pleading dialogue to follow.

Further, these were clearly performances before an audience. Here, we can ask: how involved was the audience in mooting performances? Some descriptions of the process of mooting indicate that the audience was more active than we might think. A passage from Wilfred Prest's seminal work is telling:

> At the appointed time, the two men who had prepared the case, with two students who were to recite the appropriate pleadings for and against the action concerned, took their seats on a bench facing their seniors. The pleadings, which had also been drawn up by the two 'moot-men', were first recited from memory 'in homely law French'; then the first moot-man rose as counsel for the plaintiff to address himself to the points at issue, which were agreed upon beforehand between the two disputants. [There were]...nine other individuals besides the two mootmen advancing arguments, usually by citing yearbook cases bearing on the disputed points. Finally, the mooters presented the judges with a slice of bread and a mug of beer and the exercise was over.[51]

[49] Baker, *The Oxford History of the Laws of England, 1483–1558*, 466n157.

[50] Charlton, 'Liberal Education and the Inns of Court in the Sixteenth Century', 28.

[51] Wilfred R. Prest, *The Inns of Court Under Elizabeth I and the Early Stuarts, 1590–1640*, 2nd ed. (Cambridge: Cambridge University Press, 2023; first published London: Longmans, 1972), 155–56. Not only did the moots involve multiple parties, but also multiple languages, with Law French being spoken by the Inner and Utter Barristers, and English by the Benchers—and no doubt with a fair sprinkling of Latin maxims. On law and language in this period, see, recently, Gwilym Dodd, 'Languages and Law in Late Medieval England: English, French and Latin', in Candice Barrington and Sebastian Sobecki (eds.), *The Cambridge Companion to Medieval English Law and Literature* (Cambridge: Cambridge University Press, 2019), 17–29.

At least in some moots, clearly, there were multiple parties directly involved—not only the two (or four) 'moot-men' on either side and the judges, but also others sitting in or beyond the bar, offering their own views. Further, interaction continued over dinner, and perhaps later over drinks. For all their variety, the moots clearly have in common a ludic quality, while at the same time focusing on issues of ethical and political controversy.

A Fourteenth-Century Moot

It is time, now, to look briefly at a particular example. The moot I have chosen comes from student notes probably written in the 1430s, but describing moots first devised in the 1380s and 1390s.[52] These notes include not only the moot problem but also a brief account of some of the arguments and pleas made when this problem was mooted. The case is as follows:

> Tenant in tail enfeoffs his son's daughter and a female stranger with warranty, and enters into religion and is professed; the heir brings a writ of formedon *quia habitum religionis assumpsit*; they plead his ancestor's feoffment with warranty; he pleads that he has nothing by descent, and [this being so found] he recovers; before execution is sued the father is deraigned by reason of precontract, and dies; [the heir] sues forth execution, whereby the sheriff and a stranger put him in seisin; then the son acknowledges the tenements to be the right of a stranger and [the stranger] grants and renders the same tenements to the son for term of his life, the reversion regardant to himself; then he grants reversion to the sheriff in fee, by virtue of which grant the tenant attorns; the son aliens the tenements to the two women in fee; the sheriff, perceiving the alienation to be to his disinheritance, enters in a moiety, and for the other moiety brings a writ *in consimili casu* and recovers by default; the women wish to recover.[53]

The moot is too complex for an exhaustive analysis of its issues, but I will engage with the main issues by paying attention to how, as a form of play, this moot problem might have helped generate insight into the

[52] From the Wiltshire Record Office. For further details, see Baker and Thorne, *Readings and Moots at the Inns of Court*, lxxvii. For the report, see Baker and Thorne, *Readings and Moots at the Inns of Court*, 40–41.

[53] Baker and Thorne, *Readings and Moots at the Inns of Court*, 40.

ethical and political values at stake. There is plenty of information that the moot facts withhold—this is, indeed, part of their playful character, requiring the mooters to fill in the details and consider what opportunities for argument such gaps enable. This under-specification, which requires active speculation on part of the mooters, generating and holding—especially in the course of the oral dialogue—multiple possibilities (of action and response) simultaneously, is a crucial part of the pedagogical point of these exercises.

In this moot, the father (who is an owner of entailed land) first makes a grant of the land to the two women (his son's daughter and a female stranger). The facts do not reveal the age of either the daughter or the female stranger. Thus, already here there is an ambiguity, with important repercussions on procedure: if the parties to whom land is granted are under 21, then a question arises as to whether they can bring an action immediately or whether they must wait until they are 21. Indeed, over one-third of the report made by the student concerns the moot court's reflections on the proper procedure to take when the parties making a writ of novel disseisin or *mort d'ancestor* are 'infants' (that is, under 21).[54]

This question of the proper procedure in the case of infants seeking a writ is further complicated by the presence of a warranty. The father grants the land to the two women 'with warranty'—that is to say, with the title guaranteed by himself and his heirs. Should the presence of a warranty matter to the procedure for a writ of novel disseisin or *mort d'ancestor* when the parties seeking the writ are infants? The moot court discusses this in some detail, considering various implications and consequences of allowing the infant parties to proceed immediately or later, for instance, for matters of proof. Clearly, this was something arguable: which is the better procedure: allowing immediate action or requiring the parties to wait? The moot facts as stated do not obviously raise the issue—it only appears if the mooters plead it as if the two women are infants. It is the under-specification of the facts of the moot that allows for the generation of issues and their debate. And, whenever there is a debatable topic, there

[54] The writ of novel disseisin was a procedure designed to offer someone deprived of some land holding ('disseised') to recover it swiftly. The action came before a jury, and its members were asked whether the plaintiff had been disseised unlawfully and whether the defendant was the one who did it. The writ of *mort d'ancestor* (meaning 'death of ancestor', and also an action before a jury) was available to heirs who thought that they had been deprived of their inheritance.

is also room for a normative discretion—for judgement informed by a sensitivity to the attendant ethical and political values. In this context, these values include the workability and attractiveness of procedures of proof.

Returning to the facts, when the father grants the land to the women with warranty, he is discontinuing the estate tail, or attempting to do so. He then enters holy orders. The son, relying, it seems, on the father entering the holy orders, seeks the land back, despite the land having been granted with warranty. He deploys the writ of formedon *quia habitum religionis assumpsit.*[55] This is also somewhat strange, for the writ was in theory only available when the ancestor who had alienated the land had died, and here the father had not yet died. Should the son have been allowed to do this? In their defence, the two women plead the warranty. The warranty can be challenged by the plaintiff heir (the son) through the plea of 'riens per discent', i.e. admitting the deed which had been granted. So the son says that he has not received any assets from his ancestor and so he should not be displaced by the warranty. If the jury accepts that he has no assets, he is not bound by the warranty. Here, we are told, the son wins the point, and so gains the right to the land.

However, in one of the unexpected and sudden twists of fate characteristic of the moots,[56] before the son gets execution by the judgement, the father is thrown out of holy orders. We are told that this is because the father had made a contract to marry before becoming a priest or monk (this is what is meant by being 'deraigned by reason of precontract'). After having been thrown out, the father dies. Here, we encounter arguably one of the central questions of the moot. What ought to be the effect of the father's deraignment on the rights of the son and the two women? We know from the student notes that this was indeed a question that was explored by the mooters in this case. The mooters pleading on behalf of the two women argued that the father's deraignment (his having been kicked out of holy orders) meant that it put everyone back into the position they were in both before the father had become a priest or monk and

[55] The writ of formedon was a writ available for the recovery of lands or tenements by virtue of a gift in tail. The 'quia habitum religionis assumpsit' version was where the gift had been given in a religious context.

[56] See also Karen Cunningham, '"So Many Books, So Many Rolls of Ancient Time": The Inns of Court and *Gorboduc*', in Denis Kezar ed., *Solon and Thespis: Law and Theatre in the English Renaissance* (Notre Dame: Notre Dame University Press, 2007), 197–217.

before the son had sued on the execution. In other words, they argued that the two women ought to have rights to the land—that the father's deraignment prior to execution meant that the son lost the rights to the land he had temporally acquired. This was clearly another highly debatable point. In support of their argument, the mooters pleading on behalf of the two women brought analogies that, they argued, supported their case: they said that the grant of entailed land was just like an issue of debt, and that in the latter it had been recognised that deraignment brought the parties back to their original position. Further, they proposed analogies between deraignment and becoming an outlaw and then ceasing to be one, and becoming a serf and then ceasing to be one. The court, in turn, disagreed with them, pointing to distinctions between these scenarios and the facts of the moot. Such arguments clearly invoke moral and political issues and show us once again how substantive considerations enter into what, to contemporary ears, may sound like mere matters of procedure: should the procedure be the same for entailed land as for debt, and are priests or monks the same as outlaws and serfs? One imagines this was explored, debated and discussed, not only in the performance of the moots, but also beyond, at dinner and over drinks.

I have but scratched the surface of this moot, but even this brief analysis reveals something of the ways in which the mooting process, through its distinct dynamics of play, enables the generation of insight about matters of weighty controversy and importance. What mooting problems like this did was to construct a safe, experimental space in which to explore multiple possible forms of action and the pleas one might make in relation to them, as well as different possible issues the parties might agree on. The mooters shared and discussed, on multiple occasions and over an extended period of time, different ways of constructing the facts so as to facilitate the making of different forms of actions, pleas and issues. Although the forms of moot problems resembled those of the Court of Common Pleas, the substantive problems they raised were not ones that were likely to be seen in legal practice. They thus enabled the mooters to play in the outer suburbs of the law which called for the exercise of uncertain and delicate ethical and political judgement. This was at once playful and devilishly difficult. It was also very much connected to exploring the moral stakes in any choice of form of action, plea and issue in a real case—values concerned with justice being done to one of the parties, facilitating peace between the parties and maintaining the authority, workability and attractiveness of the relevant court and common law procedure generally.

Conclusion

This chapter has argued that focusing on early modern legal pedagogy allows us to view the ludic dimensions of knowledge more clearly than we can otherwise do. It has been shown, both by reference to the broader context of life at the Inns of Court, but also more specifically by reference to the moots, just how deeply students aspiring to be serjeants were immersed in exploring ethical and political issues through a collective, embodied, sensory and affective process of making insight. It is this serious play that prepared future serjeants for the most challenging aspect of their professional life: being able to participate in pleading and judging. When we can apply this analysis of ludic pedagogy to the practice of pleading in the Court of Common Pleas, we may well find that just as with mooting, so in pleading, there are many productive relations to explore between the practice of law and that of literature.[57] This exciting prospect I leave for another occasion.

[57] See, for example, Susanne Sara Thomas, 'What the Man of Law Can't Say: The Buried Legal Argument of the Wife of Bath's *Prologue*', *The Chaucer Review*, 31:3 (1997), 256–71; and Richard McCormick Houser, 'Alisoun Takes Exception: Medieval Legal Pleading and the Wife of Bath', *The Chaucer Review*, 48:1 (2013), 66–90.

CHAPTER 10

"A Delightful Measure": Imagining Barfield's Poetic Jurisdiction

Gary Watt

Owen Barfield (1898–1997) can teach us a great deal about the territories of law and of poetry and what it means to connect them and to move between them. Barfield was one of the celebrated Oxford "Inklings", along with such luminaries as J. R. R. Tolkien and C. S. Lewis. A literature graduate, he worked as a poet and author for a decade before working for more than a quarter of a century as a solicitor in the family firm in London. On his retirement, aged 60, he continued to work for many years as an essayist and visiting lecturer. His reflections on the tensions between his literary and legal self, revealed in his book *This Ever Diverse Pair* (1950), provide a stimulating personal insight into what it means to live a life polarized between practice in literature and law.[1] His friend, rival, and fellow Inkling C. S. Lewis called it "a high and sharp philosophic

G. Watt (✉)
University of Warwick, Coventry, UK
e-mail: g.watt@warwick.ac.uk

[1] Owen Barfield, *This Ever Diverse Pair* (London: Victor Gollanz, 1950). Page references are to the Barfield Press edition (Oxford, 2010).

S. Mukherji and D. Roberts (eds.), *Literature and the Legal Imaginary*, Crossroads of Knowledge in Early Modern Literature 4,
https://doi.org/10.1007/978-3-031-74093-0_10

comedy, more fully a work of art and more original than anything I have read for a long time".[2] It is indeed a profound philosophical work, but its concern to provide an account of quotidian life from the internal perspectives of a lawyer reveals a practical path to anyone looking for a way into Barfield's works and thought. Its great revelation is that to participate in the poetic, one must perform and one must play. If one could define in English words the mellifluent trills and warbles of a blackbird's song, one might then, I suppose, be able to summarize Barfield's works and thought in a few sentences. A much more reliable approach, in the case both of Barfield and the bird, is to linger and to listen as fully as one can. Saul Bellow was a huge admirer of Owen Barfield. In many of his letters to him he writes in a humble mode that makes him sound almost like a disciple of the Englishman. In one he writes "...it wasn't until I read your book on Romanticism that I began to understand something about the defeat of imaginative knowledge in modern times!".[3] Yet, writing to another friend four years after he was awarded the Nobel Prize for Literature, this great thinker and worker of words confesses to a certain inability to express the essence of Barfield in a way that would make sense to the outsider:

> I sometimes wonder what one can get out of Barfield if one hasn't learned the "system." Some of it is very curious, the different view of physics, for certain, the conviction that the law of the conservation of energy is all a mistake (this idea has too many poetic implications to be dismissed). My friends refuse to take any of this seriously. I forgive them as a friend should, and I perform other operations, in confirmation of my right to hold peculiar views. (Or is it a privilege, not a right?) Then I feel that I'm being faithful to Truth, through thick and thin.[4]

When Bellow writes "I perform other operations", he hits upon a notion of personal performance that might have helped him to bring Barfield to a wider audience. Barfield invites playful participation. One comes closest to expressing Barfield's thought and what he can bring to thinking about law and literature when one tries to perform his ideas in practical ways. In this chapter I offer a performance of that sort. I do not offer a theory,

[2] C. S. Lewis, 'Life's Partners', *Time and Tide*, 31 (1950), 286.

[3] Saul Bellow, Letter to Owen Barfield, 24 July 1975 (Carboneras, Almeria, Spain).

[4] Saul Bellow, Letter to Ralph Ross, 15 June 1980 (Chicago).

for theory, like points of view in a theater, is the business of the spectator. I will put Barfield’s words center stage and I will play with them a little. This is Watt performing Barfield’s script and if the product is Barfield-Watt, rather than a simplistic summary of Barfield, that is exactly as it should be if we are to appreciate participatory practice in literature and law. The point is that every reader can play along in their own way. If this sounds unhelpful, I can offer by way of assistance my own conclusion that a key part of Barfield’s thought is his discovery that playing with linguistic and conceptual polarities, as poetry does and drama does, is productive of motive energy (the power to move us). As we shall see shortly, Barfield compares this to the way that magnetic polarity contributes to the production of current in a dynamo. A related insight is to say that for Barfield this playfulness and this production of energy out of the material fabric of a word is a source of pleasure and of meaningful human participation in language. To put it much too simply, wordplay is the serious connection between the practice of the lawyer and the practice of the poet. Passivity is anathema for Barfield. Consider, for instance, his warning to those who subject poetry to criticism without engaging their own creativity: “really dreadful pitfalls open at the feet of the unpoetic critic” whose “endless appraisals” must be “leavened by some creative vigor of his own” or else “he is in danger of losing all sympathy with the Poetic itself”.[5] In Barfield’s philosophy, the subject naturally participates in the object. Meaning emerges, in other words, when the subject poet practices (plays with, performs) the object that is the word.

Michael Di Fuccia’s book *Owen Barfield: Philosophy, Poetry and Theology* begins with a foreword in this vein. The foreword, which was written by Barfield’s grandson, Owen A. Barfield, concludes with a call and a challenge to the reader to attune to the sounds and rhythms of Barfield’s thought and to participate in the movement rather than being merely a passive spectator of it:

> Grandfather’s voice is like a distant drumbeat drawing us to the parade where we find like-minded revelers enjoying the rhythm of the festivities

[5] Owen Barfield, *Poetic Diction: A Study in Meaning*, first published London: Faber and Gwyer, 1928; this and subsequent page reference are to the Barfield Press edition (Oxford, 2010), 166.

> ... Grandfather's has been the quiet voice, but we may still find it to be the most persuasive.[6]

Barfield's voice has certainly been quiet in the scholarship of law and literature. James Boyd White is among a mere handful of law and literature scholars to have attended to him. White notes that when he was in law school in the early 1960s

> ... there were only a scattering of contemporary pieces explicitly about the connections between law and literature: an essay by Justice Cardozo...; a fine article on judicial style by Walker Gibson; a popular anthology compiled by Ephraim London...; and important work by Owen Barfield..., an English lawyer (of whose work at the time I was unfortunately not aware).[7]

White went on to refer to Barfield in his books *When Words Lose Their Meaning* (1984) and *Justice as Translation* (1990), and there is clearly a harmony between White's appreciation for the power of words to constitute community and Barfield's notion that legal language can be poetically productive of social progress.[8] Leonora Ledwon's summary of Barfield's approach works almost as well as a primer for White's own project, especially when one recalls that it was White who asked, "Is The Judge Really A Poet?".[9] Ledwon writes that

> the language of the law...can be at its heart what Owen Barfield calls a poetic language, not a theoretical one—a language that works by association and connotation, by allusion and reference, by the way words are put

[6] Michael Di Fuccia, *Owen Barfield: Philosophy, Poetry and Theology* (Eugene, OR: Cascade Books, 2016), viii.

[7] James Boyd White, 'The Cultural Background of The Legal Imagination', in Austin Sarat, Cathrine O. Frank, and Matthew Anderson, eds., *Teaching Law and Literature* (New York: Modern Language Association, 2011), 29–39 (31).

[8] James Boyd White, *When Words Lose Their Meaning: Constitutions and Reconstitutions of Language, Characters and Community* (Chicago: University of Chicago Press, 1984); James Boyd White, *Justice as Translation: An Essay in Cultural and Legal Criticism* (Chicago: University of Chicago Press, 1990).

[9] James Boyd White, *The Legal Imagination* (Boston: Little, Brown & Company, 1973), 761. In 2018, on its 45th anniversary, the entire book was reissued by Aspen Publishers. Reviewed in *Law and Humanities*, 31:1 (2019).

together to make a whole. In this way it can maintain connections with the terms and processes of ordinary life and ordinary language.[10]

Kathy Eden draws out from Barfield the same strand, by which I mean the idea that the practice of legal language has a rhetorical capacity to stimulate the "workings" of the mind even as it stimulates the "making" of society.[11] Another scholar of law and literature, Jeanne Gaakeer, is unusual in devoting an entire page to Barfield.[12] This is not surprising when one considers that Gaakeer is a senior judge in The Netherlands who has written extensively of her appreciation for James Boyd White and of the practical experience of judging.[13] She appreciates Owen Barfield as a fellow poet-practitioner.

These examples aside, most scholars, myself included, who have been concerned with the shared rhetorical or fictional practices of law and literature, have tended to quote Barfield only in passing or in a footnote. The rhetorical thinker and literary critic Wayne C Booth once taught a ten-week course on Barfield with his colleague Saul Bellow,[14] but scholars of law have given him nothing close to such sustained engagement. Barfield is certainly quotable, but his commitment to theosophy and the metaphysical teachings of Rudolph Steiner (which posit the possibility of an empirical and scientific understanding of the spiritual realm) has arguably positioned him as something of an outlier. That said, Steiner's ideas singled him out as an enemy of the Nazi party from its very earliest days as the German Workers' Party and for that alone he and Barfield would deserve serious attention. I cannot offer anything like a comprehensive account of Barfield's thought here, but I can offer a route to a fuller appreciation. If the reader wishes to travel further, Barfield's book *Poetic*

[10] Leonora Ledwon, *Law and Literature: Text and Theory* (New York: Garland Publishing, 1996); this quotation is from the Palgrave edition (London, 2015) at 16–17.

[11] Kathy Eden, *Poetic and Legal Fiction in the Aristotelian Tradition* (Princeton: Princeton University Press, 1986), 63–64.

[12] Jeanne Gaakeer, 'Configuring Justice', *No Foundations: An Interdisciplinary Journal of Law and Justice*, 9 (2012), 20–44 (30).

[13] Jeanne Gaakeer, *Hope Springs Eternal: An Introduction to the Work of James Boyd White* (Amsterdam: Amsterdam University Press, 1998); Jeanne Gaakeer, *Judging from Experience: Law, Praxis, Humanities* (Edinburgh: Edinburgh University Press, 2019).

[14] Wayne C. Booth, *My Many Selves: The Quest for a Plausible Harmony* (Logan, UT: Utah State University Press, 2006), 114.

Diction: A Study in Meaning (1928) and his article "Poetic Diction and Legal Fiction" (1947) are good way markers, as is his book *Saving the Appearances* (1957).[15] He has produced a significant library of works, the vast majority of which remain in print or accessible online through the good offices of the Owen Barfield Literary Estate and their website *owenbarfield.org*.

To play my part with Barfield's words, I will begin by setting out my own idea of playful polarity before taking us to Barfield for amplification, dialogue, and occasional dispute. I largely agree with Barfield—certainly in the inevitably selective way in which I represent him here—but occasionally he and I may be what Barfield calls "sweet enemies",[16] offering opposing opinions that operate productively as polarities of the same matter while sharing the hope for improved—that is, more careful and attentive—social practice. Equity and Law are "sweet enemies" in that sense, as we will see.

Let me start with a dumb show. Let us imagine that the stage lights are down, and that in the darkness we can just make out the sound of a recurrent, rhythmic thwack—sharp yet dull and weighty. As the lights go up, a table is revealed center-stage and standing over it we see that a baker is holding a ball of dough which she works with steady deliberation. She knocks it back on the table, stretching it out with the heels of her hands so that it takes the shape of a bone, long and thin in the middle with masses at each end. The stretching of the dough strengthens it by exercising the wheat proteins like strands of muscle.

This exercise is a picture of practice, and in particular that mode of practice that involves itself in the dynamic relationship between the contraction and expansion of meanings. It shows us the practical relationship between law and equity, between prose and poetry, and between law and poetry. Where law tends toward contraction, poetry tends toward

[15] Barfield, *Poetic Diction*; Owen Barfield, 'Poetic Diction and Legal Fiction', in C. S. Lewis, ed., *Essays Presented to Charles Williams* (Oxford: Oxford University Press, 1947), 106–27; page references are to the reissue in *The Rediscovery of Meaning and Other Essays* (Oxford: Barfield Press, 2013), 63–93. Owen Barfield, *Saving the Appearances: A Study in Idolatry* (London: Faber and Faber, 1957); page references are to the Barfield Press edition (Oxford, 2011).

[16] Owen Barfield, *Speaker's Meaning*, first published Middletown, CT: Wesleyan University Press, 1967; this and subsequent page references are to the Barfield Press edition (Oxford, 2011), 21.

connotation. Poetical and rhetorical figures such as metaphor and paronomasia play with words by stretching the sense of a word into relation with other senses of the word. From the point of view of legal drafting, this introduces vagueness at the expense of precision, but from a poetic point of view the sense of the word is enlarged through play and is productive of a wider range of experience and a greater depth of appreciation. Metaphor is a poetic pulling apart toward the poles, as one might tease out a ball of dough, but never to the point of breaking the center. Playful connection is everything. In its etymological sense, metaphor denotes a carrying over from one place to another. The word comes from the Greek *metaphora* (think "meta-ferry"), which in Latin is called *transferre* or *translatio*. Yet we must resist the temptation to regard metaphor as implying dislocation of one side from the other. It is crucial to keep the "ferry" central to the exercise and constantly moving. Perhaps the ideal is to see metaphor as a cable ferry that traverses a watercourse by following a line fixed between opposing shores. An example is the old chain ferry that crosses the river near Shakespeare's burial place in Stratford-upon-Avon. It is only when both sides of the metaphor are kept in constant communication and in a state of constant tension that the metaphor is poetically productive. Metaphor—as a sort of poetic movement or stretching of meanings—operates in poetry, as it can operate in law, to stretch the mind with the puzzle to know how poles of meaning may be connected. To break the bond that keeps two distinct senses in playful unity, to refuse to hold both senses at once, is to destroy the metaphor and dissipate the energy that wants to pull the senses back together and to solve the puzzle of their alienation. The legal mind, like the poetic mind, is called upon to contemplate the vast range of possible senses that can attend a word, but whereas the practice of the poetic mind is to hold several senses at once so as to make the wordplay poetically generative, the practice of the legal mind, at least in drafting mode, is to exclude all senses but one and thereby to make the word logically reductive. Only when it comes to the lawyer's effort to get around the wording of a document—draft dodging, so to speak—does the lawyer resort to the more expansive, creative, connotative, and multivalent poetic mode.

Pleasure plays a part in all this. The following passage is taken from Barfield's conclusion to *Poetic Diction*:

> If not the prime *object*, pleasure is undoubtedly an excellent test, or mark, of the presence of poetry. For what is absolutely necessary to the present

> existence of poetry? Movement. ... the experience of aesthetic pleasure betrays the real presence of movement ...
> ... Great poetry is the progressive incarnation of life in consciousness. Hence the absolute value of aesthetic pleasure as a criterion; for before we can feel it, we must have become aware in some degree of the actual progress—not merely of its results.[17]

Pleasure derives from movement having qualities of change and progress:

> the pleasure of appreciation depends upon ... change itself. If I pass a coil of wire between the poles of a magnet, I generate in it an electric current—but only do so while the coil is positively moving across the lines of force.... Current only flows when I am actually bringing the coil in and taking it away again. So it is with the poetic mood, which, like the dreams to which it has so often been compared, is kindled by the passage from one plane of consciousness to another. It lives during that moment of transition and then dies...
> ...we know instinctively that, if we are to feel pleasure, we must have change. ...poetic experience depends on a "difference of potential", a kind of *discrepancy* between two moods or modes of consciousness.[18]

The action of teasing and releasing—of puzzling and resolving—is inherently pleasing because it involves movement. The play is produced out of the drama that is the dynamic tension of opposites—protagonist against antagonist. The joint—the joining of two things—has "play" only if the articulation admits movement. To put it another way, we can say that to pull apart the poles creates a differential and this brings a sort of stored form of energy, akin to the energy stored by an electrical cell having oppositely charged poles. The puzzle of wordplay can be solved only by holding both poles at the same time and thereby discharging the poetic energy like a spark across the gap. It is exhilarating. Wordplay produces pleasure. This is the case, as noted earlier, whether we are practicing poetry or law. We might not think of legal practice as pleasurable. It is of course serious business for all concerned, but for lawyers it is vitally important that words should be dynamically engaged with,

[17] Barfield, *Poetic Diction*, 178–79.

[18] Barfield, *Poetic Diction*, 44–47.

and not used as dead letters. Legal performance, especially in its equitable mode, requires the practitioner to attend to the sorts of flexibility of interpretation and application that only wordplay can bring in.

The experience of poetic pleasure is especially intense in metaphor. Barfield sees metaphor somewhat as I see the two extremities of a ball of dough, or the opposite ends of a bridge or cable ferry: "the two should be somehow inevitably fused together into one simple meaning".[19] If the word "fused" seems unhelpfully static, let us think of it as the sort of fuse that carries an electric current. Cicero, the most famous forerunner to Barfield's philosophical endeavor to reconcile the practical rhetoric of literature and law, was deeply appreciative of the connection between metaphor and pleasure. In *De Oratore*, he writes that

> ... it often appears to me wonderful why all men are more delighted with words used in a metaphorical or foreign sense than in their own proper and natural signification ... even in the greatest abundance of proper words, men are much more charmed with such as are uncommon, if they are used metaphorically with judgment. (Cicero, 3.159)[20]

The phrase "a delightful measure" that was chosen for the title of this essay comes from Shakespeare's description of a dance in *Richard II*. As John of Gaunt attempts to engage his son, Henry Bolingbroke, to an imaginative mitigation of the king's sentence of banishment, he invites the banished Bolingbroke to suppose that the strides of his exiled tread are but steps performed in "a delightful measure or a dance" (1.3.291).[21] I have chosen this phrase for my title because it expresses qualities of pleasure and movement with overtones of law and order. Dance was important to Barfield. He married a dancer and choreographer, Maud Douie, and was himself a proficient dancer;[22] their daughter Lucy, to whom her godfather C. S. Lewis dedicated *The Lion, the Witch and the Wardrobe*, trained as a dancer and worked as a dance teacher. But it is the

[19] Barfield, 'Poetic Diction and Legal Fiction', 67.

[20] Marcus Tullius Cicero, *De Oratore* (*On Oratory and Orators*, trans. J. S. Watson (New York: Harper and Brothers, 1881)).

[21] Unless otherwise stated, quotations are from the most recent edition of the Arden Shakespeare.

[22] Marjorie Lamp Mead, *Owen Barfield: A Biographical Note* (1985): https://www.wheaton.edu/media/wade-center/files/authors/OBbio-Marj_20181114.pdf.

conjunction of rhythm and law, dance and adjudication, that makes the Shakespearean context suggestive. Through metaphoric and imaginative play Gaunt attempts to translate the strict measure of legal judgment into a measure of pleasure. Bolingbroke's response is a rebuttal that at once doubts the remedial capacity of poetic imagination and inscribes in his own body the felt sensation of legal judgment:

> O, who can hold a fire in his hand
> By thinking on the frosty Caucasus?
> Or cloy the hungry edge of appetite
> By bare imagination of a feast?
> Or wallow naked in December snow
> By thinking on fantastic summer's heat? (1.3.294–299)

The play between Gaunt and Bolingbroke exists in the tension between two notions of reality—the translated imaginary and the untranslated sensory. Gaunt's translated imaginary operates through the imaginative attribution of meaning to experience, whereas Bolingbroke's response would appear to deny that there is room for meaning to be added to an experience that has already been filled to capacity with the physical sensation of pain. On Bolingbroke's analysis, if the body and mind are full of pain, then imagined pleasures mean nothing. A body in pain is in this sense full of meaning, even if the pain in itself may not be meaningful in an abstract or higher sense. A body of law can be approached in a similar way, as being subject to an untranslated prosaicness or to a translated imaginary. An extreme positivist view of law can be characterized as the former, for it is sated by an overriding sense of law as rules. (US Supreme Court Justice Antonin Scalia was thinking in this mode when he equated "the Rule of Law" with "the law of rules".[23]) If an untranslated sensory experience of law as rules fills the law with meaning, what room can there be for the translated imaginary sense of law as something dependent upon external, including moral, considerations?[24] In a brilliant essay on H. L. A. Hart's postscript to *The Concept of Law*, Timothy Endicott

[23] Antonin Scalia, 'The Rule of Law as a Law of Rules', *University of Chicago Law Review*, 56:4 (1989), 1175–88.

[24] See H. L. A. Hart, 'Positivism and the Separation of Law and Morals', *Harvard Law Review*, 71:4 (1958), 593–629.

summarizes Hart to say that "*Meaning* is what speakers share".[25] The present question is whether a positivist concept of law as rules depends upon speakers sharing one authoritative meaning of rule and law to the exclusion of all others. In short, the question is whether there is scope in the legal appreciation of rules for the poetic and imaginative ascription of meaning? If there is not, we must conclude that the meaning-full quality of "law as rule" renders it morally, poetically, and imaginatively meaningless inasmuch as meaning is something that may be ascribed to rule *ab extra* rule itself so as to give it human worth. Such a simple portrayal of positivism may be a caricature, but there is truth in the exaggeration. What cannot be doubted is that if ever we find ourselves satisfied with the positivist notion that rules provide a full expression of law, we will have abandoned the struggle that should be central to our encounters with legal language, which is the poet's struggle to ascribe wider meaning to words in the face of law's habitual effort to close meanings down.

Barfield indicates that complex multiplicity of linguistic meanings may be the hallmark of the poetic:

> you can perhaps also have meanings that are multiple or complex without being separable; and this problem, too, has invited a great deal of attention from those interested in the study of the theory of poetry—those in particular who find in the poet's use of ambivalent, or multivalent, language his chief distinguishing mark as a poet.[26]

Contrast Justice Antonin Scalia's observation, made in jocular mode to an Arts audience that "[t]he main business of a lawyer is to take the romance, the mystery, the irony, the ambiguity out of everything".[27] This contrast brings me to what I would offer as a definitional distinction between law and poetry—I mean law in its drafting and regulatory mode and poetry in its most playful and least prosaic mode—namely that law seeks to close down meanings whereas poetry seeks to open them up.

[25] Timothy A. O. Endicott, 'Herbert Hart and the Semantic Sting', *Legal Theory*, 4:3 (1998), 283–300 (292).

[26] Barfield, *Speaker's Meaning*, 38.

[27] See Daniel J. Wakin, 'Scalia Defends Government's Right to Deny Art Funds', *The New York Times* (23 September 2005), www.nytimes.com/2005/09/23/nyregion/scalia-defends-governments-right-to-deny-art-funds.html.

Barfield suggests that "Language has two primary functions, one of which is expression and the other communication". For Barfield, expression aims at "fullness" not in the sense of excluding or capturing other meanings, but in the sense of integrating multiple meanings into a dynamic whole:

> ... The goal to which expression aspires, or the criterion by which it must be measured, is something like fullness or sincerity. The goal toward which communication aspires is accuracy.
> ...Expression could say to Communication, in the words of Alice's Duchess, "The more there is of mine, the less there is of yours"; but on the other hand the relation is a *dynamic* rather than a *quantitative* one. This means that, though each of them is exclusive of, or counted to, the other, yet they are both concurrently necessary. They are, so to speak, "sweet enemies." There is a tension, or polarity, between them. And it is in this polarity that the depths of language are to be found. The two functions conflict, they also co-operate. ...[28]

For Barfield, the multivalence of language yields something more than poetic pleasure. For one thing, it yields political utility. He points, for example, to multiple meanings of words as a defense against Nazi inquisition: "The word *Tarnung* was, I believe, extensively used under the heel of the Nazi tyranny in Germany for the precautionary practice of hiding one meaning in another".[29] For another, multivalence of language also yields hope for social progress. Language must live if it is to evolve in step with societal changes, and law, like language, must evolve too. He sees unvarying law as a restraint on law's capacity to keep pace with society:

> Phenomena exactly repeated are not life, they are mechanism. Life varies, law is of its nature unvarying. Yet at the same time it is the function of law to serve, to express, and indeed partly to *make* the social life of the community.[30]

There is nothing especially surprising in the suggestion that laws evolve as language evolves. Barfield's more radical argument, sometimes termed "objective idealism", is that human consciousness evolves alongside both

[28] Barfield, *Speaker's Meaning*, 20–22.

[29] Barfield, 'Poetic Diction and Legal Fiction', 70.

[30] Barfield, 'Poetic Diction and Legal Fiction', 86.

and that concept and conception are in some sense mutually dependent. The character of Sanderson in *Worlds Apart* expressed it this way:

> if you start from the *brain* and say it "constructs" the world it is aware of, you seem to leave out of account the fact that the brain as an object of observation is itself part of a world which you yourself have constructed. Surely you have got to *start* with the *act* of construction and not with the brain![31]

He objects that the physical human brain, without mind, can have no monopoly over the perception of reality and that scientific notions of reality are inadequate without the participation of mind operating beyond the capacities of the physical brain. The mind in this sense participates in the production of reality, hence "nature is the reflected image of man's conscious and unconscious self". This leads him to reject "the historical fallacy of born literalness".[32] He rejects the idea that a stone was ever simply a stone. For him, a stone has always been inseparable from the linguistic and poetic idea of a stone. He notes that science assumes "that the real world is a 'somewhat', in the construction of which the mind ... does not participate; of which it is purely a detached observer", and argues to the contrary that "The mind first creates what it perceives as objects".[33]

At the start of *Saving the Appearances* he illustrates this creative capacity of the mind with the example of a rainbow:

> Look at a rainbow. While it lasts, it is, or appears to be, a great arc of many colours occupying a position out there in space. It touches the horizon between that chimney and that tree; a line drawn from the sun behind you and passing through your head would pierce the centre of the circle of which it is a part. And now, before it fades, recollect all you have ever

[31] Owen Barfield, *Worlds Apart: A Dialogue of the 1960s*, first published London: Faber and Faber, 1963; this and subsequent page references are to the Barfield Press edition (Oxford, 2010), 56.

[32] Owen Barfield, 'The Meaning of 'Literal'', in L. C. Knights and Basil Cottle, eds., *Metaphor and Symbol: Proceedings of the Twelfth Symposium of the Colston Research Society* (London: Butterworth and Co., 1960), 48–57; this quotation is from the reissue in *The Rediscovery of Meaning and Other Essays* (Oxford: Barfield Press, 2013), 45–62 (60–61).

[33] Barfield, *Poetic Diction*, 8, 19.

been told about the rainbow and its causes, and ask yourself the question *Is it really there?*[34]

What other instances can we think of in which the mind might be said to have created the very thing it perceives as an object? Death may be one such. It is the one certainty of life, but it is really a metaphor by Barfield's definition, because "it attempts to arouse cognition of the unknown by suggestion from the known".[35] Was it ever possible to express the perception that something leads from the land of the living to what Hamlet (or Shakespeare) terms the "undiscovered country" of the dead (3.1.78) without making death concretely real through the metaphorical use of some "thing"; be it door, ferry, or bridge? Let us ask of death, as we ask of Barfield's rainbow, "Is it really there?" Could it be that death has no reality outside the metaphoric language that is used to describe it? To put it another way, in what sense *other* than the metaphorical, can death be "real". It is, after all, a "thing" with neither matter nor place nor time (unless it be a phantasmal spark of time—what has been called a "*scintilla temporis*").[36] The same may be said of other intangible abstractions such as love and justice, and so we find that in the description of such ideas our reliance on the concrete reality of metaphor is always inevitably strong. From the first human encounter with death, was the human mind not instantly and constantly engaged in processes of coming to terms with it, which is to say producing linguistic terms to account for it? I should clarify that I am talking of death and not of dying or of the state of being dead. Death cannot be equated to the state of being alive or to the state of being dead, but more properly describes the moment of movement between states. It is the epitome of carrying over from one place to another and is therefore in the truest etymological sense *metaphora* or *translatio*. We might now hear new meaning, or rediscover an old meaning, in Shakespeare's phrase, uttered by Touchstone in *As You Like It*: "I kill thee, make thee away, translate thy life into death" (5.2.53–4). Metaphor, that most lively and state-changing mode of linguistic expression, is naturally resorted to in order to supply a name for this most abstract and otherwise inexpressible process of passing over. If death (I say again, not

[34] Barfield, *Saving the Appearances*, 10.

[35] Barfield, *Poetic Diction*, 106.

[36] The term has been used by the judicial committee of the House of Lords, *Abbey National Building Society* v *Cann* (1991) 1 A.C. 56 (HL), per Lord Oliver at 93.

"dying" or "being dead") is not literal but only and purely metaphorical, this would explain why death has always been so readily realized in relatable form through concrete metaphors and through personification. For Shakespeare, death was a rigorous legal agent—a "fell sergeant"—making an arrest (*Hamlet*, 5.2.341). Law itself operates in poetic mode when it purports to carry the person—the mask of legal personality—over the threshold of death by such means as personal representatives and testamentary will.[37] As metaphor can prompt the imagination to see a material thing ferrying the living to the world of the dead, so likewise a physical image adorning legal texts—be it cover art, frontispiece, or emblem—can ferry in the other direction, animating the dead letter with the imagination of life. Peter Goodrich's chapter in this collection is just the ticket for a journey he describes as one "from the passive page, the *litera mortua*...into life".[38]

When Barfield sets out his definitions at the start of *Poetic Diction*, he makes a choice that at first sight is surprising. He submits that "Meaning includes the whole content of a word, or of a group of words arranged in a particular order, other than the actual *sounds* of which they are composed".[39] Here Barfield seems to urge an awareness of mechanical soundwaves existing as vibrations of air while ruling out the attribution of meaning to the sensory and cognitive effects they produce via the medium of the ear. This is despite the fact that he repeatedly acknowledges the great significance of sound as an element of the poetic, for example where he writes that "in examining the texture of poetry one of the most important elements (a mansion to itself) is rhythm, sound, music".[40] If he is purporting to exclude poetic sound effects from the meaningful content of a word or group of words, is he correct? If he is not saying that, what is he saying? One instinctively feels that the musical tones that words sound are sometimes a meaningful element in the connotations of those words. Take the word "peace". Does it not connote certain non-rational or instinctive associations of a physical or cognitive sort even as a result of its mere sound effects? On that hearing, one meaningful association

[37] Gary Watt, *Shakespeare's Acts of Will: Law, Testament and Properties of Performance* (London: Bloomsbury Arden Shakespeare, 2016).

[38] Peter Goodrich's chapter (chapter 08) in the present collection.

[39] Barfield, *Poetic Diction*, 34.

[40] Barfield, 'Poetic Diction and Legal Fiction', 63.

of the word "peace" is a felt sense of "ease" that is pleasing for reasons other than the mere echo, rhyme, or assonance of those two words; for the sequence of "ee" and "s" sounds in such words as "peace", "ease", "dozy", "drowsy", and "sleep" surely expresses and evokes the primitive musical notes and rhythms of somnolent breath. Such a primitive sense might not be meaningful in a higher or abstract way, but it is surely meaningful in a profound and unmediated sense. If Barfield is rejecting pure sensory effects as being meaningless, then perhaps it is because he is indicating a distinction between physical sense and poetical sense that is somewhat akin to the distinction I drew earlier between Bolingbroke's "untranslated sensory" and Gaunt's "translated imaginary". Or perhaps, as the next quote suggests, Barfield was simply thinking of the evolved or abstract meaning of sound as something distinct from more primal senses in which sound is meaningful (including the primal sense of pleasure that flows from musical effects):

> ...one of the most efficient causes of pleasure is—palpably—sound; the rhythm, the music, and the manner in which rhythm and music are wedded to sense. ... Though they may be indistinguishable in practice, topically it is possible to distinguish the intellectual element in poetic meaning from the tonal.[41]

According to the distinction that Barfield draws here, we would have to conclude that birdsong, for instance, is poetically meaningless no matter that the sensation it produces is pleasurable. Yet, in *Saving the Appearances*, he finds meaning in the part played by sounds in the etymological evolution of words:

> ... the Semitic languages seem to point us back to the old unity of man and nature, through the shapes of their sounds. We feel those shapes not only as sounds, but also, in a manner, as *gestures* of the speech-organs — – and it is not so difficult to realize that these gestures were once gestures made with the whole body ...[42]

He also explores the sound dimension of etymology in *Poetic Diction*. There he cites a compelling instance of a physical sound effect that has

[41] Barfield, *Poetic Diction*, 39.

[42] Barfield, *Saving the Appearances*, 142.

undergone meaningful evolution. "Ruin" derives, he suggests, from primitive attempts to express the rumbling sound of solid matter falling in such events as earthquakes, avalanches, and landslides:

> In Latin... the four letters "r–u–i–n" never lost the power to suggest *movement*. In certain contexts they may seem to modern readers to possess a purely static and material reference; but if so, it is because those readers are of the kind described by Maupassant as demanding only a "sens", a definable meaning. The *soul* of such a word as "ruina" is really inseparable from motion.[43]

To illustrate the English language evolution of the word "ruin" from its earliest moving sense to its modern, more solid and static sense, Barfield first cites Saturn in Chaucer's *The Knights Tale* who boasts to Venus: "Min is the ruine of the highe halles, / The falling of the toures and of the walles."[44] He then turns to Shakespeare's *King John*, inviting us to "listen…to Salisbury's words, when he is confronted with Arthur's body lying huddled on the stones, where the fall has killed him"[45]:

> It is the shameful work of Hubert's hand;
> The practice and the purpose of the King –
> From whose obedience I forbid my soul,
> Kneeling before this ruin of sweet life... (4.3.62–5)

Barfield observes that:

> Shakespeare has felt the exact, whole significance of his word. The dead boy has *fallen* from the walls; the sweet life, which was in him too, has crumbled away; but wait—by Shakespeare's time the word is beginning to acquire its other meaning of the actual remains—and there is the shattered body lying on the ground! He has, indeed, found a soul in the word.[46]

[43] Barfield, *Poetic Diction*, 110.

[44] Barfield, *Poetic Diction*, 111.

[45] Barfield, *Poetic Diction*, 113.

[46] Barfield, *Poetic Diction*, 113–14.

Thus by Shakespeare's day, the user of the word "ruin" "could now mean, not only the falling itself, but *the thing fallen*. It is like watching a physical process of crystallization".[47] It may be doubted that any process of philological evolution is perfectly linear, and that almost certainly goes for Barfield's exemplary word "ruin". For before the word "ruin" appeared as such, its Anglo-Saxon cognates apparently expressed, in poetic usage at least, a combined or complex sense of the "thing falling" and the "thing fallen". An example appears in the Anglo-Saxon poem known as "The Ruin" in the line "Hrofas sind gehrorene, hreorge torras" (Roofs are fallen, ruinous towers).[48] The philological process of crystallization that Barfield observes may be less linear and more cyclical in its progress, like successive winters with ever-hardening frosts.

Progressive crystallization or fossilization of language is certainly observable in the legal context. For example, the legal idea of "proving" has undergone a reductive fossilization from its original sense of a questioning process (etymologically akin to "probing") to the modern sense in which proving denotes merely the static end of the process—the point at which the probing ceases and proof is established.[49] Petrification of the word "proving" may be attributable in part to the fact that it has been uprooted from its lively origins in the moving to and fro of rhetorical dialectic and has been rendered static by the statistician's project to reduce uncertainties to stateable number.[50] The fossilizing process is also observable in the crucial legal idea of "judgment". Nowadays we are far more likely to talk of the static noun "*a* legal judgment" rather than of "legal judgment" as a process. Julen Etxabe has argued with sophistication that "judgment" is today regarded as the final outcome of a trial (we might say the static moment of the final judicial statement on the matter) when judgment should properly be used to describe a more

[47] Barfield, *Poetic Diction*, 109.

[48] William C. Johnson Jr., 'The Ruin as Body-City Riddle', *Philological Quarterly*, 59 (1981), 397–411, posits a polarity between the ruined body and the ruined city that Barfield would no doubt have appreciated.

[49] Gary Watt, *Dress, Law and Naked Truth: A Cultural Study of Fashion and Form* (London: Bloomsbury Academic, 2013), 51–77 ('Shakespeare on Proof and Fabricated Truth').

[50] Lorna Hutson, *Circumstantial Shakespeare* (Oxford: Oxford University Press, 2015), 42.

open-ended, dialectical, and moving process of deliberation.[51] The words "discernment" and "discrimination", both derived etymologically from the process of "sifting", have resisted the same fossilized fate. We seldom talk of "*a* discernment" or "*a* discrimination".

We should not be surprised that the law provides instance after instance of the fossilizing tendency in language. I have suggested that poetry, with its preference for playfulness and multivalence, is the antidote to law's reductive tendency toward contraction. As I read Barfield, he would agree. The works of Shakespeare have frequently been juxtaposed with law. Perhaps that juxtaposition is attractive and productive because Shakespeare's poetic method is one that brings play to the frozen joints of language. Barfield presents Shakespeare as someone who can melt linguistic matter so as to get the molecules of meaning moving again:

> The influence of such a mind on the language in which it expresses itself can only be compared to the effect of high temperatures on solid matter. As imagination bodies forth the forms of things unknown, each molecule of suggestiveness contained in each word gains a mysterious freedom from its neighbours; the old images move to and fro distinctly in the listener's fancy, and when the sound has died away, not merely the shape, but what seemed to be the very substance of the word has been readjusted.[52]

If Barfield appears dismissive of the capacity of mere sound to be meaningful, perhaps his criticism is, at root, a complaint that the primitive audible root of a word does not display the flower of the word in its full bloom. There is, he might say, insufficient distance between root and flower in the mere sound or the unevolved metaphor to admit scope for meaningful play and pleasure. If metaphor is a ferry across a river, the river is sometimes too narrow to permit a poetic journey of real interest. The evolving, moving, and shifting mutual referencing between the poles of a relation (as between root and flower in my example) is, for Barfield, essential to the production of poetic pleasure. As he writes in the August 1972 Afterword to his 1928 work *Poetic Diction*: "It should be noted that *Poetic Diction* does not simply exalt the Poetic at the expense of the Prosaic, but emphasises their essential relation, their dependence on each

[51] Julen Etxabe, *The Experience of Tragic Judgment* (Abingdon: Routledge, 2012).

[52] Owen Barfield, *History in English Words*, first published London: Methuen & Co., 1926; the quotation is from the Faber and Faber edition (London, 1954), at 148–49.

other, and indeed their interpenetration".[53] The Afterword thereby ties the book back (in a pleasingly polar way) to the epigraph by which *Poetic Diction* is dedicated to Barfield's friend and rival C. S. Lewis: "Opposition is true friendship". Lewis described Barfield as "The Second Friend...the man who disagrees with you about everything...each learning the weight of the other's punches, and often more like mutually respectful enemies than friends".[54] They were, to apply Barfield's term, "sweet enemies".

Earlier I suggested that law and equity are sweet enemies that are joined in cooperative opposition. It is a relation that requires a metaphor, and ideally one with a sense of movement in it. Aristotle understood this when in his *Nicomachean Ethics* he offered the pliable leaden ruler used by masons—known as the Lesbian rule—as his metaphor for *epieikeia* (forbearance, yielding) as the needful flexible counterpart to rigid legal rule (book V, chapter 10). The fate of equity in English law has been one of fossilization through institutionalization. The regularization of proceedings and judgments in the Chancery courts tended to remove the humane life and movement that had been the essence of the earliest idea of equitable justice.[55] As Barfield writes, "Equity" in its institutional sense "begins as soon as the 'relation between two persons' begins to be recognised as a thing, as an object no less 'real,' in fact though not in name, than a piece of land".[56] In the institution of the English Chancery "trust", Chancery's achievement of attributing proprietary reality to a relationship of confidence between persons has made it especially hard to keep the human actors in view: "now the trust in this court is the same as the land, and the trustee is considered merely as an instrument of conveyance".[57]

How is the modern lawyer to live expressively in legal practice without becoming an instrument fossilized by the reductive tendencies of her profession? How is the modern judge to live creatively, and not just critically (in the objective sense that insists upon a lifeless vacuum of space

[53] Barfield, *Poetic Diction*, 222.

[54] C. S. Lewis, *Surprised by Joy: The Shape of my Early Life* (London: Geoffrey Bles, 1955), 189.

[55] Gary Watt, *Equity Stirring: The Story of Justice Beyond Law* (Oxford: Hart, 2009).

[56] Owen Barfield, 'Equity Between Man and Man', *Anthroposophy: A Quarterly Review of Spiritual Science*, 7:2 (1932), 134–56; this quotation is from the abridged reissue 'Understanding Equity', *Associative Economics Monthly* (2007), 4–5, at p. 2.

[57] *Burgess v Wheate* (1759) 1W Bl 123, 162; 96 ER 67, 84 (per Lord Mansfield).

between the judge and the object of their deliberation)? One way forward is to connect the judge to the judged and to open up possibilities for their mutual relation through moving participation. This, as I read him, is the way that Owen Barfield invites us to proceed. In this way we might one day hear law speaking again in its first voice, which is its poetic voice. The voice that made the world real might then remake the world, and we, the makers, might find pleasure in it.

I say "we", but can academics be practitioners with the possibility of participation? I hope so. In *This Ever Diverse Pair*, Barfield presents the tension between his pragmatic and poetic selves as partners in a law firm, called respectively Burden and Burgeon. In *Worlds Apart*, again speaking through the medium of his alter ego Burgeon, he imagines an ideal trans-disciplinary academe:

> A Senior Common Room that boasts an eminent biologist, a Hebrew scholar, an atomic physicist, two or three philosophers, a professor of comparative religion, a chaplain, a Freudian psychologist, and a leading anthropologist, with Law and English Literature thrown in for good measure, and all dining and wining together nearly every day! What amazingly interesting conversations you must have![58]

"Law and English Literature thrown in for good measure". For those of us who work on the chain ferry between those two sides of the river that seems a suitably humble and hopeful note to end on.

[58] Barfield, *Worlds Apart*, 2.

PART V

Law and Poetics

CHAPTER 11

Gottfried von Strassburg's *Tristan* and the Allegory of Law

Conrad van Dijk

> [G]enuine allegory does not seek the 'meaning' of a work, but rather functions to reveal its structure of multiple meanings, and thereby to modify the very meaning of the word *meaning*.[1]

While the study of literature and law has involved much debate about where to draw the disciplinary lines,[2] my focus will be less on the ever-shifting boundaries and more on the method we use to cross them. After all, literature and law are not simply mirrors of each other. A literary text does more than reflect contemporary legal issues, and the law's literary moments are more than imaginative embellishments. As we'll see in the

[1] Fredric Jameson, *Allegory and Ideology* (London: Verso, 2019), 10.

[2] See especially Kieran Dolin, *A Critical Introduction to Law and Literature* (Cambridge: Cambridge University Press, 2007), 8.

C. van Dijk (✉)
Concordia University of Edmonton, Edmonton, AB, Canada
e-mail: conrad.vandyk@concordia.ab.ca

S. Mukherji and D. Roberts (eds.), *Literature and the Legal Imaginary*, Crossroads of Knowledge in Early Modern Literature 4,
https://doi.org/10.1007/978-3-031-74093-0_11

work of the medieval German poet Gottfried von Strassburg, the relation between law and literature is often an allegorical one, where the terms of one discourse are translated and reorganized in the other. In the same way that the allegorical figure of Justice can, in the words of Julie Stone Peters earlier in this volume, both hide and modulate the "messy and contentious realities of law-in-action," so Gottfried's use of allegory enables a profound examination of the legal limits of necessity.

Allegory is primarily a relational term. As Dante insisted, allegory retains an element of difference and separation: "For allegory is derived from the Greek *alleon*, which means in Latin *alienus* ('belonging to another') or *diversus* ('different')."[3] According to Dante, only God is an absolute being: all other terms are identified and transformed by their field of reference. The challenge of allegory then—beyond the perception that such a hermeneutics is outdated—is to realize how meanings are not simply shifted from one allegorical level[4] to another, but originate in their dialectical tension.

To make this case, I turn to Gottfried von Strassburg's *Tristan*, one of the most popular romances of the Middle Ages. The legal questions entertained in *Tristan* should not be read in isolation of the author's allegorical concerns. In particular, Gottfried's constant obsession with the tension between fact and law, with the notion that *necessity knows no law*, should be read in parallel with the allegory of love. Eager to guard the purity of Tristan and Isolde's love, scholars have used allegory as a technique to ignore the legal aporias exposed by the frequent appeals to necessity. Surely the meaning of the text must be different than what we encounter on the literal level. However, as I will argue, in *Tristan* love is structured as a state of exception, and only a proper allegorical interpretation will allow us to bridge the divide between law and literature.

Mark Chinca has shown that Gottfried is always keen to shift description and metaphor from one field of knowledge, or *ars*, to another. Chinca calls this process "metaphorical interartificiality,"[5] and it consists

[3] Dante Alighieri, *Literary Criticism of Dante Alighieri* (Lincoln, NE: University of Nebraska Press, 1973), 99.

[4] At the risk of anachronism, I use the term "level," even though the technical term was *sensus* (sense).

[5] Mark Chinca, 'Metaphorische Interartifizialität: Zu Gottfried von Straßburg', *Zeitschrift Für Deutsche Philologie*, 128 [Supplement] (2009), 17–36.

of a continual transposition of terms, a kind of conceptual metamorphosis. The three dominant *arts* in Gottfried's *Tristan* are Love (an *ars amatoria*), the craft of poetry (*Dichtkunst*), and the elaborate descriptions of valuable artifacts. Not only do these arts intersect, but each borrows a host of metaphors from other domains. Thus, the treatment of love is identified not only with the art of the hunt (the lover is both hunter and hunted), but also with music and medicine (the beloved as physician). For instance, in the Cave of Love episode, music is at first only a metaphor for love, but gradually becomes synonymous with the cultured act of loving. Not only are the Minnesänger described as nightingales, but the lovers are literally entertained by birdsong.[6] Nature and art, the literal and the metaphorical, are interchangeable. The same can be said for the craft of poetry, as the poet is compared to a weaver, a tailor, a magician, but also a horticulturalist, growing and grafting beautiful plants.[7]

We can extend Chinca's argument by suggesting that the law is another *ars* subject to metaphorical interartificiality, though we might equally wonder why this connection is not more obvious. Before we turn to the law, however, it is worth pointing out that Gottfried's habit of metaphorical transposing fits with his love of allegory. In the famous literary excursus (Chapter 7), Gottfried makes it clear that he prefers allegory to elaborate mythologizing. This is not to say that Gottfried avoids irony or paradox, for at the end of this rhetorically ornate chapter we discover that outward clothing pales in comparison to the wardrobe of the heart, the only place where true nobility can be found. The entire allegorical edifice has been constructed to demonstrate that external appearances matter less than an internal sincerity and mettle. Indeed, despite disavowing a false showiness, the allegory never quite arrives at a literal level, but remains a series of personifications (Mettle, Means, Discretion, Courtesy) and metaphors (the wardrobe of the heart).

[6] Chinca, 'Metaphorische Interartifizialität', 22.

[7] The general trend is to make the various discourses and symbols subservient to the topic of love. For instance, Hugo Bekker argues that the various motifs (the hunt, the musician, the pilgrim, the tossing ship, etc.) create the impression that "*Tristan* is a cohering *Entwicklungsroman*." See Bekker, *Gottfried von Strassburg's Tristan: Journey Through the Realm of Eros* (Columbia, SC: Camden House, 1987), 24. Not only is the legal dimension absent from the list of motifs, but the various discourses add up to a remarkably harmonious picture—what Bekker calls the "magic circle" that holds us spellbound.

How to explain Gottfried's choice of an allegorical poetics? We might point to the medieval love of unity in diversity, the humanism of the twelfth century, or the formality and pageantry of court ceremony. Whatever cause we favor, we will be writing the allegory of allegory.[8] Just as a plain style is never an absence of style, but a modeling of honesty and sincerity (or a rebellion against excess and decadence), so the use of allegory may represent a variety of cultural values, from faith in the cohesion of the social framework to an elitist assumption that only a select few will see below the *integumen*, the covering of the literal text. Allegory has a tendency to proliferate and produce new allegories—a process that might be termed the content of form.

On this basis we might question C. S. Lewis's famous dictum that "Symbolism is a mode of thought, but allegory is a mode of expression."[9] Lewis argued that in symbolism we see an object and perceive an inherent meaning (a glimpse of the Platonic forms), but with allegory we start with an immaterial feeling or idea and then seek to clothe it in physical form (e.g., through personifications). From this perspective, the Christian sacraments are profound symbols, not allegories imposed from above. Yet the opposition constantly threatens to dissolve. Earlier Lewis writes, "Allegory, in some sense, belongs not to medieval man, but to man, or even to mind, in general. It is of the very nature of thought and language to represent what is immaterial in picturable terms."[10] Despite their important differences, allegory is a mode of thought just as much as symbolism.

This means that the structure of allegory can be abstracted so that it persists without any obvious allegorical content. Lewis already hints that language is intrinsically metaphorical, and it is only one more step—though not one that Lewis might have taken—to Derrida's theory of language, which Fredric Jameson has characterized as a form of allegory: "Thus the very structure of the sign is allegorical, in that it is a perpetual movement from one 'level' of the signified to another from which it is expulsed in its turn in infinite regression."[11] For Jameson himself, the

[8] For this formulation, see especially Jameson, *Allegory and Ideology*.

[9] C. S. Lewis, *The Allegory of Love: A Study in Medieval Tradition* (Oxford: Oxford University Press, 1936, repr. 1967), 48.

[10] Lewis, *Allegory of Love*, 44.

[11] Fredric Jameson, *The Prison-House of Language: A Critical Account of Structuralism and Russian Formalism* (Princeton: Princeton University Press, 1974), 180.

only way to escape the prison-house of language is to historicize, though the latter movement also relies on allegory.

A similar abstraction of allegory occurs in Gottfried's *Tristan*. For example, in the detailed chapter on the courtly art of hunting, Tristan instructs the men of Cornwall in the ceremony of bringing back a quartered deer. Accompanied by horns and celebration, the courtiers are to retain the shape of the deer:

> [R]ide two and two together and keep close beside one another, preserving the shape of a hart. Let the horns go ahead, the breast follow in their track, the ribs come after the fore-quarters. Then arrange for the hind-parts to follow on the ribs. After that, you should see to it that the quarry and fourchie bring up the rear—such is true huntsmanship. (p. 83)

> wan varn ie zwêne und zwêne samet
> und rîtet rehte ein ander bî,
> alse der hirz geschaffen sî.
> daz gehürne daz gê vor,
> diu brust dâ nâch in sînem spor,
> die rieben nâch den büegen.
> dâ nâch sô sult ir vüegen,
> daz daz jungeste lit
> iesâ den rieben volge mit,
> dâ nâch sô sult ir nemen war,
> das allerjungeste var
> diu cuire und diu furkîe.
> deist rehtiu jegerîe. (ll. 3172–84)[12]

Ironically, the innards come last, and we might even say that they are the exception that confirms the rule. The essential point, however, is that structure itself signifies. It is not as if the cut-up deer has any specific symbolism, though generally speaking the ceremony represents courtliness. The focus is on the relationship between the parts and the whole. Allegory is a kind of dissection into parts, and the trick is to retain a semblance of unity. The allegory of allegory can therefore be both

[12] All citations of *Tristan* are taken from Gottfried von Straßburg, *Tristan*, ed. Rüdiger Krohn, 3 vols. (Stuttgart: Reclam, 1980). English translations are from Gottfried von Strassburg, *Tristan: With the 'Tristran' of Thomas*, trans. A. T. Hatto (London: Penguin, 2004).

inward and outward facing. Its ordered structure can impart an ideological message about courtliness and social hierarchy, but it can also disclose something about the workings of the mind—the way we organize and represent knowledge.[13]

Gottfried's interest in how the part relates to the whole—the structure of allegory—makes him investigate what Giorgio Agamben has called the state of exception found at the heart of the law.[14] We see this when Tristan berates King Mark's barons for their cowardice in giving the Irish the tribute they demand year after year:

> "You lords, one and all," he said, "to name you all by one name. ... you have laid your freedom at the hands and feet of your enemy by means of this shameful tribute, and, as in the past, you give your noble sons into serfdom and bondage, who ought to be your joy, your delight, your very life! And yet you cannot show who is forcing you to do so, or what necessity compels it, but for a duel and one man! No other necessity is involved. Nevertheless, you cannot hit on one among you all who is willing to pit his life against a single man to try whether he shall fall or prevail. ... After all, fathers should give their lives for their children, since their lives are one and indivisible: this is to go with God." (p. 123)

"ir hêrren" sprach er "alle samet,
alle mit einem namen genamet
. . . .
Nu habet ir iuwer vrîheit
iuwern vînden geleit
ze vüezen und ze handen
mit zinslîchen schanden.
und iuwer edelen kindelîn,
diu iuwer wunne solten sîn,
iuwer lust und iuwer leben,
diu gebet ir unde habet gegeben
ze schalken unde z'eigen
und enkunnet niht gezeigen,
wer iuch betwinge dar zuo

[13] For the argument that medieval allegory amounts to class propaganda (especially when it appears subversive), see Noah D. Guynn, *Allegory and Sexual Ethics in the High Middle Ages* (New York: Palgrave Macmillan, 2007), 4.

[14] Giorgio Agamben, *State of Exception*, trans. Kevin Attell (Chicago: University of Chicago Press, 2005).

oder welher hande nôt ez tuo
niwan ein einwîc unde ein man.
kein ander nôt enist hier an.
und enkunnet under iu allen
an einen niht gevallen,
der wider einen man sîn leben
an die wage welle geben
weder er belîbe oder gesige.
. . . .
Jâ suln vetere vür ir kint,
wan sî mit in ein leben sint,
ir leben geben: deist mit gote." (ll. 6063–64, 6075–93, 6103–5)

Tristan insinuates that the lords have long excused their apathy by appealing to the notion that "necessity compels." They had no choice but to obey the law and give up their sons as hostages. By contrast, Tristan does not buy their definition of necessity (*nôt*). Instead, the terms of the tribute offer a way out: either open warfare or single combat. We might say that in such dire circumstances—faced with a choice between losing their children and risking death—necessity knows no law, were it not for the fact that the agreement already includes a clause that provides a solution. The statutory terms acknowledge the possibility of a challenge. Thus, while the law (the terms of the harsh tribute) seeks to compel by necessity, it simultaneously recognizes that necessity knows no law and that on this basis a legal challenge can be sustained.

Agamben, however, has argued that the use of the maxim *necessity knows no law* was quite limited in the Middle Ages. He cites Gratian and Thomas Aquinas as proof that the adage was used not to blur the lines between fact and law but to create an exception where the law does not apply.[15] Examples include stealing bread in cases of penury or celebrating the mass in an unhallowed place. According to Agamben, we are here far removed from the political declaration of a state of emergency (*Notstand*, in German) that becomes commonplace in the twentieth century and is symbolized concretely by the concentration camp. In other words, "It is only with the moderns that the state of necessity tends to be included in the juridical order."[16]

[15] Agamben, *State of Exception*, 24–26.

[16] Agamben, *State of Exception*, 26.

I have shown elsewhere that the maxim was more widely used than Agamben may have realized,[17] and, as Agamben himself notes, more research needs to be done to trace the history of the adage.[18] It is in any case clear that Tristan feels that *not* has a legal force, for he also invokes another maxim: "violence must be met by violence, force by force" ("gewalt hoere wider gewalt / und craft wider crefte"; p. 127; ll. 6420–21). In the words of Paul Hyams, "medieval legal writers constantly deploy the tag *vim vi repellere*."[19] Not only does this argument justify personal self-defense or vengeance, but jurists made a connection with the *ius belli*, the right of a people to engage in reprisals or declare war. For instance, the fourteenth-century lawyer Bartolus of Sassoferrato argues that a person's right to defend one's own body is mirrored by a people's right to repel force with force.[20] Such a just-war theory is legitimized by divine law and the law of nations (*ius gentium*), not by civil or canon law. In some sense then, these different types of law themselves create a system of exceptions that make it difficult to say whether the medieval state of necessity is, as Agamben suggests, entirely excluded from the juridical order, or whether it represents a source of law.

However, in Gotffried's *Tristan*, the argument is not only a legal one, but also has a formal dimension. After all, Tristan's rhetoric has much in common with Gottfried's approach to allegory. Tristan points out that the term "lords" signifies a multitude of individuals: "'You lords, one and all,' he said, 'to name you all by one name …'" As with the levels of allegory, the constituent parts or individuals should add up to a unified whole. Likewise, Tristan concludes his speech by making the same point about the family unit: the lives of fathers and children are indivisible. The argument is reminiscent of definitions of the Trinity—where the persons may be distinguished, but their essence and being remain indivisible, to use the language of the Athanasian Creed. False divisions are a form of heresy,

[17] Conrad van Dijk, "'Nede hath no law': The State of Exception in Gower and Langland", *Accessus: A Journal of Premodern Literature and New Media*, 2:2 (2015), article 2. http://scholarworks.wmich.edu/accessus/vol2/iss2/2.

[18] Agamben, *State of Exception*, 24.

[19] Paul R. Hyams, 'Afterword: Neither Unnatural nor Wholly Negative: The Future of Medieval Vengeance', in Susanna A. Throop and Paul Hyams, eds., *Vengeance in the Middle Ages: Emotion, Religion, and Feud* (Farnham: Ashgate, 2010), 203–20 (203).

[20] Jacob Giltaij, 'Roman Law and the *Causa Legitima* for Reprisals in Bartolus', *Fundamina*, 20:1 (2014), 349–56 (354).

and so Tristan insists that the collective unity of the people necessitates action. The abstract structure of allegory requires legal intervention.

If this seems a stretch, we have only to observe how these formulations are worked out in the subsequent trial by combat. At every stage, the allegory demonstrates who is in the right. When Tristan arms himself, Gottfried writes, "The work of art inside [the armor] was most excellently contrived in form and conception" ("daz werc daz was dar inne / an geschepfede unde an sinne / vil lobelîchen ûf geleit"; p. 130; ll. 6649–51). As Mark Chinca writes, in *Tristan* "ist allerdings auch der Mensch metaphorisch ein Artefakt."[21] Inside and outside, art and life, justice and application—all come together in the figure of Tristan. The passage culminates in an erotic description of Tristan in the saddle, and Gottfried concludes that man and beast are so in unison (he rhymes "ein" with "zwein") that it is as if they were born and raised together (p. 131; ll. 6707–11). Having teased us with the structure of allegory, Gottfried then becomes more explicit. Whereas Morold simply has the strength of four men, Tristan represents an army of four: he has on his side God, Right, Willing Heart, and Tristan himself. On either side, then, we have "four knights under one helmet" ("under einem helme... vier ritter"; p. 133; ll. 6899–6900). Both parties are four in one and one in four. However, Morold's strength is merely literal, whereas Tristan's is allegorical.

Despite the idealism, the actual fighting is remarkably pragmatic, as neither party is opposed to fighting on unequal terms.[22] In many romances it is hardly chivalrous to fight on horse when one's opponent is on foot, yet Tristan strikes Morold while he's trying to get back on his horse and Morold wounds Tristan's horse and then tries to get back on his own. Given that Tristan has made sure that only one man can return from the island alive—he has set his own boat adrift—this is a fight to the death, and in those circumstances necessity once again compels.

Indeed, when both parties are equally brave and underhanded, it is a matter of perspective who is in the right. In such cases, the narrator's formal choices have as much weight as any legal justification. In the end, Morold is cut into pieces, and so loses the oneness that allegorically represents truth and justice. The dissolution of unity signifies that Tristan is in the right:

[21] Chinca, 'Metaphorische Interartifizialität', 32.

[22] See Bekker, *Realm of Eros*, 119.

[I]n lieu of their lord, [they] found a man hewn to pieces. . . When the Irish reach land they took up the wretched Present which had been sent by them—all three pieces, I mean. They laid them together so that nobody should lose any. (p. 136)

und vunden vür ir hêrren dâ
einen zestucketen man ...
Nu sî ze lande kâmen,
ze handen si nâmen
den jaemerlîchen prîsant,
der bî in dar was gesant.
diu stucke meine ich elliu driu.
zesamene leiten si diu
daz ieman iht dâ von verlür. (ll. 7140–41, 7143–49)

To drive the point home, Gottfried notes that King Gurmun the Gay [Morold's overlord] was far from gay ("der künec Gurmûn Gemuotheid / der haete unmuot"; p. 136; ll. 7155–56).[23] His identity has become a contradiction.[24]

Yet while Tristan has won, his own life is in danger, not only because of a poisonous wound, but also because a splinter from his sword has been left in Morold's skull. Later, the sword and the splinter will become a sexual image—Isolde observes that they "made as perfect a whole as if they were one thing" ("wâren alse einbaere, / als ob ez ein dinc waere"; p. 174; ll. 10083–84)—so that the exception is once more subsumed in the whole. In this way, love is not immune from either the violence of the law or the structure of allegory, a point to which I will return. For now, however, the splintering of Tristan's strength provides an ominous hint that the allegorical unity that Tristan represents will not always appear quite so harmonious.

Gottfried's frequent recourse to allegory (and its abstracted structure) can thus be read as itself an allegory for the manifestation of justice (the *iudicium Dei*). This formal strategy becomes necessary when the law fails to provide clarity or resolution. In exceptional cases (self-defense, feud,

[23] Hatto's translation is somewhat loose, as King Gurmun's nickname might equally be "the Bold" or "the Proud," but the play on "Gemuotheid"/"unmuot" is clear.

[24] In the Icelandic version (*Tristrams saga ok Ísoddar*), the argument from necessity found in the Morold episode becomes a *reductio ad absurdum*. See my 'Amused by Death?: Humour in *Tristrams saga ok Ysoddar*', *Saga-Book*, 32 (2008), 69–84.

etc.), *auctoritas* must be sought outside the law, so that the exception may have the force of law. In the Middle Ages, when jurisdiction of the law remains limited and is frequently supplemented by self-help (the violence of nature), it should not surprise us when a literary text investigates the liminal zone that opens up in cases of dire need and necessity. In fact, in a medieval context, private enmity is rarely simply a breakdown of the authority of the state, as if society degenerates into complete anarchy. To quote Robert Bartlett, we might rather say that "the violence of the state in the modern period can be seen not as public violence reborn but as private violence writ large."[25] Self-help is not an exception, but a right, even if a contested one.

We also observe this earlier in *Tristan*, when Tristan reclaims his fief by challenging and killing his father Rivalin's overlord, Morgan. Rivalin had been rash in fighting Morgan, though even then such youthful bravado is not without admiration. While Tristan is similarly high-spirited, he nevertheless faces an impossible situation. Morgan believes him to be a bastard, and so Tristan has no legal standing:

> "You mean that I am a bastard, and so will have forfeited my fief and my claim?"
> "Indeed, my dear young knight, that is how it strikes me and many others." (p. 115)

> "ir meinet ez alsô, daz ich
> niht êlîche sî geborn
> und süle dâ mit hân verlorn
> mîn lêhen und mîn lêhenreht."
> "entriuwen, hêrre guot kneht,
> dâ vür hân ichz und manic man." (ll. 5408–13)

When Tristan then challenges Morgan, the latter points out that he lacks the required legal standing: "You may not draw sword on anyone who was ever made free of a court!" ("iuwer slac engât ze keinem man, / der ie ze hove reht gewan" (ll. 5447–48). The problem Tristan faces is well illustrated with a passage from *The Saxon Mirror*, the most famous medieval German customary: "The following groups are excluded from

[25] Robert Bartlett, *"'Mortal Enmities': The Legal Aspect of Hostility in the Middle Ages." T. Jones Pierce Lecture* (Aberystwyth: The Registry, 1998), 1–18 (14).

feudal law: priests, merchants, villagers, women, all who are encumbered in their rights or born illegitimate, as well as all those who cannot trace their knightly status to their father and grandfather."[26] Such persons can still be invested with a fief (though no lord is obliged to do so), but any feudal rights conferred upon them are temporary and not binding on a successive lord.

When Tristan then kills Morgan in a surprise attack, the violence may seem rash and vengeful, but necessity knows no law:

> He whipped out his sword and ran at him. With a downward sweep he struck through skull and brain, ending only at the tongue, then at once plunged the sword into his heart. Thus the truth of the proverb was evident which says that debts lie, yet do not rot. (pp. 115–16)

> er zucte swert unde rande in an.
> er sluoc im obene ze tal
> beidiu hirne und hirneschal,
> daz ez im an der zungen want.
> hie mite sô stach er ime zehant
> daz swert gein dem herzen în.
> dô wart diu wârheit wol schîn
> des sprichwortes, daz dâ giht,
> daz schulde ligen und vûlen niht. (ll. 5450–58)

By ending the first stroke at the tongue, Tristan avenges Morgan's sarcastic words. By piercing to the heart, Tristan signifies that the debt has been fully paid.

The passage is offensive to some modern critics, who instinctively believe that Tristan's actions are ignoble and signify a subjective desire for revenge.[27] Hugo Bekker's solution is to allegorize the scene while ignoring the legal dimension, so that "Tristan overcomes the hunter within himself"[28] (Morgan was hunting at the time) and can continue on the path to love. By contrast, Albrecht Classen takes the scene at face

[26] *The Saxon Mirror: A* Sachsenspiegel *of the Fourteenth Century*, trans. Maria Dobozy (Philadelphia: University of Pennsylvania Press, 1999), 143.

[27] See Rosemary Norah Combridge's classic *Das Recht Im "Tristan" Gottfrieds von Strassburg*, Philologische Studien und Quellen, 15, second edition (Berlin: Schmidt, 1965), 27.

[28] Bekker, *Realm of Eros*, 103.

value. He argues that Tristan "allowed his revengeful feelings to control his behavior, disregarding all rational concerns. Only because of Rual's wise intervention does he ultimately survive."[29] Despite the fact that Tristan is not a bastard, "might has dominated over right," and both Tristan and his father are "lacking in reason, restraint, pragmatic concepts of the politically realizable, and in circumspection; both turn into victims of their erotic passions at the end, demonstrating impulsive reactions ... and recklessness regarding their social environment."[30] Although there is something satisfying about the way Classen piles it on, such a dismissal reveals a number of modern assumptions, including the idea that the feud is entirely extra-legal and irresponsible, that Tristan's recourse to self-help is selfish and lacking in pragmatism, and that a certain recklessness can never be seen as a virtue.

To gain a more nuanced perspective, it is worth considering a similar moment in Thomas Malory's *Morte Darthur*. In a memorable episode, Balin is trying to take revenge on Garlon, a knight who, somewhat comically, rides invisible, and kills his opponents unawares. When Balin finally spots his enemy at the court of the latter's brother, Balin is faced with a dilemma: "If I sle hym here, I shall nat ascape. And if I leve hym now, peraventure I shall never mete with hym agayne at such a stevyn [occasion], and muche harme he woll do and [if] he lyve."[31] Necessity compels, and the proper heroic response is encapsulated in Balin's personal motto: "I shall take the aventure ... that God woll ordayne for

[29] Albrecht Classen, 'Unjust Rulers and Conflicts with Law and Sovereignty: The Case of Gottfried von Strassburg's *Tristan*', in Robert S. Sturges, ed., *Law and Sovereignty in the Middle Ages and the Renaissance* (Turnhout: Brepols, 2011), 3–22 (9).

[30] Classen, 'Unjust Rulers', 4.

[31] Sir Thomas Malory, *Malory: Complete Works*, ed. Eugène Vinaver (Oxford: Oxford University Press, 1971), 53.

me."[32] The knights of romance give themselves up to chance and adventure, and there is much courage in a certain recklessness, even when such youthful exuberance needs to be balanced with the wisdom of a Rual or a Merlin. In fact, Gottfried draws attention to the need for moderation at the end of chapter 6 of *Tristan* ("Recognition and Reunion"), where Rual represents the avarice of age and Tristan the ambitiousness of youth. Rual cares too much for wealth and Tristan too little.[33]

Just as Tristan acts swiftly, so Balin must make a quick decision. When Garlon confronts him, Balin explains that he has come to take revenge and suddenly cleaves Garlon's head down to the shoulders. He then produces a spear, pierces Garlon's body, and makes a public declaration that poetic justice has been served: "With that truncheon thou slewyste a good knight, and now hit stykith in thy body."[34] As Robert Bartlett has argued, "[t]he formal defiance that created enmity [the state of feud] was, like similar highly visible ceremonial acts, such as homage, dubbing to knighthood or receiving the tonsure, intended as a physical and memorable moment constituting a new status."[35] Although Garlon is already dead, proper procedures must be observed.

While Tristan's actions are more ambiguous, they are hardly impulsive or irrational. Tristan could have killed Morgan without first attempting to overcome his bastard status or challenging Morgan to a duel. It is only when Morgan claims that Tristan has no legal status that Tristan faces a catch-22: the only way to demonstrate that he is not a bastard is through a trial by combat, an option that is not afforded to illegitimate children. We

[32] Malory, *Complete Works*, 40. For the ways in which Gottfried's understanding of *âventiure* differs from an Arthurian conception, see Walter Haug, '*Aventiure* in Gottfrieds von Strassburg *Tristan*', in *Strukturen als Schlüssel zur Welt: Kleine Schriften zur Erzählliteratur des Mittelalters* (Tübingen: Max Niemeyer, 1990), 557–82 (557–58). Haug astutely points out that for Gottfried *adventure* represents less a heroic quest and more a pragmatic attitude toward the inevitability of events and circumstances. My argument about necessity has much in common with Haug's attempt to determine the importance of "Zufall und Zwang" (578) in creating the laws that structure the world of the text ('das Gesetz der Welt'; 577).

[33] For the allegorical juxtaposition of prudence (Rual) and youthful bravado (Tristan), see also Jaeger, 45. Jaeger nevertheless fails to see any merit in Tristan's actions, calling them "unmoderated" and "rash." He thus privileges the prudence of old age, whereas the text seeks to find a balance.

[34] Malory, *Complete Works*, 53.

[35] Bartlett, 'Mortal Enmities', 6.

are faced with a zone of indistinction, where necessity knows no law. The point is not that Tristan's actions are either laudable or ignoble: rather, there is no way to distinguish between these options. The ambiguity is part of the law because medieval audiences were generally torn about the validity of self-help. As historians of the feud have amply demonstrated, the feud was an institution in medieval Europe.

We also see this ambiguity toward the end of Gottfried's narrative, when Tristan first meets Isolde of the White Hands (the second Isolde). Her family's lands are under siege and the family is engaged in a bitter feud. Isolde's father, the Duke of Arundel, lacks the means to defend his lands and jurisdiction against the incursions of his neighbors. Clearly, he has just cause for resistance, yet when Tristan offers to help out, the military strategy is a mixture of pragmatism and honorable conduct.[36] At first, the men of Arundel employ guerilla tactics and a scorched earth policy. When they are ready to offer open battle, they still rely on the element of surprise. In the night, they hide half of Tristan's men in two nearby castles. Then, in an act of defiance and provocation, the remaining troops ride out "openly ... [and] on foray in broad daylight" ("offenlîchen ... mit offener reise"; p. 289; ll. 18830, 18837), plundering and burning close to the enemy fortresses. Finally, after the war is won, "far-sighted Tristan" ("Tristan der nâchraete"; p. 290, l. 18936) prevents further feuds by giving the prisoners their freedom and returning their fiefs. Only now has the state of exception ended and everyone is set free.

Everyone, of course, except Tristan, who is accosted on all sides. The second Isolde's beauty has "made a conquest of the whole duchy" ("das s'al daz lant haete überkomen"; p. 290; l. 18962)—thus Gottfried ties together love and war—and her name reminds Tristan of his true love, the woman he cannot have. In a sense, the duplication of Isolde's name plays havoc with the workings of allegory. Whenever Tristan hears her name, "It is as if Cornwall had turned into Arundel, Tintagel into Karke, Isolde into Isolde" ("ich waene, ûz Curnewâle / ist worden Arundêle, / Karke ûz Tintajêle / Und Îsôt ûz Îsôte"; p. 291, ll. 19008–11). If the allegorical dismemberment of Morold showed the importance of unity, the transmutation of Isolde into Isolde leaves an insufficient difference. It

[36] As Martin H. Jones writes, "Tristan demonstrates here remarkable powers of generalship." Jones, 'The Depiction of Military Conflict in Gottfried's *Tristan*', in Adrian Stevens and Roy Wisbey, eds., *Gottfried von Strassburg and the Medieval Tristan Legend: Papers from an Anglo-North American Symposium* (Woodbridge: Suffolk, 1990), 45–65 (53).

is as if love can only be rescued through some desperate act of duplication, as if love is so riven with tension that the text can only insist on the appearance of homogeneity.

The problem of the exception therefore not only affects the text's legal passages, but also infects the treatment of love. Indeed, in the remainder of this essay, I want to argue that we should make an imaginative leap from law to love, from the structure of the exception to Tristan and Isolde's adulterous affair. There is of course something unseemly about both subjects, and we may not want to acknowledge the obvious connection that the affair is an exceptional case. In this respect, the love potion provides the necessity that justifies the lovers' fated relationship. Tristan and Isolde have no choice but to obey the laws of love, which, in the familiar medieval refrain, no one can resist. Yet scholars are hesitant to acknowledge the "metaphorical interartificiality" of these scenes. Note how Rosemary Norah Combridge, the scholar who did most to document *Tristan*'s legal character, rejects the idea that the Morgan episode might have any real connection with the subject of true love:

> The entire section depicts in various ways the victory of fact over justice, without one being privileged more than the other. Gottfried's values are to be found elsewhere, namely in the realm of courtly love and personal loyalty (Rual), as long as these do not come into conflict, as with the love potion.
> Der ganze Abschnitt stellt auf verschiedene Weise den Sieg der Tatsachen über das Recht dar, ohne daß das eine oder das andere von vornherein höher gewertet würde. Die Werte Gottfrieds sind ganz anderswo zu finden, nämlich im Bereich der Minne und persönlichen Treue (Rual), solange diese nicht, wie beim Minnetrank, in Konflikt geraten.[37]

The only way to keep love pure is to keep it firmly separate from the transgression of the law. Based on this logic, the love potion (and everything that results from it) must remain an exception to the rule. Ironically, then, Combridge affirms that the love affair is just as grounded in necessity as the law. She would put the exclusion on the outside, whereas, following Agamben, I argue for an inclusive exclusion.

Gottfried self-consciously makes this move in the opening pages of the story. *Tristan* opens with stories of needless feuding—Rivalin attacking

[37] Combridge, *Das Reht*, 44–45.

Morgan, the Saxons fighting among themselves—before seeming to switch focus to the story of Rivalin and Blancheflor. Yet their love is initially described as a feud. Blancheflor tells Rivalin, "You have annoyed me through a friend of mine" ("an einem vriunde mîn, / ... dâ habet ir mich beswaeret an"; p. 51; ll. 754, 756), meaning, of course, her heart. Rivalin is confused: "he imagined that unwittingly he must have injured a kinsman of hers" ("und wânde, daz er eteswen / ir mâge ... unwizzende ... gemachet haete schadehaft"; p. 51, ll. 761–64). He nobly asks her to "pronounce sentence" ("rihtet selbe"; p. 51; l. 778) and promises to make amends. When Rivalin finally clues in, the two lovers are reconciled and make "equal division of the kingdoms of their hearts" ("die teilten wol gelîche / ir herzen künicrîche"; p. 52, ll. 815–16). In short, the feud ends in a truce.

If Gottfried is himself keen to transpose the tension between fact and law into the domain of love—thereby reading the one discourse as an allegory for the other—perhaps we should heed the invitation. To allegorize the allegory, we might say that love and law also make equal division of their separate kingdoms, so that the text is truly the sum of its disparate parts. That said, any unification of separate realms (a desire common to law and literature) must be read as an imaginative solution to the real tensions in the text.[38] In fact, for Gottfried's *Tristan*, the problem is that in a feudal society an equal division is unusual. The story therefore constantly struggles to reconcile reality with this utopian ideal. This is why love is always political, and why after Tristan's brief co-regency with Mark fails, the united kingdom can persist only in the hearts of the lovers, who somehow remain loyal to the very end. As Alois Wolf writes, "Instead of kingship or feudal authority, the issue for Tristan is a *künecrîch des herzen* (kingdom of the heart)."[39] This displaced kingdom is meant to make up for the fact that the feudal system is founded on inequality.

What an allegorical reading thus discloses is that the tension between fact and law is not neatly resolved in the realm of love (as in a typological reading), but persists in troubling fashion. For instance, Mark catches the

[38] As Fredric Jameson has argued, romance seeks to resolve the tensions within the social unconscious. Jameson, *The Political Unconscious: Narrative as a Socially Symbolic Act* (Ithaca: Cornell University Press, 1981), 118.

[39] Alois Wolf, 'Humanism in the High Middle Ages: The Case of Gottfried's *Tristan*', in Will Hasty, ed., *A Companion to Gottfried von Strassburg's "Tristan"* (Rochester, NY: Camden House, 2003), 23–54 (27).

lovers *flagrante delicto*—a moment when the law should allow him to act without a trial—and yet he cannot summon his men fast enough to confirm what he has seen. Similarly, the lovers go into exile (Agamben calls the *ban* the classic form of the exception), and their love life can be allegorized as a triumph of love only because its setting in the wild symbolizes the dialectical relation between nature and law. Finally, when Isolde overcomes her trial by ordeal by means of an equivocal oath, and Gottfried comments disapprovingly that Christ is "pliant as a windblown sleeve" ("wintschaffen alse ein ermel ist"; p. 248; l. 15736), still Isolde's oath is merely the working out of a logic that can never leave behind the legal problem of the exception.

Perhaps the clearest example of the ubiquitous appeal to necessity (or fact) occurs at the very start of the love affair. When Tristan's true identity is discovered by Isolde, he explains that he had no choice but to come to Ireland for healing:

> "My dear ladies," said the man in the bath, "it is true that I have made you suffer, though under great duress [grôzer nôt]. If you care to recollect (as you ought), you will know that my hand was forced by nothing less than death." (p. 177)

> saeligen vrouwen beide,
> eist wâr, ich hân iu leide
> und aber mit grôzer nôt getân.
> welt ir iuch, alse ir sult, enstân,
> sô wizzet ir wol, daz diu nôt
> niht anders was niwan der tôt. (ll. 10311–16)

Literally, the need (*nôt*) was nothing less than death (*tôt*). Soon after, the love potion comes to symbolize this inexorable necessity, and it will come as no surprise that all parties view love as a kind of death.

Once we notice the pattern, less obvious details take on allegorical meaning. Consider the odd political career of Gurmun the Gay, which ostensibly tells us little about the kingdom of the heart. Unlike Tristan, who is happy to be Mark's co-regent, Gurmun refuses to be "co-heir" ("als wol erbe"; p. 121; l. 5887) with his brother after their father dies. He cannot be two in one (the allegorical structure that dominates law and love), for he refuses to share his goods: "his heart insisted that he should rule as monarch" ("sîn herze enwolte in niht erlân, / ern müese selbe ein hêrre wesen"; p. 120, ll. 5892–93). Gottfried thus takes the villain to task for preferring a path (single rule) that would have been the normal expectation for a ruler. The only way to explain this odd judgment is to realize that the idea of co-regency has gone from being a pragmatic temporary solution (as it would have been historically) to functioning as a symbolic resolution, even if the structure has an extremely brief political tenure and lasts only in the kingdom of love.

Ironically, Gurmun cannot avoid sharing, though the arrangement he enters into is much more pragmatic. After leaving Africa,

> Gurmun obtained leave and authority in writing of the mighty, illustrious Romans that he should have possession of all he could subdue, yet concede them some right and title to it. (p. 120)

> [Gurmun] nam von den maeren,
> den gewaltegen Rômaeren
> urloup unde botschaft,
> swaz er betwünge mit craft,
> daz er daz z'eigen haete
> und ouch in dâ von taete
> eteslîch reht und êre. (ll. 5905–11)

The distinction between ownership and possession is a key tenet of Roman law, and this might explain why Gurmun receives his title from the Romans. As it turns out, Gurmun has possession, but not ownership, and although possession may be nine-tenths of the law, the division is not an equal one. The somewhat sketchy arrangement has an ordinary feudal dimension in that Gurmun receives his fief from a higher lord, but since Gurmun first has to conquer the land, and since his title is limited to possession only, this is a case of might makes right—an approach to law that Tristan will both contest and confirm when he soon after challenges Morold.[40] Gurmun may disappear quickly from the narrative, but the distinction between ownership and possession stays with us until the end. After all, Mark has ownership of Isolde, but Tristan possesses her. Gurmun's pragmatic solution, which was already a step down from

[40] For feudal law, see *The Saxon Mirror*, 4.61, which insists that possession without enfeoffment and investiture is unlawful.

harmonious co-regency, opens up into a rift between de facto possession and *de jure* ownership. In the process, the exception becomes the rule.

I am thus proposing an allegorical mode of reading that recognizes and makes room for the exception. After all, allegory can all too easily become a means of forgetting and escaping from the literal level. Here, for instance, is how Stephen Jaeger reads the "meaning" of Gottfried's *Tristan*:

> When we read the poem literally, Tristan and Isolde are cunning tricksters, who maintain a shameful illicit relationship through deceit. But when we read the work as a tale of 'spiritual love,' then the 'adultery' is seen as mere wrapping, integument, and the sweet kernel of truth is the lesson that Spirit and Sense united and joined to Body represent the ideal human being.[41]

By contrast, I follow Fredric Jameson in arguing that genuine allegory is not a process of distillation, but an attempt to describe the structural tensions within a work. It will not do to limit the meaning of *Tristan* to the allegory of the cave of love, where for a brief space a more transcendent idealism is explored. After all, for Gottfried the greatest moment of passion is also the moment of greatest need. Tristan is conceived when Rivalin is dying from a wound (the great symbol of love) and what makes the sexual act necessary is that it happens *in extremis*. Necessity compels Blancheflor to act, and Tristan's own name commemorates the perilous circumstances that led to his conception and birth. When Tristan and Isolde can no longer resist their desire for each other, Gottfried writes that the lovers experienced such great "nôt" (ll. 14324, 14326) that they are each other's death and life ("ir beider tôt, ir beider leben"). "Nôt," "tôt," "Îsôt" (Isolde)—in the end it is hard to distinguish between them.

I hope I have demonstrated that allegory plays an important role in bringing literature and law to bear on one another. An author's use of allegory can even act as legal justification, as we have seen particularly in the Morold episode. Yet even when the text itself is not overtly allegorical (unlike Gottfried's *Tristan*), the reader still relies on allegory to make the law relevant both structurally and thematically. There are many ways to

[41] C. Stephen Jaeger, *Medieval Humanism in Gottfried von Strassburg's Tristan und Isolde* (Heidelberg: Universitätsverlag Winter, 1977), 178.

theorize this relationship,[42] but any figurative reading of the text requires the twin faculties of imagination and judgment. It is not always a matter of drawing the boundary between literature and law, but of deciding how far to extend the bridge.

I will end with a brief reflection on the work of Giorgio Agamben. As mentioned, Agamben suggested that the argument from necessity remained itself an isolated exception in the Middle Ages. I have argued that even if the transformation of politics into a state of exception is a modern invention, we must do more to recognize how medieval authors employed the maxim. For at the heart of Agamben's work we find a tension between reading the state of exception as a historical phenomenon and viewing it as a timeless logical structure. If the state of necessity is primarily a historical development, then the Middle Ages acts as a foil to modernity, and we can reason that the increasing use of states of emergency is itself unusual and exceptional. It was not always so, we might lament. On the other hand, if the state of exception is inherent in thought itself—there can never be a whole without an exception—then the exception becomes an allegorical key that allows us to unlock the door to any vault of knowledge. In fact, Agamben does find the exception everywhere: in Saussurean linguistics, in Heidegger's metaphysics, and the list goes on.[43] This is also how the law becomes allegorical, so that it can be transposed to other fields of knowledge, not as a set of regulations, but as a problem of knowing that influences and structures other forms of expression, including art. Only in this way can we reconcile history and allegory.

[42] Compare also the next essay in this collection (by Valérie Hayaert), which looks at the other side of the coin, namely how the law uses "jurispoetry" to distill and enshrine its legal concepts.

[43] As an example, Agamben argues that the exception is to the law as *parole* is to *langue*.

CHAPTER 12

The Versification of Legal Codes

Valérie Hayaert

On Saturday, 17 June 2017, Robert Darnton and the French Mezzo-Soprano Hélène Delavault presented a cabaret-lecture at the Paris Institute of Advanced Studies—which is housed in the Hôtel de Lauzun—during which Delavault performed a number of seditious songs which would have been common in eighteenth-century Paris. These songs would once have been belted out by street singers and memorized by people of all social ranks, but now their performance was possible only due to the discovery of copies in a number of musical archives and in the archives of the Parisian police. As a former aristocratic residence which had been broken up into apartments for artisans at the Revolution, the Hôtel de Lauzun was the ideal setting in which to listen to these politically charged songs brought back to life again. Aside from experiencing the aesthetic pleasure of listening to Delavault's interpretation of several

Warm thanks to Peter Goodrich, who commented on earlier drafts of this paper.

V. Hayaert (✉)
University of Warwick, Coventry, UK
e-mail: valerie.hayaert@warwick.ac.uk

S. Mukherji and D. Roberts (eds.), *Literature and the Legal Imaginary*, Crossroads of Knowledge in Early Modern Literature 4,
https://doi.org/10.1007/978-3-031-74093-0_12

"Poissonnades" (a pun on the maiden name of Madame de Pompadour),[1] spectators were able to enjoy an approximation of how the street singers of the *Ancien Régime* would have sounded when they were spreading their seditious messages.[2] This evocative engagement with the oral culture of eighteenth-century Paris was a source of considerable pleasure to the audience, but it also presented an opportunity for thinking about the oral transmission and reception of other types of text—particularly, as the following chapter shows, when it comes to the study of law.

Legal historians of European cultures rarely study the oral dimension of legal material. But other traditions of legal cultures have regularly underlined the orality of legal prescriptions as well as their performative nature. The dialogue between law and poetics is thus an occasion to study the oral transmission of legal *carmina* from their early antique history until the late nineteenth century. How do legal principles penetrate into the citizen's heart? Is this only a matter of teaching moral principles or are there specific forms of delivering authority that have better chances of inscribing themselves in the memory? If law is a poetic art, then how do rhythm, form, verse and tone leave an imprint on individuals?

Cicero tells us that in Roman antiquity, schoolboys were taught to memorize the Law of the Twelve Tables as a *carmen necessarium* (an indispensable and compulsory song). One of the most powerful means of transmitting legal precepts was through song. How does the singing of a legal code affect the transmission of its content? If this *carmen* was meant to be learnt by heart, then how do other audiences (not only pupils but all sorts of citizen) chant, perform and use this type of solemn hymn? More generally, how does a legal oral system of communication travel across age differences and social boundaries? This chapter will argue that the versification of legal codes in Europe has had a variety of aims from the medieval age until the nineteenth century. The oral nature of legal transmission

[1] Jeanne Antoinette Poisson, Marquise de Pompadour (1721–1764) was the chief mistress of Louis XV from 1745 to 1751.

[2] Robert Darnton, Hélène Delavault, and Claude Pavy, *Poetry and the Police: Communication Networks in Eighteenth-Century Paris* (Cambridge MA: The Belknap Press of Harvard University Press, 2012). About the early modern Parisian soundscape, see in particular: Nicholas Hammond, *The Powers of Sound and Song in Early Modern Paris* (Pennsylvania: Pennsylvania State University Press, 2019), where the author shows "how noise in the ancient regime was considered a crime in itself, and yet street singers flourished". See also the special number of *Early Modern French Studies*, 41:1 (2019), devoted to soundscapes.

may be gauged by analyzing the prosody, the metrics and the mythical roots of this tradition. The sixth-century legal compilation known as the *Corpus Juris Civilis*, undertaken early in the reign of the Roman Emperor Justinian (*r.*527–65), is seen as a living body, to which interpreters and poets may give a new form. Most of them are very scrupulous about the normative nature of Justinian's law code but, at the same time, their innovative poetry explores new ways of presenting, reordering and digesting legal writings.

The Versification of Legal Codes

During my 2008 survey of emblematic structures within forensic humanism,[3] I was intrigued by the curious work of the humanist lawyer Honoratus Draco (or Onorato Drago) (1512–1579).[4] Born in Sospel, in the south of France, Draco is known for having turned Justinian's *Institutes* into Latin hexameters in his *Elementa Juris Civilis, seu Institutiones Imperiales in carmen contractae* (1551). The contribution Draco made to legal thought has not attracted the attention of legal scholars. In the area of law, Donald Kelley mentions this work only in passing.[5] He has, however, reemerged as a prominent linguist. Recently, Maria Carla Marinoni carried out a philological inquiry on another aspect of Draco's polyvalence, a glossary of Provençal language which was compiled around 1536–1538 and which was dedicated to the Marquis Alfonso d'Avalos.[6] Draco wished to enable his patron to read an anthology of troubadour poetry which d'Avalos had in his possession. This stands out as one of the many examples of how jurists cultivated poetry. The novelty of this collection is that Draco devises a nomenclature of the troubadour chansonniers' *lexica* in Old Occitan and offers his work as an *amical munus*, a token of esteem and friendship between him as a jurist and his powerful

[3] Valérie Hayaert, *Mens emblematica et humanisme juridique: le cas du Pegma cum narrationibus philosophicis de Pierre Coustau, 1555* (Geneva: Droz, 2008).

[4] For further information on Draco's name and its variants, see the entry for him in the CERL Thesaurus: https://data.cerl.org/thesaurus/cnp01119794.

[5] Donald R. Kelley, *Foundations of Modern Historical Scholarship: Language, Law and History in the French Renaissance* (New York: Columbia University Press, 1970; edn 1992).

[6] Onorato Draco, *Il glossario provenzale-italiano di Onorato Drago*, ed. Maria Carla Marinoni (Fasano: Schena Editore, 1989).

patron. His versification of the *Institutes*, which he had published at the age of thirty-nine, is a learned and erudite work, a “compacted” version (*elementa juris in carmen contractae*) which appears in particularly dense verses. Are these lines nothing but scholastic verses, printed at the time when Thibault Payen was eager to try out new ways of publishing the fundamental textbook of Roman law? Are they an effective tool to provide innovative ways of teaching the *Institutes*, i.e. the elementary textbook for first-year law students? The evidence, as least so far as the publication history is concerned, is that it had mixed fortunes.[7] It was published four times in the 1550s, each time in a different city (Lyon, Leuven, Genoa, Basel, Cologne), but it was not until the 1580s that any further editions appeared (the Lyon edition of 1581). After this, more than two centuries elapsed before, in 1786, a Basel edition was published. The initial rush of editions suggests that an initial and geographically far-reaching effort was made to find a reliable readership—with hopes of finding one perhaps animated by the wider “interpretation boom which is detectable in all disciplines after 1550”.[8] However, the fact that only one of the original four cities saw a reprint—and then after a delay of 30 years, suggests that these efforts were not altogether successful. Whilst it is possible that whole editions have been lost (a likelihood which is increased by the low survival rates amongst the editions which are known), the impression which one gets, based only on what does survive is that *Elementa Juris Civilis* enjoyed mixed success in the sixteenth century and then saw a brief resurgence (perhaps as an intellectual curiosity) in the eighteenth century.

In her monumental work *Fabuleuse juridicité. Sur la littérarisation des genres juridiques* (2015), Anne Teissier-Ensminger has highlighted the ambivalence of what scholars have termed as “Law and Literature”: on one hand many writers are curious about law as a global social

[7] *Elementa iuris civilis, seu Institutiones imperiales in Carmen contractae* (Lyon: Thibaud Payen, 1551); *Elementa iuris civilis, seu institutiones imperiales in carmen contractae* (Leuven: Martinus Rotarius and Reinerus Velpius, 1552); *Elementorum iuris civilis, sive Institutionum imperialium metrica epitome* (Genoa: Antonio Bellone, 1553); *Elementa juris civilis, seu Institutiones imperiales in carmen contractae* (Cologne: heirs of Arnold Birckmann, 1556); *Institutionum Imperialium metrica epitome* (Lyon: Francisci Conrardi, 1581); *Institutiones Justiniani in carmen contractae* (Basel: Decker, 1786).

[8] Ian Maclean, ‘The Market for Scholarly Books and Conceptions of Genre in Northern Europe, 1570–1630’, in Georg Kauffmann, ed., *Die Renaissance im Blick der Nationen Europas* (Wiesbaden: Kommission bei Harrassowitz, 1991), 16–31.

phenomenon (this is the "*Droit en Lettres*" paradigm), whilst on the other hand, lawyers produce "*textes jurislittéraires*", especially designed to cater to a legal audience (this is the "*Lettres en Droit*" side). The idea of her book is not to consider why a lawyer will use a specific genre to carry out a plea or choose fiction to transmit the account of a cause but rather to detect the legal culture and the legal concepts that are enshrined and presupposed by the use of a literary genre to expound the law. If recent criticism has largely focused on the first movement, then the second one is less well known.

This second paradigm has nevertheless been well represented in the work of Roman law jurists. This can be seen from the twelfth century, in which Roman underwent an energetic revival, through to the fifteenth and sixteenth centuries, in which erudite and encyclopaedically minded humanists, such as Lorenzo Valla, Guillaume Budé and Andrea Alciato, championed a return to the Greek roots of Justinian's texts. Budé provides an amusing poetic pastiche of the Law of the Twelve Tables, Honoratus Draco invents *carmina* in order to reduce the prose text of the *Institutes* into mnemonic verses, and Hugo Grotius inaugurates his poems about the freedom of the seas in 1601.[9] Flowing somewhere between blind legal technicality and empty concepts, the tradition of legal songs kept inspiring some of the most ingenious wits of the law (*lucerna juris*) until its renewal through the influence of Giambattisa Vico three centuries later. Eventually, the versification of legal codes achieved a much higher ambition, as the Code Civil was promulgated in vernacular and also moulded into verses by French lawyers of the nineteenth century, who added popular illustrations to convey the legal message differently. This essay will mainly focus on the antique tradition and the inventiveness of early modern 'jurispoetry'.

[9] See Anne Tessier-Ensminger, *Fabuleuse juridicité: sur la littérarisation des genres juridiques* (Paris: Classiques Garnier, 2015), esp. Part 4, Chapter 1 ('La poésie du Droit des eaux: de Grotius (1601) à Ravasinus (1708)', 707–55). For a comparison between Draco's versification of the Institutes and Grotius' use of poetic paraphrasis of the same text, understood as a piece of "jurispoésie géorgique", see idem, 719–20.

The Verse *Institutes* of Richard d'Annebault (1280)

We may begin by trying to see the reasons offered to legitimize the use of poetical inventions to mould the law. The practice of translating legal books into poetry is not new. One of the earliest verse translations of the *Institutes* has been widely attributed to Richard d'Annebault (or d'Annebaut), a Norman poet.[10] This untitled work consists of approximately 24,000 lines, and, according to its epilogue, was finished in 1280. In the prologue, d'Annebault states that his translation is meant to educate a schoolboy (named Bertrand d'Eschalfepié, "ung enfant de gascogne") and to teach him how to understand legal Latin, such that he could read the *Institutes* in a vernacular edition with commentary. As Claire-Hélène Lavigne has shown, d'Annebault's translation is not a literal rendition of the text: he invents a versified legal language in Old French in order to adapt the *Institutes* to verse form and to add a contextual reading of it. Verse is seen as a pleasant mnemonic aid as well as a pedagogical tool.[11] But verse also provides a mythical genealogy for the transmission of laws. The Benedictine monk Theobald of Bec had travelled to Rome in 1139 and had brought a manuscript of the Digest back to the Abbaye Notre-Dame du Bec, where he had recently become Abbot. The translation from Latin to vernacular was obviously meant to widen the audience of this legal transplant, but beyond the transmission of a text, d'Annebault sees himself as the Normandy *trouvère* of a new version of the legal text. The vernacular text inspired by the imperial *Institutes* is a conversion of the laws into poetic form. To this extent, there is a parallel to be drawn with Draco, who had a particular interest in the recovery of troubadour poetry. Both are less interested in Old Occitan or Ancient Romanicist technicalities than in the vernacular and pedagogical use of a new interpretation of Justinian's textbook. It is useful to note that d'Annebault's verse rendition of the *Institutes* was not printed much later, in around 1485, under

[10] For a study of this "cas d'espèce", see Claire-Hélène Lavigne, 'Literalness and Legal Translation: Myth and False Premises', in Georges L. Bastin and Paul F. Bandia, eds., *Charting the Future of Translation History* (Ottawa: University of Ottawa Press, 2006), 145–62.

[11] "Prologue" of *Institutes*' verse rendition attributed to Richard d'Annebault (British Library, MS Harley, 4477) verses 29–32: "Il y pourra asses aprandre / Et puis legierement entendre / Le latin quand il le verra / Et trouver de que il querra".

the presses of Antoine Cayllaut.[12] In his prologue, the *trouvère* incites his pupil to "trouver de que il querra" (find what he is looking for), using the polyptotic pun on *trouver/trouvère* to indicate an initiation and a quest. This pun is a topos of the nascent "roman" of the time; it indicates an exegetical quest as well as a new genealogy of the transmission of the laws.

The work was probably written to be sung in d'Annebault's newly founded school of law. If so, then—as with the Parisian songs with which this chapter began—its musical form would mostly likely have heightened its formal capacity to mould a pedagogical content. In order to arouse curiosity, the *trouvère* would have asked his pupils to chant the legal propedeutics—or introductory elements—of the Roman law tradition. The poetical translation of the legal textbook was regarded as an empirical apprenticeship in which knowledge of the law should first be recited orally. In the law schools of the time, song was probably considered the best medium to unite a civic assembly. In this context, octosyllabic verses were traditionally used to convey epic poetry: d'Annebault insists on the oral quality of his rimes: "Si les translateray en rime/ Ou consonant ou leonine" (I will translate them into verses, whether harmonious or leonine) (Prologue v. 17–18). The *trouvère* advertizes a pedagogical and moral ambition; "a ensaigner et a duyre" (v. 34) means to teach and to conduct in a moral sense. Justinian is presented as a good Christian, "religieux et prudomme" (scrupulous about religion and a man of good morals), who achieved through his command to "tribunien le questor", "et a compaignons qu'il ot" [...] Que tout le viel droit ramenassent/ A concordance et a droite ordre/ Que nulz ne s'en peust remordre." (Tribonian the questor, along with his fellow jurists [...] was instructed to draw a selection from the old laws/ to convergence and right ordering/ to prevent anyone from generating further issues).

Justinian's prohibition of commentary in the various prefaces of the *Corpus Juris Civilis* as well as the reordering and selection of the vast corpus of legal writings is, unsurprisingly, designed to be self-sufficient. D'Annebault insists on the good faith of the compilators and the rectitude

[12] Incunabula Short Title Catalogue, no. ij00546300. This edition is studied in Claire Hélène Lavigne, 'L'utilisation des gloses comme moyen d'appropriation et de réinvention culturelle', in *Traduction juridique: histoire, théorie(s) et pratique: [actes] = Legal Translation: History, Theory/ies and Practice: [Proceedings]* (Bern: ASTTI, 2000), available online here: http://www.tradulex.com/Actes2000/lavigne.pdf.

and moral ethos of the emperor's undertaking, but the poetical prelude tells us more, if we compare two manuscript variations of the same text:

> Quant Justinien eust le cours [Quant Justinien oult le core]
> De droiz il se pourpensa lors [Que droiz il se porpensa lore]
> Qu'il feroit Institutions
> Qui sont les introductions
> Et la voie des lois savoirs.[13]

[When Justinian received the course of Law (or: When Justinian's heart became righteous) he decided to produce Institutions, which are the propaedeutics of the knowledge of laws.]

The verse variation indicates an interesting metaphor: Justinian's heart—or will—is the cause of him arrogating to himself the authority and influence of drafting laws. D'Annebault hints at another way of understanding the transmission of the legal tradition. By re-stating in various verses the imperial prohibition of commentary and interpretation, the assertive nature of imperial power refers to two models of authority. The first is the *auctoritas* granted by honesty and majesty: if anything were to appear obscure, this is to be referred by judges to the very summit of the empire and be made clear by imperial authority. This first rationale follows the text of the *De confirmatione Digestorum* (Tanta § 21). As an emperor, Justinian is thought to be the source of unquestionable authority. The second rationale is modelled onto a chivalric ethos: Justinian is the heroic character of a noble endeavour and the vernacular verses produced by d'Annebault confirm the epic nature of his engagement towards *recta ratio*. His "Institutions" are a new grail to be sought after, and in this context, the quest is more valuable than the writing itself.

These verses have been attributed to d'Annebault, but upon closer examination, they appear as the result of plural voices.[14] On an equal footing with the only interpretation authorized, the word-to-word (or "foot to foot"/*kata poda*) translation, the *trouvère* has found a form of interpretation suitable for disputants or teachers. The metric transposition of the emperor's wording may not have any necessary force. D'Annebault

[13] The first text is from Bibliothèque nationale de France (BnF), Rés. F.35 (which is accessible here: https://gallica.bnf.fr/ark:/12148/bpt6k8711814p). The variant, given in square brackets, is from British Library, MS Harley 4477. The Harley MS is discussed in Lavigne, 'Literalness and Legal Translation'.

[14] See Lavigne, 'Literalness and Legal Translation', passim.

produces a fiction about the oral transmission of legal voices. A diæresis is needed on Justini/en and Instituti/ons, as well as introducti/ons and voi/e, if we chant the verse as an octosyllable. The name of the Byzantine emperor naturally deserves a leonine rime, but also his œuvre as Justinian is heralded as the *sacrosancta auctoritas* of the *Institutions*. If we compare the D'Annebault manuscript with another extant thirteenth-century manuscript of the *Institutes* in Old French,[15] the meaning of the Latin word "Institutions" (as a legislative text) has transformed the noun "Institutes" (a textbook primarily intended for legal students). Beyond the leonine rime made possible by the use of a longer word, the *trouvère* reorchestrates the imperial authority by using a word-for-word translation of the Latin, which is also a statement about the emperor's authority in a context where feudal oral procedures and custom laws had precedence over Roman and Canon law.

As Peter Goodrich has variously voiced, the law is not only a poetic art: it has to be performed, promulgated and chanted. Anyone who has heard a conference paper by Goodrich knows that he understands the delivery and the transmission of legal culture by performing it as an oral, theatrical and performative oath first. On 2 December 2018,[16] Gary Watt gave a most stimulating paper on the oral nature of English procedures, reviving the synesthaesia of legal voices. D'Annebault's voice is also a polyphonic song, made to repeat in parts the oral transmission of legal writings, inventing a new form (heroic verses) to adapt to the context of legal textual explanation in the year 1280.

From the beginning of the revival of Roman law studies in the twelfth century, propaedeutic dialogue between student and teacher had to explore new ways of transmitting interpretative norms. The use of poetic verses—which may have had a musical element to them—would

[15] BnF, MS Français 1064. This anonymous manuscript, which is labelled "Institutes en vieil français", dates from the second half of the thirteenth century. It was probably acquired by the future French King Charles V during the time when he was only dauphin. The item features in the inventories of the Librairie du Louvre until 1424, where is consistently described as "un livre nommé Institute" or "Institutes". It has been edited by François Olivier-Martin, *Les Institutes de Justinien en français. Traduction anonyme du XIIIè siècle* (Paris: Société anonyme du Recueil Sirey, 1935). See Véronique de Becdelièvre's description: https://archivesetmanuscrits.bnf.fr/ark:/12148/cc78171t.

[16] Gary Watt, 'Jurists or Jawists? The Office of the Orifice', oral paper given at the Offices of the Jurist conference, Cardozo School of Law, New York, 2nd December 2018.

undoubtedly have helped to disseminate another way of delivering legal knowledge. The scale of their cultural impact is difficult to assess at a distance of so many centuries, and in a context where authorship was often not explicitly asserted, but the ongoing work of medievalists is gradually revealing a richer and more detailed picture of the extent to which—often through translation, rather than through the more contentious field of interpretation, per se—the *Institutes* were a lively field of intellectual activity. For example, one anonymous prose translation of the *Institutes* was found by François Olivier-Martin in the 1930s to survive in at least fourteen complete; more recently, however, through a greater scholarly appreciation of manuscript fragments (something exemplified by the *Fragmentarium* project),[17] a further three (fragmentary) copies have come to light.[18] For so many copies to survive—when so many more copies surely did not—suggests a text of considerable cultural importance.

But the success of other translations should not detract from the unique importance of D'Annebault's verses, which, through their poetic form, show that law is (also) a poetic art and that verse, as a scholastic exercise may explain more fully the connection between customary legal practices and the oral tradition of legal transmission.

The Curious Case of Honoratus Draco (1551)

I will now focus on the humanist movement and examine two telling cases. The first is Draco's Latin versification of the *Institutes* (his *Elements of Civil Law*) and the second is Guillaume Budé's pastiche of the law of the Twelve Tables, first published in the 1515 edition of his *Opera omnia*. The former is an example of brevity; Draco achieves the challenge to contract the original imperial prose into laconic verses, shorter in length than the original text. The latter is a paradoxical rewriting of the Laws of the Twelve Tables into a humanism-challenging programme.

As we have already seen, Draco's work first appeared in 1551, in an edition by the Lyonnaise publisher, Thibault Payen.[19] This edition was

[17] University of Fribourg, *Fragmentarium: Laboratory for Medieval Manuscript Fragments*: https://fragmentarium.ms/.

[18] Olivier-Martin, *Les Institutes de Justinien en français*.

[19] For an updated account of his early career, see Morgane Perrier, 'Thibaud Payen, imprimeur lyonnais du XVIe siècle, les premières années: 1530–1545' (unpublished

a small and elegant *libellus* (a quarto of 142 pages). Payen was a well-connected Protestant printer, known in particular for having published the first truly polyglot dictionary of the time (Spanish, Italian, Greek and Latin), Ambrosius Calepinus' *Dictionarium* (1559).[20] Ian Maclean has demonstrated how Sébastien Gryphe and Payen had agreed to collaborate in order to saturate the market for textbooks.[21] Payen's career was prolific and can be taken to represent representative of Lyon's polyvalence within the wider and highly interconnected European market for print. Projects such as Andrea Guarna's *Bellum grammaticale*, Erasmus' *De conscribendis epistolis opus* and Ippolito Marsili's *Consiliorum criminalium* attest the wide range of disciplines covered by Payen and his partners. But there are signs, as his career progressed, that a combination of poetry and law, within the medium of an affordable textbook, would have been especially germane to how he saw his position within the market. His long interest in poetry materialized with the publication in 1536 quarto of Jean Despautère's *Ars versificatoria*. In the same year, he published Justinian's *Institutiones* in a pocket format, consisting of four tiny sexidecimo volumes. In 1539, he collaborated with Jacques Giunta on a reprint of Andrea Alciato's *Parerga*, and in 1540 he published the moral distichs of Michele Verino, in a highly portable octavo format which one could, as the book's title suggested, keep close to one's chest (*pectore libro*).[22] The audience targeted is schoolboys wishing to learn Latin sayings promptly. Payen's innovative approach to the publication of textbooks became more pronounced in succeeding editions of this work: scholarly "notae" were added to the 1543 edition, and the 1544 edition saw the addition of helpful summaries which were described as "argumentis paragraphos singulos illustrantibus". Also of relevance is his

masters dissertation, University of Lyon, 2015), available here: https://www.enssib.fr/bibliotheque-numerique/documents/65992-thibaud-payen-imprimeur-lyonnais-du-xvie-siecle-les-premieres-annees-1530-1545.pdf.

[20] See Martine Furno, 'Du commerce et des langues: latin et vernaculaire dans les lexiques et dictionnaires plurilingues au XVIè siècle', in Frédéric Barbier, ed., *Histoire et civilisation du livre: Revue internationale IV* (Genève: Droz, 2008), 93–116.

[21] Ian Maclean, 'Concurrence ou collaboration? Sébastien Gryphe et ses confrères lyonnais (1528–1556)', in Raphaële Muren, ed., *Quid novi? Sébastien Gryphe, à l'occasion du 450è anniversaire de sa mort* (Lyon: Presses de l'Enssib, 2008), 15–32.

[22] Michele Verino, *Disticha cum luculenta expositione. Huic puer incumbas pectore libro, Fundere si prompte verba Latina velis* (Lyon: Thibauld Payen, 1540).

edition of Matteo Gribaldi [Mopha]'s *Methodus ac de ratione studendi*,[23] which includes a strong plea in favour of an alliance between poetic art and legal interpretation.

The case of Draco's *carmina* is arguably the most sophisticated form of scholastic verses moulding the *Institutes*. Notes and arguments derived from the source and commentaries are the mainstream tendency of most scholastic editors of the Justinian compendium. Draco's verses appear as the utmost example of brevity, insofar as the hexameters he produces are shorter than the initial prose. His aim is to give the shortest possible poetic account of Justinian's laws. Compare an extract from the *Institutes* with Draco's poetical reduction:

> Et quidem naturali iure communia sunt omnium haec: aër, aqua profluens et mare et per hoc littora maris. (*Institutes*, II, 1, 1)

> Aer, unda fluens, mare, littora quæ mare cingu[n]t
> Naturæ cuivis communia iure putantur.[24]

In the late seventeenth century, a Latin verse paraphrase of the *Institutes* produced by Giambattista Pisacane, in which the same text is rendered differently, this time appearing in juxtalinear fashion next to the *Institutes* themselves:

> Sunt naturali cunctis communia jure
> Aer, atque imber, vastum mare, Litora ponti.[25]

Both verse paraphrases (Draco and Pisacane) are meant to cultivate the Horatian principle of *dulcedo utilissime* by transposing vexed questions into pleasurable and witty verses. In his dedicatory epistle to his reader (addressed to Antonio de Santi), Pisacane explains that he produced these verses because rimed *elementa juris* are able to expound legal issues by playing the harmonic lyra (*Iurisprudentia elementa explanari armonico lira sonu*). The music metaphor applied to legal interpretation might

[23] See Hayaert, *Mens emblematica*, 173–74.

[24] Draco, *Elementa Juris Civilis* (Leuven, 1552), f. 15ʳ.

[25] Giambattista Pisacane, *Institutionum, seu elementorum Divi Justiniani sacratissimi principis libri quatuor* (Naples: Joseph Rosselli, 1694), 40.

be understood in two ways. On the one hand, non-verbal systems of interpretation such as music recall the topical analogy of law and music (a Platonic topos), where the analogy only serves an aesthetic claim: law is harmony and the legislator as well as the legal interpreter needs to expound its meaning. On the other hand, in other contexts, where the *jus non scriptum* is prevalent and where legal norms such as equity and custom take over the written law, the musical metaphor becomes a powerful reminder that legal interpretation is always beyond verbatim statement. It raises the question of the rhetorical status of poetic law. Legal poetry may then serve as a manifestation of legal logic and argumentation, which stands against the excess of interpretation (*cavillatio*). The tradition of humanist scientific poetry had also influenced law, and Draco's verses can be understood as an acknowledged humanist form of reflecting on legal interpretation in its widest possible applications. If legal verses are meant to be useful, then their pretence to clarity, their poetical utterance and harmonious rhythm will settle the issue and will, through the oral performance of chanting *carmina*, lead to undeniable consensus. Mnemonic verses are not only a way to store topical arguments and exercise wits. Their genealogical *substratus* also serves to anticipate, create and invent new forms of judgements. *Carmina* become the binding force of schoolboys aiming to become jurists, and their songs need to be attuned to fulfil the final cause of the law, namely the common good and public usefulness. Legal poetry stands as a battle against heavy books, a hearty joust against complicated collations and their austere forms. Draco published a poetical chest-treasure, in a compact and portable size.

In 1635, Scipion Dupleix wrote a versified version of the axioms and rules of Law (*Axiomata, sententiae et regulae juris, versibus redditae,* Paris 1635). In his preface, he reports the antique tradition of writing laws in verses and the example of the Druids, who, according to Julius Caesar, had enshrined their laws in 20,000 lines of poetry. He defends the use of rhymed laws by claiming that they will help the lawyer's memory and also divert him. These productions of poetry as a category of legal discourse or law as a poetic art might seem odd to modern proponents of the apodictic status of legal science. The frequent denial of the symbolic valence of visual and poetical jurisprudence forgets a crucial element of the force of law and its logic of supplement. Legal cultures and phenomena are beyond the *jus scriptum*, they penetrate the hearts of citizens through other ways of intellection. Nor does this mark a demise of intelligence. This chapter argues for a reconsideration of ancient legal phenomena aside from the hegemony of textual, script-based interpretation. Analyzing legal symbolic acts in their visual and aural dimension raises fundamental questions. Is Law nothing but the Empire of Text? Law has to be embodied, as texts are more powerful when they are conveyed by dense verses, legal songs or leonine rhymes. More importantly, as Peter Goodrich suggests, the very act of versifying challenged the juridical hierarchy of writing (*lex scripta*) over speech (*jus non scripta*) of sovereign prohibition of all interpretation: "Hermeneutics, *officium poetae*, rhetorical practice and theatrical play, all simultaneously expand the dominion and undo the boundaries and restraints of legal form."[26]

Poetic Justice

This brief survey has tried to expand our understanding of legal hermeneutics. Beyond the textual form of Codes or *sacrosancta auctoritas*, other traditions undo and escape the verbal summons, "Lex imperat". This motto was inserted by French painter Paul Baudry (1828–1886) onto a pedestal which features in his monumental painting *La glorification de la Loi*, a huge work (measuring (4.8 m × 3.6 m) which in 1888 came to occupy the central position in the allegorical ceiling of the *salle d'audience* of the *première chambre civile* of the first jurisdiction of France, the Cour de Cassation. At the centre of image, the tall white-clad figure of Dame Justice stands in front of the imperial throne, above a neo-classical pedestal, has a powerful gesture of *indigitatio*, a visual equivalent to the maxim "Lex imperat" which is written below in Roman capital letters. Most French magistrates, when they visit the audience chamber, will stress that the glorification of the legal order is a plain, imperial and self-sufficient message. They hardly notice the erotic, obscene presence of Innocence, a sensuous putto in a sleeping posture below Jurisprudence, a man in red "grand costume" who, in an expression of deference, has removed his cap before Dame Justice. The erotic flesh of the putto serves as a scopic delegate ("délégué scopique") indicating to the viewer where to look. Dame Justice may well ordain, summon and instruct. Her desirable body, standing out in front of the vacant imperial throne, under the double figuration of Equity (holding the scales) and Force (holding the sword), is, as in other depictions, a tiered figure. Her visual order

[26] Peter Goodrich suggested this idea in a private communication (dated 18 October 2019) whilst reading an earlier version of this chapter.

is only one of the three components of doing justice. She cannot act as a sole figure. Instead, she forms part of a secular trinity which, taken together, commands, weighs and threatens, all at the same time. Dame Justice's symbolic acts always escape the positivist writing of legal orders: *Lex imperat, corpus dominae secessit* (Fig. 12.1).

Throughout the early modern period, the value of poetic verses for the transmission of Law is regularly associated with the necessity of making these laws visible, manifest and accessible in the forum. The figure of the legislator-poet-musician Masurius Sabinus (Atheneus, *Deipnosophists*, V, 179–180) is regularly put forward. In 1601, the French lawyer and orator Guillaume du Vair dedicate an opening ceremonial discourse at the Parliament of Paris to the topic "la Justice et la Musique sont un même art". Music has the highest philosophical value: it is educational, therapeutic, and made for both bodies and minds; as such it deserves full attention from legislators, jurists and citizens alike. Most humanist jurists try to recover the Roman custom mentioned by Cicero, whereby the children learned the Law of the Twelve Tables by singing it as a required song (*necessarium carmina*) originates from *De Legibus*, II, 23. Soon the *carmen necessarium* is revamped in *carmina solemnia*. François Baudouin insists on their monumental status, carved on ivory tablets on the Rostres tribune, displaying for every Roman citizen the current legislation of the time.

Guillaume Budé's Pastiche of Roman Laws

In order to assess the sempiternal tradition of poetical defence of the beauty of law, a final example should be highlighted. Although, as it is well known, Guillaume Budé never taught law as a scholarly discipline, his humanistic achievements shed light on the reception of the *Corpus Juris Civilis* as an anthology of Roman legal history, which had suffered from the misinterpretations of various schools of law, mainly because of their ignorance of Greek language and ancient history. One example of his philological method is particularly telling: his copy of the 1489 Nerli edition of Homer, which is packed with his handwritten philological notes in Greek and Latin,[27] something which demonstrates how Budé absorbed

[27] Princeton University Library, 2681.1488q (copy 2). It is accessible online: http://pudl.princeton.edu/viewer.php?obj=m613n114v&vol=v1phys&log=v1log#page/132/mode/2up.

Fig. 12.1 Paul Baudry, *La glorification de la Loi* (1881) (Copyright Paris, Cour de cassation)

and annotated Homeric hymns with great voracity. Budé's pastiche of the most ancient Roman laws (which occurs early on in his *De asse et partibus ejus* [1515])[28] is relevant here because Budé remained a lifelong scholar without actually being charged with any teaching responsibilities. This final example will show how humanist legal culture frees itself from the weights and constraints of imperial *auctoritas*. Poetry is thus used to launch a polemical joust, where Budé mocks the solemnity with which ancient monuments were praised. As a champion of humanism, Budé sought to circumvent the famous prohibition against legal interpretation, beyond the word-to-word translation (*kata poda*) allowed by Justinian, and its legal consequences (deportation and confiscation of all property, the *poena falsi*). For most legal humanist scholars, the *auctoritas* of the written law was to be challenged only when some kind of pedagogical pretext enabled or necessitated it. For Budé, however, the challenge to its authority was, to some extent, an end in itself. His aim was that of mocking the concept of sacrosanct interpretation per se, and thereby to show that there is no such thing as an untouchable text. As Luigi-Alberto Sanchi has noted, Budé wrote "un efficace pastiche de la Loi des XII tables, grâce auquel il inscrit dans le marbre les règles d'or de la méthode critique, par opposition aux arguments d'autorité".[29] In short, all texts are corruptible and are, as such, prone to being desecrated by some sort of pastiche.

At the beginning of his masterpiece, *De asse et partibus ejus* (1515), Budé explains that an experienced and knowledgeable humanist is entitled to question the textual authority of all antique authors. If he suspects a copyist's error or a corrupted text, or if he considers that the antique author himself made an error, the humanist scholar is entitled to correct these errors. According to Budé, this argument is valid for any author: Pliny, Cicero or even Aristotle.

What is remarkable about this new philological statement is that Budé asserts these critical principles against indisputable *auctoritates* and proposes to carve them in the syntactic mould of Roman laws:

[28] Guillaume Budé, *Opera omnia* (1557), II, pp. 11–12. For a modern French translation, see Guillaume Budé, *De asse et partibus eius. L'As et ses fractions. Livres I–III. Édition critique du texte de 1541 et traduction française*, trans. Luigi-Alberto Sanchi (Geneva: Droz, 2018).

[29] Luigi-Alberto Sanchi, 'Guillaume Budé et la langue juridique', *Revue historique de droit français et étranger*, 93:4 (October–December 2015), 487–501.

For in the interest of this present time when letters are being repaired, I would not consider it useful to promulgate a law of this content:

> Eternal and sacred will be the authority of what Pliny, the elders, the first-rate authors, say and write, of everything they have left us in their works. Whoever has avoided, abrogated or replaced the *auctoritas* enshrined in tradition will therefore be despicable and cursed: all men of good letters will (at the very least) chase him away after the trial.

I would prefer to recommend the following law:

> Lovers of science will obligingly greet the majesty of any sworn writer. Whoever expresses or has expressed a doubt, who raises or has raised a question in order to restore the truth of an inaccurate expression (since these are human works) having occurred, slipped, insinuated into the works of one of them, an error that each of these authors could commit without deception or malignancy: that they incur neither fines nor discredit to honest people—which is equivalent to capital punishment.[30]

These two laws are, as Luigi-Alberto Sanchi noted, a witty pastiche of how Roman laws were drafted and exhibited as sacred monuments, indisputable, untouchable and symbolically self-sufficient. Budé uses Latin to produce a prose poem: the sequences "derogaverit abrogaverit obrogaverit" and further "irrepserit obrepserit fefellerit" echo well known debates about the vexed issue of verbal intention and legal interpretation. In adding dignity to his own principles of humanistic interpretation, Budé circumvents the famous prohibition of unauthorized commentaries ordered by Justinian. The rule of law he now wishes to obey reminds

[30] "Nec enim ætati huic nostræ literarum interpolatrici hanc legem promulgandam censuerim : Quod Plinius, quod prisci, quod primi meriti scriptores dixerint scripserint, quam rem cumque inter monumenta sua reliquerint, eiusce rei æterna ac sacrosancta auctoritates esto. Qui huic velut consecratæ sententiæ derogaverit abrogaverit obrogaverit, is ob eam rem intestabilis et sacer esto : eum literati omnes ex conventu certatim exigunto. Illam enim potius legem ipse suaserim : Qui discendi cupidi sint, iuratissimi cuiusque scriptoris maiestatem comiter conservanto ; quod secus (ut sunt humana) dictum in eorum cuiusque libros irrepserit obrepserit fefellerit, qui de eo dicto indagandæ veritatis ergo addubitet addubitaverit, quæstionem referat retulerit, quod eorum ab unoquoque absque dolo malo aut livore animi factum sit, eius rei mulcta ne sit nec bonorum offensio, quod instar est extremi supplicii" (Guillaume Budé, *De Asse*, edn. 1550, 32).

every interpreter that it is the condition of human law always to decline endlessly (C. I.17.2.18). As for the prohibition of interpretation, beyond word-to-word translation, and its legal consequences (pain of deportation and confiscation of all property, the *poena falsi*), Budé transposes it into a much harder penalty: the discredit of men of good letters and good reputation, which to him, equals capital punishment.

The use of verse, transpositions and poetic interpretations of legal codes is thus, more far reaching than most scholars of these curious texts usually admit. Jurists are often poets, but their poems are not only meant to serve as mnemonic shortcuts or didactic tools. These verses are sometimes true manifestations of the importance of the vivid voices of legal texts. In his *New Science* (1744), Giambattista Vico further elaborates this fertile ground and claims that the law was originally a serious or severe poem. In 1752, Giuseppe Aurelio Gennaro, in his *Respublica Jurisconsultorum*, produces an extensive versification of the Law of the Twelve Tables. Neo-Latin poetry has cultivated with great success this antique tradition. But the versification of legal codes cannot be reduced to an erudite and polemical fight that would not concern later exponents of legal writings. As I have tried to show, the vernacular strategies of transposing the *Institutes* into verse also deserve patient scrutiny, insofar as it aims at recovering oral systems of judicial transmission, which escape the order of textual norms.

Until the nineteenth century, the elective affinities between law and poetry are particularly visible in these recurrent attempts to versify legal codes. This brief survey has examined why a wide number of legal codes have been turned into metrical forms. Although European legal traditions rarely acknowledge these inventions, law understood as a poetic endeavour shows that between oral systems and legal writings, one cultural norm and another, verses have something to say about interpretation. Legal songs, visual jurispoetry indicate that the Code always has to encounter, and be undone by, the unwritten: the caritas of breath, of incorporation in lived interactions, occasions and events. The law longs to escape and cannot escape the rendering of the text.

CHAPTER 13

Towards a Poetics of Equality in Nineteenth-Century English Literature

Jan-Melissa Schramm

The publication of Denis Diderot's *Encyclopédie* (1751–1772) in Paris marked a crucial departure in the organization of social knowledge. Amongst the terms it sought to define and release into wider circulation were complex political concepts such as 'Egalité naturelle'. According to this entry by the prolific contributor Louis de Jaucourt, 'Natural or moral *Equality* is … based on the constitution of human nature common to all men, who are born, grow, live, and die in the same way': it is 'the principle and foundation of liberty', and from it, all other 'rights of man' flow.[1] This definition of equality is both seminal and provocative: on the one hand, it is an early landmark in the history of attempts to articulate the crucial ingredients of the so-called democratic creed of 'liberty,

[1] Louis, chevalier de Jaucourt, entry for 'Egalité naturelle', in Denis Diderot's *Encyclopédie* (1751–1772), accessed online at https://quod.lib.umich.edu/d/did (accessed 25 September 2024).

J.-M. Schramm (✉)
University of Cambridge, Cambridge, UK
e-mail: js10032@cam.ac.uk

S. Mukherji and D. Roberts (eds.), *Literature and the Legal Imaginary*, Crossroads of Knowledge in Early Modern Literature 4,
https://doi.org/10.1007/978-3-031-74093-0_13

equality, fraternity', but on the other hand, it tethers equality to an experience 'common to all men', that is, the same biological trajectory of growth, maturation, and death independent of invented social hierarchies. Yet there was no consensus about the role socio-economic inequality played in the formation of that 'human constitution' at the time, with Enlightenment philosophers divided as to whether equality was spiritual but not political (following Locke) or alternatively the only foundation on which democratization could proceed (following Diderot, Helvetius, and d'Holbach).[2] The division between the two camps could be explained by differing degrees of belief that civic hierarchies (and their foundations in primogeniture and respect for tradition) were God-given, in which case they could be ameliorated but not abolished: only the atheistic *philosophes modernes* in France felt that a complete overhaul was possible. Public discourse was shaped by shorthand expressions of binary opposition, with major figures standing as cyphers for larger conceptual arguments—for example, with the conservative Edmund Burke pitted against the radical Thomas Paine, and the great mythographer of the common law, William Blackstone, in conflict with the preeminent exponent of codification, Jeremy Bentham. For the purposes of this chapter, though, one of the more interesting questions of the period was the potential form which legal thought might take as it absorbed and catalyzed changing attitudes to inheritance and innovation. How, then, should equality be advanced as a political agenda—by the legislative programme of the revolutionary camp in France (and Bentham in England), or by more capacious ideas of cultural consent encouraged in part by literary forms which accumulate meaning over time?

According to Jonathan Israel, there is a 'deeply felt poetic and dramatic aversion to oppression clearly discernible from the 1760s onwards' in radical literature published in England, France, and Germany: by 1789, 'a revolutionary ideology of completely unprecedented power, intensity and scope [had] established itself firmly on both sides of the Atlantic'.[3] At the same time, the idea of equality was enshrined in two crucial documents—the American *Declaration of Independence* (1776) and *The Declaration of*

[2] See Jonathan Israel, *A Revolution of the Mind: Radical Enlightenment and the Intellectual Origins of Modern Democracy* (Princeton: Princeton University Press, 2010), 37–91.

[3] Israel, *A Revolution of the Mind*, 87–88.

the Rights of Man and of the Citizen, by the National Assembly of France (1789). The Preamble to the American document observes that

> We hold these truths to be self-evident, that all men are created equal, that they are endowed by their Creator with certain unalienable rights, that among these are life, liberty, and the pursuit of happiness.[4]

Despite the assertion of 'self-evidence' (which seeks to extract 'equality' from the fertile ground in which it had germinated and elevate it as a self-interpreting truth), the *Declaration of Independence* foregrounds one of the greatest philosophical problems of rights language—the question of origins, and whether the possession of rights is consistent with any form of submission to divine power. In contrast, the French text is famously secular and Republican in tone and aspiration:

> The representatives of the people of France formed into a National Assembly, considering that ignorance, neglect, or contempt of human rights, are the sole causes of public misfortunes ... have resolved to set forth ... those natural, imprescriptible, and unalienable rights.[5]

In Article 1, they set out the belief that men are born free and remain equal in their rights, with those rights defined initially in Article 2 as liberty, property, security, and resistance to oppression. Whilst the American and French documents have much in common—not least their expressive and aspirational form—they also gesture towards many points of difference, especially the para-textual authority allegedly required to underpin the idea of rights: as Israel argues (and as I have noted above), one of the foundational differences between radical and moderate Enlightenment thinkers was their attitude to the existence of the human soul and thus of the afterlife, which may be used to justify the existence of social oppression in this life with the offer of a utopian reward in the next.[6] As pressure mounted on the British parliament to undertake its own agenda of democratic reform, its members kept a close eye on

[4] Text available online at: https://avalon.law.yale.edu/18th_century/declare.asp (accessed 25 September 2024).

[5] Text available online at: https://avalon.law.yale.edu/18th_century/rightsof.asp (accessed 25 September 2024).

[6] Israel, *A Revolution of the Mind*, 1–36.

developments across the Channel and across the Atlantic, resulting in a compelling triangular and transnational debate about the contours and design of democratic governance.[7] But unlike their revolutionary counterparts, the Houses of Parliament in Westminster were constrained by what they had inherited from the past—by the continuities enshrined within the methodologies of precedential reasoning which underpinned the common law itself.[8]

In his *Commentaries on the Laws of England*, published in four volumes between 1755 and 1759, William Blackstone famously described the common law in the following terms:

> A single legislator or an enterprising sovereign [...] may at any time form a concise, and perhaps an uniform, plan of justice; and evil betide that presumptuous subject who questions its wisdom or utility. But who, that is acquainted with the difficulty of new-modeling any branch of our statute laws (though relating but to roads or to parish-settlements) will conceive it ever feasible to alter any fundamental point of the common law, with all its appendages and consequences, and set up another rule in its stead? [...] We inherit an old Gothic castle, erected in the days of chivalry, but fitted up for a modern inhabitant.[9]

For Blackstone as for Burke, this shared inheritance is the nation's uncodified constitution, an amorphous but sacrosanct vehicle for the conveyance of the accumulated customs of the people and the unique guarantor of the liberties of 'free-born Englishmen'.[10] Blackstone's interpretation of the law prioritized a constant referential comparison between past decisions and present dilemmas: historiography, in other words, lies at the heart of the law. But Blackstone's mythologizing of the common law did not go unchallenged. According to J. S. Mill, in his retrospective

[7] See for example, Ruth Livesey and Ella Dzelainis, eds., *The American Experiment and the Idea of Democracy in British Culture, 1776–1914* (Aldershot: Ashgate, 2013).

[8] On 'precedential reasoning', see Ayelet Ben-Yishai, *Common Precedents: The Presentness of the Past in Victorian Fiction* (Oxford: Oxford University Press, 2013).

[9] William Blackstone, *Commentaries on the Laws of England*, 4 vols. (Oxford: Clarendon Press, 1755–1759), vol. I, Bk III, ch.17.

[10] In Blackstone, the phase refers to the traditional domestic 'rights' accumulated over time from documents such as the Magna Carta (1215) and the Bill of Rights (1689). See also Edmund Burke, *Reflections on the Revolution in France* [1790] (Oxford: Oxford University Press, 1993).

account of Enlightenment jurisprudential development, it was Bentham 'who demand[ed to know] the why of everything' that his generation had inherited and who thus 'broke' Blackstone's spell'.[11] For Bentham, a true law (as opposed to the metaphorical ones of religion or science) was a command of the sovereign backed by a sanction, expressed as austerely and crisply as possible.[12] Ideally, such a law should be codified: it should certainly not be dependent on the decisions of courts over time or on appeal to a divine authority beyond the confines of the text. In other words, Blackstone's Gothic battlements should be measured against modern ideas of utility, and found wanting—and then replaced by the more functional legal architecture of statutes. The difference between Blackstone and Bentham opens up an important question about the form of law and whether it can be considered hermetically sealed off from the wider political and literary cultures which catalyze and sustain the formation of social norms and values. Inspired by French Republicanism, Bentham's was the vision of the revolutionary moment, when the fracturing of the inherited past allowed people to imagine what law-making based on first principles might look like.[13] But Bentham's codes fell from favour in the aftermath of the Reign of Terror and by the 1820s, even France considered Bentham's atheism suspect: a new generation returned to the rhetoric of Christian conservatism to advance the interests of political stability. What this reveals with particular clarity is the ideological baggage of two models of law-making—the declarative codes favoured by Bentham, and the cumbersome inheritance of the uncodified British constitution, eulogized by Blackstone and by Burke, and by all those who came to favour reform over revolution as a response to fears of bloodshed. And form cannot be separated from content, in law as in literary criticism: as always, style has ethical and political implications. It is primarily if law is seen as something inherited and organic—something which expresses

[11] J. S. Mill, 'On Bentham' [1838], in F. R. Leavis, ed., *Mill on Bentham and Coleridge* (Cambridge: Cambridge University Press, 1980), pp. 41–42.

[12] See Jeremy Bentham, *A Fragment on Government* [1776], ed. Ross Harrison (Cambridge: Cambridge University Press, 1988): see also John Austin, *The Province of Jurisprudence Determined* [1832], ed. Wilfred Rumble (Cambridge: Cambridge University Press, 2009).

[13] On Bentham's indebtedness to French thought, and the work of his French translator Étienne Dumont in the dissemination of his works on both sides of the Channel, see Emmanuelle de Champs, *Enlightenment and Utility: Bentham in French, Bentham in France* (Cambridge: Cambridge University Press, 2015).

the customary life of the people—that literary culture can play any active part in its formation.

The afterlife of Diderot and Jaucourt's definition of equality illustrates this process in action. In *Ancient Law*, published to great acclaim in 1861, the famous Victorian jurist Henry Sumner Maine argued that the French did not invent the idea of equality (he claims for it a Roman precedent) but they gave it its modern inflection:

> There cannot, I conceive, be any question that to the assumption of a Law Natural we owe the doctrine of the fundamental equality of human beings. That 'all men are equal' is one of a large number of legal propositions which, in progress of time, have become political. The Roman juriconsults of the Antonine era lay down that 'omnes homines natura aequales sunt', but in their eyes this is a strictly juridical axiom. They intend to affirm that, under the hypothetical Law of Nature, and in so far as positive law approximates to it, the arbitrary distinctions which the Roman Civil Law maintained between classes of persons cease to have a legal existence... [But] the modern civilian wrote 'all men are equal' in the sense that 'all men ought to be equal' ... This is the enunciation not of a legal rule but of a political dogma; and from this time the equality of men is spoken of by the French lawyers just as if it were a political truth which happened to have been preserved among the archives of their science.

Although it was allegedly Maximilian Robespierre who first used the phrase 'Liberté, Égalité, Fraternité', Maine argues that the impact of this so-called 'democratic creed' was determined not by its use by lawyers but by its rapturous reception in the literary sphere:

> Like all other deductions from the hypothesis of a Law Natural ... [the idea of equality] was languidly assented to and suffered to have little influence on opinion and practice until it passed out of the possession of the lawyers and into that of the literary men ... and of the public which sat at their feet.[14]

Maine suggests here that it is not so much the work of Bentham himself, or indeed of philosophical texts such as William Godwin's *Enquiry Concerning Political Justice* (1793), which furthered the radical cause,

[14] Henry Sumner Maine, *Ancient Law* [1861] (Cambridge: Cambridge University Press, 2002), 85–86.

but instead the fictional and poetic advocacy of rights which won the day. Godwin himself was an extraordinarily successful self-adaptor, with his wildly successful novel, *Things as they Are: or, the Adventures of Caleb Williams* (1794), exposing an audience to his ideas which the *Enquiry* itself had never reached (due to its cost as well as its intellectual density), whilst Lord Byron, Samuel Taylor Coleridge, Mary and Percy Shelley, and William Wordsworth, all mediated French and American revolutionary principles of equality and fraternity to ever-expanding English audiences. The sheer power of the democratic imagination led the government of the 1790s to categorize it as an existential threat to the political status quo: as John Barrell has shown, any attempt (even in artistic form) to encourage the reconceptualization of the uncodified English constitution in democratic directions was taken to imply a willingness to 'imagine the king's death'.[15] This was the substance of the treason charges brought against the members of the London Corresponding Society in 1793, but as Godwin noted in his 'Preface' to *Caleb Williams*, the capacity of fiction to imaginatively experiment with constitutional reform meant that when 'terror' was 'the order of the day', 'even the humble novelist might be shown to be constructively a traitor'.[16] Unsurprisingly, in this climate, intellectual and artistic self-censorship grew in intensity, leaving many writers engaging only obliquely or allegorically with the larger questions of social organization that had animated earlier Enlightenment debate.

For Sumner Maine, who counted George Eliot, Frederic Harrison, and Leslie and James Fitzjames Stephen amongst his closest friends (and Charles Dickens amongst his acquaintances), the work of literary culture was to create fictional laboratories in which the mental experiments of jurisprudence might take place, disseminating exciting new developments like the belief that 'all men ought to be equal' and dramatizing repeated acts of consent to the imposition of order—or at the very least eulogizing the rule of law. So, one consequence of England's rejection of revolutionary codes of law—its preference for evolutionary change over time—was that it afforded plenty of room for literary texts to participate in the cultural work of norm innovation. For Eliot, the novel genre was

[15] John Barrell, *Imagining the King's Death: Figurative Treason, Fantasies of Regicide, 1793–1796* (Oxford: Oxford University Press, 2000).

[16] William Godwin, 'Preface' to *Caleb Williams* [1794] (Oxford: Oxford University Press, 1995), vii.

'a set of experiments in life', in which competing grounds for deliberative decision-making—particularly self-sacrifice versus self-interest—could be tested in an 'incarnational' form which sought to 'clothe' formulas 'in some sort of human figure and individual experience'.[17] As she explained to Harrison,

> I think aesthetic teaching is the highest of all teaching because it deals with life in its highest complexity. But if it ceases to be purely aesthetic—if it lapses anywhere from the picture to the diagram—it becomes the most offensive of all teaching. Avowed Utopias are not offensive, because they are understood to have a scientific and expository character: they do not pretend to work on the emotions, or couldn't do it if they did pretend.[18]

If literary forms thus permit the careful ethical and emotional dissection of life and its choices 'in [their] highest complexity', narrative attention (in almost every case bar perhaps texts like Daniel Defoe's *Robinson Crusoe* (1719)) will inevitably fall on protagonists' relationships with the wider society in which their development as an individual is occurring. As Eliot observed in *Felix Holt* (1866), 'there is no private life that is not determined by a wider public life',[19] and almost every novel demands this careful negotiation between individual freedoms and the greater good to which that autonomy might have to be sacrificed in the interests of community survival. The critic Joseph Slaughter has illuminated with extraordinary precision the extent to which this ongoing tension between the needs of the one and the many is central to human rights law as well as to the novel genre: as he has argued in his seminal study, *Human Rights, Inc: The World Novel, Narrative Form, and International Law* (2007):

> The novel genre and liberal human rights discourse are more than coincidentally, or casually, interconnected ... They are mutually enabling fictions: each projects an image of the human personality that ratifies the other's idealistic visions of the proper relations between the individual and society

[17] Eliot to Joseph Frank, 25 January 1876, in *The George Eliot Letters*, ed. Gordon S. Haight, 9 vols. (New Haven: Yale University Press, 1954–1978), vol. 6, p. 216.

[18] George Eliot to Frederic Harrison, 15 August 1866, in *George Eliot: Selected Essays, Poems, and Other Writings*, ed. A. S. Byatt and Nicholas Warren (Harmondsworth: Penguin, 1990), 248–49.

[19] George Eliot, *Felix Holt, the Radical* [1866] (Harmondsworth: Penguin, 1987), 129.

> and the normative career of free and full human personality development ... Human rights law does indeed recognize an implicit freedom to plot a life story, and the species of person that the law describes is, in effect, *homo narrans*.[20]

According to Slaughter, the novel (and particularly the *Bildungsroman*) 'makes legible the inequities of an egalitarian imaginary' and simultaneously 'normalizes the story of enfranchisement', serving as 'the predominant formal literary technology in which social outsiders narrate affirmative claims for inclusion in a regime of rights and responsibilities'.[21] In this influential model, the literary sphere serves as a forum for para-legal advocacy—the chosen protagonist is a socially marginal representative of a wider group, and as readers watch his or her incorporation into the polis, they are educated though feelings of sympathy and identification which work to foster reconciliation across divisions of class and gender. The strength of this model depends on the wider political efficacy of the sympathy generated for a representative protagonist: 'That a character like [Esther or Jo in *Bleak House*] may be both particular and yet representative of the interests of a group reminds us of the ways in which a "social problem" novel is something like a class action.'[22] To use the language of Equity and Chancery law, the novel can then serve as what I have called elsewhere a litigative aggregation device,[23] making claims on behalf of a wider community providing they can show they have an interest in the outcome of proceedings.

Yet, as Slaughter rightly notes, the novel only illustrates successful processes of social incorporation when the chosen protagonist deviates from 'the norm' in a fairly limited fashion:

> [T]he exemplarity of the affirmative *Bildungsroman*'s protagonist lies in its relatively modest marginality, a model marginality that is capable of being transcended or transformed by proper training in the socially acceptable forms of speech and the social norms of the bourgeois reading public.

[20] Joseph Slaughter, *Human Rights, Inc.: Narrative Form, the World Novel, and International Law* (New York: Fordham University Press, 2007), 4, 40.

[21] Slaughter, *Human Rights, Inc.*, 104.

[22] Jan-Melissa Schramm, 'Dickens and the National Interest: On the Representation of Parties in *Bleak House*', *Law and the Humanities*, 6 (2012), 217–42 (234).

[23] Schramm, 'Dickens and the National Interest', 238.

> Thematically and sociologically, the viability of a candidate for affirmative *Bildungsroman*'s incorporative work appears largely pegged to the historical conditions of the public sphere itself—to the actual or imminent expansions and contractions of the franchise, which the novels both reflect and catalyze.[24]

Such 'modest marginality' is on display in the mid-Victorian social problem novel, in which working-class protagonists demonstrate sophisticated skills of literacy and oratory whilst minor characters speak in dialect (for example, in almost all of Dickens's, Eliot's and Elizabeth Gaskell's works). A text like Charlotte Brontë's *Jane Eyre* (1847) further reveals the limits of rights claims in England. Brontë's eponymous protagonist furiously rebuts Rochester's assumptions that self-respect is tethered to gender and social standing, arguing instead that dignity is innate—a quality with which all humans are endowed:

> Do you think I am an automaton?—a machine without feelings? and can bear to have my morsel of bread snatched from my lips, and my drop of living water dashed from my cup? Do you think, because I am poor, obscure, plain, and little, I am soulless and heartless? You think wrong! –I have as much soul as you, –and full as much heart! And if God had gifted me with some beauty and much wealth, I should have made it as hard for you to leave me, as it is now for me to leave you. I am not talking to you now through the medium of custom, conventionalities, nor even of mortal flesh;–it is my spirit that addresses your spirit; just as if both had passed through the grave, and we stood at God's feet, equal,–as we are![25]

Novels such as *Jane Eyre* performed important political work, encouraging readers to feel that regardless of their birth status, they had a stake in the country's national interest—in Franco Moretti's analysis, an interest of sufficient promise to stave off the threat of revolutionary violence.[26] Although denied a vote at present, the para-parliamentary forum of fiction seemed to suggest that their political enfranchisement

[24] Slaughter, *Human Rights, Inc.*, 156–57.

[25] Charlotte Bronte, *Jane Eyre* [1847] (Harmondsworth: Penguin, 1996), 350.

[26] Franco Moretti, *The Way of the World: The Bildungsroman in European Culture* (London: Verso, 1987).

(their entry into full and active citizenship) would follow in due course.[27] Whether this aesthetic representation subsequently catalyzed real change (as Maine suggested), or simply anaesthetized the masses against the need for wholesale social reconstruction, remains to this day a moot point.

Even if the status of the novel genre as an agent of political change is given the benefit of the doubt, however, its representation of equality remains flawed at best. Insofar as the affective impact of a novel depends upon an investment in the detailed depiction of the plight of its protagonists, it is sentenced to continually repeat the limitations of aristocratic social formations. As Alex Woloch has noted so perceptively,

> The realist novel is infused with the sense that any character is a potential hero, but simultaneously enchanted with the freestanding individual, defined through his or her interior consciousness. In the paradigmatic character-structure of the realist novel, any character can be a protagonist, but only one character is; just as increasing political equality, and a maturing logic of human rights, develop amid acute economic and social stratification. On the one hand, the asymmetric structure of realist characterization—which rounds out one or several characters while flattening, and distorting a manifold assortment of others—reflects actual structures of inequitable distribution. On the other hand, the claims of minor characters on the reader's attention—and the resultant tension between characters and their functions—are generated by the democratic impulse that forms a horizon of nineteenth-century politics.[28]

Whilst the rise of the novel—with its portrayal of the lives of ordinary men and women—can then be understood as one expression of the spirit of democratization sweeping Europe in the eighteenth and nineteenth centuries, it remains limited in its formal capacity to represent all characters *equally*: no matter how much work is performed by the representative function of its *dramatis personae*, the protagonist must inevitably remain *primus inter pares*. Minor characters, on the other hand, remain formally and spatially marginal.

[27] See Catherine Gallagher, *The Industrial Reformation of English Fiction: Social Discourse and Narrative Form, 1832–1867* (Chicago: University of Chicago Press, 1985), particularly Ch. 3. Gallagher's classic study notes that fiction played both a conservative and a radical role in the enfranchisement of the working classes.

[28] Alex Woloch, *The One vs. the Many: Minor Characters and the Space of the Characters in the Novel* (Princeton: Princeton University Press, 2003), 31.

The passage of the First Reform Bill in 1832 was a significant step towards the extension of the franchise, but many felt its achievements (enfranchising at best one in five men) were more symbolic than real: by the end of the decade, Chartism had emerged as a working-class movement to demand (amongst other things) universal suffrage for adult males. Whilst the democratic creed of 'Liberty, Equality, Fraternity' remained tainted by its association with the Reign of Terror, Chartism reconfigured its claims in powerful and appealing ways, combining stories of local experience with the rhetoric of universalism. Whilst Lynn Hunt has suggested that the discourse of rights falls into abeyance in nineteenth-century England, others have pushed back against that claim, contending instead that rights claims remain a crucial ingredient of Chartist agitation, the campaign for the abolition of slavery in the British Empire and then the United States, and the outcry against Governor Eyre's brutal suppression of rebellion in Jamaica in 1865.[29] Appeals for the liberation of the 'universal we' continued apace, and Christopher Warren is right to argue that we can identify a 'literary history of the International' prior to its emergence in formal socialist structures in the second half of the nineteenth century.[30]

Whether equality extended to the economic realm (in addition to the political and spiritual ones) had been a subject of debate for centuries: as Susan Marks has argued, rights to equal political representation were of little use to those forced into poverty by the parliamentary Enclosures Acts and the impact of the Industrial Revolution. There was little value in a right to liberty if there was no pre-existing right to life.[31] Yet mid-Victorian campaigners for political equality were as divided as their predecessors as to whether or not there was any right to hold private property: once admitted, inequality seemed a given. Although

[29] See Lynn Hunt, *Inventing Human Rights* (New York: Norton, 2003), Gary Bass, *Freedom's Battle: The Origins of Humanitarian Intervention* (Manchester University Press, 2008), Jenny Martinez, *Slave Trade and the Origins of International Human Rights Law* (Oxford: Oxford University Press, 2012), and Siep Stuurman, *The Invention of Humanity: Equality and Cultural Difference in Global History* (Cambridge, MA: Harvard University Press, 2017).

[30] Christopher Warren, 'Big Leagues: Specters of Milton and Republican International Justice Between Shakespeare and Marx', *Humanity* (Winter 2016), 365–97 (365).

[31] See Susan Marks, *A False Tree of Liberty: Human Rights in Radical Thought* (Oxford: Oxford University Press, 2019).

English Chartism was largely suppressed in 1848—and its leaders transported to penal colonies abroad or imprisoned—the *Manifesto* of the Communist League was published in English in George Julian Harney's *Red Republican* in 1850, the same year that the Chartist leader Ernest Jones was released from prison for sedition: there is significant overlap, in other words, between the weakening of one movement and the subsequent expansion of European internationalism. Jones's writings—across the genres of journalism, epic poetry, and fiction—offer compelling insights into the English strand of socialist thought at mid-century, prior to the establishment of the First International (also known as the International Workingmen's Association) in London in 1864. In pausing for a moment to consider Jones's arsenal of rhetorical tropes, my interest is less the history of social thought per se and more a question of the ethics of style: what language speaks most insistently to a given audience, allowing concepts such as 'equality' to ignite and capture the imagination in particularly compelling ways at a given point in time?[32]

Jones's background was cosmopolitan: born in Berlin whilst his father served as equerry to the future King of Hanover, he was called to the English Bar in 1844—although he soon abandoned any hope of long-term legal practice for journalism in the Chartist cause.[33] Jones's rhetorical agenda, both before and after the period of imprisonment which followed his trial, lay in exploring the parameters of shared national and international interest—whether it was class-based, or nation based, and if not, how widely the boundaries of the universal could be drawn. To give an example of the symbolism which accompanied the meetings of the various Democratic societies in the 1840s, John Saville describes the annual banquet of the German Democratic Society for the Education of the Working Classes, held at the White Hart Tavern on Drury Lane on February 8, 1847. According to newspaper reports, Jones spoke in front of a painting depicting the defeat of tyranny beneath the rising sun of liberty 'which lights up the happy homes of the emancipated millions': the editor noted,

[32] See discussion in Peter de Bolla, *The Architecture of Concepts: The Historical Formation of Human Rights* (New York: Fordham University Press, 2013).

[33] Miles Taylor, *Ernest Jones, Chartism, and the Romance of Politics, 1819–1869* (Oxford: Oxford University Press, 2003), ch. 1.

The whole is surrounded by a golden wreath (on crimson ground) of oak leaves and acorns, with which is entwined a riband, bearing the society's motto:

ALL MEN ARE BRETHREN

in twelve different languages: German, English, French, Swedish, Danish, Dutch, Italian, Greek, Spanish, Polish, Hungarian, and Russian.
[Ernest Jones]: "Citizen Chairman and Brother Democrats! When we recollect that the time was, and not long ago, in which a Frenchman could not walk the streets of London without men calling after him, "There goes a French frog!' or an Englishman the streets of Paris, without being greeted as an "English bif-steak!" When his appellation in Berlin or Vienna was a "*verrükter Englander*"; when we remember that a celebrated Italian author, Goldoni, ridiculed him in one of his plays as "Milord Round-o'beef", and a Frenchman satirised him as "Milord God-damn", when we think that bloody battles were the upholders of these prejudices and that Rossbach, Fontenay and Waterloo, the shame of humanity, were the glories and results of kingcraft; recollecting these things, I say, we can but feel a proud hope, in seeing here united, members of those different countries, banded for the cause of democracy, who, a few years back would have been cutting each other's throats in the cause of kings ... We are met here on a convivial occasion ... Every glass is a health to equality..."[34]

The twelve languages of the fraternal declaration gesture towards the emergence of a cultural commons which Marx describes in the almost contemporaneous Communist *Manifesto*: 'The intellectual creations of individual nations become common property. National one-sidedness and narrow-mindedness become more and more impossible, and from the numerous national and local literatures, there arises a world literature'.[35] Jones deploys the rhetoric of equality in his speech to imagine ever closer levels of transnational cooperation: in subsequent lectures, he takes this strategy even further:

I stand here by a higher title. I am not an Englishman alone—I am a man. I—we all—have a wider and a greater country than these narrow isles. It

[34] John Saville, *Ernest Jones: Chartist. Selections from the Writings and Speeches of Ernest Jones* (London: Lawrence & Wishart, 1952), 92.

[35] Karl Marx and Friedrich Engels, *The Communist Manifesto* [1850] (Oxford: Oxford University Press, 2008), 7.

> embraces the Frenchman and the German—it includes the Hungarian, the Italian and the Pole—my country is the world, and the nation I belong to is the most numerous of all; the nation of the oppressed. I acknowledge but two nationalities in existence, the tyrant and the slave. To me, the world forms but two great camps: the rich and the poor—and in the latter, I am a soldier. The language I speak, the men of every country understand. It was the universal tongue before tyranny's rude Babel brought confusion upon earth. It is the language of liberty—the first lisping of the new-born babe—the last aspiration of the dying saint. The creed I follow is the rights of man. Its trinity is Equality, Liberty, Fraternity. Its altar is the human heart. Its priesthood are the captive, the exile, and the martyr in the cause of truth. Its Litany is the Sufferers' cry of pain. Its revelation is the coming glory of the human race. Its commandments—it has but one: Strike! Till the last tyrant falls before the freeman or the last slave has fallen before the tyrant...[36]

As I noted earlier, the catch-cry of 'liberty, equality, fraternity' was seen as tainted by the revolutionary Reign of Terror, yet Jones embraces it freely, defending violence in the service of self-determination. The 'watchword of [his] struggle' is for each man to be 'masters in [their] own land, independent of any foreign influence'[37]: whilst this is hardly the language of global citizenship, Jones at least extends this right to all oppressed communities: for example, he assures the Irish that the English populace is on their side: 'Those who slew you at Rathcormac, slew us at Peterloo; those who imprisoned you in the Dublin Newgate, imprisoned us in the London one.'[38] Jones differs here from the eloquent Young Irelander John Mitchel, whose moving appeals for Irish liberty, founded on eyewitness evidence of the horrors of the Great Famine, countenanced no claims of ethical equivalence with the poverty of the English working classes.[39] Even more unusually for his times, Jones also understood the Indian Mutiny as a legitimate expression of revolt against English oppression:

[36] Ernest Jones, 'Speech at a Meeting in the Hall of Science, City Road, London, on 4 December, 1854', reprinted in the *People's Paper*, 9 December 1854: Saville, 215.

[37] Jones, 'To the Men of Ireland', *People's Paper*, 8 March 1856: Saville, 218.

[38] Jones, 'To the Men of Ireland', *People's Paper*, 8 March 1856: Saville, 216–17.

[39] See for example, John Mitchel, *Jail Journal: or, Five Years in British Prisons* [1854] (Dublin: Fisher Unwin, 1913).

> How any one can hesitate which side to take is inconceivable to us. England—the people, the English people—sympathise with liberty. On which side were they when Poland struggled for its freedom against Russia? On the side of Poland. On which side were they, when Hungary struggled for its rights with Austria? On the side of Hungary [...] Was Poland right? Then so is Hindostan. Was Hungary justified? Then so is Hindostan [...] We bespeak the sympathy of the English people for their Hindu brethren. Their cause is yours—their success is, indirectly, yours as well.[40]

Whilst acknowledging the possibility that 'Jones's attitude to the uprising in India ... was relentlessly opportunistic, involving the manipulation of news and events to mould it in the image of the renewed Chartist movement he now hoped to revive and lead', Priyamvada Gopal detects a more generous and inclusive impulse at work in passages such as these:

> What makes Jones's reading of the rebellion more active and dialogical than a mere annexation of events to a pre-existing framework would invoke is the way in which he repeatedly identifies the rebel as a speaking subject with a voice who can be heard in sundry texts and who, as such, ought to be heeded. Engaging with and interpreting these utterances enabled Jones to elaborate a discourse which ran counter to the one being forged in the British public sphere.[41]

But for Jones, universal equality (which includes an equal division of national lands and an equal distribution of individual wealth) is nevertheless both masculine and restricted to those who labour: the rights of indigenous peoples at the edge of Empire who eschewed Thomas Carlyle's gospel of work as a consequence of very different (but equally complex) social structures are not accommodated by this pan-European model. For example, there is no principle here which would enable English socialism to challenge the classification of colonies such as New South Wales and Van Diemen's Land as *terra nullius*—allegedly 'unoccupied' despite their large aboriginal populations, with their cherished landscapes 'uncultivated' for any commercial purpose recognizable to English settlers/invaders.

[40] Jones, 'The Indian Struggle', *People's Paper*, 5 September 1857: Saville, 219.

[41] Priyamvada Gopal, *Insurgent Empire: Anticolonialism and British Dissent* (London: Verso, 2019), 33.

Like Godwin before him, Jones disseminated his revolutionary commitment to liberty in fictional form as well, although his prose rarely attains the complexity of Eliot's ideal textual painting—he frequently descends instead to the diagram which she considers to be the least efficacious form of aesthetic teaching. For example, *The Maid of Warsaw, or the Tyrant Czar: A Tale of the Last Polish Insurrection* (1854) depicts the suffering of the country during the 1830 rebellion against Russian rule, subtitled 'a tale of revenge': Jones opens with the observation that '[a]s with individuals so with nations. Oppression ever breeds resistance that shows itself according to the powers of the oppressor, in open revolt or secret conspiracy'. When a rebellion is planned, '[s]ecret meetings were appointed and held, and an invisible thread spun between the betrayed of Poland and the oppressed of Russia'.[42] A thinly sketched cast of characters then dramatize these two political theses—the justification of armed resistance, and the creation of transnational sympathies between members of each country's labouring communities. Yet whilst the Polish figures eulogize liberty, the plot falls far short of treating all equally. Instead, Jones seeks resolution for conflict in the principles of tragic sacrifice that power the fiction of competition and capitalism (for example, Dickens's *Bleak House* [1852–1853], *Hard Times* [1854] and *A Tale of Two Cities* [1859]): as Woloch noted so perceptively, the socialist geometry of fairness is so often abandoned at the point of narrative closure when the less fortunate must pay for the benefits awarded to others, and find value only in a para-Christian celebration of the martyrdom they are forced to embrace. In a moment of Eucharistic substitution, the virtuous figureheads of the Polish resistance are murdered in front of the altar of the national church whilst the hymn of liberty rings out.[43] Although Poland's autonomy was erased when Russia crushed this rebellion in 1831, the scene of sacrifice which ends the novel heralds its eventual renewal and restoration, reminding readers of Benedict Anderson's definition of a nation state in *Imagined Communities*: whilst literacy and mass consumption of newspapers and novels were the most influential factors in the affective conception of the state as what he calls a 'deep horizontal companionship', its persistence may be explained by the fact that it is the

[42] Ernest Jones, *The Maid of Warsaw, or the Tyrant Czar: A Tale of the Last Polish Insurrection* (London, 1854), 25.

[43] Jones, *Maid of Warsaw*, 98.

largest entity for which so many million people in the last two centuries have shown themselves willing to die, to make 'such colossal sacrifices'.[44] For Jones as for Dickens, the state feeds perpetually on the blood of the marginalized—their labours support it in life and their deaths in battle (when required) subsequently sustain the founding myths of its identity. For Anderson, this explains, at least in part, the persistence of the nation state despite Marxism's prediction of its eventual demise.

The close but complicated correlation between revolutionary sacrifice and Christian martyrdom troubled writers throughout the nineteenth century, from Lord Byron's *Cain* (1821) and Percy Bysshe Shelley's 'Mask of Anarchy' (1819/1832) to Dickens's *A Tale of Two Cities* and Eliza Lynn Linton's *History of Joshua Davidson* (1872). Linton's representation of her eponymous protagonist engages most explicitly with the claim that if Jesus had lived in the 1840s, he would have been a Chartist: after travelling to Paris to participate in the uprising of 1872, Joshua is killed by a mob of Anglican clergymen enraged by the challenge his doctrine of equality offers to the established social order in England. As Joshua's biographer and 'disciple' records immediately after witnessing his murder,

> I know no more—no more than this, that the man who had lived the life after Christ more exactly than any human being ever known to me, who had given himself to humanity and poured out his strength like sacred water for the cause, who had been loving, tolerant, pitiful to all—that man was killed by the Christian Party of Order; his memory denounced on the one hand as that of a blood-thirsty revolutionist who was justly punished for his crimes, on the other, as that of a presumptuous and heretical enthusiast who had insulted God and dishonoured the true faith. But the same things were said of the early Christians as have been said of him, and of all reformers of all times.[45]

Christianity both valorizes the martyr and disciplines them to consent to the sacrifice, thus attempting to give equal weight to both sides in this contest between two important but incommensurable values—the needs of the one for autonomy and the demands of the many for conformity.

[44] Benedict Anderson, *Imagined Communities: Reflections on the Origins and Spread of Nationalism* (London: Verso, 1983), 24.

[45] Eliza Lynn Linton, *The True History of Joshua Davidson* [1872] (London: Strahan & Co. 1873, 4th ed.), 274–75.

As I have argued elsewhere, this doctrinal suppleness perhaps accounts for the popularity of sacrifice as a mechanism for dispute resolution in nineteenth-century narratives: it works with strategic ambiguity to serve a variety of purposes (ideological, sectarian, aesthetic, political) whilst seeking to bind all readers together in the common language of kinship sealed in blood.[46] The conceptual complexity of the Christian narrative is also one reason for the traction it continues to exert over the historical imagination: in Moyn's analysis, 'unlike Christianity, human rights do not give much of a chance for spiritual transfiguration for the rare authentic seeker of transcendence':

> And one doubts that human rights will ever move true believers to self-sacrifice or even martyrdom, giving themselves as witnesses to the truth of their faith. Secular nationalism found ways to win that level of devotion from its followers, but secular post- and supranationalism so far has not.[47]

As Jonathan Kertzer has noted so insightfully, equality (with its larger sense of each receiving their due) belongs to the jurisdiction of comedy: at best, '[j]ustice permits [comic] restoration' whilst tragic 'sacrifice promises transformation' but only through immersion in an economy of cruelty where the innocent are often punished or discarded.[48] Tragedy—predicated on inequality and exclusion—retains an extraordinary imaginative traction precisely because its affective power can exceed the logic of equality. Despite the self-evident inhumanity of sacrifice, art cannot renounce it: both genres are needed to give a full account of the complexity of human experience.

This returns us to our opening question of how the principles of equality should best be promoted. Despite his preference for legislative clarity, Bentham famously asserted that foreclosing any argument by playing 'liberty, equality, fraternity' as some kind of trump card was the equivalent of 'raising [his] voice to the people' or 'bawling upon paper: it proceeds from the same temper and the same sort of distress as produces

[46] Jan-Melissa Schramm, *Atonement and Self-Sacrifice in Nineteenth-Century Narrative* (Cambridge: Cambridge University Press, 2012), 1–32.

[47] Samuel Moyn, *Christian Human Rights* (Philadelphia: University of Pennsylvania Press, 2015), 176.

[48] Jonathan Kertzer, *Poetic Justice and Legal Fictions* (Cambridge: Cambridge University Press, 2015), 10.

bawling with the voice'. So sure was Bentham that this creed was rhetorically violent that he called it 'terrorist language', whilst the substance of rights was only 'nonsense upon stilts'.[49] Universal 'rights' language was excluded from Bentham's otherwise capacious sympathy for French Republicanism because there should be no recourse to values or powers outside a legal text to support its claims—by definition, then, any 'rights' of a subject could be guaranteed only by the commands of a sovereign operating at the level of national or domestic law. Jones's transnational sympathies—in which the 'English' workers should 'feel for' the plight of their similarly oppressed comrades in Poland or India—retains a strong basis in national identity, despite his enthusiasm for the rhetoric of 'universal' equality. That 'rights' language in the Enlightenment was a product of citizenship is one of the reasons for Moyn's renowned suspicion of the historiography of human rights. For Moyn, rights—supra-national, perhaps even global, and available for enforcement against states—emerge only in the 1970s:

> The universalism of the Enlightenment and revolutionary eras clearly does bear some affinity to contemporary forms of cosmopolitanism. Yet what it put forward as "the immortal rights of man" was nevertheless part of a political project strikingly distinct from contemporary human rights (which, in fact, were born out of a criticism of revolution). The rights of man were utopian, and evoked emotion ... Unlike later human rights, however, they were deeply bound up with the construction, through revolution if necessary, of state and nation. It is now the order of the day to transcend that state forum for rights, but until recently the state was their essential crucible.[50]

As I noted earlier, a number of historians have disagreed with this rather adversarial stance,[51] and what is at stake in the disagreement between the two camps is (at least partly) the role that cultural forms like the novel have played in the formulation of rights language—in a recapitulation of earlier competitions between codification and the common law

[49] Jeremy Bentham, Philip Schofield, Catherine Pease-Watkin, and Cyprian Blamires, eds., 'Nonsense upon Stilts', in *Rights, Representation, and Reform* (Oxford: Clarendon Press, 2002), 330.

[50] Samuel Moyn, *Human Rights and the Uses of History* (London: Verso, 2014), 20.

[51] See texts cited in footnote 29.

played out at various intervals in the late eighteenth and early nineteenth centuries, the disagreement focuses our attention on whether the law alone, as a command backed by some form of sanction, produces changes in behaviour, or whether law is simply one social practice amongst several that moulds moral norms and educates people for active citizenship.

What, then, does the citizenship sketched out by the global republic of letters—Marx's 'world literature'—look like? Clearly its aspirations are 'extraterritorial' in Homi Bhabha's phrase, powered by the 'emancipatory work of the imagination'.[52] This is the sphere in which Slaughter's understanding of the novel as a technology of incorporation possesses its greatest explanatory power. In this model, literary culture affords an opportunity to create an equitable imaginary of global citizenship in which everyone stands for one, and none for more than one (Bentham's definition of an ideal utilitarian polity).[53] But is this a chimaera, a weak consolation in a world in which sovereign power operates very differently within and without national borders or at the edge of Empire, and much turns on the luck of one's place of birth? As Bhabha notes, whilst Mill was completing his work *On Liberty* (1859), his status was that of a democrat at home but a despot in India[54]: in Nathan Hensley's detailed application of such contrapuntal reading practices to the Victorian novel, 'the images we take to characterize the world's first liberal empire should include not just the middle-class hearth or the democratic ballot box but the war zones and boneyards of England's global periphery, where mutiny, and its suppression, were all but universal. Emancipation and death advanced together.'[55] This is precisely the reason that for Marx the institutions of international law remained tainted by their imperial origins. The utopian declaration that 'All men are equal' erases the history of oppression which literature can explore so effectively. As jurists have noted, '[t]he underlying principle of natural law is that all human beings are of equal worth.

[52] Homi Bhabha, 'Democracy De-Realized', *Diogenes*, 197 (2003), 27–35 (31).

[53] See discussion in Mill, 'Utilitarianism' (1860), in Mill and Jeremy Bentham, *Utilitarianism and Other Essays* (Harmondsworth: Penguin, 1987), 335–36.

[54] Bhabha, 'Democracy De-Realized', 29.

[55] Nathan Hensley, *Forms of Empire: The Poetics of Victorian Sovereignty* (Oxford: Oxford University Press, 2017), 97.

But how the worth of a particular group of people is to be affirmed today depends in great part on how it was denied some other day'.[56] Storytelling must seek to do that crucial work of retrieval and correction for us.

[56] Robert E. Rodes Jr., 'On the Historical School of Jurisprudence', *American Journal of Jurisprudence*, 49:1 (2004), 165–84 (178).

CHAPTER 14

The Beatitude of the Berrigans: Jurisprudential Drama and the Poetics of Martyrdom

Alex Feldman

> *They entered the draft board office near Baltimore in broad daylight and ransacked the drawers […] Outside, in front of journalists they had summoned, they dumped the files of would-be soldiers […] and incinerated them with a napalm-like mixture made from gasoline and Ivory soap. History would remember them as the Catonsville Nine.*[1]

So begins a *New York Times* article of May 2018, commemorating the fiftieth anniversary of an historic protest by a group of Catholic laity and clergy against the war in Vietnam. Across the street from the Knights of

[1] Maggie Astor, 'Their Protest Helped End the Draft. Fifty Years Later It's Still Controversial', *New York Times*, May 18th, 2018.

A. Feldman (✉)
University of Haifa, Haifa, Israel
e-mail: bfeldman@univ.haifa.ac.il

S. Mukherji and D. Roberts (eds.), *Literature and the Legal Imaginary*, Crossroads of Knowledge in Early Modern Literature 4,
https://doi.org/10.1007/978-3-031-74093-0_14

Columbus Hall, Catonsville—the site of their incendiary protest—there now stands an historical marker dedicated to the Nine's infamous action and its role in the antiwar movement, inspiring as it did more than 250 similar acts of civil disobedience throughout America. For all of the public recognition accorded this protest half a century later, in 1968, neither the local community, nor the Catholic Church, nor indeed the Baltimore District Court looked so kindly upon it. As the plaque points out, "in a highly-publicized trail, the nine, who included priests Daniel and Philip Berrigan, were convicted and sentenced to prison."[2] In identifying the celebrated Brothers Berrigan, the plaque links the history of Baltimore to two of the most prominent members of the Catholic Left in the second half of the twentieth century. As we shall see, it also registers a controversial aspect of the Catonsville Nine's legacy: the disproportionate attention paid to the Berrigan fraternity in commentary upon the events of May 17th.

Philip, the elder Berrigan, was a Josephite priest, and the most prominent activist among the Nine at the time of Catonsville. Six months earlier, he and three others (who became known as the Baltimore Four) participated in a draft-board raid at the Baltimore City Custom House, in which they poured blood over selective service records. Philip hatched the plan for Catonsville with one of his former Baltimore companions, the artist, Tom Lewis, who hit upon the idea of using home-made napalm as the flammable agent. They were joined by three ex-Maryknoll priests, Thomas and Marjorie Melville, and John Hogan, whose opposition to the Guatemalan government, as missionaries, had brought them into disfavour with the Guatemalan regime, with the American government and with their own order, thereby precipitating their return to the United States. Also among the Nine were George Mische, a Peace Movement organizer, who had worked with Maryknoll Society missionaries in Mexico, his friend, Mary Moylan, a nurse-midwife recently returned from Uganda, and David Darst, a Lasallian Christian Brother. Finally, Philip succeeded in recruiting the man whose presence he deemed most important, his own younger brother, Daniel a Jesuit minister, and, during this period, the assistant director of the Cornell United Religious Work. In spite of the encouragement he offered to student activists, Daniel Berrigan had yet to join a raid himself, but "counselling other people

[2] Ibid.

to be heroic" was beginning to feel inadequate, and a visit from Philip to Ithaca convinced him.[3] "I simply say that I was saved at the last moment," he would later write; "Toward dawn, I can remember seeing the light. I told Philip that I was with them."[4]

Marking a significant turning point in Daniel Berrigan's life—his decision to supplement prayer and preaching with radical activism—the Catonsville protest and the trial that followed it generated a proliferation of essays, poems, and meditations from Berrigan's pen. The following words, read into the record during the trial, are perhaps the most resonant and memorable among them:

> Our apologies, good friends, for the fracture of good order, the burning of paper instead of children, the angering of the orderlies in the front parlor of the charnel house. We could not, so help us God, do otherwise.
> For we are sick at heart, our hearts give us no rest for thinking of the Land of Burning Children. And for thinking of that other Child, of whom the poet Luke speaks.[5]

Characteristic of Berrigan's writing by virtue of their capacity to speak both candidly and allusively, these words are concrete in their claims, vivid in their imagery, and rhetorically powerful, if a little stagey, in their self-conscious archaism. This quasi-prophetic utterance leaves no doubt as to the moral opprobrium in which Berrigan casts the war-mongers. The Catonsville Nine "hoped", in Berrigan's words, that their "experiences would urge others to discover alternatives to the imposition of death," with a view to "achieving a future for man."[6] The protestors "wished to question our way of dealing with the living, and, by implication, with the unborn."[7] Far from an unintended consequence of their activism, the Catonsville trial created the forum in which this radical questioning took place.

During the trial, the Catonsville Nine detailed their experiences of missionary and ministry work among the world's dispossessed as having

[3] Daniel Berrigan, *No Bars to Manhood* (Eugene OR: Wipf and Stock, 2007), 15.

[4] Ibid.

[5] This meditation is printed as the Preface (xiii–ix) to Daniel Berrigan, *Night Flight to Hanoi* (New York: Macmillan, 1968), xvi.

[6] Berrigan, *No Bars to Manhood*, 35.

[7] Ibid.

shaped their resolve to raid the Catonsville draft board. "We have chosen to be powerless criminals in a time of criminal power," Berrigan later wrote, emphasizing the voluntarism of the protestors' clash with the law: "We have chosen to be branded as peace criminals by war criminals."[8] Their counsel, celebrated defender of dissidents, William Kunstler, pursued a strategy based upon the doctrine of "jury nullification," encouraging the jury to consult their consciences as to the validity of the laws under which the protestors had been arraigned, rather than the defendants' adherence to or transgression of them. The judge rejected the doctrine and instructed the jury to deliberate strictly upon the basis of the law. All nine defendants were sentenced to time behind bars.

Determined not to allow the protest and its attendant legal proceedings to disappear from the public consciousness, Berrigan sought a means of immortalizing the events, and their challenge to the justice system, in another form. The primary Catonsville action had been "a dramatic 'homily' against the evils of militarism," complete with ritualized utterance of the Lord's Prayer, which the protesters recited as the draft files burned.[9] The trial was then a secondary extension of this theatricalized protest, marked by the same liturgical ritual. Berrigan requested the Court's permission "to recite the 'Our Father' with our friends"—a request unopposed by the prosecution and granted by the judge.[10] In composing *The Trial of the Catonsville Nine*—the play which forms the subject of this chapter—Berrigan was determined to harness this dramatic power for a tertiary iteration, in the modality of theatre.

The argument that follows first establishes the prophetic characteristics of the Nine's protest, and then the martyrological discourses deployed in Berrigan's prose, poetry, and drama of the period, which (in addition to the notable plaudits garnered by his play) provoked adverse reactions on Catholic Left. My intention is to examine the complexity of these responses by contextualizing the play—and its treatment of Catonsville's

[8] Daniel Berrigan, 'Sermon from the Underground,' August 2nd, 1970, in Stephen Halpert and Tom Murray, eds., *Witness of the Berrigans* (Garden City NY: Doubleday, 1972), 140–41.

[9] Robert Drinan, quoted by Jim Forest, *At Play in the Lion's Den: A Biography and Memoir of Daniel Berrigan* (Maryknoll, NY: Orbis, 2017), 120.

[10] Daniel Berrigan, *The Trial of the Catonsville Nine* (Boston: Beacon Press, 1970), 3. Subsequent page numbers in the text refer to this edition.

dissident defendants—within developments in the genre of jurisprudential drama, in the mid-to-late twentieth century.

"For Them We Have One Message": Berrigan's Theatres of Prophecy and Presumption

Berrigan was already an acclaimed poet—his verse had won the admiration of Marianne Moore and his 1957 collection, *Time Without Number*, had been awarded the Lamont Poetry Prize—but *The Trial of the Catonsville Nine* would be Berrigan's most ambitious creative project to date. In May 1969, he was in negotiations with the Beacon Press to produce "an edited version of the Catonsville Nine record," which, in spite of the necessary "compression and changes in the text," would remain "faithful to the spirit which brought [the Nine] together at Catonsville."[11] Fidelity to the revolutionary spirit here entailed the inclusion of much of the Nine's testimony, versified, and the inclusion of Berrigan's own meditations and original compositions which had been read into the record during the trial. "In composing this book," Berrigan's preface asserts, "I have worked directly with the data of the trial record, somewhat in the manner of the new 'factual theatre'" (vii). But the documentary character of the work was by no means a guarantee of forensic objectivity.

Versifying the language of the play's defendants, while retaining the legal practitioners' prose, Berrigan's play transforms the court record into a quasi-scriptural document. The differentiation of poetic and prosaic utterance is not only an attempt to distinguish between roles in the legal system—privileging, indeed, sanctifying the language of the accused—but also an attempt to distinguish between the adherents of opposing normative systems, governed by alternative sets of legal or quasi-legal commitments: those of secular law-enforcement in contrast to those of the Christian liturgy. The resulting work is an economical condensation of one of the most extraordinary trials in American legal history and a prophetic text in its own right. Berrigan's original version formed the basis for the play's premiere under the direction of Gordon Davidson at the Mark Taper Forum in Los Angeles, in 1970. When the play transferred to New York, Davidson commissioned the playwright Saul Levitt to

[11] 'Letter from Daniel Berrigan to Catonsville Nine, May 7, 1969', *Fire and Faith: The Catonsville Nine File*, Enoch Pratt Free Library, 2004. http://c9.digitalmaryland.org/artifact.php?ID=CUCN012&VW=S.

produce a more concentrated version of the text. Though Levitt's adaptation rendered the work entirely into prose, it retains the lapidary phrasing, the rhythm, and cadences of Berrigan's words, harnessing the dramatic power of the material, with considerable economy.[12]

In Berrigan's original text, the play begins, in prose, by identifying some important legal facts: the first being the defence counsel's abstention from jury selection. Elsewhere in his prose of the period, Berrigan explains that he and his fellow activists "were attacking the assumption that lawyers are capable of embodying a legal tradition and of serving us."[13] The play's next crucial detail is an account of the charges: "That the defendants did willfully injure and commit depredation against property of the United States; [...] obliterate records of the Selective Service System [...] and interfere with the administration of the Military Selective Service Act of 1967" (3–4). As Berrigan saw it, however, the government's legal indictment was a rearguard action, responding to the Catonsville Nine's own verdict against the American elites. "The burning of draft files by men and women like us," he writes; "is a kind of preliminary and particular judgement," aiming both "at the law" and "beyond the law, at a social change, in a time of paralysis and dread."[14]

After a second, short, prose section, "The Day of the Facts of the Case," containing the draft-board clerks' testimony, the play launches into "The Day of the Nine Defendants," which contains more than sixty per cent of the play's dialogue, and consists of the versified testimony of the accused. Establishing the grounds of their opposition to the war, and to the American justice system, the defendants speak expansively of their work as missionaries, aid workers, and clerics, of their encounters with economic injustice and state-sponsored violence, detailing the effects of these experiences upon their moral and political educations. Philip Berrigan's work in the slums of New Orleans, John and

[12] While Berrigan's Beacon Press edition provides the most reliable record of the playwright's initial conception of the work, Levitt's adaptation (used for the off-Broadway and Broadway runs, and the play's return to L.A.'s Mark Taper Forum) is the version to which the majority of reviewers responded. Both versions are therefore relevant to my analysis. Except where indicated, all of the quoted text appears in the original Beacon Press edition and Levitt's adaptation. See Daniel Berrigan, *The Trial of the Catonsville Nine*, text prepared and adapted by Saul Levitt (Samuel French, 1971).

[13] Berrigan, *No Bars to Manhood*, 50.

[14] Ibid., 50–51.

Marjorie Melville's witness to the American government's exploitation of Guatemala, Mary Moylan's experiences as a nurse-midwife in Uganda, and George Mische's confrontation of the vicious Trujillo regime in the Dominican Republic, all converge upon Catonsville. When his testimony turns to Vietnam, Philip Berrigan speaks of "prayer vigils/ with meals of reconciliation/ with a few tentative marches," or demonstrations at military bases, of letters to political and military officials registering their protest against the war: but "the military were immune/ from any citizen influence./ They were a law unto themselves" (26). Throughout this section of the play, Berrigan's selections from the defendants' testimony emphasize the Nine's repeated and frustrated attempts to conduct antiwar protests within the law, which accounts for their decisions, individual and collective, to make their protest heard by illegal means instead.

From the perspective of the American justice system, this appears to be a movement from legality to criminality, but it in fact bespeaks the defendants' adherence to an alternative set of commitments entirely. The fundamental irreconcilability between the demands of American foreign policy and Christian worship is given in David Darst's words: "We have not been able/ to let sacred life/ and total death/ live quietly together within us" (37). And there is, embedded in this pronouncement, something of the Pauline distinction between the letter of the law that kills (that kills American soldiers, that kills Vietnamese civilians, that imprisons those who campaign against killing) and the spirit of divine justice that gives, preserves and sustains life—the lives of both body and soul. Though the Pauline maxim, in the post-Reformation consensus, bespeaks the distinction between the Old Testament (as lettered law) and the New (as incarnate spirit),[15] rather than applying to the dictates of secular law-enforcement, nonetheless, the general sense of law as uncompromising, unresponsive to spiritual life, unaccommodating to the operations of grace and inimical to the ethical demands of Christian faith, is threaded through the Berrigans' protest.

Berrigan's first words on the stand articulate the conflict between the law of the American courts and the alternative jurisdiction of the liturgy: "one could not indefinitely obey the law," he explains, in the face of "structures of compassion breaking down" (81). "My thinking," explains Darst, articulating the basis of their opposition to the power structures by

[15] See Regina Schwartz, 'The Letter and the Spirit: Portia's Case,' the present volume, pp. XX–XX.

which they stood accused, "is part of an ethic/ found in the New Testament/ You could say/ Jesus too was guilty/ of assault and battery/ when he cast the money changers/ out of the temple/ and wasted their property and wealth" (36). "You could say" this, Darst implies, if you shared the normative perspective of secular law-enforcement. Those with whom Thomas Lewis associates their protest have not, however, always adhered to this code: "Civil disobedience was practiced/ by the early Christians," who obeyed instead "the primary law of love and justice/ toward other men" (43). For the Catonsville Nine, to command obedience, the laws of the American courts would have to derive from the "ineffable unity" and "radical simplicity" of God's First Eternal law, "comprising within it all derivative species of law," and would be invalidated by originating in another source, or by opposing the tenets of Christian faith.[16] "We say: killing is disorder." Berrigan declares; "life and gentleness and community and unselfishness/ is the only order we recognize" (94).

That these claims or their expression might appear grandiose, or self-aggrandizing, did not escape the attention of Berrigan and his co-defendants, who were well aware of the risks and potential pitfalls of notoriety. Elsewhere, in his prose of the period, Berrigan speaks of the need for "something modest [...] in intent and style," fearing lest "such a criterion as 'making it big in the press' violates the long-hauling patience that produces true history."[17] And yet he can barely resist the following "dizzying thought": "Could it be that your humble servant, without script or staff, might be an instrument for demythologizing Big Bro Justice?" (74). Berrigan admits to being seduced by the idea of his own prophetic vocation, "even as a voice reminds [him] it is fraught with presumption."[18] This presumption did not go unnoticed by the protest's critics: "Those priests and sisters! I admire their courage and dedication but not their arrogance" (128), declared Dorothy Day.[19] "Who do they

[16] Torrence Kirby, 'Configuring God as Law: Richard Hooker's Neoplatonic Poetics of Law', in the present volume, pp. XX–XX. Though, of course, Richard Hooker's *The Laws of Ecclesiastical* is a foundational work of Anglican philosophy, the treatment of God *as* law, and as the origin of law, holds true for orthodox Catholic theologians as well.

[17] Daniel Berrigan, *America Is Hard to Find* (London: SPCK, 1973), 74.

[18] Ibid., 63.

[19] Nancy L. Roberts, *Dorothy Day and the Catholic Worker* (Albany NY: SUNY, 1984), 160. Quoted in Peters, *The Catonsville Nine*, 128.

think they are," Berrigan's own brother asked, in a letter to the *Minnesota Tribune*, "to take the law into their own hands?"[20]

Berrigan responded, implicitly, to these and similar protestations in the play, where the charge of arrogance is broached twice, and repudiated with reference to the defendants' and their accusers' alternative commitments:

> We have been accused of arrogance
> But what of the fantastic arrogance   of our leaders
> What of their crimes against the people   the poor and powerless
> Still no court will try them   no jail will receive them
> They live in righteousness   They will die in honor. (30)

The righteousness and honour to which the political elites lay claim and those to which the Catonsville Nine aspire are ironically juxtaposed, while the arrogance of "our leaders," secure in their impunity, is manifest in their exploitation of the weak. Darst reiterates the theme:

> We have cried out on behalf of life
> The government has chosen
> to see our cry
> as anarchy and arrogance
> Perhaps real anarchy lies
> in the acts of those
> who loose this plague of war
> upon a proud people. (37)

But if Daniel Berrigan had hoped to head off criticism of the Catonsville Nine's protest, their testimony, and its subsequent dramatization by means of these arguments, he did not entirely succeed.[21]

The play did receive fulsome praise from numerous quarters. Reflecting upon the *Catonsville*'s capacity "to make us all deeper, more compassionate, perhaps more understanding and critical human beings," one

[20] Letter to the *Minnesota Tribune*, quoted in Murray Polner and Jim O'Grady, *Disarmed and Dangerous: The Radical Life and Times of Daniel and Philip Berrigan, Brothers in Religious Faith and Disobedience* (Oxford: Westview Press, 1998), 209.

[21] The charge of arrogance was widespread. See, for example, Joseph Morgenstern, 'Morality Plays, Legality Plays', *Newsweek*, March 1st, 1971.

reviewer declared that "No thinking citizen should miss this play"—a sentiment that recurs throughout the play's press coverage.[22] "One does not have to agree with the political and international overtones of *Catonsville*," wrote Charles Faber, "to be moved by the sweeping sincerity of the nine, and to feel their anguish expressing for us all [...] the dark night of the American soul."[23] Indeed, there were also those who took it upon themselves to answer the charge of arrogance themselves: "[the play] is easily dismissed as profitable, alienating, foolish, arrogant. It exists nevertheless," protested Dan Finlay, "singularly powerful, singularly imaginative."[24] Not all of the commentators, however, were so forgiving.

In a letter to the *New York Times*, Ned O'Gorman, a prominent voice in the Catholic Peace Movement, declared himself sceptical as to whether "renewal in the Church will come solely from political and social action" and rejected the doctrine that "the essential Church is the politically active Church," represented by "the Berrigans and their crusade."[25] Disavowing the protestors' "crippled, howling, petulant, spoiled brat anger," O'Gorman repudiated "the self-importance that traps revolutionaries in their own will and leaves their zeal, their visions and their hope abandoned to their egos."[26] Having sought "the solitary, searing voice of the prophet," he found only "a community of parasites who free-load off the Gospels."[27]

A month later, the *New York Times* published a group of letters to the editor, written in response to O'Gorman's review. While some reflected upon the incoherence of O'Gorman's argument, others endorsed his assessment of the play's "incredible moral pretentiousness."[28] In some cases, this critique was motivated by certain aesthetic choices. Thus Daniel

[22] Robert C. Wylder, 'The Trial of the Catonsville Nine', *Long Beach Independent*, July 2nd, 1971, 23. See also R. H. Gardner, '*Trial of the Catonsville Nine* Opens Center Stage's Tenth Season', *Baltimore Sun*, November 1st 1971.

[23] Charles Faber, '*Trial of Catonsville 9*: An Impassioned Dialogue', *Entertainment Today*, June 25th, 1971.

[24] Dan Finlay, 'The Law Versus Justice and The Catonsville Nine', 4–5.

[25] Ned O'Gorman, 'Berrigan, the Church and the "Nine"', *New York Times*, May 30th, 1971.

[26] Ibid.

[27] Ibid.

[28] 'Drama Mailbag: Readers Discuss Father Berrigan', *New York Times*, June 13th, 1971.

Finlay confessed his disappointment at the play's opening speech, which involved "the use of Daniel Berrigan as commentator," when, in reality, "none of the nine at the trial [had] pointed to each other in that self-conscious way."[29] The reference here was to the speech that begins "On a June morning, I lay before the altar in the chapel—to be ordained a priest," in which Berrigan describes "the priesthood [as] a pallid, vacu-umatic enclosure, a sheepfold for sheep," who "made Jesus mild as milk, a temple eunuch."[30] Elsewhere, the critics were troubled by the Nine's self-righteousness, judging *The Trial of the Catonsville Nine* "a disturbing play, a frightening picture of selfless fanaticism merging into holy terrorism."[31] And yet, most commonly, the critics were perturbed by "the author's calling attention to his own nobility",[32] and passed judge-ment upon those elements of "self-dramatization and even glorification in a play that depicts the author as a heroic crusader in the cause of justice."[33]

The specific charge levelled above, accusing the author of self-dramatizing as an "heroic crusader," exemplifies a recurrent strain of commentary that identifies the Berrigans with certain mythic or historic character types. Should they be dubbed "true religious 'prophets', or genuine 'heroes', or quintessential American 'patriots'"?[34] Among the commentaries, the category that emerges with the greatest regularity, and least contestation, is that of *prophet*. In consideration of passages such as the following, one can see why:

> For them we have one message   for those
> in whose manicured hands   the power of the land lies
> We say to them
> Lead us   Lead us in justice

[29] Halpert and Murray, *Witness of the Berrigans*, 73.

[30] This text does not appear in Berrigan's Beacon Press edition, published prior to the first performance, but the evidence of the archive suggests that it was written for inclusion in the original production. The speech is retained in Levitt's adaption. See Berrigan, *The Trial of the Catonsville Nine*, 5.

[31] Peter Coleman, 'And Another Thing: Burning Draft Cards in the Name of God', *The Bulletin*, October 23rd, 1971.

[32] *New York Post*, February 27th, 1971.

[33] R. H. Gardner, '*Trial of the Catonsville Nine*', *Baltimore Sun*, November 1st, 1971.

[34] John Dear, *Apostle of Peace: Essays in Honour of Daniel Berrigan* (Maryknoll, NY: Orbis, 1996).

and there will be no need to break the law. (30)

As Richard Fenn explains in his book *Liturgies and Trials*, which provides (to my mind) the definitive account of the conflict, enacted at the trial, between secular and religious jurisdictions:

> The prophet's claim to credible speech rests on the "I say unto you": on the relation between prophet and hearer […] and in the force of prophetic utterance itself […] It is the *we say* that is the guarantee of prophetic credibility, since the prophet speaks only what the prophet truly knows. But in a secular courtroom the *we say* of the prophet is out of order, in the sense that it violates or ignores judicial rules for crediting testimony.[35]

Barbara Arizti has argued that "*The Trial of the Catonsville Nine* is a polyphonic artifact which exposes frictions between authoritative and alternative discourses of the law."[36] But as Fenn suggests, the designations of authority and alterity depend entirely upon the discursive context. The defendants' courtroom strategy was to challenge the court's jurisdiction over the conscience of the American people, and to declare their allegiance instead to the Divine Word and its accompanying doctrines, statutes, and professions of faith. More radically still, their intention was thus to supplant the epistemology of positive law, its truth claims and its authority, by appeal to an epistemology originating in the sacred—"what the prophet truly knows"—legitimizing their claims to superior

[35] Richard Fenn, *Liturgies and Trials: The Secularization of Religious Language* (Oxford: Blackwell, 1982), 58.

[36] Barbara Arizti, 'The Word Made Flesh: Law, Literature and Ethical Responsiveness in Daniel Berrigan's *The Trial of the Catonsville Nine*', *Atlantis*, 32:1 (June 2010), 29–44, 35.

wisdom.[37] Just as the Catonsville protest has been aligned with the tradition of prophetic activism,[38] so the Catonsville trial can be viewed within the linked tradition of prophetic utterance. The defendants' speech may not have proved authoritative in the Federal courtroom but when they re-articulated their protest as theatre, performed at New York's Good Shepherd Faith Church, the environment seemed all the more auspicious for the transmission of their message.

"Self-Appointed Martyrs to a Cause": Berrigan's *Imitatio* and the Self-Sacrificial Gesture

While the identification of Berrigan as a prophet, per se, is not my chief interest, it is relevant to my argument in so far as it bespeaks a movement from the designation of a character *trait*—say, arrogance or self-importance—to the delineation of a character *type*, from personality to persona, or from psychology to typology, and thence to genre. And while neither "heroic crusader" nor "prophet" conjures a rich dramatic heritage, describing the protestors as "self-appointed martyrs to a cause" certainly does.[39] "All martyrs," writes Dan Sullivan of the *Los Angeles Times*, "are a little smug about it."[40] "From the viewpoint of hagiography," writes John T. Elson, in *Time* magazine, "the martyr is the ultimate Christian hero" but "[s]ociology [...] sees him as something else; a special kind of social deviant", whose self-sacrificial behaviour may be little more than "an expression of primary narcissism"[41] Of course, Berrigan's biography and its dramatization fall rather short of martyrdom's criteria, by dint of the defendant's death of natural causes, almost half a

[37] Readers of the present volume will note that the conflict between alternative jurisdictions dramatized in Berrigan's play recalls the "collision between natural justice and positive law" imaginatively explored by the Inns of Court plays of the 1560s, as discussed by Doyeeta Majumder (p. 5). Staging conflicts of law, interpretative collisions and "jurisdictional rivalries" (5) has been the province of jurisprudential drama—indeed, its defining feature—from *Antigone* and the *Oresteia* to the "liberal martyrologies" of mid-twentieth century (discussed below) and beyond.

[38] See Richard J. Clifford, S.J., 'The Berrigans: Prophetic?', in William Van Etten Casey, S.J. an Philip Nobile, *The Berrigans* (New York: Avon, 1971), 35 and Harvey Cox, 'Tongues of Flame', in Halpert and Murray, *Witness of the Berrigans*, 21–22.

[39] R. H. Gardner, '*Trial of the Catonsville Nine*', *Baltimore Sun*, November 1st, 1971.

[40] Dan Sullivan, 'Once a Sermon, Now a Play', *LA Times*, June 18th, 1971.

[41] John T. Elson, 'Styles in Martyrdom', *Time*, October 11th, 1971.

century after his trial, at Fordham University's Jesuit Infirmary in 2016. And yet the recurrence of the term in commentary upon the Catonsville protest and play bears closer scrutiny.

Firstly, Berrigan's own writing betrays an inclination towards self-sacrifice. "We have tried to underscore with our tears," Berrigan writes, "*and if necessary with our blood* [...] that death may not be inevitable, that a unified and compassionate society may still be possible."[42] The emulation of Christian sacrifice was first introduced into the Peace Movement of the 1960s by the Baltimore Four, who, as Philip Berrigan testified, "took [their] own blood and [...] attempted to anoint [the Baltimore Custom House draft] files with the Christian symbol of life and purification" (29). Confronting "the great sinfulness/ of modern war" that "renders concrete things abstract" (82), Berrigan's testimony dwells, with ethical intent, upon images of carnality. He recalls "the bodies of children the hearts and organs and limbs of woman" observed in Hanoi, where "America had been experimenting/ upon the bodies of the innocent/ [...] improv[ing] our weapons/ on their flesh" (90). Following "the self-immolation/ of a high school student/ [...]/ in the spring of 1968," Berrigan "smelled the odour of burning flesh" at the victim's bedside, and acknowledged, in a transformative moment, that "this boy's death/ was being multiplied/ a thousandfold/ in the Land of Burning Children" (92).[43] Such experiences persuaded Berrigan that he could no longer "announce the gospel/ from a pedestal" but "must act as a Christian/ sharing the risks [...] and anguish/ of those [...] placed in the breach by us" (93). "Like the earliest Christians," Mary Mollin explains, "the Nine sought literally to enflesh the message of Christ's Sermon on the Mount and its call to nonviolence and peacemaking, and to use that doctrine, and the self-sacrifice and risk-taking it required, to follow the Christian mystery of crucifixion, sacrifice, and redemption."[44]

[42] Berrigan, *No Bars to Manhood*, 52. [My italics.]

[43] The corporeality of these images bespeaks Berrigan's resistance to the "sanitization" that Alex Houen and Jan-Melissa Schramm observe in nineteenth-century images of sacrifice, informed as they are by "the Protestant aversion to the depiction of vulnerable flesh" (Alex Houen and Jan-Melissa Schramm, eds., *Sacrifice and Modern War Literature: from the Battle of Waterloo to the War on Terror* [Oxford: Oxford University Press, 2018], 3, 11).

[44] Marian Mollin, 'Communities of Resistance: Women of the Catholic Left in the late 1960s', *The Oral History Review*, 31:2 (Summer–Autumn 2004), 29–51.

Secondly, then, one cannot escape, either in Berrigan's own writing or that of his disciples, the persistent alignment of his own life with the life of Christ. "The soul of peacemaking," Berrigan recalls in his autobiography, "was simply the will to give one's life"—one of many phrases echoing what Jan-Melissa Schramm describes as the doctrine of "Christ's voluntary submission and self-surrender to the forces marshalled against him."[45] There is thus a kind of martyrdom-by-association, or a proxy martyrdom, implicit in, or extrapolated from, Berrigan's *imitatio.* Crucial to this relationship is Berrigan's encounter, and its resemblance to Christ's encounter, with the law. It is *on trial* that Berrigan's life comes closest to the point in Christ's life at which he paid (on earth) the ultimate price for his opposition to the prevailing teachings of his own religion and secular state power. The Nine's *guarantee* of their protest "with the gift of [their] liberty/ if necessary [their] lives" (95) was an affirmation of their liturgical commitments, in so far as "martyrdom tests with compelling clarity the values for which a man is prepared to die."[46] During the Catonsville trial, William Kunstler declared that the proceedings "share[d] the historic meaning of other great contests of law. The trial of Socrates was not merely a question of a man sowing confusion and distrust among the youth of the Athens; the trial of Jesus could not be reduced to one of conspiracy against the Empire" (103). And when the verdict was handed down, Kunstler's typological exegesis was echoed by an anonymous cry from the public gallery: "You have just found Jesus Christ guilty" (121).

Berrigan's prose of the period further extrapolates this theme. "Have you ever heard," Berrigan asks, "of death by solitude, by ostracism? [...] (He was born, says the author of the Letter to the Hebrews, outside the walls, *extra muros*, to die; extradited [...] cut off from the privileges of community and citizenship.)"[47] Berrigan's sense of the combined hostility of the wider American community, the Catholic Church and the Society of Jesus is palpable here. During the trial, he spoke of being "exiled" by his Church (89). "One of history's resolute (and persecuted)

[45] Berrigan, *To Dwell in Peace*, 165; Jan-Melissa Schramm, '"Let Us Carve Him as a Feast Fit for the Gods": Girard and Unjust Execution in Nineteenth-Century Narrative', in Pierpaolo Antonello and Heather Webb, eds., *Mimesis, Desire, and the Novel: Rene Girard and Literary Criticism* (East Lansing: Michigan State University Press, 2015), 161–174 (163).

[46] Schramm, '"Let Us Carve Him"', 164.

[47] Berrigan, *America Is Hard to Find*, 79.

outcasts," writes Robert Coles, Berrigan felt "very much connected, mind, heart, and soul [...] with the historical Jesus," whose "travail, nourished Dan [...] as he lived the jeopardy of a 'wanted man'."[48]

It may be instructive to dwell upon Coles's final word above. As Marian Mollin has observed, "a notable masculinity dominated the perception and reality of the draft board raids [...]; it was men who were cast as the true resisters and who ultimately dominated the community's circles of power."[49] The invocation of masculinity, dominance, and power implies an un-Christ-like challenge to the Peace Movement's egalitarian and communitarian ideology, remarked by a number of prominent commentators on these events. According to the Berrigans' friend and mentor, Thomas Merton, "the language of spurious nonviolence is merely [...] a different method of expressing one's will to power."[50] These remarks anticipate Terry Eagleton's account of the process by which the "vulnerable victim [...] rises to a sense of their own infirmity [...] appropriates this infirmity [...] and embark[s] on a transition to power."[51] As Eagleton astutely observes, as "a matter of voluntary self-giving, the institution of sacrifice crosses over from Nature to culture, myth to tragedy, cult and ritual to ethics and politics."[52] Eagleton's "transition to power", in so far as it represents the movement from myth to tragedy, is also, crucially, a transition to drama. The martyr's self-consciousness enables, or precipitates, a move towards the status of protagonist.

The Trial of the Catonsville Nine in the Field of Jurisprudential Drama

In the remainder of this chapter, my intention is to read *The Trial of the Catonsville Nine* as a work of jurisprudential drama—play distinguished not solely by courtroom scenes but by a pervasive preoccupation with the philosophy and ideology of law. And by interrogating *Catonsville*'s

[48] Dear, *Apostle of Peace*, 38.

[49] Mollin, 'Communities of Resistance', 41.

[50] Charles Meconis, *With Clumsy Grace: The American Catholic Left, 1961–1975* (New York: The Seabury Press, 1979), 38.

[51] Terry Eagleton, *Radical Sacrifice* (New Haven and London: Yale University Press, 2018), 51.

[52] Ibid.

complex relationship to its genre, and jurisprudential drama's trajectory in the mid-to-late twentieth century, I hope further to contextualize, and thus partially to explain the range of reactions to Berrigan's play.

In the original, Beacon Press text, Berrigan punctuated the versified testimony of the defendants with quotations from Jean-Paul Sartre's *The Condemned of Altona* (25), Bertolt Brecht's *The Life of Galileo* (46), Heiner Kipphardt's *In the Manner of J. Robert Oppenheimer* (47), Peter Weiss's *The Investigation*, Jean Anouilh's *Becket* (49) and Sophocles' *Antigone* (66), attesting to Berrigan's desire to position his play within the context of jurisprudential drama.[53] And while this network of allusions was (largely) removed from the play in Saul Levitt's pared-down version of the text, reviewers still responded to *The Trial of the Catonsville Nine* in New York in the context of other legally oriented plays. Thus, Tom Prideaux observed that "[r]ecently, American playgoers have judged the trials of Robert Oppenheimer and the Rosenberg family [and] attended the damning of Winston Churchill and Pope Pius XII."[54] Narrowing his purview to "the last few weeks," Prideaux adduces Jerome Lawrence and Robert E. Lee's *The Night Thoreau Spent in Jail* and Stanley Greenburg's *Pueblo* (both produced by Washington, DC's Arena Stage Theatre, in 1970 and 1971, respectively), two further dramatizations of "men obeying their conscience rather than obeying the law."[55]

The elevation of the private conscience over laws enforced by the ruling elites is also the theme of another play that recurs among the reviews. *The Trial of the Catonsville Nine* "echo[es] in part the theme of Robert Bolt's play *A Man for All Seasons*," observed Murray Polner and Jim O'Grady, "which centres on the fatal clash between Henry VIII and Sir Thomas

[53] I have discussed the role of these allusions in detail in a recently published article. See Alex Feldman, '"As Inspiring as the Muses, as Righteous as the Supreme Court": *The Trial of the Catonsville Nine* and Jurisprudential Drama', *Modern Drama*, 63:3 (Winter 2020).

[54] Tom Prideaux, 'Stage Left: Current Events—An Epidemic of Documentaries', *Life: Theatre Review*, April 17th, 1971. Prideaux refers here to: Heinar Kipphardt's *In the Matter of J. Robert Oppenheimer* (Mark Taper Forum, 1968); Donald Freed's *Inquest* (Music Box Theatre, 1970); Rolf Hochhuth's *Soldiers* and *The Deputy* (Brooks Atkinson Theatre, 1964).

[55] Ibid.

More [...] over religious faith and politics and conscience."[56] Berrigan, of course, avoided the *fatality* of this clash, but the comparison is nonetheless an instructive one, and crucial to an understanding of the conflicted reactions to Berrigan's work. My suggestion here is that the judgments given against Berrigan were not merely reflections upon the Catonsville Nine's conduct during the protest or the trial, of which audiences were *reminded* by the play. Rather, the retelling of these events *as* jurisprudential drama contributed another layer of hagiographic self-fashioning to Berrigan's image, by recalling the canonical works of the genre with which the Catonsville protest could be associated.

A Man for All Seasons belongs to a sub-genre of jurisprudential drama, on the mid-twentieth century, Anglo-American stage, which might be termed the "liberal martyrology," encompassing, for example, Arthur Miller's *The Crucible* (1952) and Jerome Lawrence and Robert E. Lee's *Inherit the Wind* (1955)—the most prominent American legal-historical dramas in the period preceding *Catonsville*. Animated by liberalism's "structure of feeling," as Raymond Williams defines it, these plays are "liberal in [their] emphasis on the surpassing individual."[57] Pitting the dissident defendant-protagonist against the dominant institutional tyrannies of his or her day, they promote the sovereignty of the individual conscience, "embod[ying] all ultimate values" as the primary ethical lodestone around which the plays' conflicts revolve.[58]

Williams's focus, in *Modern Tragedy*, is on the development and, subsequently, the decline of a particular *tragic* form—where "liberalism in its heroic phase begins to pass into its twentieth-century breakdown," where the once-heroic protagonist enters "the self-enclosed, guilty and isolated world; the time of man his own victim."[59] But there is, discernible throughout Williams's work, a series of partial acknowledgements that certain critically significant texts, linked by their dramatization of a martyred protagonist's legal ordeal, do not entirely fulfil the criteria of modern, liberal tragedy as he defines it. Shaw's *Saint Joan, for example,*

[56] Polner and O'Grady, *Disarmed & Dangerous*, 212. See also John T. Elson, 'Styles in Martyrdom', *Time*, October 11th, 1971, p. 64.

[57] Raymond Williams, *Modern Tragedy*, 87.

[58] Ibid., 68.

[59] Ibid., 68, 100.

portrays "the heroic and liberating individual destroyed by a false society" and yet "fails to include any of the deepest human energies and problems."[60] *Saint Joan* fails in other words, to rise to Williams's vision of true, tragic stature, as "the problem of the frustrated individual is masked by [her] theatrical transformation into a movement."[61] Similarly, *The Crucible*'s protagonist, John Proctor, dies to preserve "the truth of himself and of others, in opposition to the lies of the persecuting authority." While *Death of a Salesman's protagonist is "the victim: the disconnected individual," The Crucible* maintains a vision of "the liberal martyr."[62] Suffering, in these liberal martyrologies, is not the precondition for victimhood, but of spiritual heroism, around which the "commemorative community" coheres.[63]

The incommensurability of Christian sacrifice with the tragic sensibility is the province of George Steiner, who writes, of the Passion of Christ, that while it is undoubtedly an "event of unutterable grief [...] it is also a cypher through which is revealed the love of God for man. In the dark light of Christ's suffering," Steiner continues, "original sin is shown to have been a joyous error (*felix culpa*)." When it comes to the martyrdom of the saint, then, "being a threshold to the eternal, the death of a Christian hero can be an occasion for sorrow but not for tragedy."[64] Thus for Steiner, as for Williams, martyrdom changes the paradigm, diverting the play's conclusion from tragedy towards salvation. The protagonist's death, though "drastic and irrefutable [...] does not carry the major or the final meaning of the play."[65]

Williams addresses this point when discussing Eliot's *Murder in the Cathedral*, a work of jurisprudential and liturgical drama, concerned with the martyrdom of Henry II's Archbishop of Canterbury, Thomas Becket.

[60] Ibid., 102.

[61] Ibid.

[62] Ibid., 104.

[63] See Clayton Fordahl, *The Ultimate Sacrifice: Martyrdom, Sovereignty, and Secularization in the West* (Routledge, 2020), 40.

[64] George Steiner, *The Death of Tragedy*, 332.

[65] While, for Steiner and Williams, Christian salvation precludes, or redeems, tragedy's ruin, for Terry Eagleton, the crucifixion *can* be regarded as a tragic gesture, according to an alternative, affirmative tragic vision (*Radical Sacrifice*, 30–58) See also ch. 3 'Failed Oblations and the Tragic Imagination', in Douglas Hedley, *Sacrifice Imagined: Violence, Atonement, and the Sacred* (Continuum, 2011), 91–108.

In accordance with "the special character of [the] rhythm of sacrifice in the Christian tradition, [...] the sacrificial victim becomes the redeemer or the martyr."[66] Invoking yet another jurisprudential play, Williams then goes on to describe the difference between *Murder in the Cathedral* and *A Man for All Seasons*, arguing that "Bolt's play is not sacrificial but [...] ethical: this good man against the rest."[67] The potential confusion here, Williams explains, derives from the fact that "the structure of [*Murder in the Cathedral*] pushes Becket towards an heroic position which is in fact irrelevant."[68] In other words, much to Williams's consternation, the truly Christian play—*Murder in the Cathedral*—risks presenting its protagonist as heroic; that is, it risks the kind of treatment that Bolt gives Thomas More.

Bolt speaks of More as "a man with an adamantine sense of his own self."[69] In taking an oath—"an invitation to God [...] to act as witness, and to judge"—More "offers himself as guarantee" of his contractual obligations to his Creator.[70] While "the self [might be regarded as] an equivocal commodity" for twentieth- or twenty-first-century spectators, to More it was sacrosanct, which serves as Bolt's "explanation and apology for treating Thomas More, a Christian Saint, as a hero of selfhood."[71] The heroism of the self, although perhaps appealing from a certain historical distance, is theologically problematic (as Bolt is well aware) because it compromises the self-abnegation, and the devotion to divinity, requisite to sainthood. This is the dramatically effective misreading of More's confessional commitments for which Bolt is apologizing. It is also, undoubtedly, one source of his play's tremendous appeal to bourgeois, secular audiences.

[66] Williams, *Modern Tragedy*, 162.

[67] Ibid., 163.

[68] Ibid.

[69] Robert Bolt, *Three Plays: Flowering Cherry; A Man for All Seasons; The Tiger and the House* (London: Heinemann, 1963), 94.

[70] Ibid., 95.

[71] Ibid. 96.

Liberal humanism's account of the self—interiorized, reflexive, rational, the origin of free will and moral agency—would be unthinkable in the absence of Pauline and Augustinian theology,[72] but the conflict with Christian orthodoxy arises in the elevation of the self to a position of eminence as the origin of all value. And while, as Douglas Hedley authoritatively asserts, "the key to sacrifice is [...] renunciation," martyrdom always seems fraught with the possibility of self-possession.[73] For Lacey Baldwin Smith, martyrdom is "a display of individuality sealed and sanctified by death".[74] As she elaborates:

> Self-confidence reinforced by deadly self-seriousness is the common property of all martyrs, scarred only by the cry of dereliction from the cross. But even in the Gospels the 'I' predominates. Jesus was no self-effacing messenger [...] and he repeatedly replaced the Old Testament formula 'thus saith the Lord' with 'I say unto you.'[75]

This perspective is by no means an orthodox account of Christian martyrdom, but even the martyr's authentic "radical self-dissolution" leaves him susceptible to the crucifixion's transformative effects.[76] Christ's death was "a sacrificial act," Eagleton explains, "because it concerns the passage of a humble, victimized thing from weakness to power."[77] Mistaking the nature of this power—the power to signify, not to inhabit, the "revolutionary transitus" from an old order to a festive future—as a mode of earthly authority, the would-be martyr risks the sin of pride.[78] This, of course, is the subject of Eliot's *Murder in the Cathedral* and

[72] See, for example, Kevin Crotty, *Law's Interior: Legal and Literary Constructions of the Self* (Ithaca, NY: Cornell University Press, 2001), Ch. 2 and Larry Siedentop, *Inventing the Individual: The Origins of Western Liberalism* (Cambridge, MA: Harvard University Press, 2014), Ch. 4–8.

[73] Hedley, *Sacrifice Imagined*, 109.

[74] Lacey Baldwin Smith, *Fools, Martyrs, Traitors: The Story of Martyrdom in the Western World* (New York: Alfred Knopf, 1997), 10.

[75] Ibid., 363.

[76] Eagleton, *Radical Sacrifice*, 88.

[77] Ibid., 31. Fordahl makes a similar observation when he describes martyrs as "figures of weakness and strength, triumph and loss, inertia and action." *Radical Sacrifice*, 3.

[78] Ibid., 93.

the basis of Becket's temptation by, and ultimate rejection of, heroic self-regard, "doing the right deed, for the wrong reason."[79] Recent theorists of martyrdom commonly turn to Eliot's play in order to find this martyrological paradox most eloquently articulated.[80] Indeed, in spite of its ritualistic function, its liturgical verse, its doctrinal orthodoxy—features which make *Murder in the Cathedral* the serious work of Christian drama that it is—Eliot's play, like Bolt's, retains a tension between the heroism of self, or individualism, and the self-dispossession required of the Christian martyr.

The Trial of the Catonsville Nine is neither a tragedy nor, in any strict sense, a martyrology, but it is a jurisprudential play composed in a hagiographic key, which dwells upon sacrifice and the mortification of innocent flesh. There were those among the reviewers who both acknowledged and celebrated these aspects of the work. Thus, John Simon declares himself ignorant as to how to write about the playwright and his co-defendants: "I would like simply to canonize them [...] If there were halos around their heads, these nine could not be more clearly clothed in sanctity."[81] And yet Berrigan's opponents were unable to accept the hagiographic self-fashioning of the playwright-protagonist. In view of the martyrological paradox established above, it may be that the Berrigan's perceived "self-glorification" felt doctrinally unsound. It would certainly have appeared indecorous to more conservative adherents of the American Catholic Church, which officially supported U.S. foreign policy during the Vietnam War. Furthermore, in the 1960s, jurisprudential drama was undergoing a significant transition, directing its attention away from the plight of the dissident individual, and towards the configurations and corruptions of power.

Coda

On Monday, June 24th, 2019, Robert Schenkkan's verbatim play, *The Investigation: A Search for the Truth in Ten Acts* was performed at New York City's Riverside Church, and live-streamed across the world to

[79] T. S. Eliot, *Murder in the Cathedral* (London: Faber and Faber, 1935), 39.

[80] See Smith, *Fools, Martyrs, Traitors*, 364; Eagleton, *Radical Sacrifice*, 93.

[81] John Simon, 'Saints for Our Time', *New York Magazine*, February 22nd, 1971.

millions. The play is a read-through—part narrative, part performance—of excerpts from the Mueller Report into the White House's alleged links to the Kremlin and President Trump's alleged obstruction of justice. Every word belongs to the Report, and thus to the American people. The play's target is the investigation's subject, placed figuratively, if not literally in the dock: Donald Trump, at that time the most powerful man in the world. This is very much in keeping with jurisprudential drama's trajectory in recent years—the Tricycle Theatre's *Tribunal Plays* attest to the same phenomenon—towards an increasingly forensic focus on legal proceedings and matters of public record, designed to interrogate the culpability and the accountability of the elites. Rather than serving as the backdrop against which the defendant-protagonist's struggles are enacted, in the present day, abuses and asymmetries of power, the corruption and criminality of the ruling class have taken centre stage, as the hagiographic subject has faded from view. This transition began, though it did not end, in the era of Catonsville.

Two notable differences began to distinguish the jurisprudential drama of the 1960s from the liberal martyrologies of the preceding generation. Firstly, courtroom dramatists began to depict recent, even contemporary legal-historical events, rather than dwelling upon the Mediaeval Church or the early American colony. Secondly, the liberal trial play's domestic scenes, which had provided considerable scope for imaginative, authorial invention in earlier plays—at home with John and Elizabeth Proctor, in *The Crucible*, or with Thomas and Alice More, in *A Man for all Seasons*, for example—began to disappear. The increasing proportion of stage time devoted to the legal proceedings in the public arena necessitated a concomitant withdrawal from the private sphere, from the delineation of character, and thus from the liberal trial play's concern with the protagonist's conscience. The combined effect of these two phenomena was that the dissident protagonists of legal-dramatic works were becoming markedly less prominent, in structural terms and, in ethical terms, conspicuously less saintly.

This movement has been serviced by an aspiration towards the fetishized, albeit illusory, transparency of documentary form. And while contemporary documentary plays often adhere strictly to the dictates of verbatim drama, the documentary plays of the sixties, while dispensing with the naturalism of their predecessors, were far from forensic in their aesthetics. I began with an account of *The Trial of the Catonsville Nine*'s complex, aesthetic hybridity—its combination of prose and verse, of transcript and quotation, of documentary and prophecy—in order to indicate the play's transitional status within jurisprudential drama's development. In this respect it might be aligned with a number of seminal plays of the 1960s.

In Michael Hastings's *Lee Harvey Oswald* (1966), for example, the majority of the play's dialogue derives from the transcript of the Warren Commission into the Kennedy assassination, and Oswald's own diaries and notes, but supplements the documentary material with imaginary scenes between Oswald and his wife, *based upon* the historical evidence but nonetheless fictive. *In the Matter of J. Robert Oppenheimer* derives its dialogue *almost exclusively* from the transcripts of hearings conducted by the Atomic Energy Commission's Personnel Security Board, but the playwright, Heinar Kipphardt, supplements the historical record with soliloquies composed for each of the Board's members. These elements of authorial invention do not serve entirely to exonerate the protagonist, J. Robert Oppenheimer, but rather reflect upon the complexity of establishing his culpability or innocence. Peter Weiss's *The Investigation* is another of these transitional texts. The dialogue is mined from the records of the Frankfurt Auschwitz trials, but the playwright versifies the text, as Berrigan does, arranging it into cantos, in Dantean fashion, and with Dantean implications.[82] Weiss's desire, controversially, is to present the Holocaust as the inevitable terminus of industrial capitalism. Rather than drawing the sharp, ethical distinctions—foundational to the liberal trial play—between the individual and the ruling elites, these plays interrogate the interpellation of individuals within dysfunctional systems, which are themselves the chief subjects of scrutiny. And of course, though Lee Harvey Oswald, J. Robert Oppenheimer, and the Concentration Camp Commandants exhibit varying degrees of culpability, none of them can be said to be entirely innocent.

Berrigan's inclusion of quotations from Kipphardt's and Weiss's plays in the original version of *Catonsville*, reveals his intention to align his play with the jurisprudential drama of the 1960s. As my commentary has shown, *The Trial of the Catonsville Nine* is committed to a critique of the political *status quo*. The Nine's testimony reveals the unscrupulous

[82] *The Investigation*'s relationship to *The Divine Comedy* is addressed by Erika Salloch in 'The *Divina Commedia* as Model and Anti-Model for *The Investigation* by Peter Weiss', *Modern Drama*, 14.1 (1971), 1–12.

conduct of successive American regimes, charging the military industrial complex and its masters with innumerable depredations, both foreign and domestic. But in dwelling so extensively upon the motivations of its protagonists, their anguish, their consciences, their righteous indignation, *The Trial of the Catonsville Nine* also harks back to a dramatic form preparing to make an exit from the stage. There is thus a productive tension between the affective charge of the defendants' appeal, enhanced by the poetic lyricism of its expression, and the forensic authenticity constructed by the play's aesthetics. The spoken words of the play also derive their legitimacy from *what is written*: the epistemological claims of prophetic wisdom, echoing the scriptures, are reinforced by those of the legal record, marked by textual authority.

Thus, Berrigan's play belongs at a mid-point in jurisprudential drama's development: between the historical martyrologies, representing clashes between the dissident individual and the ecclesiastical or political establishment—*A Man for All Seasons*, *Saint Joan*, *Murder in the Cathedral*, *The Crucible*, *The Life of Galileo*—and the verbatim plays of the present, which interrogate the functioning of power, by dwelling upon the culpability of the elites. If certain reviewers were disinclined to regard Berrigan as a latter-day More, or Becket, this resistance was only compounded by their reluctance to identify the American justice system with the Inquisitions of Mediaeval surveillance states. But the play's tremendous power, and its appeal to those who considered it essential viewing for thoughtful Americans, can be explained precisely by these same criteria. *The Trial of the Catonsville Nine* encourages its audience to know injustice by anatomizing the corruption of power, *and* by bearing witness to the martyrdom of the innocent.

PART VI

Afterword

CHAPTER 15

Afterword

Kathy Eden

In his effort to defend poetry against the charges of falsehood and immorality, leveled most damagingly by Socrates in Plato's *Republic*, Philip Sidney sets in motion a competition among the humanistic disciplines designed to demonstrate that, on the contrary, *poetry* (by which he means *fiction*) best serves the "ending end of all earthly learning being virtuous action" (13).[1] Excluded from this competition, not incidentally, is the study of the law on the grounds that it instills in its followers fear of punishment (*formido poenae*) rather than love of virtue (*amor virtutis*) (15). On the other hand, the poet's fictions, Sidney argues, closely resemble the lawyer's hypotheticals in that both depend on the particularity of circumstance to arrive at a compelling representation of events—one that discloses a truth about events that transcends mere historical accuracy. Sidney further epitomizes this shared dependence on

[1] *Sidney's "The Defence of Poesy" and Selected Renaissance Literary Criticism*, ed. Gavin Alexander (London, 2004), 13. Hereafter page numbers will be cited parenthetically in the text.

K. Eden (✉)
Columbia University, New York, NY, USA
e-mail: khe1@columbia.edu

S. Mukherji and D. Roberts (eds.), *Literature and the Legal Imaginary*, Crossroads of Knowledge in Early Modern Literature 4,
https://doi.org/10.1007/978-3-031-74093-0_15

particulars by foregrounding the legal and fictional practice of assigning agents to the actions represented. "Their naming of men," Sidney explains about poets and lawyers, "is but to make their picture the more lively.... Painting men, they cannot leave men nameless" (35).

Centuries before Sidney writes his *Defence of Poesy* (c. 1580), Quintilian draws attention to the deep homologies between what we would call *literature* (by which we usually mean *fiction*) and the *law*. Like Sidney, Quintilian acknowledges the special property of *fictiones* to resolve legal and ethical questions and to foster sound judgments (*Inst. orat.* 5.10.95–99). Throughout his first-century *Institutio oratoria*, in fact, Quintilian bolsters rhetorical training for the aspiring orator with illustrations of forensic practice borrowed not only from works of epic and dramatic poetry but from the fictionalized discourse of Plato's Socrates. For the Roman schoolmaster can find no better practitioner of the rapid-fire question and answer that characterize both tragic stichomythy and legal interrogation than the Athenian philosopher famously contemptuous of both the law court and the tragic stage (*Inst. orat.* 10.1.35–36). On the other hand, Quintilian alerts his readers, as does Sidney, to the stark differences between stage and forum. Among them is one obvious contrast between this same tragic dialogue and legal cross examination. Whereas in tragedy the *dramatis personae* always say exactly what the dramatist wants them to say, in legal debate the litigants more often than not contest their opponents' statements, thwarting their best-laid plans. For this very reason, Quintilian records, the Roman tragedian Accius scoffed at the opportunity to transfer his talent for writing the give-and-take of dramatic dialogue to the rough and tumble of the courtroom (*Inst. orat.* 5.13.43).

The deep and abiding relationship between the literary and the legal, as the essays in this volume set in high relief, is defined, in other words, no less by their differences than by their commonalities; and both are best appreciated in terms of the complex questions they are invoked to solve. One longstanding complexity involves the status of a law and a literary work as a *made thing*. In the *Symposium* (205BC), Socrates reminds his listeners that linguistic usage has tended to limit the activity of making or *poiēsis* to what we call *poetry*, before he challenges them with an extended analogy between procreativity (making babies) and literary creativity (making poems). In the end, Plato has Socrates exploit this generic connection in order to subordinate both the procreator and the poet to the philosopher—a subordination that is not lost on his disciple

Aristotle. For Aristotle builds his taxonomy of the disciplines, decisive for Quintilian's *Institutio oratoria* as for Sidney's *Defence of Poesy*, around the dialectical division of human activity into making, thinking, and acting.[2]

In the *Nicomachean Ethics*, an inquiry into the etiology of human action, Aristotle's concern with acting (or doing) prompts him to consider the conditions of making. Whereas action (like contemplation or thinking) is an end in itself, a *product* or *made thing* is a means to some further end. Doing and making (*praxis* and *poiēsis*) "are generically different," Aristotle insists, "since making aims at an end distinct from the act of making, whereas in doing the end cannot be other than the act itself: doing well is in itself the end."[3] On the other hand, making is unlike doing (but like thinking) because we judge the *thing made* in and of itself apart from the moral disposition of the maker, while human action can only be fairly judged in terms of the intentions and moral disposition of the agent (*Nic. Ethics* 2.4.3).

In keeping with this key distinction, Aristotle further distinguishes skill (*technē*) from virtue or moral excellence (*aretē*). The physician who kills his patient unintentionally may be a better person than the one who plots his patient's death, but he is for all that a less skillful practitioner of the art of medicine (*Nic. Ethics* 6.5.7). Sidney puts this Aristotelian distinction into his own words not only when he charges the mathematician with "draw[ing] forth a straight line with a crooked heart" (13) and faults Thomas More the man but not the poet (17) but when he reasons that "the saddler's next end is to make a good saddle, but his further end to serve a nobler faculty, which is horsemanship, so the horseman's to soldiery, and the soldier not only to have the skill but to perform the practice of a soldier" (13). For Sidney as for Aristotle, it is in the nature of *poetics* of all kinds to look beyond themselves to their products, whether that product (or *made thing*) is a saddle or a poem.

In the *Poetics* (6. 1449b24–28), therefore, Aristotle defines tragedy in terms of not only *what* is represented and *how* that representation is made, but to what end or *why*. As a *made thing*, tragic poetry looks beyond itself to its effect on the audience through the arousal of fear and pity—the same two emotions at play in the law courts. In the *Rhetoric* and

[2] For a more detailed discussion of this division, see my *Poetic and Legal Fiction in the Aristotelian Tradition* (Princeton, 1986; rpt. 2014).

[3] Aristotle, *Nicomachean Ethics*, trans. H. Rackham (Cambridge, MA, 1926; rpt. 1975), 6.5.3. See also 6.2.5. All subsequent references are to this edition and cited in the text.

Nicomachean Ethics, moreover, Aristotle addresses the law itself as a *made thing*, reframing Plato's characterization of law in his final dialogue as the finest tragedy (*Laws* 817B). For a law differs from a tragedy in terms of its investment in universality. Tragic fiction's access to the universals that render it more philosophical and thereby more worthwhile than history derives from its imposition of causality on the particular actions (the plot or *mythos*) represented through the moral characters (*ēthē*) and intentions (*prohairēseis, dianoiai*) of the agents. Stating in no uncertain terms that *ēthos* and *dianoia* are the second and third constituent parts of tragedy, Aristotle neglects to spell out explicitly that they are no less the causes of the first constituent part, the *mythos*, also characterized as the beginning (*archē*), the end (*telos*), and the soul (*psyche*) of tragedy (6. 1450a38, 1450a22, 1450a38). Once again, Sidney echoes Aristotle's argument on fiction's behalf when he attributes poetry's being "*philosophōteron* and *spoudaioteron*" to the "universal considerations" that are part and parcel of the poet's "imposed names" (18–19).

The law's universality, in contrast, bars it from taking particular cases into account in its general statement (*Nic. Ethics* 5.7.6, 5.10.4–7); and this limitation constitutes its deficiency. To remedy this deficiency, understood as the mismatch between the generality of legal statute and the infinite particularity of human actions, the law requires fiction in the form of an inference concerning either how the absent lawgiver would decide the case in question if he were present or how he might reformulate the law itself with this set of circumstances in mind (*Nic. Ethics* 5.10.5, *Rhet.* 1.13.17–19). As Aristotle, Quintilian, and Sidney agree, in other words, there is no legal *poetics* without fiction.

With his provocative and frequently quoted claim that "poetry makes nothing happen," W. H. Auden challenges not only W. B. Yeats but some of his most authoritative ancient and early modern predecessors with a poetry that is not, in their terms, *poiēsis* at all. Whereas the law, a *made thing*, makes us fear punishment, to repeat Sidney's helpful contrast, poetry, also a *made thing*, makes us love virtue. In spite of this marked difference, however, neither is an end in itself. Both serve precisely to make something happen—just as the saddle serves to make the horseman, who serves, in turn, to make the soldier. On some occasions, as the essays in this volume show, legal and literary making work in tandem; on other occasions, they come into conflict. Either way, law and literature are profoundly responsive to one another as they set their sights on what Sidney calls a "judicial understanding" of human action (16).

Index

A

affect, 10, 14, 23, 37, 166, 169, 176, 184, 185, 195, 256, 264
Agamben, Giorgio, 13, 83, 246–248, 256, 258, 261
State of Exception, 13, 246, 247, 261
agelasts, 166
Alciatus, Andreas, 167
Emblematum liber, 167
allegory, 3, 14, 30, 50, 123, 242–246, 248–250, 257, 260, 261
allegory of allegory, 244, 245
Ambrose of Milan, 136
Aquinas, Thomas, 56–59, 76, 113, 116, 130, 132, 136, 139, 247
Summa Theologica, 57, 130–132, 136, 139
Aristotle
Nicomachean Ethics, 114, 115, 121, 236, 335, 336
Poetics, 132, 335, 336
Rhetoric, 12, 144–149, 153, 335
artem ludicram, 169
Auden, W.H., 336
audience, 32, 35, 62, 63, 86, 87, 102, 146, 148, 150–152, 154, 190, 202, 210, 227, 264, 267, 273, 276, 289, 295, 322, 324, 329, 335
Augustine of Hippo, 124, 138

B

Bacon, Francis, 150, 151
Baker, John, 74, 197, 200, 202, 207–211
Barfield, Owen, 12, 173, 217–222, 224, 225, 227–237
barrister, 128, 201–203, 210
Barthes, Roland, 4
bastards, 82, 251, 253, 254
Bentham, Jeremy, 284, 287, 288, 301–303
Berman, Harold J., 80

S. Mukherji and D. Roberts (eds.), *Literature and the Legal Imaginary*, Crossroads of Knowledge in Early Modern Literature 4,
https://doi.org/10.1007/978-3-031-74093-0

Berrigan, Daniel, 13, 306–308, 310, 312, 313, 315, 316
  Trial of the Catonsville Nine, 13, 308, 310, 315, 329
Berrigan, Philip, 306, 310, 311, 318
Bhabha, Homi, 303
Bible, 11, 15, 35, 41, 109–113, 123, 124, 127, 128, 137, 138, 329
Blackstone, William, 58, 284, 286, 287
Bolting, 202
Bolt, Robert, 321, 324, 326
  A Man for All Seasons, 321, 324
Bornitius, Jacob, 171
Brant, Sebastian, 31, 173
Brecht, Bertolt, 321
  The Life of Galileo, 321, 329
Brontë, Charlotte, 292
Bry, Theodor de, 169, 185–187
Budé, Guillaume, 267, 272, 277, 279–281
Burton, Robert, 167, 168

C
cabaret-lecture, 263
caltrops, 174, 175
carmen necessarium, 264, 277
Castoriadis, Cornelius, 5
Catholic Left, 306, 308
Catonsville Nine, 306, 307, 309, 310, 312, 313, 322
Cats, Jacob, 178
Chamberlayne, Edward, 190
character, 9, 16, 22, 34, 61, 80–88, 90, 91, 93–95, 98, 100, 124, 146, 152, 171, 175, 188, 212, 229, 270, 291, 293, 299, 309, 317, 336
Chartism, 294, 295
Chinca, Mark, 242, 243, 249
Christian/ity, 4, 23, 111, 120, 124, 136, 193, 300, 301, 323
civil law, 12, 57, 74, 146, 157, 158, 160, 161, 288
Cohen, Leonard, 94
Coke, Sir Edward, 77, 171, 173
Combe, Thomas, 178
comedy, 6, 37, 40, 86, 166, 170, 173, 175, 176, 178, 179, 184, 190, 194, 198, 218, 301
contronym, 90
co-regency, 257, 259, 260
Corinthians, 110, 112, 113, 117, 118
Courtly love, 13
  Cave of love, 243
  In extremis, 260
Court of Common Pleas, 60, 75, 198, 202, 214, 215
Cunningham, Karen, 28, 197, 205, 206, 213
Curtius, Ernst, 184

D
d'Annebault, Richard, 268–272
Darling, Charles J., 166, 171
Day, Dorothy, 312
death, 9, 32, 62, 63, 66, 70, 71, 85, 94–96, 117, 122, 123, 230, 231, 249, 258, 284, 300, 307, 317, 319, 323, 335
Del Mar, Maksymilian, 9, 12, 15, 16, 18, 19, 171, 195
Democritus, 167, 169, 193
Derrida, Jacques, 15, 80, 244
Despautère, Jean, 273
dialogue, 8, 14, 16, 18–20, 41, 45, 46, 98, 118, 166, 210, 212, 222, 264, 271, 310, 328, 334, 336
Diderot, Denis, 283, 284, 288
dies nec fasti, 169
disputation, 202, 207, 208
Draco, Honoratus (Onorato Drago), 265, 267, 268, 272, 274, 275
Drama/theatre, 13, 20, 308

documentary, 13, 327, 328
jurisprudential, 15, 55, 309, 317, 320–323, 326–329
Duplicem sententiam, 170
Durkheim, Emile, 82
du Vair, Guillaume, 277

E
Eagleton, Terry, 320, 323, 325, 326
Ecclesia and Synagoga, 36
Eliot, George, 289, 290
Eliot, T.S., 326
Murder in the Cathedral, 323, 325, 326
Elizabeth I, 41, 203
emotion, 11, 22, 23, 31, 33–35, 39, 152, 171, 199, 290, 302, 335
Engels, Friedrich, 296
epieikeia, 74, 75, 114–116, 119, 123, 236
episteme, 14
epistemology, 6, 8, 11, 12, 21, 28, 38, 101, 138, 146, 193, 316, 329
equity, 4, 11, 30, 45, 74, 75, 77, 85, 100, 112, 114, 115, 117, 120, 123, 124, 222, 236, 275
evidence, 11, 39, 51, 95, 145, 149, 153, 154, 167, 171, 199, 208, 266, 297, 315, 328
exception, 6, 14, 16, 56, 74, 75, 82, 94, 116, 209, 242, 245, 247, 248, 251, 255, 256, 258, 261
expression, 27, 94, 114, 141, 153, 167, 194, 208, 227, 228, 230, 244, 261, 276, 280, 284, 297, 317, 329

F
feuds and extra-legal violence, 251, 253, 255
Flitner, Johann, 175, 176, 179, 181, 182, 184
Nebulo nebulonum, 175, 181, 182
foolosophy, 193
form, 12–16, 24, 28, 35, 36, 62, 64, 65, 85, 91, 96, 100, 102, 134, 140, 152, 158, 167, 169, 175, 178, 185, 190, 203, 204, 207, 211, 214, 224, 244, 248, 258, 264, 269–271, 275, 281, 284, 286, 287, 291, 297, 299, 302, 303, 308, 336
Fortescue, John, 58, 116
Fortuna, 173, 175, 185, 194
Foucault, Michel, 173
Fraus, 175, 176, 179

G
Gascoigne, George, 56, 205
Jocasta, 56, 205
Gennaro, Giuseppe Aurelio, 281
genre/s, 10, 14, 16, 20, 22, 138, 206, 207, 267, 290, 293, 301, 309, 317, 321, 322
Gismond of Salerne, 56, 60, 71, 205
Godwin, William, 288, 289, 299
Goltzius, Hendrick, 187, 188
Goodrich, Peter, 7–9, 12, 15, 21–24, 203, 231, 271, 276
Gratian, 57, 58, 140, 247

H
hagiography, 317
Hart, H.L.A., 80, 98, 226
Hayaert, Valérie, 13, 15, 16, 21, 30, 166, 173, 185, 189, 190, 261, 274
Heraclitus, 90, 165, 167, 169
hermeneutics, 4, 6, 10, 11, 14, 15, 109, 110, 114, 116, 120,

122–124, 128, 184, 193, 242, 276
Hobbes, Thomas
Briefe of the Art of Rhetorique, 12
De Cive, 146, 151, 153, 157–161
Elements of Law, 144, 146, 153, 154, 156, 161
Leviathan, 56, 77, 144, 153
Hooker, Richard, 11, 15, 127–133, 135, 137–142, 312
Of the Lawes of Ecclesiasticall Politie, 128, 129
Horace, 166, 170, 171, 181, 184
Hughes, Thomas, 55, 71
Misfortunes of Arthur, 55, 56, 71
Huizinga, Johan, 195, 198
human rights, 13, 285, 290, 291, 301, 302
Hutson, Lorna, 8, 18, 21, 116, 197, 205, 234

I
image/s, 4, 6, 15, 23, 27, 28, 30, 31, 34–41, 44, 47, 83, 118, 167, 169, 173, 175, 176, 182, 184, 185, 187, 190, 193, 199, 229, 276, 298, 303, 318, 322
imagination, 13–15, 17, 18, 21, 28, 67, 87, 100, 185, 206, 207, 226, 231, 235, 261, 295, 303
in flagrante delicto, 258
Inns of Court, 11, 12, 19, 55, 56, 60, 71, 128, 167, 195, 198–201, 205–207, 215, 317
interdisciplinary, 7, 9, 12, 14, 17–19, 21, 24
interpretation, 11, 35, 90, 109, 110, 112, 113, 120, 122, 148, 169, 188, 225, 263, 268, 270, 272, 274–276, 279–281, 286
In vitam humanam, 167, 175
Israel, Jonathan, 110, 118, 284, 285
Ius ridiculus, 166

J
Jameson, Fredric, 5, 241, 244, 257, 260
James VI and I, 47, 50
Jaucourt, Louis de, 283, 288
Jones, Ernest, 295–297, 299
Judaism, 111, 124
Reformation, 124
judgment, 27, 28, 31, 33, 34, 37–41, 51, 52, 54, 77, 98, 102, 188, 225, 226, 234, 236, 259, 261, 322, 334
jurisdiction, 8, 11–13, 16, 56, 61, 74, 171, 184, 195, 255, 276, 311, 316, 317
jus non scripta, 171, 276
justice, 3, 4, 6, 17, 18, 20, 27, 30, 32, 37–41, 45, 46, 49, 54, 57, 60, 62, 63, 69, 70, 74, 84, 86, 96, 114, 115, 117, 119–121, 125, 155, 174, 175, 185, 186, 188, 190, 214, 227, 242, 250, 254, 277, 286, 308, 311, 312, 317, 329
Justinian, 57, 265, 267–271, 273, 274, 279, 280
Digest, 169
Institutes, 265, 267, 268, 271, 274
Justitia, 4, 27, 28

K
Kinwelmersh, Francis, 56, 205
Jocasta, 56, 205
knowability, 14, 15, 22
Knowledge, 5–7, 10–16, 18, 19, 30, 34, 37, 55, 68, 88, 93, 96, 97, 100–102, 118, 133, 138, 141, 145, 146, 151, 153–157, 159–161, 175, 179, 197–199,

215, 223, 242, 258, 261, 269, 272, 283, 329
Kunstler, William, 308, 319

L
law and literature, 7, 14, 19, 22, 23, 28, 55, 217–221, 225, 241, 242, 260, 261, 266, 336
legal *carmina*, 264
legal imaginary, 5, 6, 10, 16, 28
Leonine rhymes, 276
Lewis, C.S., 217, 218, 222, 225, 236, 244
Linton, Eliza Lynn, 300

M
Maclean, Ian, 273
Maine, Henry Sumner, 288, 289
Malory, Thomas, 253, 254
  Morte Darthur, 253
martyrdom, 13, 299–301, 319, 323, 325, 326, 329
Marx, Karl, 296, 303
masks, 97, 165, 175, 176, 178, 179, 181, 231
maxims
  Necessity compels, 247
  Necessity knows no law, 247
  Vim vi repellere, 248
McCabe, Richard, 71–73
meaning, 6, 27, 40, 81, 83, 87, 100, 101, 113, 117, 122, 124, 145, 159, 166, 167, 170, 174–176, 179, 181, 193, 202, 208, 212, 223, 225, 226, 228, 230–233, 235, 242, 244, 257, 258, 260, 271, 275, 284, 319, 323
Melancholia juridica, 166
mercy, 4, 20, 37, 62, 84, 87, 96, 101, 113, 115, 119, 120, 125, 189
metaphor, 13, 51, 117, 118, 129, 132, 135, 141, 142, 223, 225, 230, 235, 236, 242, 274, 275
metaphorical interartificiality, 242, 243, 256
Meyler, Bernadette, 18–20
Miller, Arthur, 322
  The Crucible, 322
  Death of a Salesman, 323
Mill, J.S., 286, 287, 303
Mirandola, Pico della, 97
mooting, 12, 198, 199, 202, 205–207, 209, 210, 214, 215
Mopha, Matteo Gribaldi, 274
More, Thomas, 202, 204, 322, 324, 335
movement, 17, 24, 99, 173, 223–225, 236, 244, 267, 294, 298, 306, 311, 317, 323, 327
Moyn, Samuel, 301, 302
Murner, Thomas, 175, 179

N
Nebrija, Antonio de, 166, 193
  Aenigmata iuris, 193
Nequitia, 175, 176, 179
Nietzsche, Friedrich, 109, 110, 119, 175, 193
Norton, Thomas, 56, 205
  Gorboduc, 56, 205
Noses. *See* proboscation

O
Oppenheimer, J. Robert, 321, 328
ownership and possession, 259

P
Parson, Robert, 65
participation, 21, 57, 134–136, 218, 229, 237

pastiche, 267, 272, 279, 280
Paul, Saint, 110
Peace Movement, 306, 314, 318, 320
pectore libro, 273
performance, 6, 9, 12, 14, 19, 20, 24, 42, 49, 81–83, 100, 122, 166, 176, 179, 199, 201, 204, 210, 214, 218, 225, 275, 315, 327
Perrière, Guillaume de, 176, 178, 190, 193
Plato, 13, 82, 134, 159, 160, 333, 334, 336
  Republic, 333
  Symposium, 334
play, 4, 9, 12, 13, 15, 17, 19, 41, 62, 63, 68, 69, 71, 73, 84, 85, 87–89, 95, 96, 100, 102, 119, 122, 124, 166, 171, 175, 178, 184, 190, 195, 197, 204–206, 209, 214, 219, 222–224, 226, 235, 308–310, 313, 315, 320, 321, 326–328, 335
pleading, 12, 39, 74, 198, 199, 208–210, 214, 215
pleasure, 9, 12, 15, 149, 166, 176, 190, 198, 219, 224–226, 232, 235, 237, 264
poetic, 6, 12–14, 16, 56, 198, 218–220, 223, 224, 226, 227, 229, 231, 234, 235, 237, 264, 267, 268, 271, 274, 275, 277, 281, 289, 309
polyphonic song, 271
proboscation, 181, 184
Proclus, 134–136
  Elements of Theology, 134
prophecy, 68, 328
Pseudo-Dionysius the Areopagite, 136
  On the Divine Names, 136
punctum, 11
punishment, 3, 4, 37, 40, 44, 73, 280, 281, 333, 336
Pykeringe, John, 56, 61, 62, 67
  Horestes, 56, 61, 62

Q
Quintilian, 13, 334–336
  Institutio oratoria, 334, 335

R
Rabelais, François, 174
Raphael, 189
reading. *See* Inns of Court
reality, 6, 7, 9, 27, 81–83, 90, 100, 123, 132, 135, 176, 229, 230, 242, 315, 320
Reisch, Gregor, 28, 30, 31
representation, 4–7, 9–12, 16, 20, 22, 50, 56, 94, 171, 178, 293, 294, 333, 335
revels, 12, 171, 173, 190, 195, 201, 203, 204, 206
rhetoric, 16, 22, 61, 67, 89, 90, 114, 144, 145, 148–150, 154, 157, 158, 160, 225, 248, 287, 296, 302
Rose, Gillian, 94
Ruggle, George, 166, 167
  Ignoramus, 166

S
Sabinus, Masurius, 277
Sackville, Thomas, 56, 67, 205
  Gorboduc, 56, 64
sacred, 80–83, 92, 95, 96, 98, 100, 111, 114, 280, 300, 316
Sanchi, Luigi-Alberto, 279, 280
sanctimony, 89
Sartre, Jean-Paul, 5, 6, 321
  The Condemned of Altona, 321
satire, 166, 175, 176
Saturnine, 165, 166

Schmitt, Carl, 83
scientia. *See* Knowledge
Selden, John, 76, 77, 171
Jani Anglorum facies altera, 171
serio-ludere, 171, 173
Shakespeare, William
Hamlet, 17, 230, 231
King John, 233
King Lear, 84
Measure for Measure, 11, 80, 82, 205
The Merchant of Venice, 11, 117, 121
A Midsummer Night's Dream, 80, 82
Richard II, 225
The Tempest, 97
Shaw, George Bernard, 322
Saint Joan, 322
Sidney, Philip, 13, 333–336
Defence of Poesy, 334, 335
Skinner, Quentin, 22, 145, 146, 149, 152, 154, 157, 197
Slaughter, Joseph, 290–292, 303
Socrates, 319, 333, 334
Solomon (King), 27, 28, 31–38, 40, 41, 43–45, 49, 50, 52, 53, 131
Sophocles, 68, 321
Antigone, 321
sound, 96, 116, 121, 125, 190, 214, 218, 219, 222, 231, 232, 235, 334
Starkey, Thomas, 64, 74
Steiner, George, 221, 323
St German, Christopher, 59, 60, 75–77, 114–116
Doctor and Student, 59, 60, 75, 114
Strassburg, Gottfried von, 13, 242, 245
Tristan, 13, 242, 245
Strauss, Leo, 79, 81, 98, 143–145, 160
suspicion, 84, 88, 119, 145, 302
sword, 4, 30, 33, 34, 37, 47, 50–52, 54, 173, 185, 189, 250, 252, 276
syllogism, 148, 152, 161

T

Tessier-Ensminger, Anne, 267
tragedy, 6, 37, 40, 71, 301, 320, 323, 326, 335, 336
Trajan (Emperor), 27, 28, 31–33, 37–40, 45–47, 51–54
troubadour chansonniers, 265
trouvère, 268–271

V

veritas falsa, 176
Vico, Giambattista, 267, 281
Vietnam War, 13, 326

W

Warren, Christopher, 21, 294, 328
Watt, Gary, 9, 12, 13, 15, 16, 23, 115, 117, 123, 173, 193, 197, 198, 219, 231, 234, 236, 271
Weisberg, Richard, 8, 22
White, James Boyd, 220, 221
Williams, Raymond, 322
Williams, Rowan, 129, 131
Wilson, Luke, 8, 9, 205
Winston, Jessica, 19, 111, 204, 205
Woloch, Alex, 293, 299
writ, 80, 208, 211–213, 251

Kolibri 360 GmbH
Ferdinand-Jühlke-Straße 7
99095 Erfurt, Deutschland
produktsicherheit@kolibri360.de